Henryk Zins

England and the
in the Elizabethan era

translated by H. C. Stevens

Manchester University Press
Rowman & Littlefield, Totowa, N.J.

Sponsored by the Lublin Scientific Society

Published by the University of Manchester at

THE UNIVERSITY PRESS

316–324 Oxford Road, Manchester M13 9NR

UK ISBN 0 7190 0471 3

USA

ROWMAN & LITTLEFIELD

Totowa, N.J. 07512

US ISBN 0 87471 117 7

Printed in Great Britain by Butler & Tanner Ltd
Frome and London

Contents

List of tables

Preface to the English edition

This book was first published in Polish in 1967. It has been translated by Mr H. C. Stevens, F.I.L., who has added some explanatory footnotes. These have been denoted accordingly. A few more explanatory notes have been added, and these have been put in square brackets. A little material in the Polish edition, consisting of matter with which an English reader would already be familiar, has been omitted. It has not been felt necessary to indicate these omissions in the text. In addition, the opportunity has been taken to amend chapter nine at several points in the light of recent research.

H. Z.

Acknowledgements

The author has the pleasant duty of expressing his gratitude to all those persons and institutions who gave him assistance while he was writing the book. First and foremost I must thank Professor S. T. Bindoff and J. J. Scarisbrick of the University of London, during whose seminar in the Institute of Historical Research in 1959 the first outline of the subject came into being. I must also express my gratitude to the great expert on the Elizabethan era, Professor Sir John Neale, of London University, for the suggestions I derived from his Tudor seminars. My thanks must also be expressed to Dr A. M. Millard of London, for making available to me her work, not as yet published, on London's import trade in the first half of the seventeenth century. For a similar service I have to thank R. W. K. Hinton, of Cambridge, whose book on the Eastland Company in the seventeenth century has now been published. I greatly regret that I cannot convey my thanks to that outstanding investigator of the Tudor and Stuart period, Professor R. H. Tawney, whose death some years ago was an incalculable loss. Professor Tawney took much interest in my work and encouraged me to continue with it. My thanks are also due to the British Council, who helped me during the writing by providing me with various publications not available in Poland, and who facilitated many research activities of mine during my stay in England in 1957–59.

In conclusion I also wish to express my thanks to Professor S. Hoszowski and Dr H. Samsonowicz for their valuable critical observations, and to Professor T. S. Willan for his help with the English edition of this book.

Abbreviations

Annales U.M.C.S. *Annales Universitatis Mariae Curie Skłodowska*
A.P.C. *Acts of the Privy Council*
B.M. British Museum
Cal.S.P.Dom. *Calendar of State Papers, Domestic*
Cal.S.P.For. *Calendar of State Papers, Foreign*
Ec.H.R. *The Economic History Review*
E.H.R. *The English Historical Review*
H.R. *Hanserecesse*
H.U. *Hansisches Urkundenbuch*
L.P. Henry VIII *Letters and Papers, Foreign and Domestic, of Henry VIII*
P.H. *Przegląd Historyczny* (*Historical Review*)
P.R.O. Public Record Office
R.D.S.G. *Roczniki Dziejów Społecznych i Gospodarczych* (*Annals of Social and Economic History*)
S.P.Dom. State Papers, Domestic
T.R.H.S. *Transactions of the Royal Historical Society*
V.C.H. *Victoria County History*
W.A.P.Gd. Wojewódzkie Archiwum Państwowe w Gdańsku (Provincial State Archives in Danzig)
Z.W.G. *Zeitschrift des westpreussischen Geschichtsvereins*

Introduction

In many respects the Elizabethan era is a turning point in English history. Above all, it was a time of economic expansion in which Shakespeare's kinsmen were led to search for new markets in various parts of their contemporary world. It meant the achievement of a greater initiative on the high seas, and a decisive settlement of accounts with Spain, brought about by the defeat of the Great Armada in 1588. That victory marked the beginning of English domination of the Atlantic. But the Elizabethan era was also a time of enormous progress in the realm of English culture, a time when Renaissance literature flourished and advances were made in the theatre, in the arts and in science, and in the whole field of material and artistic achievement. This noteworthy advance in civilization was to a large extent the result of England's economic and social development during the sixteenth century. After the Hundred Years War, which had been catastrophic for England, and the Wars of the Roses, which had brought extensive ruin to the economy as well as causing political chaos, in the sixteenth century the country very slowly began to recover, largely through the rise of the middle class, the gentry and the burgesses, who were one of the pillars of the Tudor monarchy. One of the most notable demonstrations of Elizabethan England's economic growth, and a pre-condition of her later importance in world economy and politics, was the development of her foreign trade during the second half of the sixteenth century.

Northern Europe, the lands lying around the North and the Baltic seas, was one of the earliest and initially most important areas of England's commercial expansion. For a long period her trade with the nearby Netherlands and north-west Germany remained in foreign hands, despite her early experiences in the organization of her own trading companies (the Merchants of the Staple, the Merchant Adventurers). Her trading expansion in the Baltic area was achieved after a severe struggle with the powerful Hanseatic League, which had long played a predominant role in the area and functioned as a troublesome middleman in England's trade with the Baltic countries.

Two fairly definite periods can be distinguished in England's early relations with the Baltic area. The first, running from the end of the fourteenth century to the end of the sixteenth, covered England's prolonged and determined struggle to break down the German Hanse's monopoly and to achieve a more independent position in her trading relations with the Baltic countries. Parallel with her attempts to restrict the Hanse's privileges within her own borders she made persistent attempts to obtain and maintain a permanent base, an entrepot for her trade, in the Baltic area. In this struggle the prize she aimed at was the capture of the lucrative Baltic market for her cloth production, while tapping a rich source of supplies of the raw materials and semi-manufactured goods necessary for shipbuilding, such as timber, cordage, flax and hemp, iron, tar, and pitch, and also, in times of poor harvests at home, of grain. Thus the climax of the struggle came naturally in the years that marked the beginnings of the expansion of her trade and navigation, in the Tudor era, but especially in the reign of Elizabeth I. Those years saw not only England's struggle with Spain and the numerous voyages of English navigators and buccaneers—Francis Drake, Walter Ralegh, Frobisher, Gilbert and others—but also persistent attempts and manœuvres on the part of English merchants to develop commercial organizations for trade with, in some cases, remote parts of Europe and the world. It was to a certain extent a precondition of England's later world expansion that the Hanse domination should be overthrown and that the Tudor merchants should take over a greater share in northern European trade. And it was precisely in the area of the North, the Baltic and the White seas that they gained their first experience in organization.

The second period in England's relations with the Baltic dates from the beginning of the seventeenth century; so far as the forms and methods adopted were concerned it was of a somewhat different nature from its predecessor. In this period the Baltic was still of considerable, though gradually diminishing, importance to England as a market for supplying her basic needs in naval stores, though now she was mistress of the seas and was developing her policies and commercial expansion on a world scale. During the seventeenth century the Baltic also became an important factor in English foreign policy.[1] During that century England, threatened during the Dutch wars[2] and the struggle for *dominium maris Baltici* with being cut off from her

Baltic imports, became involved in extensive diplomatic activity in the area, following her historic policy of seeking to maintain the balance of power in Europe.[3] The words Oliver Cromwell spoke before Parliament in 1658—'If they can shut us out of the Baltic Sea, and make themselves masters of that, where is your trade? Where are your materials to preserve your shipping?'[4]—help to provide a key to the understanding of the essential motive behind England's Baltic policy in those years.

The present work deals with the first period of England's relations with the Baltic countries,[5] but more especially with the Elizabethan era, when she succeeded in eliminating the Hanse from her Baltic trade and set up a trading company of her own to develop exchange with the Baltic countries. After a discussion of England's early relations with those countries and of the Anglo-Hanseatic rivalry, in the first five chapters are specified the political, economic and social factors which led in 1579 to the foundation of the Eastland Company, and the capture of its administration by the wealthy London wholesalers. The second part of the book, chapters six to ten, is devoted entirely to an analysis of England's Baltic trade in the second half of the sixteenth century, to its organization, and to English navigation in the Baltic.

Thus we are primarily concerned with England's commerce with the Baltic countries, but especially with Poland, which had the largest share of England's Baltic trade. From 1579 onward that trade was organized through the Eastland Company. Thus by the nature of things our work deals primarily with English trade with the Polish Commonwealth, which, with Gdansk (Danzig) and later Elblag (Elbing) as its ports was the dominant factor in Baltic commerce with Western countries during the period in question. In addition to the trade with Poland, England's trade with Russia is also taken into account on a rather broader scale, especially in connection with the problem of the Narva navigation, with the aim of establishing the relative proportions of the Polish and Russian markets in England's Baltic trade.

On the other hand, comparatively little space is devoted to the problems of English trade with the Scandinavian countries, which had not yet obtained any large share in England's commerce or were developing it outside the Baltic area,[6] and had only a few entries in the Sound toll registers. Only Norway's importance as a supplier of timber to England has been given rather more emphasis, taking the

English port books as our basis. The nature and state of the surviving sources have meant that our work is concerned mainly with the Baltic trade carried on by English merchants, not with England's Baltic exchange as a whole; this is impossible to cover more fully because of the existence of foreign intermediaries, especially the Dutch, and the part played by Amsterdam as a great warehouse and distribution point for Baltic products. Owing to the gaps in the English port books and the lack of general computations of England's total import and export trade in the sixteenth century our analysis of the English Baltic trade has been based in many instances on the material available for London, Hull, Newcastle and other ports of eastern England, and not on data for England as a whole. A total presentation of England's Baltic commerce was possible only by taking the Sound toll registers as a basis, but these could provide a fairly safe criterion only in regard to English exports (see the introductory remarks to chapter seven).

In geographical terms our work covers the Baltic area, the region closed by the Sound and lying beyond the Sound, as English contemporary documents defined it, but especially Elizabeth's 1579 charter, in which the area of the Eastland Company's monopoly was defined. By naming Danzig as the most important port in the area, these documents identified England's Baltic trade with her exchange with Danzig, and therefore with Poland. (This point will be discussed later.) In attempting to define this economic area we have to accept with Małowist[7] that in the sixteenth century the Baltic was primarily a region for exploitation by Western European capital. This capital, which from the end of the fifteenth century was mainly Dutch[8] but which from the second half of the sixteenth century was also English to an increasing extent, obtained from the area the raw materials and semi-manufactured goods necessary for the development of Western industry. One may accept that the distinctive feature of the Baltic area at this time was as the source of supply of the raw materials and semi-manufactured goods, such as agricultural produce, timber and all the varieties of forestry manufactures and products indispensable to the development of north-western Europe's industrial production.[9]

The chapters of this work which are devoted to an analysis of England's Baltic trade cover the period from 1562 to the end of the sixteenth century, although, to obtain a better perspective, the analysis is at times extended considerably beyond these chronological limits. The initial date is established by reference to the basic source: the

Sound toll registers contained detailed data on goods passing through the Sound only from 1562 onwards. On the other hand, the terminal date is fixed by analysis of England's Baltic trade, which, after growing perceptibly during the second half of the sixteenth century, towards the close of the period began to reveal clear signs of crisis. At the turn of the sixteenth century the export of English cloth to the Baltic began to decline, partly as a result of increasing Dutch competition and partly through the development of a local cloth industry, especially in Silesia. English cloth, the basis of England's entire trade, was becoming too expensive for the Baltic consumers, and from the beginning of the seventeenth century there was an increasingly serious decline in its export to the area.[10] At the turn of the sixteenth century England's trade with Moscow *via* Archangel also began to be affected by Dutch competition, which gradually robbed the English merchants of their importance in this commerce.[11] Thus the period covered by our work is the comparatively short space of time during which England played an important part in Baltic trade, after the Hanse intermediaries had been eliminated and the Hanse monopoly broken, but before Holland gained the complete mastery of Baltic navigation and trade, already considerable though it was even in the sixteenth century.[12]

In conclusion, it should perhaps be emphasized that the object of this work was to cover the broader aspect of Anglo-Baltic commercial and political relations, from the point of view of the history of Elizabethan England, against the background of the country's social and economic development during the turning point in time marking the beginnings of her economic and political expansion, and the rapid development of England's trade and of her merchant class. For this reason I have considered it expedient not to overload the text with such well known and rather petty problems as the antagonism between Danzig and Elbing, or the Eastland Company's attempts to get the Polish court to confirm the English residence in Elbing. For the same reasons the generally well known problems associated with analysis of the socio-economic changes which occurred in the Baltic countries during the sixteenth century, and the problems of these countries' trade and commercial policy, have also been ignored in so far as they were not directly connected with the main subject of the book. To make the work readable and to free the text from the ballast of a large quantity of statistical data, a number of tables have been compiled, providing quantitative data on England's Baltic trade, English navigation in the Baltic, etc. The great majority of these tables contain information never before published on this theme, information based on various kinds of customs records not always easily accessible or legible (this relates especially to the English port books), which is our justification for including a relatively large amount of such statistical material.

Notes

1 Cf. A. Szelągowski, *Walka o Bałtyk* (*The struggle for the Baltic*), Lwów, 1921, p. 82.

2 Of recent works on this subject see Charles Wilson, *Profit and power: a study of England and the Dutch wars*, London, 1957.

3 There is extremely interesting and little-known material on the problem of English policy in the period of the Altmark armistice in the correspondence of the English mediator, Sir Thomas Roe. See 'Letters relating to the mission of Sir Thomas Roe to Gustavus Adolphus, 1629–30,' in *The Camden miscellany*, ed. S. R. Gardiner, vol. VII, 1875.

4 G. J. Marcus, *A naval history of England*, vol. I, London, 1961, p. 149.

5 Recently M. Małowist has drawn attention to the absence of studies of this problem in 'Z zagadnień popytu na produkty krajów nadbałtyckich w Europie zachodniej w XVI wieku' ('On problems of Western Europe's demand for the products of Baltic countries in the sixteenth century'), *P.H.*, vol. L, 1959, 741. H. Zins has discussed the state of research into the history of England during the Elizabethan era extensively in 'Angielska historiografia elżbietańska' ('English Elizabethan historiography'), *Odrodzenie i Reformacja w Polsce* (*The Renaissance and Reformation in Poland*), vol. VIII, 1963, pp. 157–209.

6 Cf. A. Mączak and H. Samsonowicz, 'Z zagadnień genezy rynku europejskiego: strefa bałtycka' ('On problems of the genesis of the European market: the Baltic zone'), *P.H.*, vol. LV, 1964, No. 2, pp. 198*ff*, in which the authors, utilizing the extensive literature on the subject, provide a comprehensive analysis of the concept of the Baltic zone.

7 M. Małowist, 'Ryga i Gdańsk oń wybuchu wojny trzynastoletniej do końca XVI stulecia' ('Riga and Danzig from the outbreak of the Thirteen Years War to the end of the sixteenth century') in *Polska a Inflanty* (*Poland and Livonia*), Gdynia, 1939, p. 124.

8 Cf. M. Małowist, *Studia z dziejów rzemiosła w okresie kryzysu feudalizmu w zachodniej Europie w XIV i XV wieku* (*Studies in the history of crafts during the crisis of feudalism in Western Europe in the fourteenth and fifteenth centuries*), Warsaw, 1954, pp. 90, 385, 390, 439 and elsewhere.

9 Mączak and Samsonowicz, *op. cit.*, p. 201.

10 Cf. A. Mączak, *Sukiennictwo wielkopolskie, XVI–XVII wiek* (*The Great Poland cloth industry, fourteenth to seventeenth centuries*), Warsaw, 1955, p. 232.

11 A. Attman, *Den ryska marknaden i 1500-talets baltiska politik, 1558–95*, Lund, 1944, pp. 407*ff*.

12 The problem of England's trade with the Netherlands in the fourteenth and fifteenth centuries has been studied by N. J. M. Kerling, *Commercial relations of Holland and Zeeland with England from the late thirteenth century to the close of the Middle Ages*, Leiden, 1954. For the ensuing period down to the seventeenth century, which has been more fully studied, see, among others, G. Edmundson, *Anglo-Dutch rivalry, 1600–53*, Oxford, 1911. But the existing works on the subject of Anglo-Dutch relations do not go deeply into the problem of Dutch activities as intermediaries in England's Baltic trade.

one *Early trading relations between England and the Baltic to the middle of the sixteenth century*

Written sources indicative of England's interest in the Baltic exist as early as the time of Alfred the Great.[1] From the ninth century we have the well known narrative of Wulfstan's journey to Truso and the land of the Prussians.[2] The name Estland (the land of the Ests)[3] also dates from this period, and together with this name the term Eastland came into the English language at a later date. From about the fourteenth century 'Estland' signified the Baltic area,[4] and especially Gdańsk Pomorze (Danzig Pomerania). In English sources these regions are defined as the 'east countries', or 'east parts', as their most important trading centre was Danzig (Gdansk), with its enormous Polish hinterland; in the sixteenth century they were also called the 'east parts or Danske' or 'Danske and the east parts',[5] and even 'Danske or Eastland'.[6] Hence also the official title of the Eastland Company, founded by English merchants in 1579 to develop the Baltic trade, was 'The Governour, Assistants and Fellowship of the Merchants of Eastland'.[7]

England's commercial relations with the Baltic countries were among the oldest, most constant and enduring in her early history. Unlike the trade with the Mediterranean, whose ports sent mainly luxury goods, from early times the Baltic attracted the attention of English merchants as a rich source of supplies of food products, especially grain, as well as the raw materials indispensable to the construction of the English fleet. Together with the North Sea, the Baltic constituted the most important area of English trade in the sixteenth century.

England's interest in the Baltic and northern trade, in commerce with Poland and Russia, marked the first stage in her economic expansion on a larger scale. Although this trade was decidedly second in importance to her commerce with the Netherlands, which had long been fundamental to her economic needs, in essence it was the first important venture of English merchants on to the broad sea routes, a successful attempt on the part of English trade to render itself independent of foreign intermediaries.[8]

Again and again in the fifteenth, sixteenth and seventeenth centuries the English themselves emphasized the importance of the Baltic trade to their national economy, calling the Baltic countries the 'root' of all their sea trade, and a granary. A long poem entitled *Libelle of Englyshe Polycye*, published in 1436, indicated the essential value and the variety of the goods imported from Prussia, and, among the commodities which for many years had been imported from Danzig, mentioned iron, copper, steel, timber, wooden bows, tar, pitch, flax, skins, furs, canvas, beer, meat, wax, etc.

> Now bere and bacone bene fro Pruse ibroughte . . .
> Osmonde, coppre, bowstaffes, stile and wax,
> Peltre ware and grey, pych, terre, borde and flex
> And Coleyne threde, fustiane and canvase,
> Carde, bokeram; of olde tyme thus it was.[9]

This work also drew attention to the role of the Baltic market in English cloth exports. At the beginning of the sixteenth century two treatises said to be by Clement Armstrong summed up the importance of the Baltic area,[10] especially Prussia, to England in similar terms. An interesting footnote to this question is the adoption into English from the end of the middle ages of the name 'spruce' to signify the fir (at that time Prussia was called Spruceland in England), which testifies to the general association of Prussia with certain kinds of timber imported from Poland.[11]

As diplomats, merchants and writers on economics observed in the sixteenth and seventeenth centuries, the importance of the Baltic market for England consisted primarily in the importation of ships' supplies[12] and the export of cloth. In 1568 two English merchants, Thomas Bannister and Geoffrey Duckett, drew William Cecil's attention to the benefits to be obtained from the Moscow trade; they wrote that by developing that trade it would be possible to free England from her great dependence on Danzig in respect of imports of cordage, masts, sails, pitch, etc, which were so vital to the English fleet.[13] Cecil, Elizabeth's Privy Councillor and Secretary of State, knew quite well the importance of the Baltic market in this respect and was of the opinion that 'the commodities which we bring out of the East parts are necessary for the use of this land'.[14]

Nothing better characterizes the importance of trade with Poland for Elizabethan England than English diplomatic activity in 1590. Through her ambassador in Turkey, Edward Barton, England tried to persuade the sultan to abandon his planned attack on Poland because she needed many Polish commodities which 'were necessary for the navy'.[15] In the event of war with Turkey, Barton argued, Poland would hold up the export of these raw materials to England, and this in turn might have the effect of England withdrawing help from the Netherlands during that country's struggle with Turkey's chief enemy, Spain. In a letter to Elizabeth the sultan admitted that he had refrained from attacking Poland at the Queen's request, as, among other reasons, he did not wish to be the cause of restricting the export from Poland of such commodities as masts, gunpowder, grain, etc, which, as he judged, were needed by England in the war with Spain.[16]

Not only the pronouncements of diplomats and merchants, but the observations of English travellers, who in certain cases spent many years in Poland, emphasized the importance of the trade with the Polish Commonwealth and the Baltic area. Two of these deserve further attention: the narrative of Fynes Moryson, published in 1593,[17] and that of William Bruce, published in 1598.[18] Both writers expressed amazement at the Commonwealth's natural riches and the cheapness of Polish commodities. Bruce called Poland 'the common grenary and arsenall of all Europe', especially in regard to naval stores. But he was astonished that a country so rich in raw materials, and abundant in produce which was sought all over Europe, was not at all wealthy; he ascribed this state of affairs to the benefits which the port cities, especially Danzig, derived from the export of Polish goods.[19]

The events associated with the founding of the Eastland Company in the time of Elizabeth I did not mark the beginnings of England's commercial penetration of the Baltic. English merchants had called there as early as the thirteenth century, as is evidenced by, among other sources, a Dutch proposal to Lübeck in 1286 to close the Baltic completely to the English.[20] English merchants themselves pointed to the close of the thirteenth century as marking the beginning of England's relations with the Baltic countries, especially with Pomorze (Pomerania).[21] But we have no further information on this point, and it would appear that these relations grew stronger and more important only in the fourteenth century. The English themselves, and in particular the Eastland Company, maintained in 1659 that only in the middle of the fourteenth century had their ancestors started trading with the Baltic.[22] It certainly follows from statements in certain documents that from the beginning of the first half of the fourteenth century English citizens frequently travelled to Danzig, and quite often settled and acquired civic rights there.[23] English merchants sailed to the Baltic with cloth; the export of this commodity increased greatly during the second half of the fourteenth century.[24] And they brought back, mainly from Danzig and Elbing, pitch, ashes, timber, grain and other products of Polish and Pomeranian origin,[25] as well as timber from Norway. In the fourteenth century the English also arrived in the Baltic area as knights to aid the Teutonic Order in its struggles with Lithuania,[26] as Chaucer noted in his description of the knight in the *Canterbury Tales*:

> At Alisaundre he was, when it was wonne;
> Ful ofte tyme he hadde the bord begonne
> Aboven all naciouns in Pruce,
> In Lettow hadde he reysed and in Ruce,
> No Cristen mann so ofte of his degree [27]

Apart from the voyages of individual English merchants to the Baltic, and especially to Danzig, towards the end of the fourteenth century we observe the first attempts to organize these activities in a form reminiscent of the later trading companies. At the end of the fourteenth and the beginning of the fifteenth centuries 'privileges' were issued in England, and these were the first official recognition of the so-called regulated companies. These were monopolistic trading organizations, with a fairly loose structure, within the bounds of which the members carried on individual trade, as distinct from the later joint stock companies, which had a centralized structure and in which the companies themselves traded. Privileges dating from the end of the fourteenth and the beginning of the fifteenth centuries covered England's trade with the North Sea and the Baltic, and this clearly indicates those areas as the earliest regions of England's early trading expansion overseas. The oldest of these documents was issued by Richard II in 1390 to English merchants trading with Prussia and other Baltic countries.[28] They were granted the right of free trade within the area of the lands of the Teutonic Knights and the right to put in at all the Order's Prussian ports.[29]

At this stage it must be emphasized that from the very beginning all England's trading ventures in the Baltic came up against the antagonism of the dominant trading power in northern Europe, the German Hanseatic League, which jealously guarded its supremacy in the area.[30] English expansion in the Baltic was accomplished against the background of intense rivalry with the Hanse; the foundation of the Eastland Company was the final chapter in this struggle, it was one of the indications of the Hanse's collapse.

The fact that the Hanseatic merchants possessed extensive privileges in England caused real difficulties in her relations with the Hanse and the area under its commercial control. These privileges had been obtained in the early days of the League's contacts with England, and especially in the time of Edward I, with his privilege of 1303, entitled *Carta Mercatoria*, which conferred, *inter alia* the right of retail trading, direct exchange with foreigners, etc.[31] Edward III greatly enlarged the scope of the privileges granted to the Hanse by his Plantagenet predecessors, freeing its merchants from various imposts, with the result that at the beginning of the fifteenth century Hanseatic merchants were paying lower customs duties on the export of English cloth than English merchants themselves. In these circumstances, owing to the weakness of the English merchants, the Hanse had a substantial share in middleman activities connected with England's Baltic trade, and, in accordance with its monopolistic policy, did not allow English merchants to avail themselves even partially of similar advantageous privileges in Danzig and other cities members of the League. So it is not surprising that from the end of the fourteenth century England's endeavours to obtain a greater share of the Baltic trade were buttressed repeatedly by reference to the principle that her merchants should have the same rights in Hanseatic cities as the Hanse enjoyed in England, and that if the League refused it should be deprived of the special rights enjoyed by its London residence, the Steelyard.[32] But this was an extreme demand and at the time not a very realistic one. Until the Elizabethan era England was too weak in the sphere of Baltic trade to be able to enforce this principle. None the less, in constant conflicts with the Hanse over the question of the reciprocal rights of English and Hanseatic merchants, England regularly and consistently advocated and defended it. One may add that in the case of Danzig, which was the chief opponent of English trading expansion in the Baltic, there were times when English merchants found themselves in a more favourable situation, because two contradictory trends affected that city's policy concerning them. Danzig attempted to prevent the English entering the local market, but simultaneously, even during the severest Anglo-Hanseatic conflicts aimed to maintain commercial relations with England, since they were so advantageous to the city.[33] Besides the growing lack of unity and the contradictions in the Hanseatic world, especially at a later period, another fact of some significance was that one member and patron of the League, the Teutonic Order, adopted a rather distinctive attitude to the question of English trade at times, and especially in the fifteenth century.[34]

Passing over the course of England's conflicts with Hanse, which grew very frequent and severe from the last quarter of the fourteenth century onward, and the mutual repressions and chicanery, the suspension of privileges, the confiscation of goods, etc (the two source works, the *Hanserecesse* and *Hansisches Urkundenbuch*, are packed with information on the question), it needs to be observed that it was, in fact, towards the end of the fourteenth century that England's interest in Baltic trade increased considerably. In connection with one dispute we learn that eighty-eight English merchants traded with Danzig in 1385.[35] Sources mention repeated cases of English merchants settling in Danzig in those years, and more than one of them acquired civic rights.[36] Hanseatic sources also refer to English merchants trading with Elbing in the middle of the fourteenth century.[37] Trade with Norway had even older traditions, and went back to the thirteenth century.

Towards the end of the fourteenth century there was some improvement in England's relations with the Hanse, and this in turn affected the position of English merchants in Prussia. In 1388 an agreement was reached between England and the Teutonic Order[38] which confirmed the Hanse's privileges in England but on the other hand guaranteed English merchants their ancient rights in Prussia, the possibility of settling in that country, and carrying on free trade. A month earlier, on 28 July 1388, an English mission was received by the Grand Master of the Order in Marienburg (Malbork); the English emissary demanded, *inter alia*, that the English trading post in Danzig should be recognized.[39] As a result of these agreements[40] —which, however, did not regulate the question of the trading post— conditions were established for the founding at Danzig of the first, as already mentioned, English trading company of its kind in the Baltic, to which Richard II issued a privilege first on 20 December 1390 and then on 17 January 1391.[41] To judge from this privilege, it appears that the organization had a governor, took the form of a corporation, and had a defined range of jurisdiction, its own meeting house, the right to elect its governing bodies, etc. On the strength of this privilege the first governor appointed was John Bebys,[42] who in 1388 had taken part on England's behalf in the negotiations between the English mission and the Grand Master in regard to the elimination of disputes and the conclusion of a trade agreement.[43]

The organization headed by John Bebys had no definite name; the documents refer to him as the governor of the English merchants in the area of Prussia, Scania, and the Sound[44] and the Hanseatic possessions,[45] and so in effect within the area of Eastland.[46] But Hanseatic sources simply speak of English merchants 'liggende' in Danzig.[47]

An interesting fact which has so far escaped notice is that the memory of this oldest English trading organization in the Baltic was still vivid among the members of the Eastland Company quite late in the sixteenth century. When the English ambassador, John Rogers, was endeavouring to persuade the Polish court to confirm privileges for the English merchants in Elbing he appealed to the existence in the late fourteenth century of an English trading organization in Danzig, and to the privilege granted by Richard II.[48]

Little information is available on the early fortunes of this English trading post in Danzig at the end of the fourteenth and during the fifteenth century; the same applies to the volume of England's trade with the Baltic at that time, though trade would seem to have been quite active.[49] In any case there must have been a considerable export of English cloth to Prussia, since only a few years after the Marienburg agreement of 1388 the Danzigers' attacks on the English merchants' privileges in their city grew more and more frequent, as did the charge that owing to the import of English cloth Danzig and other Prussian cities were being impoverished.[50] This attitude, in association with disputes with England over customs dues, the depredations of pirates, etc, led to renewed exacerbation of Anglo-Prussian relations. In 1396 restrictions were placed on the right of Englishmen to remain in Prussia under the Teutonic Order, and in 1397, as a result of Danzig's pressure, an order was issued forbidding the purchase of English cloth anywhere outside England,[51] which clearly indicates the real motives behind Danzig's policy in regard to English merchants—who furthermore, when the Grand Master revoked the Marienburg agreement, were called on to leave Prussia.[52] In 1404 at the request of Hanseatic cities the Order prohibited the export of pitch and timber to England, and the import of English cloth.[53] Again, in 1405 a Hanse congress at Lübeck passed a resolution banning trade with England.[54]

However, these official interdictions were not in general followed by executive measures. Anglo-Danzig trade brought both parties too much profit for it to be given up even in the years of the severest repressions and restrictions. In practice, despite the expulsion order, the English did not leave Danzig, nor did England's trade with the lands belonging to the Teutonic Knights in Prussia come to an end.

During this very period, on 6 June 1404, English merchants trading with Danzig obtained further privileges from the Crown[55] which confirmed their 1390 organization and moreover granted the right to issue statutes and ordinances. English merchants trading with Holland, Zeeland, Brabant and Flanders obtained a similar privilege on 5 February 1407 [56] as, on 1 March 1408, did English merchants trading with Norway, Sweden and Denmark; these merchants too were predecessors of the Eastland Company.[57] The privilege granted by Henry VI on 20 June 1428[58] makes no distinction whatever between these two areas of activity; it refers to English merchants 'in partibus Pruciae, Daciae, Norweiae, Hansae et Swechiae'. These merchants active in the Baltic and North Sea areas did not as yet constitute definite separate organizations; they established various branches of the Merchant Adventurers, a term which, as Carus-Wilson's researches have shown,[59] down to Tudor times embraced all the English merchants engaged in foreign trade who were not members of the Merchants of the Staple Company, which was originally concerned with exporting wool from England to Calais. The common feature of all these trading measures and exertions was a search for markets for English wool and cloth. The Continental entrepots for these commodities, which were at first established at Calais and in the Netherlands, but later at Emden, Stade, Hamburg, Danzig and Elbing, clearly indicated the direction of England's trading penetration eastward, along the coasts of the North Sea and the Baltic, where she also found a valuable source of food products and naval stores.

Thus at the turn of the fourteenth century England was taking the first step towards freeing herself from dependence on the extensive middleman activities of the Hanse and taking a larger share of the Baltic trade into her own hands. In 1689 N. Tench, later a Governor of the Eastland Company, himself dated the beginnings of England's Baltic trade to this period.[60] Its prerequisite was the breakdown of the Hanseatic monopoly. Towards the end of the sixteenth century the English would be speaking of the Hanse as an institution 'upon whose ruynes we were built'.[61] The importance of the Hanseatic problem even at the beginning of Elizabeth's reign is evidenced by the fact that Thomas Gresham, when formulating the plan for a new English economic policy, included among the most important tasks the necessity to restrict the extensive privileges of the

London Steelyard[62] which had long assured the Hanse of greater rights in English trade than were enjoyed by native merchants, while at the same time the English were discriminated against in Hanseatic ports.

The problem of the considerable Dutch role in England's Baltic trade, which arose later, was different. It was of far-reaching importance, but it is difficult to reduce to figures, and, although essential to the elucidation of England's growing penetration of the Baltic, it has not so far been given thorough study.[63] We know that in the sixteenth century England depended to a great extent on the Antwerp market and Dutch transport. As we shall be discussing later, the decline of Antwerp formed one of the essential factors in the genesis of the Eastland Company and England's greater activity in the realm of overseas trade. But these issues refer to a later date: in the fourteenth and fifteenth centuries Dutch competition was not yet felt in England as a danger to her Baltic trade (as was the case with the Hanse), which could not be carried on without Dutch intermediation even in the sixteenth century because the English merchant fleet was so small. The danger of Dutch intermediation began to arouse more and more alarm only from the beginning of the seventeenth century. The problem was stated with particular force by John Keymer in 1620.[64] In his *Book of observations* he discussed the technique of the Dutch middlemen, their methods of warehousing grain and other products of the Baltic countries, keeping them for sale in years of poor harvests, with great profit to themselves.[65] He also pointed to the causes of the Dutch ascendancy over the English in the realm of navigation (see below). He drew attention to the danger to England from Dutch middleman activities also in regard to the export of English cloth. This the Merchant Adventurers exported to Holland undressed and undyed; the Dutch finished it and sold it at a profit of about £60,000 sterling per annum.

Returning to our sketch of England's earlier trading relations with the Baltic, we have to observe that in the fifteenth century, despite her persistent endeavours, she suffered defeat in her attempts to penetrate the Baltic area and to break through the German Hanse's restrictions on her foreign trade. After a brief increase of trade with Danzig towards the end of the fourteenth century England's Baltic trade collapsed. The Hundred Years War and the Wars of the Roses long exhausted her economic resources, and diminished her political importance,[66] though we no longer accept earlier opinions as to the extent of the devastation and losses they caused.[67] For a long time

England was forced to hand over most of her Baltic trade to foreign merchants, though she did not give up her attempts to diminish the extent of this dependence.

Despite the very great difficulties and chicanery it met with from the Danzig city council, the English trading post hung on in Danzig until the 1470's. We learn as much from reports of the numerous disputes, for instance the arrest of the Governor and twelve assistants[68] of this first English Baltic company, and the restrictions imposed by the Danzig council on English use of the house they owned there. The Danzig aldermen's registers for 1430 and 1431 name two aldermen of this English corporation, Niclas Gare and Willem Everhart.[69] Data cited by Simson show that in 1422, for instance, there were fifty-five English merchants resident in Prussia,[70] which suggests that quite active trading contacts were still maintained. More than one of these merchants achieved considerable affluence in the town, and mixed marriages were common.[71] Despite its many difficulties the English colony in Danzig was numerous and well organized; periodic attempts to expel it were never completely successful.[72] The lack of cohesion and solidarity which began to show in the Hanse in the fifteenth century, the differing economic interests of its members, urban revolts (e.g. in the Wend towns), political difficulties—all weakened the unity of the League's activities.[73] The defeat of the Teutonic Knights at Grunwald* also conduced to a temporary improvement in the situation of English merchants in Danzig.[74] Unfortunately, we have no details of the extent of their trade or of England's exchanges with the Baltic in the first half of the fifteenth century. It would seem to follow from the complaints of the Danzig council and merchants that the trade was quite extensive, at least down to the middle of the century.[75]

In the fifteenth century England's main export to the Baltic was cloth. Other commodities, such as tin, fruits from southern Europe, skins, etc., in practice played no great part. Cloth alone made it possible for the English merchants to obtain from the Baltic countries the raw materials and semi-manufactured goods their country needed. The figures for Hanseatic exports clearly reveal the growth in demand for English cloth in central and northern Europe. In 1307 the Hanse

* The battle of Grunwald (in German history Tannenberg), fought on 15 July 1410 between a composite force of Poles, Lithuanians, Ruthenians, Bohemians, etc, commanded by the Polish King Jagiello and Witold, Grand Duke of Lithuania, and the Teutonic Knights, led by Ulrich, Grand Master of the Order, in which the Order was defeated and Ulrich slain—*Translator.*

exported from London six pieces of cloth;[76] in the years 1406–27 its annual export reached an average of about 6,000 pieces; in the years 1438–59 the figure was about 10,000 pieces, while in the years 1479–82 it was about 13,500 pieces of cloth per annum.[77] In Henry VIII's time the figure rose to an average of 23,352 pieces per annum,[76] which represented about 40 per cent of the total exported by English merchants. Only a small part of this export went to the Netherlands, where it was sold or further processed. The majority of the English cloths destined for the Baltic were transported directly by English and Hanse merchants (later by the Dutch also), mainly to Poland, Prussia and Lithuania.

Taking as basis the detailed data obtained from the enrolled customs and the subsidy accounts[78] one can obtain a precise idea of the Hanse's and English merchants' respective positions in the export of cloth from various English ports in the fifteenth century. In the case of London, where the greater part of this trade was concentrated, the English merchants had a slight advantage over the Hanse all through the century.[79] So far as Ipswich was concerned, this preponderance was achieved only at the beginning of the fifteenth century, and it lasted till about 1437,[80] which date marks the collapse of England's political position in relations with the Hanse in the Baltic. English merchants had a decided preponderance over the Hanse in Hull,[81] Lynn—especially in the first half of the century[82]—and in Yarmouth,[83] to name only the English ports of most importance in the Baltic trade. In these years Newcastle exported only a small quantity of cloth.

The customs statistics enable us to determine the respective shares of English, Hanseatic and other foreign merchants (the data do not enable us to differentiate among these last) in the export of cloth from England in the second half of the century (see table 1.1). Speaking generally, throughout this period the English merchants maintained a slight ascendancy (a little over 50 per cent). Unfortunately, it is not known how much of this export went to Baltic countries.[84] In any case, it seems that the Baltic region's share was by no means small, in respect of both English and Hanse merchants. It is also worth remarking that Danzig merchants occupied second place, after Cologne, in the total Hanse export of cloth from England.[85] The cloth was distributed widely over Poland, Lithuania and Ruthenia (Ukraine), was carried south to Hungary and Wallachia, and penetrated even to the Black Sea coast. From the middle of the century Holland also greatly increased her exports of cloth to the Baltic countries.[86]

The chief item in England's imports from the Baltic in the fourteenth and fifteenth centuries was forest products, such as various kinds of timber (England imported Norwegian and Prussian timber as early as the thirteenth century), especially staves, oaken staves, masts, bow staves, and pitch, ashes, etc. One must also mention grain, imported in years of poor harvests.[87] The Teutonic Order's accounts for 1404 specify various commodities exported from Prussia to England, including 600 *korcy* [one korzec = $3\frac{1}{3}$ bushels] of wheat, 18 lasts of malt, one *sachcyk* and 4,500 hundreds of oaken staves.[88] In certain years the quantity of grain England imported from Danzig

Table 1.1 *English cloth exports, 1446–82*

Years	*Total (Pieces)*	*English* *Pieces*	%	*Hanse* *Pieces*	%	*Other* *Pieces*	%
1446–48	53,699	29,633	55	11,289	21	12,777	24
1448–50	35,078	18,774	54	5,929	17	10,375	29
1450–53	38,928	22,508	58	7,420	19	9,000	23
1453–56	37,738	19,424	51	9,650	26	8,664	23
1456–59	35,059	19,831	57	10,289	29	4,939	14
1459–62	31,933	15,950	50	9,801	31	6,181	19
1462–65	25,855	15,278	59	7,157	27	3,420	14
1465–69	39,664	20,802	52	6,220	16	12,642	32
1469–71	27,610	17,532	64	3,620	13	6,458	23
1471–76	43,129	24,927	58	4,721	11	13,481	31
1476–79	51,889	33,052	69	9,133	18	9,704	18
1479–82	62,586	36,728	59	13,907	22	11,951	19

Source *Studies in English trade in the fifteenth century*, ed. E. Power and M. M. Postan, London, 1951, appendix A, p. 401. The figures cover only exports of the costly broadcloth.

was considerable; for instance, in 1441 it amounted to 1,100 lasts.[89] Among other commodities must be mentioned flax, canvas, copper (Hungarian), wax, etc.

Unfortunately, the surviving source materials do not yield any basis for a more exact determination of the size of England's Baltic trade in the fifteenth century. Neither English sources nor, as Samsonowicz has pointed out,[90] Hanseatic documents enable us to get to grips with this problem for the first half of the century. However, some light is thrown on the question by the surviving Danzig registers of mooring dues for the years 1460, 1468 and 1474–76, which render it possible to get some idea of the movements of vessels and Danzig's foreign trade in those years.[91] From these it appears that in 1460 four vessels arrived in Danzig from England; in 1468, six; in 1474, only two; in 1475, seven; in 1476, twelve. Thus the total English shipping to Danzig in those years was thirty-one, a very small figure by comparison with the 912 ships which arrived during the same period from the coasts of Mecklenburg, Pomerania, Prussia and Lübeck, the 320 from Scandinavia, Bornholm, Osland and Gottland, the 155 from Holland, etc. But it needs to be explained that in the case of England's trade with Danzig the mooring dues registers give reduced figures,[92] as is revealed by comparing them with the losses England suffered in the struggle with the Hanse. The well developed smuggling of the time also favours this conclusion. England's trade with Danzig brought both sides such considerable profit that it was carried on even in face of the severest conflicts and various kinds of restrictions. At such times it went on secretly, for instance through Hel or Puck, which was obviously a disguised form of trading with Danzig. The possibility of foreign middlemen also has to be taken into account, especially in the years when political conditions were unfavourable to England. None the less, on the basis of the meagre data available, there was a clear tendency for England's trade with the Baltic to decline in the fifteenth century. While, for instance, in the first half of the century there were times when some thirty English ships were lying in Danzig harbour,[93] in the 1470's the figure barely reached ten, while at the very end of the century it appears from the registers of the Sound tolls, kept from 1497 onwards,[94] that English ships hardly figured at all. (But in 1503 some ten English ships passed through the Sound on their way to the Baltic.)

Nothing better explains England's obstinate attempts to continue with her Baltic trade, despite the enormous difficulties, than a comparison of the Danzig and English prices for certain commodities transported to England. The comparison reveals the tremendous profits which both the English and the Danzig merchants derived from this trade. (Table 1.2.)

Samsonowicz has compared the prices in Danzig, England, Holland and certain Hanseatic cities, taking freight charges into account when calculating the profit. From his studies it appears[95] that in the case of grain the profits of merchants engaged in Danzig's trade with England in the years 1460 and 1470 came within the range of 84–127 per cent. Materials preserved in Danzig sources relating to

Thomas Kruse's trading transactions in London in 1468 reveal that on the sale of ten hundreds of oaken staves, two hundreds of staves, five lasts of ashes, four pounds of tar and three pounds of flax, plus small quantities of other commodities he cleared 220 Prussian marks, which brought him 38·9 per cent net profit. In that year the price of staves in London was 700 per cent higher than in Danzig, oak staves were 471 per cent higher, tar was 150 per cent higher and flax 100 per cent higher; which clearly shows the profitability of this trade.[96] We obtain a similar picture of profit from the correspondence of the Danzig factors of the London merchant Thomas Sexton in the middle of the sixteenth century, which we shall be discussing later, as well as the correspondence of Lionel Cranfield's Danzig agents at the beginning of the seventeenth century. This latter source indicates

Table 1.2 *Prices of the chief commodities exported from Danzig to England, 1443 (Prussian marks)*

Commodity	*Unit*	*Danzig*	*England*
Rye	Last	13–15	42
Wheat	Last	36	76
Ashes	Last	9–17	24
Pitch	Last	9	20
(Wood) tar	Last	5–5·5	32
Staves	Large hundred	7–9	32–34
Oak staves	Large hundred	4–5	24

Source Fiedler, 'Danzig und England', *Z.W.G.*, vol. LXVIII, 1928, p. 91.

that in 1609 the English paid 35–50 florins for one last of grain in Danzig, and obtained 106–110 florins for it in Holland, 'which was greatt profytte', as Parrott wrote to Cranfield.[97] Of course, it has to be remembered that the merchants of those days suffered considerably through the loss of cargo in transit (storms, capture by pirates and privateers, confiscations) or as the result of difficulties in selling and warehousing. Their receipts were also reduced by various imposts, customs duties, etc. But even when all this is allowed for, the profitability of the Baltic trade for both English and Hanseatic or other foreign merchants is obvious.

As we have already remarked, the documents that have survived do not, unfortunately, allow one to determine more exactly the dimensions of English Baltic trade in the fifteenth and the first half of the sixteenth centuries. But they provide a great deal of information on the subject of the unending Anglo-Hanseatic conflicts, which broke out again and again against a background of commercial rivalry, the attacks of pirates, etc.[98] This is not the place to tell of the enduring, and at times severe, conflicts between England and the Hanse, especially Danzig, in the fifteenth century, with all their mutual chicanery, repression and political complications. These have been the subject of several studies by, *inter alia*, Fiedler, Schulz, Stein, Koppmann, Schanz and Daenell, and, among English historians, by Postan especially. The details are well known and there is no need to return to them. The role played by the Merchant Adventurers, who took an important part in England's later achievement of independence of the Hanse, is also well known.[99]

Without going more deeply into the course of the Anglo-Hanseatic conflicts, one must stress the importance of the year 1437, which marked the end of an era in which England had come off well and had even managed to achieve certain successes. In 1437, after years of severe clashes, an agreement was concluded in London between England and the Hanse which for the last time in the fifteenth century gave some advantage to England. The compromise ending of prolonged disputes, which threatened a complete severance of relations, was made possible by the moderate attitude of the leader of the Hanseatic delegation, Heinrich Vorrath, the burgomaster of Danzig. For the last time in the fifteenth century, the 1437 agreement was based on the principle of equal rights in Anglo-Hanseatic relations. On the one hand, the Hanse gained confirmation of its former privileges in England, liberation from new obligations, and freedom from customs dues. On the other, the English gained confirmation of their old privileges in the Hanseatic cities, the right of free settlement in Prussia, the privilege of free trade, liberation from new taxes, etc.[100] This agreement—which, however, was not confirmed by the Teutonic Order and was not recognized by Danzig[101]—constituted England's maximum legal achievement in regard to the Hanse in the fifteenth century. From that time there was a distinct decline in England's position in the Baltic, the consequence of, among other things, the crisis of general chaos and economic collapse she experienced towards the end of the Hundred Years War and during the Wars of the Roses.[102]

In the second half of the century her relations with the Hanse, and especially with Danzig, deteriorated sharply,[103] particularly after Danzig had supported Denmark against England in 1468, when the

Danish and Danzig fleets operating in the Sound confiscated English ships carrying cloth to Poland.[104] The subsequent reprisals (closing down the London Steelyard, confiscation of Hanse property, the arrest of Danzig merchants in England) led to war between England and the Hanse and the proclamation of a ban on the import of English cloth into Danzig which was confirmed by the King of Poland, Casimir Jagiellon.[105] The Treaty of Utrecht, concluded in 1474, was a further success for the Hanse and a defeat for England's Baltic policy.[106] By virtue of its provisions the Hanse retained all its privileges in England, and even obtained new ones, together with compensation to be paid by the English. In addition it obtained as its own property its residences in London and Boston,[107] as well as a house in Lynn, which it had previously only rented. On the other hand, in the Treaty of Utrecht the English merchants were certainly guaranteed their former privileges in the Hanseatic cities; but this was of no great practical importance, especially as Danzig was unwilling to accept the condition.[108] Source references to the governor of the English trading post in Danzig come to an end more or less from the time of the Peace of Utrecht. During the several decades following, the English rarely turned up in the Baltic ports.[109] On the other hand, the Hanse maintained and even increased the extent of its intervention in England's trade with the Baltic countries. The Dutch trade in England's imports from the Baltic also increased in importance. The English confined their direct trading mainly to the Netherlands and France, while the Merchant Adventurers gathered into their hands, apart from the Merchants of the Staple, all English foreign trade activities down to the middle of the sixteenth century, to the time of the genesis of England's modern foreign trade and the steadily growing expansion of her merchant class.

As early as the days of the first two Tudors England more than once initiated attempts to free herself from Hanse intermediation in the Baltic trade,[110] and she also endeavoured to secure the return to her merchants of the house they had formerly owned in Danzig.[111] But all these efforts achieved no tangible results, especially as Henry VIII aimed in effect at maintaining friendly relations with the Hanse, partly in recognition of England's increasing need of Baltic commodities. The continual disputes between England and the Hanse[112] during the first half of the sixteenth century did not lead to such serious conflicts as had marked their relations in the previous century. During this period England's Baltic trade grew very slowly, and the Hanse continued to extract great profits from its middleman services.

Half-way through the sixteenth century England's relations with Danzig took another sharp turn, owing to the English merchants' increasing activity in the Baltic and English royal policy, which supported the trading aspirations of the country's middle class. Hanseatic documents report more and more new cases of mutual reprisals and double-dealing.[113] One of the consequences was the imposition by Danzig in 1557 of a temporary ban on trade with the English,[114] the more general resolution of a Hanse congress being used as justification. These issues will be discussed more extensively in chapter three when we examine the circumstances attending the foundation of the Eastland Company. Here we only add that, independently of the various disputes, in the first half of the sixteenth century England was still availing herself to a large extent of Hanseatic intermediaries in Danzig, Lübeck and Hamburg, and also of the Dutch (cf. chapter six). The statistics for exports of English cloth show that in the first half of the century the Hanse still had a large share,[115] maintaining its interests at approximately the same level (about 30 per cent) as the figure for the second half of the fifteenth century.[116] On the other hand, in respect of England's imports from the Baltic foreign intermediaries were still predominant. Even in the middle of the sixteenth century the English Crown negotiated with the Hanse for the purchase in Baltic countries of such commodities as, to quote the Acts of the Privy Council,[117] 'are necessary to His Royal Majesty for equipping the fleet, such as cordage, masts, anchors, pitch, flax, etc'. And at the start of the second half of the century Hanse merchants were shipping various Baltic commodities to England in quite large quantities;[118] as we shall see, we come across their names in the English port books even later, though the entries grow steadily fewer. The process of reducing the Hanse's share in England's imports from the Baltic was accompanied by another, the growth of Dutch intermediaries, but the extent of the latter's intervention cannot be precisely expressed in figures.

England's trading penetration of the Baltic, which became possible on any large scale only after the Hanse had been eliminated and after the disintegration of the League's internal cohesion and economic role, constituted one of the earliest branches of English expansion in the times of Elizabeth I. It was a part of the same economic trend which directed the country's trading interests eastward and southward, to Moscow, the Baltic, the Levant and Africa, to the Iberian peninsula, etc, and which gave birth to several great companies: the Muscovy and the Eastland, the Levant, the African and the Spanish companies.[119] These organizations became the preserve of the wealthy English merchant class of great wholesalers, who monopolized the benefits arising from the conquest of new markets for English trade and capital.

The fifteenth and sixteenth centuries were marked, in England as in certain other western European countries, by increasing intensification of early capitalistic production. In England, Holland, France and certain parts of Germany, a system of manufacture developed which constituted an important stage in the development of crafts and industry in those countries. Because many fundamental features of the feudal social structure were maintained at the same time, this industry could not count on mass consumption in its parent countries, and it vigorously sought markets for the disposal of its products, particularly in areas where local production was weak. These factors explain the economic pressure exerted by England and other western European countries, especially Holland, on the countries of eastern Europe, which for many years had bought numerous products of foreign craftsmanship. These western countries were the more interested in the economic penetration of the Baltic area because they were able to obtain in return large quantities of needed commodities, in England's case primarily naval stores and grain.

Thus the English were stimulated into seeking more and more new and distant markets, not only by the enlargement of navigational possibilities and the 'adventurous spirit of the age', but above all by clear economic necessity. In consequence of the shrinking and closing of the old commercial markets near at hand which had been England's traditional customers and suppliers ever since the Middle Ages, she was faced with the urgent necessity to find new outlets for the disposal of her cloth, on which the country's economic progress hinged. A few months before Elizabeth ascended the throne England lost Calais, which had for long been an entrepot for her wool. Not long after, a new blow to English trade came with the closure of the Antwerp market. The trading post which England obtained in Hamburg in 1567 not only signified her conquest of a new, convenient base for the support of her trade on the Continent, it also made a broad breach in the Hanse monopoly.

England's expansion in the Baltic during the sixteenth century was an excellent reflection of the trend and nature of the changes that took place in Tudor England. During this period of great increase in economic, political and demographic dynamism, in the development of mining, crafts and industry, especially of cloth manufacture—all of which entailed an important restriction of the agricultural economy —the Baltic market, with its as yet poorly developed crafts production, was of great significance to England, since it was a considerable outlet for English cloth, while it supplied the English fleet with all kinds of good-quality yet cheap raw materials. A clear proof of England's growing interest in trade with the area in Tudor times is provided by the activities of Crown agents in Danzig from 1538 onwards; known as the 'king's merchant for Danske' and also as 'King's merchant in the east parts beyond the seas', their chief task was precisely to keep the English fleet supplied with masts, cordage, tar and other naval stores. In the time of Henry VIII, Edward VI and Mary one of these agents was William Watson,[120] who was later a member of the Eastland Company. Through his mediation Henry VIII negotiated with the Danzig city council in 1546 for the purchase of cordage, masts and other naval stores.[121] Through him Queen Mary communicated with the king of Poland, Sigismund Augustus, in 1558, asking him to allow Watson to export materials necessary for the English fleet from Danzig free of customs duty.[122] The Acts of the Privy Council repeatedly cite Watson's name in connection with his mission in Danzig.[123] For a brief period his successor in Danzig was John Borthwick,[124] and after him the Crown agent for Baltic trade for many years was Thomas Allen, later a member of the Eastland Company, and simultaneously treasurer of the company which financed Frobisher's voyages in search of the North-west Passage.[125] By the example of Allen and many other merchants who were members of the Eastland Company (see chapter four), one can best grasp the scope and range of England's foreign trading and explorative activities during the age in which her economic and maritime power was born.

Notes

1 Because of the introductory nature of this chapter, remarks on the subject of England's early relations with the Baltic area have been confined to fundamental issues.

2 Cf G. Labuda, *Źródła, sagi i legendy do najdawniejszych dziejów Polski* (*Sources, sagas and legends of Poland's earliest history*), Warsaw, 1960, pp. 13–90.

3 *Ibid.*, pp. 51*f*, 86.

4 *Oxford English dictionary*, vol. III, Oxford, 1961, p. 20 E.

5 *A.P.C.*, vol. X, pp. 272, 277, 280, etc.

6 *Calendar of Patent Rolls, Philip and Mary*, vol. I, London, 1937, p. 386; vol. II, London, 1936, pp. 266*f*.
7 P.R.O., Patent Rolls, 21 Elizabeth, c. 66/1185.
8 A. Szelągowski, *Z dziejów współzawodnictwa Anglü i Niemiec, Rosji i Polski*, Lwów, 1910, p. 92, even called the Baltic trade 'the cradle of England's modern commercial might'. See also E. Volckmann, *Der Grundstein britischer Weltmacht: geschichtliche und handelspolitische Studien über die Beziehungen zwischen Altpreussen und England bis auf Jacob I*, Würzburg, 1923, p. vii.
9 *Libelle of Englyshe polycye*, ed. G. Warner, Oxford, 1926, p. 16. The circumstances surrounding the writing of this poem have been discussed comprehensively by G. A. Holmes, 'The *Libel of English policy*', *E.H.R.*, vol. LXXVI, 1961, No. 299, pp. 193–216.
10 The text is given in *Tudor economic documents*, ed. R. H. Tawney and E. Power, vol. III, London, 1953, pp. 90–129, especially p. 108.
11 The name 'Spruceland' and the noun 'Spruce' obviously did not enter the English language as an adaptation of the Polish expression *z Prus* ('from Prussia'). This derivation was suggested by M. Aurousseau in 'What's in an English geographical name?', *Geographical Journal*, vol. CXVIII, 1952, p. 193, but it was rejected by E. Słuszkiewicz, 'Czy ang. spruce "rodzaj jodły" pochodzi z pol. "z Prus"?' ('Does the English word "spruce" derive from the Polish expression "z Prus"?') *Język Polski* (*Polish Language*), vol. XXXIV, 1954, pp. 309–11. See also B. Wojciechowski, 'Język angielski świadkiem polskości Gdańska' ('The English language a witness to the Polish character of Danzig'), *Problemy* No. 2, 1953, p. 137.
12 In *Britain in world affairs: Henry VIII to Elizabeth II*, London, 1961, p. 55, Lord Strang expressed the view that England's dependence on Baltic supplies of naval raw materials in the sixteenth century was akin to her present dependence on imports of crude oil.
13 Letter from T. Bannister and G. Duckett to William Cecil, 12 August 1568. *Cal.S.P.For. Elizabeth, 1566–68*, p. 518. In this letter England's dependence on imports from the Baltic was even called 'the bondage of . . . the town of Dantsick'.
14 *Calendar of the manuscripts of Major-General Lord Sackville, Cranfield papers, 1551–1612*, ed. A. P. Newton, vol. I, London, 1940, p. 36.
15 William Cecil's letter to Lord Talbot, dated 23 October 1590, which contains the following passage: 'The Turk, had he not been prevented by our Ambassador, intended to set upon the King of Poland with 60,000 men; but, understanding her Majesty had great need of many things from the country necessary for her navy, he withdrew his force, though he was assured of victory, only for her Majesty's sake, who received great thanks from the King of Poland.' Cf E. Lodge, *Illustrations of British history, biography, and manners in the reign of Henry VIII, Edward VI, Mary, Elizabeth and James I*, vol. II, London, 1838, p. 414.

16 H. Lippomano to the Doge and Senate, under date 6 August 1590—*Cal.S.P. Venice*, vol. VIII, No. 946. Cf also W. Camden, *Annales rerum Anglicarum et Hibernicarum regnante Elizabetha*, Amsterdam, 1677, p. 605. On this issue R. Heidenstein remarked in *Dzieje Polski od śmierci Zygmunta Augusta do roku 1594* (*History of Poland from the death of Sigismund Augustus to the year 1594*), vol. II, Petersburg, 1857, p. 293*f*, that the English ambassador had convinced the Vizier that 'if Poland begins war with Turkey she will not be able to supply either grain, or timber for the fleet, things which are absolutely necessary to England'. In his *Kronika* (*Chronicle*), vol. III, p. 1647, Bielski was rather less precise, saying that the English ambassador was to put forward the argument to Turkey that 'if the Poles are occupied with a Turkish war they will also certainly want to use those things against you, with which hitherto they have saved my mistress, obtaining from Poland food, materials, and other requisites for ships of war'. Cf also J. U. Niemcewicz, *Dzieje panowania Zygmunta III* (*History of the reign of Sigismund III*), vol. I, Cracow, 1860, p. 107. J. Jasnowski, *England and Poland in the sixteenth and seventeenth centuries*, Oxford, 1948, p. 22, also discussed the subject in a similar manner.

17 F. Moryson, *An itinerary containing his ten years' travel . . .*, vol. IV, Glasgow, 1908, pp. 69–70.

18 B.M. MSS, King's 18 BI. The authorship of this narrative has not been definitely established; it has also been attributed to George Carew. Cf 'Relation of the State of Polonia and the United Provinces of that Crown, *anno* 1598', ed. C. H. Talbot, in *Elementa ad fontium editiones*, vol. XIII, Rome, 1965, pp. xiii–xv. Cf also E. A. Mierzwa, 'Angielska relacja o Polsce z roku 1598' ('An English narrative concerning Poland dated 1598'), *Annales U.M.C.S.*, section F, vol. XVII, 1965, pp. 87–118.

19 B.M. MSS, King's 18 B I, f. 168. This author called Poland 'the common grenary and Arsenall of all Europe for tackling and other appraile of shipping'. But Moryson (*op. cit.*, vol. IV, p. 69) wrote that Poland 'is so aboundeth with corne and pastures, as it supplies all Europe with corn'.

20 J. M. Lappenbach, *Urkundliche Geschichte des hansischen Stahlhofes zu London*, vol. I, Hamburg, 1851, p. 37. Cf also *H.U.*, vol. I, No. 1154, p. 399.

21 T. Hirsch, *Danzigs Handels- und Gewerbsgeschichte unter der Herrschaft des deutschen Ordens*, Leipzig, 1858, pp. 100 and 112. Cf also A. Horn, 'Alt-England und Alt-Preussen', *Altpreussische Monatsschrift*, vol. I, 1864, p. 64.

22 Letter of Eastland Company, 17 December 1659, *Cal.S.P.Dom.*, 1659–1660, p. 283.

23 Cf H. Fiedler, 'Danzig und England: die Handelsbestrebungen der Engländer vom Ende des 14 bis zum Ausgang des 17 Jahrhunderts', *Z.W.G.*, vol. LXVIII, 1928, p. 71; also P. Simson, *Geschichte der Stadt Danzig*, vol. I, Danzig, 1913, p. 103.

24 H. L. Gray, 'The production and exportation of English woollens in the fourteenth century', *E.H.R.*, vol. XXXIX, 1924, pp. 13*ff.*

25 For England's trade with Danzig in the fourteenth century see P. Simson, *Geschichte . . .*, vol. I, p. 69. For Elbing see E. Carstenn, *Geschichte der Hansestadt Elbing*, Elbing, 1937, p. 99.

26 *Scriptores rerum Prussicarum*, vol. II, Leipzig, 1863, pp. 479, 531, 792, 795.

27 *Chaucer: works, Canterbury tales*, prologue, Oxford Edition, ed. W. W. Skeat (n.d.), p. 419.

28 *Foedera, conventiones, litterae et cuiuscunque acta publica . . .*, ed. T. Rymer, vol. III, The Hague, 1740, part 4, p. 66.

29 R. Hakluyt, *The principal navigations, voyages, traffiques and discoveries of the English nation*, vol. II (London, 1962 edition), pp. 20–2.

30 Among the most important works on the question see E. R. Daenell, *Die Blütezeit der deutschen Hanse: hansische Geschichte von der zweiten Hälfte des 14 bis zum Letzten Viertel des 15 Jahrhunderts*, vol. I, Berlin, 1905; D. Schäfer, *Die Hanse*, Bielefeld–Leipzig, 1903; F. Schulz, 'Die Hanse und England von Edwards III bis auf Heinrichs VIII Zeit', in *Abhandlungen zur Verkehrs- und Seegeschichte*, vol. V, Berlin, 1911; and others. Of English contributions to the subject, M. M. Postan's work, cited in the Bibliography, remains of basic importance.

31 K. Kunze, *Hanseakten aus England, 1275–1412*, Halle, 1891, pp. iii–xxii, discusses the Hanse's privileges in England in the thirteenth and fourteenth centuries in great detail.

32 As early as 1378–79 English merchants' complaints included a demand of this nature: see *H.R.*, Abt. I, vol. II, No. 212. At that time the English demanded that the Hanse should allow them to enter its trading area on similar advantageous conditions to those the Hanse enjoyed in England. They also demanded the non-application of collective responsibility in cases of repressive measures.

33 M. M. Postan, 'The economic and political relations of England and the Hanse, 1400–75', in *Studies in English Trade in the fifteenth century*, pp. 100*ff.*

34 Cf *Acten der Ständetage Preussens unter der Herrschaft des deutschen Ordens*, ed. M. Toeppen, vol. I, Leipzig, 1878, No. 335. See also. K. Höhlbaum, 'Preussen und England im 13 und 14 Jahrhundert', *Altpreussische Monatsschrift*, vol. XV, 1878. H. Świderska discusses this problem in 'Z dziejów stosunków angielsko-krzyżackich, XIII–XV wiek' ('History of relations between England and the Order of the Cross, thirteenth to fifteenth centuries'), *Teki Londynskie* (*London portfolios*), vol. X, 1959, pp. 103*ff.*

35 In 1385 goods belonging to eighty-eight English merchants were detained in Danzig: *H.R.*, Abt. I, vol. III, No. 404, pp. 405–07. More or less at the same time the Grand Master of the Teutonic Knights ordered the confiscation in Danzig and Elbing of goods belonging to sixty-nine English merchants. Cf Hirsch, *op. cit.*, p. 99.

36 For example, such rights were granted to John Bade in 1370, to John of London in 1374, to Robert Nixon in 1380, etc.: Hirsch, *op. cit.*, p. 98.
37 *H.U.*, vol. III, No. 685, p. 487.
38 *H.R.*, Abt. I, vol. II, Nos. 236, 402–6.
39 *Ibid.*, vol. III, Nos. 375 and 402.
40 Hakluyt, *op. cit.*, vol. I, pp. 122*ff.*
41 *H.U.*, vol. IV, No. 1042, p. 462.
42 *Ibid.*, pp. 462–3.
43 *Ibid.*, No. 928, p. 395. Bebys also took part on behalf of the English court in negotiations with the Hanse in 1390; *ibid.*, No. 1040, p. 461*f.*
44 The term 'Sounde', which occurs in the privilege, was explained by the editor of the volume, Kunze, as meaning Stralsund (*ibid.*, p. 509). Koppmann gives the same explanation in his 'Die preussisch-englischen Beziehungen der Hanse, 1373–1408', *Hansische Geschichtsblätter*, vol. XII, 1884, p. 121. But it would seem that in fact not Stralsund, but the Sound, was intended.
45 Richard II's privilege of 1390 and that of Henry IV in 1404 refer to the English merchants 'in partibus Pruciae et de Scone ac in aliis partibus de Hansa': *H.U.*, vol. IV, No. 1042, p. 462; vol. V, No. 616, p. 317.
46 *H.U.*, vol. IV, No. 1042, p. 462. On the subject of the English trading post in Danzig, see the meagre references in Simson, *Geschichte . . .*, vol. I, p. 102; Hirsch, *op. cit.*, p. 100; Schulz, *op. cit.*, p. 51; Daenell, *Die Blütezeit der deutschen Hanse*, vol. I, p. 64.
47 *H.U.*, vol. VI, No. 732, p. 403.
48 J. Rogers' report to Walsingham, dated 1 April 1581: P.R.O., S.P. 88/1, No. 9.
49 Koppmann drew attention to this fact: *op. cit.*, p. 117; also Małowist, *Studia z dziejów rzemiosła . . .*, p. 97. The erroneous opinion was long maintained in Danzig historiography to the effect that in 1392 as many as 300 English vessels arrived at that city to take on grain; it has no basis whatever in the source material. Cf, for example, K. Lohmeyer, *Geschichte von Ost- und Westpreussen*, Gotha, 1908, p. 306; Simson, *Geschichte . . .*, vol. I, p. 103; Fiedler, *op. cit.*, p. 74, and others. As E. Waschinski showed in his article 'Haben im Jahre 1392 300 englische Schiffe gleichzeitig im Danziger Hafen Getreide geladen', *Weichselland*, vol. XXXVIII, No. 4, 1939, pp. 73–9, this faulty opinion was the result of a distortion of the narratives of sixteenth- and seventeenth-century chroniclers, who noted only that in 1392 probably an aggregate of 300 Dutch, French and English ships arrived at Danzig. As Waschinski demonstrated, the main share in this figure went to French vessels.
50 *H.R.*, Abt. I, vol. IV, No. 345; also *Acten der Ständetage . . .*, vol. I, p. 52.
51 *H.R.*, Abt. I, vol. IV, No. 409. At a Hanse congress in Danzig on 2 July 1397 the resolution was passed: 'das keyn koufman us der Deutscher hense beussen Engeland von den Englischen gewant koeuffe, sonder in Engeland alleyne'.

52 Cf Fiedler, *op. cit.*, p. 77.
53 *Acten der Ständetage* . . ., vol. I, No. 70.
54 *H.R.*, Abt. I, vol. V, Nos. 205, 225, etc.
55 *Foedera* . . ., vol. IV, part I, p. 165; also *H.U.*, vol. V, p. 317.
56 *H.U.*, vol. V, p. 317, comment I.
57 *Foedera* . . ., vol. IV, part I, p. 125.
58 *H.U.*, vol. VI, No. 736, p. 413.
59 E. M. Carus-Wilson, 'The origin and early development of the Merchant Adventurers' organization in London', *Ec.H.R.*, vol. IV, 1933, pp. 147*ff*.
60 N. Tench, *Reasons humbly offered by the Governor, Assistants, and Fellowship of Eastland-Merchants*, London, 1689, p. 6: 'About the time of King Henry the 4th the English began to trade themselves into the Eastparts.'
61 B.M. Sloane MSS, 25, f. 13.
62 J. W. Burgon, *Life and times of Sir Thomas Gresham*, vol. I, London, 1839, pp. 484*ff*.
63 For example, D. W. Davies, *A primer of Dutch seventeenth century overseas trade*, The Hague, 1961, discusses the various trends of Dutch trade in the second half of the sixteenth and in the seventeenth centuries but gives very little attention to the Dutch role in England's Baltic trade, even though his work attempts to cover Dutch trade as a whole in the period. In his *Dutch trade to the Baltic about 1600: studies in the Sound toll register and Dutch shipping records*, Copenhagen–The Hague, 1941, A. E. Christensen also ignores the issue.
64 P.R.O., S.P.Dom. 14/118, No. 114. The full title of Keymer's tract reads: *Keymer's book of observation for your most excellent Majestie touchinge trade and traffique beyond the seas and in England.* It is not included in J. R. McCulloch, *Early English tracts on commerce*, Cambridge, 1954 (reprint of the 1856 edition). But in 1653 Keymer's tract was published, in an edition now not easily obtainable, as being from the pen of Sir Walter Ralegh. Cf W. Raleigh, *Observations touching trade and commerce with Hollander and other nations* . . ., London, 1653.
65 Keymer wrote that the Dutch 'make store-houses of all foreign commodities, wherewith, upon every occasion of scarcity and dearth, they are able to furnish foreign countries with plenty of those commodities, which before in time of plenty they engrossed and brought home from the same places . . .': P.R.O., S.P.Dom. 17/118, No. 114.
66 Cf Małowist, *Studia z dziejów rzemiosła* . . ., pp. 229, 278, etc.
67 K. B. McFarlane, 'War, the economy and social change: England and the Hundred Years War', *Past and Present*, No. 22, 1962, pp. 3*ff*.
68 Hirsch, *op. cit.*, p. 106.
69 *Ibid.* In the Danzig aldermen's register both these men were called 'Olderlude der Englischen'.
70 Simson, *Geschichte* . . ., vol. I, p. 156.
71 Cf the letter from the Danzig council to the Grand Master in 1440: *Acten der Ständetage* . . ., vol. II, pp. 140*ff*. Attacking the English merchants

sojourning in Danzig, the council reported that certain English 'lose weiber nemen, die do gehen hoher gekleidet, dan ein ander erbar frau. Darumb ist unser begeren noch, das sie kein gastung oder gastheuser halden und kein haubstrosse inwonen.'

72 For instance, on 21 July 1402, as can be deduced from the records of the Marienburg congress, 'die Engelschen, die myt wyben unde kynderen her int land sint gekomen, sullen czwisschen hir unde czu vorjoren heym czheen, unde lengh sullen sy hir im lande nich wonende blibin.'—*H.R.*, Abt. I, vol. v, No. 101. In July 1404 at a congress in Danzig it was resolved: 'dy Engelschen czu Danczk wesende, dy nicht borgere syn, sullen czwisschen hiir unde Michaelis von hynne usme lande rumen'—*ibid.*, No. 203.

73 A good illustration of this is provided by, for instance, certain incidents in 1423, when the Hanse congress at Lübeck recommended the Hanseatic cities to arrest any English merchants residing in them and to confiscate their goods as an act of revenge for England's policy towards the Hanse. The Prussian cities and the Teutonic Order paid no attention to this recommendation because of their trading interests—*H.R.*, Abt I, vol. VII, Nos. 461, 708, 746, 773, 800, 821, etc.

74 Cf Postan, '. . . England and the Hanse', p. 111.

75 Fiedler, *op. cit.*, p. 84.

76 G. Schanz, *Englische Handelspolitik gegen Ende des Mittelalters mit besonderer Berücksichtigung des Zeitalters der beiden ersten Tudors Heinrich VII und Heinrich VIII*, vol. II, Leipzig, 1881, p. 28.

77 *Studies in English trade in the fifteenth century*, ed. E. Power and M. M. Postan, London, 1933, p. 407.

78 *Studies in English trade . . .*, pp. 330–60; also *England's export trade, 1275–1547*, ed. E. M. Carus-Wilson and O. Coleman, Oxford, 1963, pp. 75*ff*.

79 *Studies in English trade . . .*, pp. 343–6.

80 *Ibid.*, p. 339. There was a marked decline in the export of cloth from Ipswich in the second half of the century.

81 *Ibid.*, pp. 341*f*.

82 *Ibid.*, pp. 347*f*.

83 *Ibid.*, pp. 359*f*.

84 Cf H. L. Gray, 'English foreign trade from 1446 to 1482' in *Studies in English trade . . .*, p. 25.

85 Postan, '. . . England and the Hanse', p. 143.

86 Cf Małowist, *Studia z dziejów rzemiosła . . .*, p. 101.

87 Hirsch, *op. cit.*, p. 99.

88 C. Sattler, *Handelsrechnungen des deutschen Ordens*, Leipzig, 1887, pp. 21 and 77.

89 Hirsch, *op. cit.*, p. 116.

90 H. Samsonowicz, 'Handel Gdańska w pierwszej połowie XV wieku' ('Danzig's trade in the first half of the fifteenth century'), *P.H.*, vol. LIII, 1962, pp. 695*ff*.

91 H. Samsonowicz, 'Handel zagraniczny Gdańska w drugiej połowie XV wieku' ('Danzig's foreign trade in the second half of the fifteenth century'), *P.H.*, vol. XLVII, 1956, No. 2, pp. 282*ff*; also V. Lauffer, 'Danzig's Schiffs- und Wahrenverkehr am Ende des XV Jahrhunderts', *Z.W.G.*, vol. XXXIII, 1894, pp. 2*ff.*

92 Samsonowicz, 'Handel zagraniczny Gdańska . . .', p. 334.

93 *H.R.*, Abt. 2, vol. II, No. 36.

94 *Tabeller over skibsfart og varetransport gennem Öresunde*, 1497–1660, ed. N. E. Bang and K. Korst, Copenhagen–Leipzig, 1906–33, vol. I, p. 2.

95 H. Samsonowicz, *Badania nad kapitałem mieszczańskim Gdańska w II połowie XV wieku* (*Investigations into Danzig burgher capital in the second half of the fifteenth century*), Warsaw, 1960, p. 47. Cf also his 'Studien über Danziger Kaufmannskapital im 15 Jahrhundert', *Forschungen zur mittelalterlichen Geschichte*, vol. VIII, *Hansische Studien*, Berlin, 1961, pp. 334*ff*.

96 Samsonowicz, 'Studien über Danziger Kaufmannskapital', p. 335.

97 P.R.O., Cranfield papers, MS S. 637 (no page numbers).

98 Exceptionally rich source material on these problems is contained in the two main publications of documents on the history of the Hanseatic League, *Hanserecesse* and *Hansisches Urkundenbuch.*

99 Cf G. Unwin, 'The Merchant Adventurers' Company in the reign of Elizabeth' in *Studies in economic history: the collected papers of George Unwin*, ed. R. H. Tawney, London, 1958 (first edition, 1927), pp. 133*ff.*

100 *H.R.*, Abt. 2, vol. II, No. 84.

101 When in 1438 the English, placing a broad interpretation on the passage in the London agreement which said that their relations in the Hanseatic cities were to be constituted the same 'as had been the custom before 10, 20, 30, 40, 50, and 100 years', demanded a series of privileges, for instance freedom from mooring dues and poundage, the right to settle freely, to possess their own house, various trading liberties, etc., there was considerable indignation in Danzig, and a hostile attitude to Vorrath developed. (Cf Fiedler, *op. cit.*, p. 90.) Despite the fact that the representatives of Toruń (Thorn), Elbing and Königsberg all expressed their support of the agreement at the congress of estates in Marienburg, on 12 May 1438, Danzig spoke against its confirmation.—*Acten der Ständetage*, vol. II, p. 40.

102 Postan, '. . . England and the Hanse', p. 121. Cf also E. F. Jacob, *The fifteenth century, 1399–1485, Oxford history of England*, vol. VI, Oxford, 1961, p. 359.

103 W. Stein, 'Die Hanse und England beim Ausgang des hundert-jährigen Krieges', *Hansische Geschichtsblätter*, vol. XXVI, 1921, pp. 27*ff.*

104 *Scriptores rerum Prussicarum*, vol. IV, p. 730, and vol. V, p. 443.

105 *H.R.*, Abt 2, vol. VI, Nos. 418–21, 436, 589.

106 K. Pagel, *Die Hanse*, Brunswick, 1952, p. 378. R. Pauli, 'Die Haltung der Hansestädte in den Rosenkriegen', *Hansische Geschichtsblätter*, vol. IV,

1874, p. 90, endeavours one-sidedly to explain the peace conditions of Utrecht, which were advantageous to the Hanse, by reference to the obligations which Edward IV had entered into with Danzig in return for its aid during the Wars of the Roses. The explanation of the Utrecht peace conditions is to be found in the entire complex of England's and Hanse's political and economic situations.

107 Despite this agreement, the Hanse did not return to the house in Boston. Cf J. D. Mackie, *The earlier Tudors, 1485–1558, Oxford history of England*, vol. VII, Oxford, 1952, p. 221.

108 Postan, '. . . England and the Hanse', p. 150.

109 J. D. Mackie, *op. cit.*, p. 221, is even of the opinion that the English 'posts in Danzig and Bergen were lost and they were excluded from the Baltic trade', which would appear to be too extreme a view.

110 Schanz, *op. cit.*, vol. I, pp. 172–246. L. Boratyński's statement, in 'Stefan Batory, Hanza i powstanie Niderlandów' ('Stefan Batory, the Hanse and the Netherlands rising'), *P.H.*, vol. VI, 1908, p. 56, that the Hanse had already had the ground cut from under its feet in England at the beginning of the sixteenth century is obviously erroneous.

111 Schulz, *op. cit.*, p. 21.

112 *Danziger Inventar*, Nos. 783, 784, 785, 808, 819, 1362, 1375, 1378, 1405, 1463, 1547, 1554, 1614, 1617, etc.

113 *Ibid.*, Nos. 2505, 2527, 2545, 2549, 2640, 2643, 2644, 2653, 2673, 2685, 2696, 2885, 2923, 3116, 3117, 3122, 3124, 3130, 3133, 3143, 3151, etc.

114 P.R.O., S.P. Supplementary 46/9.

115 Schanz, *op. cit.*, vol. II, pp. 102–3.

116 *Ibid.*, vol. II, p. 105.

117 *A.P.C., 1547–50*, p. 61.

118 For example, at the end of May 1560 the English court negotiated with the merchants of Lübeck for the supply to England of Danzig ships' cables, which at the time were much cheaper than the Dutch variety. Cf *Cal.S.P.For. Elizabeth, 1560–61*, London, 1865, No. 138, p. 88.

119 The basic literature on this problem has been discussed in Zins, 'Angielska historiografia elżbietańska', pp. 182*f.*

120 *L.P. Henry VIII*, vol. XX, part I, pp. 193*f.*

121 *Ibid.*, vol. XXI, part I, pp. 107, 660.

122 Letter from Sigismund Augustus to Mary Tudor, dated 15 May 1558: *Cal.S.P.For., 1553–58*, No. 769, p. 375.

123 *A.P.C.*, vol. I, p. 321; vol. II, p. 120; vol. III, p. 297, etc.

124 *Ibid.*, vol. III, p. 365. The Acts of the Privy Council in 1551 name him as 'the Kinges Majesties Agent in Danske' in connection with the task entrusted to him of securing the release of a load of ninety-six pieces of cloth detained in Danzig which belonged to the London merchant Thomas Bannister.

125 *Cal.S.P.Dom., 1547–80*, p. 608; also *A.P.C.*, vol. X, p. 415.

two *The Muscovy Company and the Narva route in England's Baltic trade*

During the Elizabethan era England's foreign trade developed rapidly, branching out in many directions. In the majority of cases, whether in the Levant or in Africa, the English followed in the tracks of Portuguese and other explorers and merchants, and thus inevitably coming into conflict with them. In the Baltic area also England's penetration was accompanied by bitter rivalry with the Hanse. However, in the middle of the sixteenth century she found a direction for trading expansion which did not expose her to conflicts with the seafaring might of Spain or Portugal, although it brought difficulties of a different kind, chiefly of a climatic and navigational nature. This new direction was the northern route to Russia, which, in contemporary eyes, promised to lead not only to the realm of the tsars but also to the riches of the East, to the legendary treasures of China and India.[1] The expedition which set sail in 1553 to discover the north-eastern passage to China and India resulted in the establishment of a trade route through the White Sea to Moscow and the foundation of the Muscovy Company, the first organization of the joint-stock type of company in English foreign trade.[2]

The genesis of the Muscovy Company is associated with the initiative of some 240 London merchants, among them many Merchant Adventurers, who, with the support of the court, financed the 1553 expedition to discover the north-eastern route to the sum of £6,000 sterling in shares of £25 each.[3] The idea of such an expedition was not entirely novel. It had been suggested in Henry VIII's time, and in 1527 Robert Thorne had argued that 'out of Spain they have discovered all the Indies and seas occidental, and out of Portugal all the Indies and seas oriental', in view of which the north was left as the natural area for Englishmen to explore.[4]

The plan to reach the treasures of the East was not the only motive for sending an expedition to the White Sea.[5] There can be no doubt that fundamentally it was inspired by the necessity to find new markets for English cloth, which in the middle of the century was experiencing a certain export crisis. During the first half of the

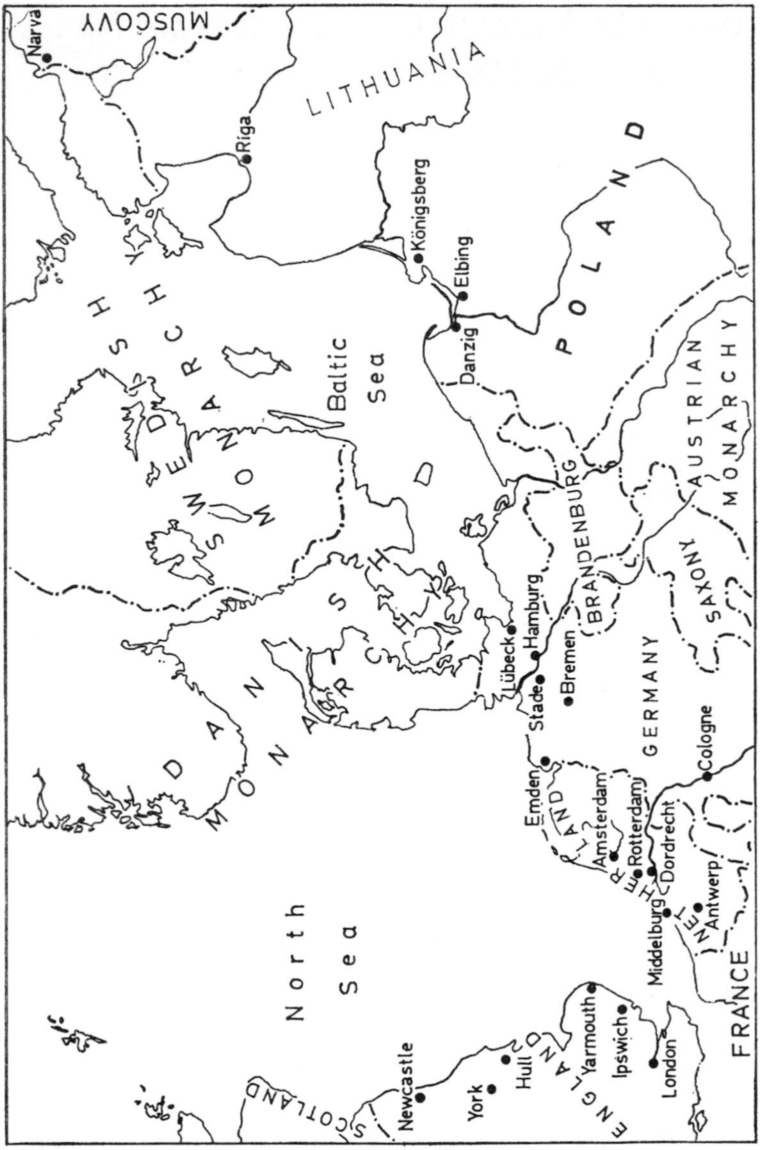

Fig. 1 Northern Europe about 1560 *Marketing centres of the Merchant Adventurers and of the Eastland merchants*

century cloth exports from London had increased by some 150 per cent, but after 1550 there was a decline, from 132,767 cloths in that year to 84,969 in 1552. During the 1550's and 1560's exports remained at a level much below that of the first half of the century.[6] In this connection a noteworthy statement was made about this time by Clement Adams, who associated the origins of the 1553 expedition more with the search for new markets than with the desire to find gold, and added:

our marchants perceived the commodities and wares of England to bee in small request with the countreys and people about us, and neere unto us, and that those Marchandizes which strangers in the time and memorie of our ancestors did earnestly seeke and desire, were nowe neglected, and the price thereof abated . . .

In these circumstances 'certaine grave Citizens of London' decided to develop a new and hitherto unknown direction of trade and navigation.[7] Towards the end of the Elizabethan era the Muscovy Company itself attributed its foundation to these factors, declaring that

in the time of King Edward the Sixthe, the king and his councell, finding it inconvenient that the utterance of the commodities of England, especiallie clothe, should so muche depend upon the Lowe Countries and Spaine and that it should be beneficiall to have a vent some other waies, did encourage his subjectes the merchauntes to adventure for discoverie of the new trades northe warde. . . .[8]

This pronouncement becomes even more understandable when we recall that many of the members of the Muscovy Company were also Merchant Adventurers who depended heavily on the export of cloth to Holland. T. S. Willan's researches have shown that among the original members of the Muscovy Company were some twenty-six Merchant Adventurers, as well as sixteen other merchants who probably belonged to both companies.[9] Willan also established that some thirty per cent of the founders of the Muscovy Company were cloth exporters, which still further confirms the opinion expressed above.

Among the organizers of the expedition 'to China', as the 1553 voyage was officially called, though the ships were to sail to Russia *via* the White Sea, the most important were the famous navigator Sebastian Cabot, son of John Cabot,[10] Hugh Willoughby and the pilot, Richard Chancellor. The fleet consisted of three vessels: the *Bona Speranza*, 120 tons, the *Edward Bonaventure*, 160 tons, and the

Bona Confidentia, 90 tons. In addition to the crews, three doctors and a chaplain, eighteen merchants sailed in the ships, which clearly indicates the expedition's trading objectives. This was further emphasized in Edward VI's letter, addressed to 'all the kings, princes, rulers, judges and governors of the world',[11] which not only extolled the mutual economic benefits that could be derived from trade but reasoned that it conduced to a greater *rapprochement* and friendship among all the peoples of the world.

Of the three ships only one, the *Edward Bonaventure*, commanded by Chancellor, reached the mouth of the Dvina. The others were stranded on the coast of Lapland, and their crews died of cold and starvation. At the court of Ivan IV Chancellor was given a friendly reception, and in 1554 he returned to England bearing a letter from the Tsar to the King in which Ivan expressed the desire to develop trade with England, and to grant English merchants privileges to carry on trade all over his tsardom.[12] A year later, on 26 February 1555, Queen Mary issued a charter setting up the Muscovy Company for trade with Russia[13] and detailing the nature of its organization, its entitlements, and members' obligations, etc.[14] The Company at once developed an active trade with Russia *via* the White Sea, with the support of Ivan IV, who at the end of 1555 conferred extensive trading privileges on the Company. Passing over these well known details as outside the scope of our study, we shall simply consider the nature of the Anglo-Russian trade, and then discuss rather more broadly the issue of the Narva route, which for a brief period enabled England to engage in trade with Russia *via* the Baltic also.

Russian products had long since found their way to England, mainly through the Hanse, which played an essential part in the trade.[15] By this route *via* the ports of Livonia Russian furs, wax and grain were brought to England from Novgorod, and by the same route English cloth[16] had long been exported to the east *via* Gotland and Scandinavia, though it is difficult to give the trade a quantitative value. The English mariners' development of the northern route, which had not hitherto been frequented to any great extent, not only showed that the English merchants had gained independence of the Hanse in their trade with Moscow, but was also a sign that Anglo-Hanseatic rivalry was now extended to the realm of Russian trade, to the further weakening of the Hanse.

We have only fragmentary data on England's trade with Russia at the beginning of the second half of the sixteenth century. They enable us to learn the actual nature of the trade but do not enable more detailed, quantitative estimates to be formed. At the same time they do reveal the serious difficulties which had to be overcome in this northern trade due to the climatic and navigational hazards. For instance, in 1556 three out of four English ships were wrecked on the return voyage.[17] Conditions of this kind[18] meant that in practice only once a year—usually in May or June—did a fleet, consisting usually of several larger ships, make the four weeks' voyage from England to the White Sea; they remained in Russia a month, taking Russian commodities on board, and returned in August or September. Usually an agent of the Muscovy Company supervised the course of the trading operations and, in accordance with the constitution of a joint-stock company, carried the transaction through from beginning to end, acting on behalf of the organization.[19] As we have mentioned, in the case of regulated companies each merchant carried on trade on his own account.

Analysis of the cargoes of the vessels engaged in trade with Moscow at the beginning of the latter half of the sixteenth century reveals the basic role played by cloth exports, while imports consisted chiefly of wax, tallow, flax cordage and furs.[20] Three ships which sailed to Russia in 1560 carried 276 broadcloths, 100 kerseys and small quantities of groceries, salt, tin, etc.[21] In 1564 four ships transported more diversified cargoes;[22] in addition to lead, tin, sulphur, groceries and paper they carried expensive woven goods, silks, etc. The London port book for 1565 shows that in that year 317 broadcloths and 830 kerseys were exported to Moscow.[23] Comparing the data for English exports to Russia with those to the Baltic, we reach the conclusion (which we shall discuss more extensively in chapter eight) that in the second half of the sixteenth century the Russian market was not yet a serious rival to the Baltic area and its dominant Polish ports. During this period the Muscovy ports received only a small percentage of the total English cloth exports to eastern Europe by sea.

So far as England's imports from Russia were concerned, only in respect of flax and cordage did the Russian market prove a serious rival to the Baltic market, partly because of the cheapness of its commodities, as the Muscovy Company itself emphasized in 1557.[24] We shall be making a more detailed analysis in chapter eight. In 1568 two merchants, Bannister and Duckett, drew William Cecil's attention to the benefits to be derived from importing ships' cordage, sails, pitch and other ships' commodities from Moscow, and emphasized that this trade enabled England to be 'delivered out of the bondage of the King of Denmark and the town of Dantzick'.[25] In 1580

Richard Hakluyt, arguing the necessity for further exploration of the north-eastern route 'to China,' expressed the hope that the north Russian market would prove as rich in products requisite to the English fleet as the Baltic market.[26]

Queen Mary's 1555 privilege gave the Muscovy Company the monopoly of trade with Russia and all the countries 'lying to the north, north-east and north-west' which before the English voyage to Russia in 1553 had not been known to English merchants.[27] As at this date Russia had not yet gained access to the Baltic, the Company's trading operations were confined to the northern route *via* the White Sea.[28] The situation changed and became complicated when in 1558 Russia conquered part of Livonia, with its important port of Narva on the mouth of the river Narova in the Gulf of Finland. Ignoring the political aspect of this question,[29] we shall here discuss only its

Table 2.1 *Narva's share in English Baltic sailings, 1563–78 (per cent)*

1563	1564	1565	1566	1567	1568	1569	1574	1578
1·3	18·2	16·6	54·5	30·2	28·9	6·9	17·5	2·6

Source *Tabeller over skibsfart* . . ., vol. 1, pp. 35*ff*.

commercial significance for England in respect of the Baltic trade and the complications it gave rise to for the Muscovy Company.

It is an interesting fact that the Muscovy Company was not immediately interested in the possibility of trading with Russia *via* Narva and that even after 1558 it continued to use the northern route exclusively.[30] We do not know exactly when English merchants first took the Narva route; the Sound toll registers note only one English vessel returning westward from Narva in 1563. But there were six vessels in 1564, forty-two in 1566 (the highest number)and 16 in 1567. In the following years the number of English ships voyaging to and from Narva gradually declined, and after 1574, when there were thirteen, English exploitation of this route to all intents and purposes came to a halt, apart from a few further contacts (for instance, four ships in 1578). So that, with the exception of 1566, when English vessels returning from Narva constituted 54·5 per cent of all the English shipping passing out of the Baltic through the

Sound, and again in 1567 and 1568, the Narva calls were a relatively small proportion of the total Baltic sailings of English vessels.

The merchants of Hamburg had already entered into trading relations with Narva, in 1560, when ten of their ships returned from that port through the Sound.[31] The Dutch also developed trade with Narva in this period.[32]

The opening of the Narva route faced the Muscovy Company with the quite serious danger of losing its monopoly of the Russian trade if English merchants not belonging to the Company were to be allowed to trade with Russia *via* the Baltic, a development which, of course, the Company's founders could not foresee in 1555, when they drew up the plans for their privilege. In addition, as a joint stock company, it did not allow its members to engage in individual trading activities and considered trade with Narva, which certain members undertook on their own account, as illegal.[33] It regarded Narva as a port coming within its sphere of influence, ostensibly because from 1558 onward Narva was situated in territory taken over by Moscow.

About 1564 a group of London merchants began trading with Narva. The chief figures in this development were George and William Bond, and John Foxall. Their activities on this new route for Moscow trade attracted the attention of the Privy Council, which sought the opinion of Sir Nicholas Bacon (father of Francis Bacon, the philosopher), on the issue. Bacon's reply, dated 4 April 1564, included an unexpectedly positive estimate of the new route and the prospects of trade with Narva; trade with Moscow he even declared to be 'the best traffique for the commoditie of the realme that hath bene founde in our age . . .' because of ' . . . the necessitie of the wares, their easye pryces, the shortenes of the journey, and the vente of our commodities considered'.[34] He was of the opinion that in deciding the question of the route to Moscow, the northern one or that *via* the Baltic to Narva, it was necessary to be guided by the interests of the country, and not those of individual merchants. The shorter route and the cheaper freightage cost—about 20 per cent less than that for the northern route—told in favour of Narva. Bacon's own opinion was decidedly for maintaining and developing the Moscow trade *via* Narva and against its monopolization by the Muscovy Company. He considered that this trade should be accessible without restrictions to all English merchants.

The great importance attached at the time to trade with Moscow is indicated by a speech the Swedish ambassador made at the English court on 3 April 1560. Canvassing the possibility of a marriage between Elizabeth and the King of Sweden, he considered that many benefits would arise from a union of the two kingdoms, and among them would be a considerable improvement of England's position in trade with Russia.[35]

However, Nicholas Bacon's memorial supporting the case for individual trade with Narva did not meet with the approval of the Privy Council, which finally adopted the position of the Muscovy Company and therefore of the great London monopolists. Towards the end of 1564 the Privy Council ordered William Bond to cease trading with Narva on his own account, and for a short time he was even held under arrest because of his refusal to obey. The three London merchants mentioned above made an attempt at this time to defend their trade with Narva, appealing even to Magna Carta and the statutes of Edward III dealing with trade, as well as to the Muscovy Company's 1555 privilege, which, obviously, made no mention of Narva. In the opinion of the Bond brothers and John Foxall, Narva could not fall within the Muscovy Company's area of monopoly, since it had not been discovered by the Company.[36] They considered that financial factors also told in favour of individual trade with Narva. It could bring the English Crown an income of £500 from customs duties, for they estimated it would employ nine vessels annually to import such cheap and useful Russian products as wax, tallow. flax, hemp, etc.

In reply to the arguments of the advocates of free trade with Narva the Muscovy Company appealed to the fact that no English merchant had ever traded with Narva before the issue of the 1555 privilege, and so, in accordance with the terms of that privilege, Narva had to be regarded as falling within the Company's area of monopoly. It also challenged the argument appealing to the lower costs of the Narva route, pointing out the political complications and dangers of war involved in this route as compared with the greater safety of the northern voyage. And the northern route should be cheaper too; for example, cordage imported by this route would be two shillings cheaper per hundred than cordage bought in the Baltic area.[37]

In considering the question of the Narva route the Privy Council took into account chiefly factors of a political nature and the difficulties of Baltic navigation during the northern war and the struggles for Livonia. Without going deeply into the issue, we may recall that in the years 1558–61 as many as four States—Poland with Lithuania,

Ivan the Terrible's Russia, Denmark and Sweden—all had pretensions to the heritage of the disintegrating State of the Knights of the Sword in Livonia. The clash of these countries' interests led to a conflict of European significance embracing a large area of northern Europe. Livonia was particularly important to Russia, for previously the State had been a barrier to Moscow's access to the Baltic and to her trading, political and cultural relations with the West. However, Ivan IV's political programme aimed not only at gaining access to the Baltic ports but also at the complete domination of Livonia. The Polish Commonwealth took alarm at this policy, and in 1557 declared war on the Order of the Sword; in the spring of 1558 the Tsar invaded Livonia and occupied Narva and Dorpat. The opening of Narva as a port for Russia was opposed by the Polish court, which called on various States and cities to discontinue using it and to institute a Baltic blockade of Russia. We may add that in 1560 Denmark exploited the crisis in the Order of the Sword in Livonia by acquiring considerable possessions from the Bishop of Ösel; Sweden followed suit in 1561, occupying Estonia with the port of Reval. Poland with Lithuania also had designs on Livonia, and in 1561 the Master of the Order, Gotard von Kettler, made Livonia subject to the Polish Commonwealth, asking for its help and protection. The situation grew still more complicated when Moscow gained the support of Denmark, which was interested in developing the Narva route because of the income it would derive from the Sound tolls. On the other hand Sweden in possession of Finland, although she was in dispute with Russia over Ingria, and moreover was on bad terms with Moscow after the occupation of Estonia and Reval, at first ranged herself with Moscow in the northern Seven Years War, which began in 1563. The opposition to Russia and Sweden consisted of Poland, Denmark and the Hanseatic cities, but each of these temporary partners had its own separate aims and interests, and their links were ephemeral and inconstant.[38]

From the point of view of our subject the most important factor in the problem is the difficulties English merchants came up against in trading with Narva due to the political situation which had developed in the Baltic, and the Privy Council's consequent attitude to the dispute between the Muscovy Company and the London merchants who wished to trade individually with Moscow.

The difficulties these merchants encountered in their attempts to trade with Narva on the eve of the northern war were due primarily to Poland's blockade of the port, a step intended partly as a reply to the alleged English exports of arms to Moscow. It is worth noting that Ivan IV counted on importing arms from the West, and that this encouraged him to support the Muscovy Company. As early as 29 July 1555, some years before Russia's seizure of Narva, the Venetian ambassador to London reported that the Polish Commonwealth was demanding England's guarantee that the Muscovy Company would not supply the Tsar with weapons and war materials.[39] About the same time the king of Sweden also protested against England's supplying arms to Moscow.[40] In 1558 Thomas Alcock, one of the Muscovy Company's agents, was detained in Poland and interrogated as to the extent of arms consignments to Moscow.[41] After Ivan IV's capture of Narva, charges that the Muscovy Company was supplying Russia with arms grew more and more frequent. In a letter to Elizabeth dated 17 August 1558 Emperor Ferdinand I pointed out the dangers that could arise from Moscow's having access to the Baltic,[42] and a year later he observed that Ivan's position in the war he was waging for Livonia had been greatly strengthened as a result of the material help he had received from outside.[43] In April 1561, in letters to Elizabeth I, the city councils of Hamburg and Cologne accused England of supplying Ivan with a large quantity of guns and other weapons, offensive as well as defensive.[44] England had acquired these weapons in Germany, whence they were to be transported to Narva in English ships. In a letter to Elizabeth dated 31 May 1561[45] the Emperor again protested against the supply to Moscow of war materials, especially firearms, gunpowder, oil, iron, etc, as well as foodstuffs, including herrings and salt, and such commodities as cloth and silk. At the beginning of May 1561, in a letter to Hamburg, Elizabeth gave her royal word in denial of the rumours that England was aiding Moscow with arms and ammunition, and promised to punish the authors of these rumours ruthlessly.[46] But they continued, none the less. At the end of May 1561 the Emperor complained again, mentioning the despatch from England to Moscow of soldiers trained in the arts of war. In her reply dated 7 July 1561 Elizabeth stated that she had strictly forbidden her subjects to export arms to Russia.[45] And in fact, on 28 June 1561 she had issued an order to the Lord Treasurer that he was to watch over the ban,[47] which was finally issued on 8 July 1561.[48] But rumours that war materials were being sent to Russia in English ships still continued. On the very same 8 July came news that a considerable part of the armaments Elizabeth had ordered in Hamburg had been shipped to Russia, 'to the damage of Christendom'.[49] On 11 July 1561 William Cecil was informed that it was quite a widespread belief in Germany that Russia had succeeded in capturing Livonia partly through England's help. Some years later, on 6 January 1565, Denmark accused England of supplying arms to Sweden and even threatened to close the Sound.[50] The Queen protested against such a step, and appealed to the Anglo-Danish treaty dating from the times of the first two Tudors, which it would violate.[51] As for Denmark's charge that England was supporting Sweden, the Queen expressed her readiness to punish any English merchants who aided Denmark's enemies with arms and food.

Sigismund Augustus's blockade of Narva and detention of vessels sailing to the port was the result not of military considerations only, but—as S. Bodniak justly pointed out—of economic motives also.[52] It was Poland's way of defending herself against Russian competition, which was in rivalry with the Commonwealth's exports of a number of raw materials exported to the West. In the attempt to control and restrict Narva's trade with England and other countries, Sigismund Augustus in 1565 issued a kind of passport entitling the possessor to sail to Narva and Sweden. For instance, in 1568 two English vessels sailing to Narva, the *Primrose* and the *Mayflower*, were issued such passports by the King of Poland.[53] But these concessions were rather exceptional; the sea blockade of Narva was intended to protect the Commonwealth politically and economically from the effects of Moscow's rivalry. How seriously Poland regarded the danger of Narva's competition in the Baltic trade with the West is indicated by certain opinions expressed at the time. For instance, Jan D. Solikowski, who had an excellent grasp of political and commercial affairs, wrote in *Rozmowa kruszwicka* (*The Kruszwicka Conversation*) that the Crown had allowed itself to 'pollute' the port of Danzig, which was the eye of the whole world and the source of the nation's wealth, through Moscow's domination of Narva, to which port French, English, Dutch and Hansards were now travelling with their commodities. As a result of Narva's competition, he wrote, 'we lose a maritime State with its 200 miles of coastline, with great ignominy and everlasting stain'.[54] And in the times of the first Interregnum* an anonymous author wrote: 'all the benefits and riches come to the Crown through our ports, which when they go to ruin through

* First interregnum: from the death of Sigismund Augustus in 1573 to the election of Henry of Valois as king, in the next year. Second interregnum: from the flight of Henry to be king of France, in 1574, to the election of Stefan Batory, in 1576.—*Translator.*

Narva, bring poverty and indigence to Poland'.[55] In the light of these utterances the economic aspect of the Polish naval forces' blockade of Narva is clear.[56] In the years 1562–68 Queen Elizabeth protested against this blockade, both directly to Sigismund Augustus[57] and to the Danzig council,[58] demanding the release of vessels, merchants and goods detained. On 3 March 1568 Sigismund Augustus replied to the Queen's charges, explaining that he had indeed ordered Polish naval vessels to detain and confiscate cargoes going to Russia, with which country he was still in a state of war.[59] To England's protest on 3 July 1568, demanding the return of arrested vessels and goods consigned to Narva, the Danzig council referred to the Polish king's order, and advised the Queen to address herself to him on the subject.[60] English sources have various references to the detention by Polish privateers of vessels voyaging from England to Narva.[61] Letters from Sigismund Augustus dated 26 May 1566 and 13 March and 5 September 1569 indicate that the King of Poland clearly emphasized the importance of the blockade of Narva.[62] In a letter to Elizabeth dated 13 July 1567 he explained that he had had to take this step because it was *via* Narva that Russia was being supplied with arms, food and craftsmen.[63] The importance Poland attached to extinguishing Narva's competition is also evidenced by the demand made to the French candidate, Henry of Valois, during the first Interregnum, that French ships should cease sailing to Narva.[64] It is of interest that Archbishop Stanisław Karnkowski, defending Henry of Valois against the candidature of the Emperor, Ferdinand, adduced the argument that Poland needed a king capable of preventing the use of Narva.[65]

We may point out that the memory of Poland's blockade of Narva survived a long time in England—excellent testimony to the scope and effectiveness of Sigismund Augustus's naval strategy. When in 1597 Sigismund III's ambassador to Queen Elizabeth, Paweł Działyński, demanded the restoration of freedom of navigation to Spain, and compensation for the damage done to Polish subjects, he was reminded of how Sigismund Augustus had banned shipping to Narva and had established naval patrols to enforce the ban, with consequent serious losses to English merchants.[66]

The political circumstances attending the issue of the Narva route, as outlined above, could explain to some extent the Privy Council's attitude to the question of forbidding individual English merchants to trade with Moscow *via* the Baltic. In the end the Council cast its verdict in favour of the Muscovy Company. On 14 December 1564 it decided that the northern route was much safer for Moscow trade than that *via* Narva, partly because it did not expose merchants to conflict with Denmark and Sweden and other powers 'of these eastern lands'.[67] The Council's ban on merchants trading *via* Narva connoted the victory of the Muscovy Company's monopoly over the unorganized merchants and those of its members who had defied its orders and had attempted to develop this trade on their own account.

However, data derived from the Sound toll registers for 1564–78 show that the Privy Council's decision was not fully enforced, and that in subsequent years English merchants carried on quite a lively trade with Narva. During these years the Muscovy Company also made use of the Baltic route to the Moscow market,[68] despite its previous attitude. In 1566 it no longer objected to the use of Narva, and argued only that it, the Company, alone had the right to make use of the port in trade with Russia. Parliament passed an Act on these lines in December 1566, recognizing the Muscovy Company's monopoly of Russian trade *via* Narva also. Any merchant violating this privilege was to be punished by confiscation of his vessel and goods, half of which were to go to the Queen and half to the Company. English merchants who were not members of the Company had until 1568 to withdraw their goods and ships from Russia, or they could join the Company, provided they had had at least ten years' experience of the Moscow trade. This order applied to the merchants of Hull, Newcastle, York and Boston. The 1566 Act, which extended the area covered by the Muscovy Company's monopoly to Narva, also laid down that English vessels were to be used exclusively in trade with Russia, and that cloth sent to Moscow was to be in a finished and dyed state.

It is difficult to determine how far the Privy Council's orders and the Act of Parliament were respected. One comes across much evidence that individual merchants continued to penetrate the area covered by the Company's monopoly. These were the 'interlopers', as they were called.[69] We know too that the Company itself occasionally chartered foreign vessels to transport to England goods purchased in Russia.[70]

Turning to an estimate of Narva's role and importance in England's Baltic trade, we need first and foremost to stress the transient nature of England's use of this port. The circumstances outlined above were restricted in time mainly to the decade 1564–74; in those years exports through Narva formed quite a large item in England's imports of furs, wax and flax, as well as hemp in the years 1566, 1569, 1574 and 1578. Exports of flax through Narva in 1566–68 amounted to half the entire Baltic exports of this product to England; in 1564–66 and again in 1569 English merchants shipped wax mainly from Narva.[71] Almost all England's imports of Baltic furs and skins in those years came *via* the port (see Table 2.2).

Table 2.2 *Narva's share in England's imports of flax, hemp, wax, skins and furs from the Baltic, 1563–78 (per cent)*

Year	*Flax*	*Hemp*	*Wax*	*Skins and furs*
1563	0·9	–	–	–
1564	19·9	–	100·0	100·0
1565	20·0	–	87·2	94·3
1566	55·4	90·4	100·0	99·1
1567	51·0	5·2	–	80·6
1568	42·6	7·2	26·6	100·0
1569	13·9	39·7	65·1	100·0
1574	28·0	44·1	13·2	99·7
1578	6·1	17·4	–	98·3

Source *Tabeller over skibsfart...*, vol. IIA, pp. 8–70; vol. IIB, pp. 98–100, 156, 237*f.*, 254.

Table 2.3 *Narva's share in English exports to the Baltic of cloth, salt, lead and alum, 1565 and 1575 (per cent)*

Year	*Cloth*	*Salt*	*Lead*	*Alum*
1565	7·6	29·5	1·8	40·1
1575	2·1	4·9	–	–

Source *Tabeller over skibsfart...*, vol. IIB, p. 223.

For only two years in the second half of the sixteenth century—1565 and 1575—do the Sound toll registers enable us to draw a more precise picture of the nature of England's exports to Narva as compared with English merchants' total exports to the Baltic. From these registers we learn that England exported to Narva chiefly cloth, then salt, lead, alum and some groceries (see table 2.3). In both the years mentioned, Narva's share in England's Baltic exports was minimal, if we except alum in 1565.

The exploitation of Narva as a port formed only a brief episode in England's Baltic trade in the second half of the sixteenth century. As the Sound toll registers indicate, it contributed only a minimal percentage of all England's Baltic trade, which passed mainly through the Polish ports. After the fall of Narva English merchants continued to develop their trade with Russia by the northern route *via* Archangel, which was founded in 1584.[72] But here too they met with increasing competition from the Dutch.

Notes

1 As early as 1527 Robert Thorne had pointed out that the north constituted a natural area for English economic expansion, free from the threat of quarrels with Spain and Portugal.—Hakluyt, *op. cit.*, vol. I, pp. 212*f.*

2 There is a voluminous literature on the subject of the origin and foundation of the Muscovy Company, and we need not cite all of it. Among the most recent works the most important are T. S. Willan, *The Muscovy Merchants of 1555*, Manchester, 1953; also his 'The Russia Company and Narva, 1558–81', *Slavonic Review*, vol. XXXI, 1953; also his *The early history of the Russia Company, 1553–1603*, Manchester, 1956. Of earlier works one must mention I. Lubimenko, *Les Marchands anglais en Russie au XVe siècle*, Paris, 1912, and several other works by the same author. There is material of value in J. Hamel, *England and Russia*, London, 1854; also his *Tradescant der ältere in Russland: der Handelsverkehr zwischen England und Russland in seiner Entstehung*, St Petersburg-Leipzig, 1847. Lubimenko has listed the most important Russian and Soviet writings on the subject in her 'Anglia a Rosja w XVII wieku' ('England and Russia in the seventeenth century'), in *Angielska rewolucja bürżuazyjna XVII wieku* (*The English bourgeois revolution of the seventeenth century*), vol. II, Warsaw, 1957, pp. 377–8. On the importance of the Moscow market in Baltic trade in the latter half of the sixteenth century A. Attman, *Den ryska marknaden i 1500-talets baltiska politik, 1558–95*, Lund, 1944, is basic. Among Polish writers only Szelągowski, *Z dziejów wspótzawodnictwa . . .*, pp. 20*ff*, has dealt more broadly with the Narva issue.

3 Hakluyt, *op. cit.*, vol. I, pp. 266*ff.* The documents and narratives contained in this volume provide basic source material on this problem.

4 See E. Lipson, *The economic history of England*, vol. II, London, 1956, pp. 326*f.*

5 Anglo-Russian relations are dealt with by M. S. Anderson, *Britain's discovery of Russia, 1553–1815*, London, 1958, pp. 1–32.
6 F. J. Fisher, 'Commercial trends and policy in sixteenth-century England', in *Essays in economic history* . . ., p. 153.
7 Hakluyt, *op. cit.*, vol. I, pp. 266–7.
8 P.R.O., S.P. Russia, vol. I, p. 171.
9 Willan, *The Muscovy Merchants* . . ., p. 24.
10 *Dictionary of national biography*, vol. VIII, p. 171.
11 Hakluyt, *op. cit.*, vol. I, pp. 241*ff*.
12 *Cal.S.P.For., 1547–53*, p. 241; also Hakluyt, *op. cit.*, vol. I, p. 273.
13 The company's name read in full: 'Merchants Adventurers of England for the discovery of lands, territories, iles, dominions, and seignories unknown, and not before that late adventure or enterprise by sea or navigation, commonly frequented'. See *Calendar of Patent Rolls, Philip and Mary*, vol. I, *1554–55*, pp. 55–9.
14 The shares, which were issued in values of £25, rose in 1564 to £175, in 1572 to £200, and later even to £450. See Willan, *The Muscovy Merchants* . . ., p. 6.
15 See A. Winckler, *Die deutsche Hanse in Russland*, Berlin, 1886; N. G. Riesenkampf, *Der deutsche Hof zu Nowgorod bis zu seiner Schliessung durch Iwan Wassilewicz III im Jahre 1494*, Dorpat, 1854; E. R. Daenell, 'Der Ostseeverkehr und die Hansestädte von der Mitte des XIV bis zur Mitte des XV Jahrhunderts', *Hansische Geschichtsblätter*, vol. X, 1902. Of more recent works, see A. Kersten, 'Kontakty gospodarcze Wielkiego Nowogrodu z Litwą, Polską i miastami południowoniemieckimi, w XV wieku' ('Economic contacts between Great Novgorod and Lithuania, Poland and the south German cities in the fifteenth century'), *Slavia Orientialis*, vol. I, 1958, pp. 130*ff*.
16 See A. Nahlik, *Tkaniny wełniane importowane i miejscowe Nowogrodu Wielkiego X–XV w.* (*Imported and local woollen cloths of Great Novgorod, tenth to fifteenth centuries*), Wrocław, 1964, p. 102.
17 Willan, *The early history of the Russia Company*, p. 50.
18 The navigational hazards were so great that in 1573 there was a suggestion that the trade with Moscow should be given up altogether, transferring the entire commerce with eastern Europe to Danzig 'for the benefit of the Polish nation and for the convenience of the English, the voyage being much shorter'.—Letter from Bishop Antonio Maria Salviani to Cardinal Palema Galla dated 26 September 1573: *Cal.S.P. Venice*, vol. II, *1572–78*, p. 129. The English ambassador in Paris, Dr Dale, even tried to persuade Elizabeth to forbid her merchants to trade with Moscow and to transfer all the eastern trade to Danzig, where the King of Poland, as he judged, would considerably increase the privileges and advantages accorded to English merchants.—Letter from Sigismondo di Cavalli to the Doge and Senate, 9 September 1573: *ibid.*, vol. VII, *1558–80*, No. 560, p. 493.

19 During an attack on the monopolistic and oligarchic tendencies of the Muscovy Company it was stated in the 1604 Parliament that this company, 'consisting of eight score or thereabouts, have Fifteen Directors, who manage the whole Trade; these limit to every Man the Proportion of Stock of all, and consign it into the Hands of One Agent at Moscow, and so again, at their Return, to One Agent at London, who sell all, and give such Account as they please'.—*Tudor economic documents*, vol. II, p. 88.

20 Hakluyt, *op. cit.*, vol. I, pp. 357, 382, etc.

21 *Ibid.*, pp. 404–05.

22 Willan, *The early history of the Russia Company*, p. 53.

23 P.R.O., E 190/2/1.

24 Hakluyt, *op. cit.*, vol. I, pp. 382*f.*

25 *Cal.S.P.For., 1566–68*, p. 518: Letter to Cecil dated 12 August 1568.

26 *Tudor economic documents*, vol. III, p. 233.

27 *Calendar of Patent Rolls, Philip and Mary*, vol. II, *1554–55*, p. 57.

28 The general political background to this question has been broadly discussed by Attman, *op. cit.*, *passim*.

29 The literature on this subject is ample, and there is no need to give many details here. Of Polish authors, Szelągowski has discussed it more extensively in *Z dziejów współzawodnictwa . . .*, pp. 9–87. W. Czapliński has recently returned to the subject in 'Stanowisko państw skandynawskich wobec sprawy inflanckiej w latach 1558–61' ('The attitude of the Scandinavian States to the Livonian issue in 1558–61'), *Zapiski historyczne*' (*Historical Notes*), vol. XXVIII, 1963, pp. 379*ff.* Of non-Polish authors not mentioned in note 2 above, we must add W. Kirchner, 'Die Bedeutung Narwas im 16 Jahrhundert', *Historische Zeitschrift*, vol. CLXXII, 1951, pp. 265*ff*, and his *The rise of the Baltic question*, Delaware, 1954, pp. 248*ff*.

30 Willan, *The early history of the Russia Company*, p. 67.

31 *Tabeller over skibsfart . . .*, vol. IA, p. 27.

32 I. Lubimenko, 'The struggle of the Dutch with the English for the Russian market in the seventeenth century', *T.R.H.S.*, fourth series, vol. VII, 1924, p. 29, declares that the Dutch annually sent 200–300 vessels to Narva.

33 See Winckler, *op. cit.*, p. 98.

34 Nicholas Bacon's letter to Lord Dudley, dated 5 April 1564: P.R.O., S.P. 12/33, No. 42. See also *Cal.S.P.Dom., 1547–80*, p. 237.

35 *Cal.S.P.For., 1559–60*, No. 942, p. 500.

36 P.R.O., S.P. 12/35, No. 21.

37 *Ibid.*, No. 23.

38 Of the more important studies in this subject we must mention S. Bodniak, 'Komisja Morska Zygmunta Augusta' ('Sigismund Augustus's Marine Commission'), *Rocznik Gdański* (*Danzig Yearbook*), vols. IV and V, 1930–31, pp. 41*ff*, and his *Polska a Bałtyk za ostatniego Jagiellona* (*Poland and the Baltic in the times of the last Jagiellon*), Kórnik, 1946. Among recent Soviet works, V. D. Koroluk's *Livonskaya voyna* (*The Livonian

war), Moscow, 1954, deserves mention. The old work by G. V. Forsten, *Baltiiskii vopros v XVI i XVII stoletiiakh* (*The Baltic problem in the sixteenth and seventeenth centuries*), vol. 1, St Petersburg, 1893, is still of value. Attman's work, already mentioned, is of first-rate importance.

39 *Cal.S.P. Venice, 1555–56*, p. 143.

40 *Ibid., 1556–57*, p. 1005.

41 Willan, *The early history of the Russia Company*, p. 64.

42 *Cal.S.P.For., 1558–59*, pp. 484*f.*

43 *Ibid., 1560–61*, p. 204.

44 *Ibid., 1561–62*, pp. 59, 90.

45 *Ibid.*, pp. 126*f.*

46 *Ibid.*, p. 102.

47 *Cal.S.P.Dom., 1547–80*, p. 178.

48 *Ibid.*, p. 179.

49 *Cal.S.P.For., 1561–62*, No. 294, p. 171.

50 *Ibid., 1564–65*, No. 912, p. 279.

51 *Ibid.*, No. 913, p. 279.

52 Bodniak, *Polska a Bałtyk* . . ., pp. 139*ff.*

53 *Ibid.*, p. 140.

54 *Pisma polityczne z czasów pierwszego bezkrólewia* (*Political writings in the time of the first interregnum*), ed. J. Czubek, Cracow, 1906, p. 479.

55 Bodniak, *Polska a Bałtyk* . . ., p. 143.

56 Bodniak, 'Komisja Morska . . ., pp. 44*ff.*

57 *Calendar of Clarendon State Papers*, vol. 1, ed. C. Ogle and W. H. Bliss, Oxford, 1872, Nos. 109, 156, 165, pp. 479, 485, 486.

58 *Ibid.*, Nos. 110, 157, 228, 231, 248, pp. 479, 485, 492. See also *Cal.S.P. For., 1566–68*, pp. 506–8.

59 Sigismund Augustus to Elizabeth I, 3 March 1568: *Cal.S.P.For., 1566–68*, p. 424.

60 Danzig council to Elizabeth I, 25 August 1568: *Ibid.*, p. 530.

61 Letter from Lionel Duckett to the Marquess of Winchester dated 28 August 1568, to which is attached the protest of many merchants of London, Hull and Newcastle against the detention by Danzig vessels of several English ships: P.R.O., S.P. 12/47, No. 46; see also No. 44. In a letter dated 9 September 1568 Duckett wrote to Cecil concerning the detention of as many as sixteen English ships, which had caused 'a very greate losse and hynderance to our nation': *ibid.*, No. 63. A letter from John Marsh to William Cecil dated June 1568 indicates that English vessels voyaging to Narva had been pursued by Danzig privateers, which lost three ships in the battle: *Cal.S.P.For., 1569–71*, p. 594. In the British Museum Cotton MSS (Nero, B II, ff. 117–24) are copies of letters from the Danzig council to Elizabeth I dated 19 March and 8 November 1568, and from Sigismund Augustus to Elizabeth, dated 27 April 1568, on the question of the mutual repressive measures taken by England and Poland against the background of the Narva issue.

62 *Cal.S.P.For., 1569–71*, p. 161.

63 See W. Borowy, '"*Kompania Wschodnia*" i kampania wschodnia. Karta z historii stosunków polsko-angielskich' ('The Eastland Company and the eastern campaign: a page from the history of Anglo-Polish relations'), *Wiedza i Życie* (*Knowledge and Life*), Nos. 6–7, 1936, p. 404.

64 S. Bodniak, 'Morze w głosach opinii w dawnej Rzeczpospolitej' ('The sea in voices of opinion in the former Commonwealth'), *Rocznik Gdański*, vols. IV–V, 1930–31, p. 72.

65 *Ibid.*, p. 79.

66 *Elementa ad fontium editiones* . . ., vol. IV, Rome, 1961, No. 133.

67 *A.P.C.*, *1550–70*, pp. 178*ff.*

68 Willan, *The early history of the Russia Company*, p. 74.

69 For instance, in 1574 the 'interloper' Richard Woodgate of Yarmouth sailed in the *Elizabeth George* to Narva, where he purchased 2,040 skins (see *Select pleas in the Court of Admiralty*, vol. II: *The High Court of Admiralty*, A.D. *1547–1602*, ed. R. G. Marsden, *Publications of the Selden Society*, vol. XI, London, 1897, pp. 150*f.*). As Attman pointed out (*op. cit.*, p. 49), the English interlopers carried on a particularly extensive trade with Narva, so that the data available for England's Narva trade underestimate that trade.

70 For example, in 1576 the Muscovy Company had to make use of the services of three ships belonging to Lübeck: *Cal.S.P.Dom., 1547–80*, p. 523.

71 In the 1560's a considerable share of Russia's trade passed through Narva; it amounted to 31 per cent of Baltic exports of flax and hemp, 94 per cent of tallow exports, and 81 per cent of skin exports; see Attman, *op. cit.*, p. 50.

72 See P. Laszczenko, *Historia gospodarcza Z.S.R.R.* (*Economic history of the U.S.S.R.*), vol. I, Warsaw, 1954 p. 292; also Attman, *op. cit.*, pp. 406*ff.*

three *The commercial and political preconditions for the foundation of the Eastland Company*

The foundation of the Eastland Company in 1579 came at a time when England was experiencing a period of greater economic well-being, when trade, crafts and mining were developing, and there was a strong demand for luxury goods.[1] After the crisis of the years 1569–74, which was partly due to poor harvests, came eleven 'good years' during which harvests were satisfactory, and the rich booty captured from Spanish ships greatly improved the country's economic balance.[2]

The affluence of the years 1575–86 followed the crisis in the third quarter of the century which—as Fisher's researches have shown[3]—was closely connected with the emergence of the English trading companies. The fall of Antwerp, and its prior closure to English commodities, compelled England to seek new entrepots in place of this commercial and credit market, which she had found so convenient.[4]

As the balance of Europe's economic life shifted from south to north after the great geographical discoveries of the fifteenth century, Antwerp replaced the hitherto powerful Italian centres, took over the heritage of Bruges, and became Europe's main centre for trade and finance. While other medieval cities forbade foreign merchants to carry on business within their walls and imposed numerous restrictions upon them, in Antwerp foreigners enjoyed many trading liberties. On the walls of the Antwerp exchange, where merchants, brokers and bankers from all parts of the world congregated, were carved the words 'For the use of merchants of all nations and tongues',[5] a motto which summed up the city's commercial magnetism.

From the end of the fifteenth century Antwerp became a great entrepot for English cloth and the Merchant Adventurers' main market—one much better situated than their former trading posts, especially so far as the possibilities of selling cloth were concerned. Over the years Antwerp replaced Bruges as the centre of financial operations for north-western Europe and grew into an enormous market for the exchange of products between north and south, east and west, 'an unceasing market place', as Guicciardini wrote at the time.[6] Here the English merchants found a close and conveniently situated entrepot for their cloth, and a market supplying them with all kinds of necessary commodities, including some from the Baltic. About 1560 the English commercial colony in Antwerp was quite large, numbering some 300 to 400 persons, concentrated around the Merchant Adventurers' residence.[7] From the close of Henry VIII's reign to the first decade of the Elizabethan era England was heavily dependent on Antwerp as regards both trade and finance.[8] For many years from 1551 onward, one of the greatest financiers of the sixteenth century, Thomas Gresham, acted as her agent there.[9] The fall of Antwerp goes far to explain the intensity of England's commercial drive in the Baltic and the Mediterranean; now the enterprise and initiative of the English merchant class had full scope, after its long repression through the convenient proximity of the great Antwerp market.

In England, too, favourable conditions existed for the foundation of the Eastland Company. In view of the decisive struggle with the Hanse, the government was ready to give the newly organized company considerable support, and to grant it privileges in order to 'vindicate the trade from the usurpations of strangers'.[10] One can to some extent agree with Ramsay's view that the basic cause of the Eastland Company's foundation was, at least in part, England's desire to deal a final blow to the German Hanse.[11] Another fact not without significance for the genesis of the Company was the decline in the Merchant Adventurers' organization, which at the time was experiencing a number of difficulties. The schism within the Adventurers had a close connection with the birth of the Eastland Company. One may recall, too, England's trading problems with Russia, mentioned in the previous chapter, and the voices that were raised in the 1570's suggesting a restriction of the Moscow trade and the transfer to Danzig of all England's commerce with north-eastern Europe.[12]

England's Baltic policy in the Elizabethan era had one other, much broader, aspect for it was associated with her rivalry with the Spain of Philip II as well as with the German Hanse. Without going into the details of this wide-ranging and complex issue, we need only recall that the period of the emergence and early activities of the Eastland Company was marked by increasingly severe conflict between Spain and the Netherlands, which were fighting for their independence,[13] between Spain and England for the hegemony of the Atlantic, and, finally, between England's growing might and the Hanse's growing enfeeblement over participation in the northern trade. In the nascent configuration of the two camps England, the Netherlands and the Scandinavian countries were on one side, and Spain and the Hanse, seeking to enlist Poland's aid, on the other. In discussing this question Boratyński[14] drew attention to the political, economic and to some extent religious preconditions of these alliances, at the same time stressing Poland's independent attitude, adopted because she depended on the one hand on England's neutrality and on the other on the help of Danzig and the Hanse in face of the difficulties arising from Stefan Batory's wars on Moscow. The chief personage working for an understanding between the Hanse, Spain and—though in general ineffectively—Poland was one of the most eminent and energetic of the contemporary Hanseatic politicians, Heinrich Sudermann. Sudermann struggled vigorously to restore the Hanse's declining power.

A transient proof of Batory's interest in the policies of the Hanse and Spain was his 1576 plan for the joint conquest of Denmark by Spain, Sweden and Poland; at the time Batory was also ready to stop the export of Polish grain to the Netherlands and England in order to assist Philip II in his foreign policy[15]. One may add that England made repeated protests to the Polish court about Danzig merchants supplying Polish grain to Spain.[16] Another frequent cause of protests and irritation was the activity of English privateers, which—during the battle of the Armada, for instance—detained vessels sailing to Spain with grain, masts, cordage and other Polish commodities 'to reinforce . . . [Philip II's] decayed navy'.[17]

The English privateering attacks on Danzig ships resulted from Elizabeth's ban on the transport of arms and food to Spain. The consequence was a series of retaliatory measures and the exchange of stern notes between England and Danzig. In consequence 1597 witnessed the ill-starred mission of the Polish ambassador Paweł Działyński, who vehemently demanded that Elizabeth should lift the blockade of Spain so far as the king of Poland's subjects were concerned, and grant compensation for Polish ships and goods seized or sunk by English privateers.

Here one may well mention a little-known fact. Two years before the Armada Stefan Batory drew up a contingency plan, which was never acted upon, for a future war between Spain and England. The plan provided for the occupation of the Sound in order to secure supplies of Baltic food to Spain,[18] and recommended that the Spanish fleet should invade Ireland and the Isle of Wight, which the Spanish forces would find a convenient *point d'appui* and operational base for an invasion of England itself.[19]. In thanking Batory for proposing this plan the Duke of Parma informed him that Madrid had resolved to confer on him the Order of the Golden Fleece as a token of gratitude, since it was fully realized 'how important is the matter of maintaining friendly relations with a king so valiant and wise'.[20] This is not the place to attempt an analysis of Batory's plan, but it does prompt the reflection that it was a good deal more judicious than the one the Spanish command adopted in 1588.

Ignoring more general questions, one must stress the significance of the final and decisive phase of England's rivalry with the Hanse to the genesis of the Eastland Company, from the middle of the sixteenth century onwards.[21] It occurred during a period which saw two opposing historical processes at work, of which only one—that being accomplished in England—was an expression of contemporary progressive tendencies and embodied the aims of a modern State. Under the patronage of the Tudors' centralized monarchy, representing the national aspirations of a society moving away from feudalism, the English mercantile class, overcoming medieval particularism, even if only by organizing national general trading companies, took up the struggle to find new markets for its expanding commerce. During this same period diametrically contrary processes were occurring within the Hanse. The medieval concept of the Hanseatic League was in contradiction to contemporary national trends. The Hanse had long been in a state of crisis due to various circumstances, notably internal dissolution, the break-up of the League's solidarity, but above all the formation of economic areas which no longer needed the services of medieval middlemen.[22] Moreover, the commercial might of Holland was swiftly gaining a dominant position in the northern trade. From 1544 especially, when Charles V, as sovereign of the Netherlands, obtained the right of free passage through the Sound for his subjects, Holland's importance in the Baltic trade increased rapidly, as is shown by her overwhelming preponderance in the Sound toll registers.

The first crucial date in England's struggle with the Hanse in the latter half of the sixteenth century was 1552.[23] At a session of the Privy Council held on 24 February 1552 the Hanse's activities were subjected to severe criticism, and numerous instances were cited of its violation of obligations entered into with England. Danzig especially was accused of not conforming with the decisions of treaties previously entered into. We read in the minutes of the Council that 'the Anglo-Hanseatic understanding of Edward VI's day hath been and is dayly much broken, and specially in Danzick, not only by prohibiting Englishmen frely to buy and sell there, but also in leving uppon them new exaccions and impositions contrary to the said Treaty'.[24] And further: 'In consideracion of which the premisses and such other mattier as hath appered in th'examinacion of this mettier, the Lordes of the Kinges Majesties Pryvey Counsell, on his Hieghnes behalf, decreyd that the pryvelege, liberties and frauncheses claymed by the foresaid Merchauntes of the Stillyard shall from hensforth be and remayne seased and resumed . . .' It is true that later the Hanse's privileges were partly restored, but it never again recovered its former position in English trade.

The second important date in the process of eliminating Hanseatic middlemen from English trade was 1578, when the Hanse merchants were reduced to the same level in trading and fiscal matters as other foreign merchants in the country.[25] In that same year the English were finally expelled from Hamburg. And these two facts are closely connected with the foundation of the Eastland Company a year later. In 1578 negotiations to found the Company and to obtain a privilege for it opened in London.[26] A direct causal connection between England's struggle against the Hanse and the genesis of the Eastland Company can thus be clearly seen.[27]

This struggle was carried on over a wide geographical area which covered the extensive region of the northern trade, around the North and Baltic seas. In the North Sea area efforts to break down the Hanse's role in England's German and Dutch trade were made by the Merchant Adventurers, who made a breach in the Hanse's monopoly in this area by establishing their residence, first in Emden in 1564, and then in Hamburg in 1567. The Hanse's internal disintegration, which by now had become obvious, was clearly favourable to this kind of effort. In the Baltic area the struggle was marked by a similar development when the Eastland Company founded its entrepot in Elbing, a city which, though still a member of the Hanseatic League, was breaking free of its shackles.

The fortunes of the English residence in Hamburg—which after the fall of Antwerp marked, together with Emden and Stade, one of the stages in the advance of England's trading expansion eastward—is well known through Ehrenberg's work, which we have already mentioned.[21] After the withdrawal from Calais and the first abandonment of Antwerp in 1564, despite that city's protests, the Merchant Adventurers set up their staple in Emden. However, the new location proved unsuitable, and after some months they returned for a short time to Antwerp. Political events, religious disturbances and trading difficulties forced them to leave the Netherlands again, to find at last a welcome for their entrepot in Hamburg, on a ten-year lease. Hamburg had previously attempted to attract the Merchant Adventurers in 1564. Thus for the first time a serious breach was made in the Hanse monopoly.[28] Hamburg granted the newcomers extensive privileges similar to those enjoyed by its own citizens,[29] notwithstanding the condemnation of certain Hansards, and especially of Danzig.[30]

When, ten years later, at the beginning of 1578 the Merchant Adventurers applied for a renewal of their residence[31] they received a decided rebuff.[32] Under pressure from other Hanseatic cities the Hamburg city council reminded England of the poor treatment Hamburg merchants had received in London, such as the illegal imposition of and increases in various monetary dues, and the non-fulfilment of former obligations. Its letter observed that ten years ago the city had hoped its merchants would obtain in England advantages similar to those the English enjoyed in Hamburg. As things had turned out differently, the Hanse congress at Lübeck had answered the Merchant Adventurers' petition in the negative.

In his reply dated July 1578[33] Lord Burghley attempted once more to defend England's Hamburg residence, appealing to her ancient privileges in the Prussian area, and especially in Danzig. He cited the previous agreements between England and the Teutonic Order in 1409, 1437 and 1473, and other privileges which at various times had assured English merchants various freedoms. His memorandum made two points in particular: the necessity for renewal of the agreement enabling English merchants to continue residence, and the need for renewal by all the Hanseatic cities of agreements guaranteeing the same trading freedoms for Englishmen as Hanse merchants enjoyed in England. If the Hanse did not accept these conditions, Burghley considered that its existing privileges in England would have to be cancelled, and its attitude towards English merchants dealt with on the principle of retaliation.

Burghley's memorandum was of no great practical significance. In a letter dated 10 January 1579 the deputy governor of the Merchant Adventurers[34] informed him that the English residence in Hamburg had been finally closed down towards the end of November 1578, and that the key to the building had been returned to Hamburg city council the same day. Two weeks later the London city council forbade the Hanse Steelyard to carry on trade anywhere in England,[35] to which the Hansards responded with further repressive measures against English merchants.[36]

England's attempts to penetrate the Hanseatic trading area and to gain a foothold in the Baltic zone met with unusually favourable conditions as a result of the Danzig revolt in 1577 and the effects of the Danzigers' attack on Elbing in the September of that year. On learning of this attack and of the devastation the Danzigers had caused, Christopher Hoddesdon, who was to be one of the leading members of the future Eastland Company, wrote to Lord Burghley on 5 October 1577[37] that the attack on Elbing would do the Danzigers no good, since it would turn the king of Poland still more against them.

Thanks to Lepszy's researches, the course of Batory's dispute with Danzig is well known.[38] The crisis of two interregna in Poland had rendered it possible for the Danzig patricians to reject Karnkowski's 1570 statute.* In defending its privileged position Danzig declared itself in favour of Maximilian II (as king of Poland) and refused to recognize Stefan Batory. The Danzigers were supported in their resistance by Denmark, which was alarmed by Poland's naval aspirations. On the other hand, Spain, which was engaged in the attempt to suppress the Netherlands revolt, endeavoured to reach an understanding with Batory.

Passing over the course of Batory's struggle with Danzig, we must note that on 7 March 1577 the king banned all trade with Danzig and ordered that all Polish exports were to pass through Elbing. Hence Elbing became an entrepot for foreign merchants.[39] Very soon after, on 8 June 1577, Batory issued a privilege to Elbing which permitted foreign merchants to carry on direct trading operations in that city—in other words, the law on guests, which had been oppressive to foreigners was lifted.[40] Thus an exceptionally favourable opportunity arose for English merchants to establish a trading post in Elbing and to transfer the main centre of England's Baltic trade to that city, free from all the restrictions they had suffered in Danzig.

In September 1577 Danzig once more tried to render its rival harmless. A joint Danzig and Danish fleet attacked Elbing, destroying the port installations, sinking a dozen and more merchant ships,

* In 1569 a Polish *sejm* commission headed by Bishop Karnkowski was sent to Danzig to reach an agreement with the rebellious Danzigers. The result was a statute, confirmed by the *sejm* in 1570, aimed at linking the city more closely with the Commonwealth. Owing to the Danzigers' intransigence and Poland's internal dissensions it never came into force. —*Translator.*

and seizing sixty others lying in the port.[41] Despite its serious losses the city quickly restored the damage, thanks partly to the help granted it by Batory from the funds of the mooring dues treasury. But Elbing did not succeed in gaining a customs privilege, and from the moment Batory concluded an agreement with Danzig in December 1577, at Marienburg, the city gradually declined in importance. The one more lasting gain that accrued to Elbing from the events of 1577 was the attraction of English merchants to the city just at the time they were organizing the Eastland Company. The web of events on the Polish coast proved extraordinarily advantageous to the English merchants. Elbing's independent policy within the Hanseatic sphere and its antagonism to Danzig helped them to obtain trading privileges in Elbing that lasted half a century. This favourable situation was not worsened even by the city's natural conditions and geographical situation, which were far from suitable for navigation—for instance the difficulties of the approach to the port, the silting up of the channel,[42] the customs policy of the Duke of Prussia. On the other hand, the English trade became a source of economic strength and prosperity for Elbing.[43] The city grew and prospered.[44]

Hanseatic documents reveal that a full year before the foundation of the Eastland Company, as the English residence in Hamburg was being closed down, conversations were being carried on between English merchants and the Elbing city council as to the possibility of locating an English trading post there. The Hanse, especially Danzig, was opposed to this plan from the very beginning of the negotiations, both within the Hanseatic League[45] and at the Polish court.[46] Two eminent Hanseatic diplomats played an especially prominent part in these activities: the syndic Heinrich Sudermann[47] and the secretary of the London Steelyard, Georg Liseman.[48] Sudermann developed extensive diplomatic activity within the Hanse itself and at the imperial court, while Liseman endeavoured at the English and Polish courts to prevent English merchants settling in Elbing.

Liseman's narrative provides us with our earliest information concerning the conversations between the English merchants and the Elbing council on the possibility of starting an English residence there. It appears that despite the pressure of the Prussian Hansards the Elbingers were reluctant to take part in the Hanse congress arranged for 11 August 1578, partly because it was to be held in Danzig, which was hostile to Elbing.[49] Liseman's personal intervention was not very successful, and, as we learn from the minutes of this congress of Prussian Hansards,[50] he brought back from Elbing not only a refusal but also the news that the Elbingers intended to come to an agreement with the English despite the Hanse resolutions of 1576. His arguments and warnings to Elbing, adducing the fate of the English residence in Hamburg and Emden, had been without effect. While expressing their fear that in the end an agreement would be signed between England and Elbing, on 18 August 1578 the Prussian Hansards came to the characteristic conclusion that excluding the English from Hanseatic cities would not be of any benefit to the Hanse, since the Dutch and other foreign merchants who acted as intermediaries rendered pressure of this kind ineffective. These merchants would continue to supply England with Baltic goods, whereas the Hansards would be deprived of English goods, and their London residence would not recover its privileges.

Danzig's and the Steelyard's agitation against an English residence in Elbing continued during the later months of 1578 and the beginning of 1579, which would indicate not only that conversations between England and Elbing were still going on but also that Danzig was watching closely. In October 1578 Liseman reported to the Steelyard that the English were intending to raise the question of a residence in Elbing with Elbing itself and with the king of Poland.[51] In January 1579 the Steelyard called on Danzig to put up energetic opposition at the Polish court to the English attempts to secure privileges in Prussia.[52] Poland's political situation, the war which Batory was preparing against Moscow, and his need for the Hanse's aid, both in materials and in support for his resistance to the use of Narva,[53] led to his intervening more than once on behalf of his Prussian subjects in notes to Elizabeth.[54] But as he was at the same time anxious to curb Danzig, he supported Elbing and the plan for English merchants to settle there.[55] In any event, the Hansards counted on Poland's support in their struggle against England throughout this period, and they gave expression to this feeling at the Hanse congresses held in May and June 1579.[56] None the less, on 6 June 1579 the Steelyard gave a warning through Zimmermann that the English had not given up the idea of establishing an entrepot at Elbing.[57] By way of counter-action, in a letter to Liseman from London on 31 October 1579 Zimmermann suggested the possibility of closing the port of Narva to the English and forbidding them to trade with Danzig, Elbing and Königsberg; he considered that over 200 English vessels were intending to call at these ports during 1579.[58] In fact the Sound registers reveal that the total was 103.[59] Again, at the end of 1579 Zimmermann reported from London that English merchants engaged in trade with Danzig were spreading the story that they had already concluded an agreement with Elbing. None the less he still hoped that Elbing would not violate the resolutions of the Hanse congresses.[60] Emissaries of the Eastland Company, which had been founded on 17 August 1579, had already been negotiating with Elbing three weeks earlier.[61] On 14 December 1579 the Danzig council informed its emissaries at the Polish court, Konstanty Ferber and Konrad and Henry Lembke of this development, and instructed them to represent to Batory and Jan Zamoyski, the chancellor, the city's strong opposition to the English plans to establish a staple in Elbing.[62]

One other factor must be taken into consideration when discussing the genesis of the Eastland Company, namely Denmark's policy in the Sound. From the very start of the development of England's interest in trading with the Baltic countries, Denmark, as mistress of the Sound, saw the possibilities of profit to be derived through larger incomes from her customs office.[63] For this reason also Denmark reacted unfavourably to the foundation of the Muscovy Company and the northern route which it opened up. When England and Moscow concluded a trade agreement the king of Denmark protested to London. Christian III pointed out the danger that might threaten the Scandinavian kingdoms if England supplied Russia with war materials. But in fact it was only after Christian's death in 1559 that his successor, Frederick II, adopted a more resolute policy towards England. The new king involved himself in various broad political plans, which he was not always in a position to carry through to success; he displayed much enterprise and versatility, and played an important part in the politics of northern Europe in the second half of the century. Anxious to prevent the marriage mooted between the Swedish prince Eric and Elizabeth, which would have led to an Anglo-Swedish alliance, Frederick decided to sue on his own behalf for the hand of England's queen, and instructed his ambassador in London to wear on his chest the emblem of a scarlet heart pierced by an arrow.[64] These offerings were not taken seriously in London, but the court endeavoured to maintain friendly relations with Denmark,[65] among other reasons on account of France.[66] For it was feared that a break in friendly relations with Denmark might lead to a Danish–French alliance, which could be a threat to England now she had lost her entrepot in Calais. This danger emerged clearly when Frederick II sought the hand of the widow of the French king Francis II, Mary Queen of Scots.[67]

Obviously an even greater threat to good Anglo-Danish relations than these matrimonial problems arose from the activities of the pirates and privateers of both countries, and the repressive measures Frederick II had consequently instituted in the Sound in connection with his toll policy.[68] This policy gave England especial trouble from 1560 onward, when, as a result of Denmark's arbitrary increase of the tolls, English merchants were placed in a worse position than Hansards. [69]

At the beginning of the northern Seven Years War (1563–70) Anglo-Danish relations improved temporarily when Denmark sought England's aid in her struggle with Sweden, and asked Elizabeth at least to maintain neutrality and not to aid Sweden. Denmark also tried to persuade England to abandon the northern route to Moscow,[70] a proposal to which, obviously, she could not agree, especially as in time of war the route through the Sound had decided perils. After the peace of Stettin in 1570 England again became dependent on Danish policy in the Sound, especially as in that year Ivan IV temporarily withdrew the Muscovy Company's privileges. From 1576 onward Anglo-Danish relations worsened still further, as a result of the development of the northern route to Moscow, the activities of pirates and privateers,[71] and Denmark's toll policy in the Sound.

Interesting light is thrown on this last issue by an Eastland Company memorial in 1602.[72] This document outlines in detail Denmark's unfavourable tolls policy, which had systematically increased the tolls levied on English ships passing through the Sound and inflicted various kinds of imposition on English merchants. Whereas formerly in the Sound, the Company complained, a last consisted of forty-eight barrels of sturgeon, now the doubled tax allowed only twenty-four barrels to the last. Skins and other goods had been treated similarly. The company further protested that one hundred of timber should not be reckoned as 100 items in the Sound, since it had long been generally accepted that it consisted of 112 items or more, according to the kind of goods. The Danes had introduced these and similar impositions as early as 1566, during the northern war, and they rendered it difficult for England to develop her northern trade. Further losses, the memorial stated, were caused by yet other forms of chicanery on Denmark's part. English vessels were held up in the Sound a very long time, and were subjected to particularly rigorous customs control. The customs officers demanded that English shipmasters should present excessively detailed lists of all the goods they were carrying, specifying every item of cloth separately, with its price, etc;[73] other countries' merchants were not treated by any means as strictly. English shipmasters were compelled to sign a declaration that they understood that in the event of their making false statements they would lose their ship and their goods. It was also demanded that they should inform Denmark of any damage done by English persons to Danish subjects.[74] Particularly detrimental, in the view of the authors of the memorial, was the disproportionate severity of the punishment were an English merchant to commit an offence under Danish law. Even petty cases of smuggling incurred heavy monetary fines and confiscation of the smuggled goods; the Danish authorities even claimed that in such cases the entire vessel with its cargo should be forfeit.[75] The Eastland Company declared itself for the principle of punishment proportionate to the offence, and demanded that its merchants should be treated no more harshly than the Dutch or the Hansards.[76]

A serious threat to English shipping in the North and Baltic seas arose from the depredations of privateers of various kinds, both English and foreign.[77] We find frequent references to them in English documents of the 1570's.[78] Among the London merchants who suffered at their hands were members of the Eastland Company, including its first governor, Thomas Pullison.[79]

The issue of the privateers has its bearing on the emergence of the Eastland Company, not only because this type of trading organization reduced a little the risks attendant on long voyages, but also because English merchants trading with Baltic countries were placed in a difficult position with regard to Denmark because of the depredations of the English pirate, Hicks. To carry on protracted negotiations with Denmark on the matter of compensation for Hicks's victims an organization was necessary, and the attempts at the time to establish an entrepot in Hamburg or Elbing also made some sort of organization necessary.

In the spring of 1577 Jan Peterson, a Danish subject, was attacked and pillaged by the English pirates Hicks and Callice.[80] In consequence of Denmark's demand that England punish them and return the pillaged goods,[81] the pirates were caught and Peterson recovered his ship.[82] In order to mitigate the dispute which arose over this issue the Privy Council recognized that Peterson should receive the compensation claimed for the losses he had suffered out of the sums imposed as fines on various English privateers. England paid him a provisional £200 sterling instead of the £1,300 which was the

Danish merchant's estimate of his losses. He was to receive further sums at a time not precisely specified. Peterson thought this procedure too dilatory, and he turned to his own country with a complaint of England's negligence.[83] In the circumstances the Privy Council, afraid of repressive Danish measures against English merchants, requested the Lord Mayor of London[84] to call on merchants engaged in the Baltic trade to allocate among themselves the £1,100 outstanding to Peterson. The Lord Mayor drew up a list of merchants in London, Hull, Newcastle, Ipswich and Harwich who carried on trade with Baltic countries. The result was a long list of 141 names which is still preserved in the Public Record Office.[85] Against each merchant's name is the sum allocated to him, in amounts ranging from £2 to £15.

The Acts of the Privy Council indicate that a certain number of English merchants 'tradinge Dantzige and the East Partes', with Thomas Pullison at their head, bound themselves on 6 July 1578 to pay Peterson the compensation[86] which the Lord Mayor was to extract under the threat of arrest.[87] On 9 July 1578 the Mayor again conferred with merchants interested in the Baltic trade over the question of extracting compensation for Peterson and sending a delegation to Denmark for the purpose of discussing various issues in dispute.[88] A week later Pullison, with 'certain other merchauntes tradinge Dantzig and the East Partes',[89] pledged themselves to the Privy Council to pay the compensation; but, as would appear from the Privy Council's urgent representations, the issue was not finally settled at once. The English merchants were faced more and more clearly with the need for an organization which would set itself the task of guarding their trading interests and taking political or diplomatic action if necessary.

From a letter which Elizabeth wrote to Frederick II on 22 May 1579 it appears that even then conversations were proceeding between the English government and a group of merchants about the organization of an Eastland Company,[90] to the discontent of merchants engaged in trade with Spain, as well as some of the Merchant Adventurers.[91] Two months later, on 26 July 1579, English merchants trading with Baltic countries presented to the Queen, through the Privy Council, a petition, based on the plan presented to the government in 1578, which began:

> . . . merchauntes trading into the East Partes are humble suters unto her Majestie that by her Majesties' Letters Patentes she would vouchsafe to make

them a Companie and Fellowshippe Incorporate, and in that respect to graunte unto them certain priviledges . . .[91]

The 1578 plan took broadly into consideration the interests of the medium-scale merchants of the ports of northern and central England who had been engaged in the Baltic trade over many years. It was to their interest that members of the Company should be such merchants as carried on trade exclusively with the Baltic.[92] The acceptance of this principle would have rendered it possible for the medium-size merchants of these cities as well as of London to exclude the great wholesalers who were trading as members of other companies with various parts of the world from membership of the Eastland Company. But in the end the medium-size merchants failed to win their case; the charter creating the Eastland Company which Elizabeth issued on 17 August 1579 allowed the great London wholesalers who belonged to the Merchant Adventurers and the Spanish Company also to be members.[93]

Even before the Company was founded, John Langton arrived at Elbing in March 1578 to take the preliminary steps towards opening an English warehouse there.[94] One month after the charter was announced George Ruchs, Robert Walton, Matthew Gray, Thomas Gourney and John Briks[95] appeared before the Elbing city council in the capacity of representatives of the Company and began negotiations to obtain trading privileges for English merchants. A letter from the Elbing council to Walsingham dated 24 November 1579[96] reveals that these representatives proposed to transfer all the English trade from Danzig to Elbing on condition that the Eastland Company obtained considerable trading and taxation privileges and the guarantee of unrestricted withdrawal from Elbing with all their property and goods if the Company's terms were not fulfilled. In its letter the council expressed its readiness to grant English merchants freedom of trade and exemption from all new taxes and customs dues, excluding those already in force.[97] In its concluding paragraph the council assured Walsingham that it would intervene with the King of Poland in the interests of English merchants. On 27 January 1580 the Privy Council issued the order that English ships sailing to the Baltic from London, Hull, Newcastle, Ipswich and Lynn were to be unloaded only in Elbing.[98] So from that moment Elbing became the sole Baltic entrepot for English goods; though, in fact, the transference of the residence from Danzig to Elbing was not finally completed until about 1583.

The next step of the court and the Eastland Company was to attempt to obtain confirmation of the Elbing residence from the Polish court. On 30 January 1580 Elizabeth wrote to Stefan Batory on this subject, asking him to recognize English merchants' right to free trade.[99] At the same time she appealed to the King of Denmark, Frederick II,[100] and the Grand Duke of Prussia, George Frederick,[101] for support for the merchants of the Eastland Company. On the same day she sent a letter to the Elbing council,[102] but in a separate note she empowered Dr John Rogers to undertake a mission to Denmark and Elbing on behalf of the Eastland Company.[103] Rogers was to take the opportunity to deny, both at the Polish court and with the Elbing council, rumours being spread by Danzig to the effect that England had supplied Moscow with arms and ammunition.

These measures did not come as a surprise to the Danzig council, and from the very beginning they met with its energetic counter action at the Polish, Danish and Spanish courts and, above all, through the Hanse. The council sent a request to the king of Poland on 15 January 1580 that he should not confer any privileges on English merchants within the territory of the Commonwealth.[104] Even earlier, in December 1579, the Danzig council had presented a memorial to Stefan Batory entitled 'Informatio in causa anglicana',[105] which included the demands that the king should not permit the Eastland Company to set up a residence in Elbing, that the English should be expelled beyond the frontiers of the Commonwealth and that all trade relations with them should be forbidden until the privileges England had withdrawn from the Hanse the previous year had been restored. This last condition clearly reveals the broad politico-economic background to the issue of the English residence in Elbing and the context of Anglo-Hanseatic rivalry in which it has to be considered. In their struggle to prevent the English entering Elbing, Danzig's emissaries to the Polish court resorted to the argument—well chosen, especially at that moment, on the eve of Batory's war against Moscow—that the English had supported Moscow with arms, and for this reason the Elbing residence might become a threat to the Commonwealth.[106] Jesuit propaganda also was directed against the English having a residence in Elbing, by threatening that it would lead to a spread of heresy.[107]

Emissaries from Danzig were also sent to the Danish court to carry on the agitation against the English;[108] they attempted—ineffectually, on the whole—to draw the king of Denmark's attention to the harm that could be done to Denmark too if the English entered the Baltic.[109] Above all, numerous sources demonstrate the very active steps Danzig took in the Hanse itself, where the city's emissaries demanded, *inter alia*, that Elbing should be expelled from the Hanseatic League because it had granted the English the right to found an entrepot. The Danzig council's instruction to its representatives at the Hanse congress held on 21 October 1580 reveals that it even proposed a plan to appeal to Spain for help against England.[110]

The attitude adopted by Poland was of critical importance to the question of an English residence in Elbing. Both England and Danzig appealed, directly to Stefan Batory or indirectly through leading Polish dignitaries, with Jan Zamoyski, the chancellor, at their head, to this arbiter. The Polish court clearly resorted to the tactic of procrastination on the issue. Batory, who was preparing for a war with Russia, depended on the maintenance of good relations with Danzig and the Hanse, as is proved by the king's announcement on 8 May 1580 of a ban on the issuing of privileges to English merchants.[111] Indirectly this implied that the royal agreement to an English residence in Elbing would not be forthcoming. It is a clear instance of Batory's moderation: he was not prepared to take action against England, though the Danzigers were by no means satisfied with such half-measures. The Polish court's tactic is further confirmed by Batory's refusal of Liseman's request to take sterner action against English merchants and to intervene at the English court on behalf of the Hanse.[112] A further instance of Batory's procrastinating policy due to his involvement in the Moscow war was evident at the Warsaw *sejm* of 1581, at which representatives of the Hanse, Danzig and England were all present. Aware of the Polish court's lack of any decisive policy in regard to the Elbing residence, Dr Rogers engaged in very energetic diplomatic activity at the court and in Elbing, and towards the end of November 1581 he drew up a provisional plan for an agreement between the Eastland Company and Elbing.[113] It assured the Company complete freedom of trade, unrestricted liberty of exchange and navigation in Elbing, and the import and export of all commodities with the exception of ammunition and arms. The English were to be granted favourable customs conditions, but the question of anchorage rights was left unsettled. Commodities imported by English merchants were to be sold wholesale only in Elbing, but sales were not restricted solely to Elbing merchants, since this would have been contrary to Hanse practice.

F

Because of the thorough studies made by Simson and Lepszy the course of the negotiations between the Polish court and England, with the Eastland Company represented by John Rogers, John Herbert and the Company's deputy governor, William Salkins, is well known. So there is no need to relate the story of these protracted negotiations, which continued from 1581 to 1585. They were finally ended negatively by Batory, who in 1585 granted rights of anchorage to Danzig and refused to confirm England's proposals. To conclude this chapter we need only discuss the content of the agreements between England and Elbing of 1583 and 1585, which, though they never received the royal confirmation, became the legal basis for the existence of the English residence in Elbing.

The English court's proposed conditions for the Eastland Company's possession of an entrepot in Elbing were sent to the Elbing council[114] and to Batory[115] in the form of thirty articles in September 1582. Analysis of this document enables us to see how the English merchants conceived of their privileges in the area of the Polish port and which of the proposals were accepted by the Elbing council in 1583 and 1585.

The 1582 plan put forward by the English side contained demands for far-reaching privileges which were only partly accepted by the Elbing council. The plan made free trade for English merchants the chief request, and not only in the entrepot but throughout the territory of the Commonwealth (article 1.). Members of the Company were to be granted the right to hire dwelling houses, buildings for warehouses and shops, granaries, etc (article 15). At their request they could obtain civic rights in Elbing, and this would entitle them to own real estate (article 27). In this last instance English residents were to pay the taxes on real estate acquired in the city, but they were to be free from certain imposts laid on the inhabitants of Elbing (article 28). Any Company members who committed some transgression of English law or the Company's ordinances while in Elbing and who refused to agree to return to England to answer the charges made against them (in any case, all members were under obligation to return to England every three years) would be denied the privileges postulated in the 1582 plan (article 30).

Several of the articles in this plan related directly to trade. English merchants were to sell their goods in Elbing only in places designated for that purpose, or in granaries, etc, and they were not allowed to sell goods on their vessels (article 20). Goods bought in Elbing could be exported from the city, or they could be resold, but then only for the same price as was paid for them in Elbing. If it proved impossible to export goods bought in Elbing, English merchants could resell them, but only wholesale, first to inhabitants of Elbing, and only thereafter to foreign merchants (article 18). In such a situation the plan permitted the retail sale only of costly kinds of cloth, and then only within a restricted range. In the loading of vessels English merchants were to use only the services of Elbing inhabitants: only if it proved impossible to find manpower at the established rate on the spot could they resort to foreign labour (article 21). Jointly with the Elbing council the Eastland Company had the right to appoint and dismiss workers serving the scales, cranes, etc (article 24).

By the 1582 plan the Company would have the right to own parcels of land and a house in Elbing for its needs, or it could build itself a house on a site purchased locally (article 3). Giving corresponding application of the clauses of Elizabeth's 1579 charter, article 4 of the plan recommended the annual election of the head of the English residence in Elbing (the 'deputy'; see chapter five). It also mentioned meetings of Company members to be held there (article 5). It further regulated the question of how disputes between English merchants and Elbing citizens, and between Company members themselves, were to be decided (articles 6, 7 and 14), and the question of securing the property of a Company member who died while in Elbing (articles 25 and 26), etc. The English were also to be given guarantees of free performance of their religious practices and to bury their dead in accordance with their customs (article 2).

In 1583 this plan became the basis of the negotiations carried on by John Herbert and William Salkins for the English side, and by the Elbing council, led by the burgomaster, Jan Sprengl, on the other side, with a view to concluding a permanent agreement between the Eastland Company and Elbing. After months of discussions during August and the beginning of September 1583,[116] a formal agreement was drawn up, which, while differing in many respects from the earlier English plan, took that plan as the basis of the agreed conditions.

The 1583 agreement[117] first and foremost restricted the right of English people to settle freely in Elbing. Without the agreement of the Elbing city council neither inhabitants of the city nor Englishmen residing therein could allocate dwelling space to newly arrived English merchants (article 24). Only the Company's deputy governor in Elbing had the right to take English merchants into his house, but in any case not more than forty. In order to obtain civic rights in Elbing the English applicant had to present a certificate of good behaviour (article 28). When they obtained civic rights Company members were not to pay any new contributions imposed by the King (article 30); on the other hand, the Queen of England for her part was to assure Elbing merchants favourable conditions in England (article 31).

The 1583 agreement particularly emphasized Elbing's privileged position in England's Baltic trade. The city was to be the sole entrepot in her trade with Poland: exchange between the two countries was to proceed only through Elbing (article 2). Articles 20 and 21 set out in precise terms the postulates of the 1582 plan concerning the English merchants' trade in Elbing. Only the most expensive kinds of cloth, priced at 60 *groshen* and upwards per *lokiec** could be sold retail (article 22).

Article 3 regulated the question of the Company's headquarters in the entrepot. Until it had built its own house the Company was to make use of accommodation assigned to it by the city at a fixed rent.

Generally speaking, it can be said that the 1583 agreement was based on the English 1582 proposals, and it testified to Elbing's very favourable attitude towards the establishment of an English residence. This was evidenced even more clearly when the council placed the arms of the English emissary, John Herbert, on the Elbing town halls together with the inscription:

> Angelicos fructus Herbertus apostulus olim,
> Quem bona Drusicolis misit Elisa, tulit.[118]

England's and Elbing's attempts to get Batory to confirm this agreement were unsuccessful, despite John Herbert's and Jan Sprengl's vigorous endeavours.[119] A commission consisting of the Bishop of Chełmno, Piotr Kostka, the *voyevods* of Brześć-Kujawa, Piotr Potulicki, the Crown treasurer, Jan Dulski, the castelain of Nakiel, Stefan Grudziński, and the chamberlain of Chełmno, Stanisław Kostka, specially set up by the King in 1584, was to acquaint itself with the contents of the England–Elbing agreement and, after conversations with Herbert, present its opinion on the matter to the King. Passing over the course of these negotiations, Elbing's endeavours, and Danzig's very effective counter-action, we may only add that during sessions in Lublin and Lewartow the commission drew

* Polish *lokiec* = 576 mm, or about $22\frac{1}{2}$ in.—*Translator.*

up a memorial in which it expressed itself in principle in favour of Elbing's rather than Danzig's proposals, pointing out the benefits that would accrue to Poland from free foreign trade, the abolition of the law on guests, etc. all of which would reduce prices and restrict Danzig's monopoly. The commission confirmed that the establishment of an English staple in Elbing would not be contrary to Poland's rights and privileges, especially as by his universal dated 7 March 1577 King Stefan Batory had himself designated Elbing as an entrepot for Polish foreign trade. One must also explain that the Lewartow commission conceived of an agreement with England based on the principle of a temporary royal privilege, and not, as Herbert had proposed, a permanent trade treaty between Poland and England confirmed by the *sejm*.

None the less, the Lewartow commission's opinion did not have any great influence on the fortunes of the English residence in Elbing. At the *sejm* in February and March 1585 it was not Elbing but Danzig which was successful, first by the securing of a mooring agreement, and then because of Batory's refusal to confirm the Anglo-Elbing agreement. In this situation, despite the failure to obtain the Polish court's agreement, on 3 May 1585 Sprengl, the burgomaster of Elbing, concluded on his own authority an agreement with the Eastland Company,[120] which formed the legal basis of the English residence in Elbing for the following half-century. This agreement, consisting of twenty-one articles, was formulated very circumspectly, with the clear intention of not violating the rights of the King of Poland in any respect, and obviously in the hope that sooner or later Poland would confirm England's privileges in Elbing. The agreement also took certain suggestions of the Lewartow commission into consideration, and it was rather in the nature of a provisional agreement than a final treaty.

In comparing the 1585 with the 1583 agreement, one is struck by the absence of articles mentioning English rights to free trade throughout the Polish Commonwealth, of articles referring to Elbing as the sole entrepot for English goods in England's trade with Poland, of English merchants' privileges in selling goods in Elbing granaries and warehouses, their freedom of religion, the acquisition of civic rights, privileges for Elbing merchants in England, etc. Thus the general demands in the plan of 1582, which represented the most extreme English claims, were eliminated. And other articles were worded more prudently, so as not to give offence to the Polish monarchy.

The building of Company houses in Elbing now became dependent on the royal consent (article 1). The widely defined 1583 jurisdiction of the Company authorities in Elbing was by the new agreement confined only to questions of good order and petty disputes in cases of violations of discipline by Company members (article 2). The quantity of cloth which English merchants were free to sell retail was raised to the value of three florins (article 15). Other 1583 articles, apart from those just specified, were included in the 1585 agreement with only minor changes.

It would seem from the Elbing Convent chronicle that as early as 1583 the English merchants had completely transferred their warehouse from Danzig to Elbing,[121] where they had obtained—without royal consent—a spacious building in the centre of the city: and this building thenceforth constituted the centre of their commercial, social and religious life in Elbing.[122] Later they built themselves other warehouses and commercial accommodation,[123] and acquired landed estate. A large number of English people settled in Elbing; many of them were very affluent merchants, disposing of considerable capital,[124] who with their trade contributed to the growth and development of the town.[125]

The Elbing archives yield information concerning some fifty English merchants who were settled in the city towards the end of the sixteenth century. They obtained civic rights, and gradually merged into the local community, often coming to have considerable importance in the city's political and cultural life (table 3.1).

Table 3.1 *List of Englishmen who had acquired civic rights in Elbing towards the end of the sixteenth century*

Name	*Origin*	*Date civic rights acquired*
Atkinson, Ralph	Newcastle	1596
Bargkley, H.	London	1594
Begkwart, Robert	Newcastle	1597
Blandt, Gregory	London	1599
Buck, Robert	Newcastle	1594
Cockaine, William	London	1600
Coxe, William	?	1588
English, John	London	1594
Gart, Thomas	London	1585
Gorney, Thomas	London	1586

Name	*Origin*	*Date civic rights acquired*
Harrison, Ralph	London	1594
Hopkins, Robert	?	1596
Hunfrey, R.	Ipswich	1599
Kolbeck, Thomas	York	1594
Komin, William	London	1597
Larding, George	?	1596
Laurin, Jacob	?	1600
Lewis, Jacob	London	1594
Lewis, George	?	1599
Morell, John	?	1598
Morell, Robert	?	1598
Morell, Samuell	London	1598
Moor, William	London	1596
Nelson, William	?	1599
(Offley, Thomas)	(London)	(1605)
Payne, William	Ipswich	1596
Packthon, George	?	1585
Pagenton, John	London	1594
Philips, John	London	1594
Preus, R.	London	1594
Salbey, John	Newcastle	1597
Salbey, Thomas	Newcastle	1599
Salkyns, William	London	1583
Schwinborn, William	Newcastle	1586
Schwyster, John	?	1599
Simon, Thomas	?	1581
Struder, Robert	London	1597
Suter, Henry	London	1599
Sylvester, Nathanaell	London	1597
Taranthon, R.	Hull	1586
Tauler, Robert	York	1594
Walley, Thomas	London	1594
Willock, Richard	?	1598
Willson, Henry	?	1586
Wilmson, E.	?	1590

Source W.A.P.Gd., Archiwum m. Elbląga, 111/40 and 40/69. The names have been transcribed from the documents, hence the Germanization in some cases.

The great majority of these merchants were from London; second place was occupied by arrivals from Newcastle. Other English cities, such as York, Ipswich and Hull, were only sparsely represented. The list in table 3.1 is not complete, as one can judge from, among other sources, the register of the Elbing grammar school at the turn of the sixteenth century. The volumes of this register for the years 1598–1601 contain the names of Englishmen studying in this famous school as listed in table 3.2.

Additional light is cast on English merchants' active relations with Elbing at the turn of the sixteenth century, and on their participation

Table 3.2 *English persons studying at the Elbing grammar school, 1598–1601*

1598	1599	1600	1601
Jacob Lewis	William Grünweidt	Dawid Gwinn	William Cockaine [a]
John Morell	George Lewes	Zacharias Gwinn	Henry Larding [b]
Robert Morell	William Nelson	Albert Hödshen	George Larding [b]
Samuell Morell	John Schwyster	Paul Lewes	John Lewes
Jacob Mylins	John Quide	Jacob Ludewell	Nathanaell Sylvester
John Quide		William Ludewell	Cornelius Wilmson
		Thomas Peterson	Leonard Wilmson
		Richard Smith	

Notes

[a] 'Die Matrikell . . . ,' p. 19. Against the name of William Cockayne is the note 'Elbinga Britannus'.

[b] *Ibid.* Against the name of the Larding brothers is the note 'fratres Elbingo-Britanni'.

Source W.A.P.Gd., Archiwum m. Elbląga, III/40; also 'Die Matrikelle des Gymnasiums zu Elbing, 1598–1768', ed. H. Abs, *Quellen und Dasrtellungen zur Geschichte* Westpreussens, vol. XIX, Danzig, 1936, pp. 5–19.

in the city's social life, by the list of members of the two Elbing brotherhoods, that of St George and that of St Martin, in the years 1582–1624, in which we find as many as *c.* 500 English names.[126] Among them are creators of the Eastland Company who figure in Elizabeth's 1579 privilege, including Thomas Allen[127] and Roger Fludd,[128] as well as the sons and other relations of many of the founders of the Company (see chapter four), such as Richard Barne,[129] Thomas Gourney,[130] Thomas and Robert Offley[131], Christopher Osborne,[132] Henry Russell[133] and others.

Down to the 1620's Elbing remained the Eastland Company's entrepot in the Baltic trade, despite the well known natural difficulties of the port. All through this period it was the main intermediary in trade between England and Poland; but in 1628 it surrendered the primacy again to Danzig, and for many years lost all commercial importance.

Notes

1 L. Stone, 'Elizabethan overseas trade', *Ec.H.R.*, second series, vol. II, 1949, p. 43.

2 W. R. Scott, *The constitution and finance of English, Scottish, and Irish joint-stock companies to 1720*, vol. I, Cambridge, 1912, pp. 81, 87. Drake's freebooting expeditions in 1577–80 resulted in booty worth some £300,000 sterling.

3 F. J. Fisher, 'Commercial trends . . .', p. 169.

4 Of recent works, see H. van der Wee, *The growth of the Antwerp market and the European economy*, vols. I–III, The Hague, 1963. Also E. Sabbe, *Anvers métropole de l'Occident, 1492–1566*, Brussels, 1952, and S. T. Bindoff, 'The greatness of Antwerp' in *The new Cambridge Modern History*, Cambridge, 1958, pp. 50*ff.*

5 See L. Huberman, *Z czego żyje ludzkość?* (*What does humanity live by?*), Warsaw, 1964, p. 103.

6 J. Kuliszer, *Powszechna historia gospodarcza średniowiecza i czasów nowożytnych* (*Economic history of medieval and modern times*), vol. II, Warsaw, 1961, p. 239.

7 G. D. Ramsay, *English overseas trade during the centuries of emergence*, London, 1957, p. 18. There is extensive discussion of the latest literature devoted to the Netherlands in the sixteenth and seventeenth centuries in M. Bogucka's 'Z problematyki gospodarczo-społecznej Niderlandów w XVI i XVII w.' ('The economic and social problems of the Netherlands in the sixteenth and seventeenth centuries'), *Kwartalnik Historyczny* (*Historical Quarterly*), vol. LXXI, 1964, No. 1, pp. 119–36.

8 O. de Smedt has written a large monograph on this subject: *De engelse Natie et Antwerpen in de 16e eeuw, 1496–1582*, vols. I–II, Antwerp, 1950–54.

9 See J. W. Burgon, *Life and times of Sir Thomas Gresham*, which remains the basic monograph.

10 The Company's own words, in the middle of the seventeenth century: *Cal.S.P.Dom., 1659–60*, p. 283.

11 Ramsay, *op. cit.*, p. 109.

12 Letter from Sigismondo di Cavalli to the Doge and Senate, dated 9 September 1573: *Cal.S.P. Venice*, vol. VII, *1558–80*, p. 493; also Bishop Antonio Maria Salviani's letter to Cardinal P. Galla dated 26 September 1573: *Cal.S.P. Rome*, vol. II, *1572–78*, p. 129.

13 England's policy in regard to the Netherlands rising has been discussed by R. B. Wernham, 'English policy and the revolt of the Netherlands',

in *Britain and the Netherlands*, London, 1960. See also A. N. Chistozvonov 'Angliiskaya politika po otnoshenii k revolutsionnym Niderlandom, 1572–85' ('English policy in regard to the Dutch rising, 1572–85'), *Srednia Vieka* (*The Middle Ages*), vol. v, 1954.

14 Boratyński, *op. cit.*, pp. 55*f.*

15 W. Nowodworski, 'Stosunki Rzeczypospolitej ze Szwecją i Danią za Batorego' ('The Commonwealth's relations with Sweden and Denmark in Batory's time'), *P.H.*, vol. xii, 1911, p. 29.

16 *A.P.C.*, vol. xvii, *1588–89*, p. 192; vol. xviii, *1589–90*, p. 29. See also P.R.O., S.P.Dom. 14/125, No. 177, which gives a letter from C. Parkins to Lord Burghley dated 19 July 1595 in which the writer explains that the King of Poland's subjects exported grain to Spain, despite Elizabeth's protests, because 'it is necessarie for the use of their revenews'. He wrote that the Danzigers explained that this was a purely commercial question, and had nothing to do with politics. They had the support of the Polish nobility, who were strongly interested in this export. The Polish nobility, he continued, would suffer considerable losses if the export of Polish grain to Spain were stopped. He was also of the opinion that in view of the struggle England was waging against Spain 'for life or death' she had the right to detain ships carrying food to Spain, since in his view, it was justified 'by the Law of Nations'. See also Parkins' letter to Robert Cecil, dated 17 July 1595: P.R.O., S.P.Dom. 14/125, No. 173. Two years before the Armada the Duke of Parma sought Batory's help to hold up Polish grain exports to the Netherlands; see Kestner, 'Die Handelsverbindungen der Hanse speziell Danzigs mit Spanien und Portugall seit 1583', *Z.W.G.*, vol. v, 1881.

17 Hakluyt, *op. cit.*, vol. iv, p. 340 (the reference dates from 1589). Drake at that time commanded a fleet which detained some sixty vessels belonging to Danzig, Stettin, Lübeck and Hamburg.

18 Boratyński, *op. cit.*, p. 189.

19 Letter from the Venetian ambassador in Madrid, Hieronimo Lippomano, to the Doge and Senate, dated 24 August 1586: *Cal.S.P. Venice*, vol. viii, *1581–91*, p. 200. Authors of monographs devoted to England's 1588 war with Spain seem ignorant of Batory's 1586 plan. See, for example, G. Mattingly, *The Armada*, Boston, Mass., 1959.

20 Boratyński, *op. cit.*, p. 329.

21 There is a very extensive literature on this subject, and one cannot cite all the works which have been laid under contribution. Above all R. Ehrenberg's *Hamburg und England im Zeitalter der Königin Elisabeth*, Jena, 1896, is of basic importance. But in regard to the Emden issue the primary work is B. Hagedorn's *Ostfrieslands Handel und Schiffahrt vom Ausgang des 16 Jahrhundert bis zum Westfällischen Frieden*, 1580–1648, vols. i–ii; this is found in *Abhandlungen zur Verkehrs- und Seegeschichte*, vols. iii and vi, 1910–12. Among smaller works that of D. Schäfer, 'Deutschland und England im Welthandel des 16 Jahrhunderts', *Preus-*

sische Jahrbücher, vol. LXXXIII, 1896, pp. 268*ff*, is still of value. The question of the Hanse's decline has been broadly discussed by, among others, R. Häpke, *Der Untergang der Hanse*, Bremen, 1923. England's relations with Germany at the time of the emergence of the Eastland Company have been discussed by J. R. Marcus, *Die handelspolitischen Beziehungen zwischen England und Deutschland in den Jahren 1576–85*, Berlin, 1925, and her relations with the Hanse and Germany towards the end of the sixteenth and the beginning of the seventeenth centuries by L. Beutin, *Hanse und Reich im handelspolitischen Endkampf gegen England*, Berlin, 1929. New light has been cast on the final chapter in Anglo-Hanseatic relations by R. Grassby, 'Die letzten Verhandlungen zwischen England und Hanse, 1603–04', *Hansische Geschichtsblätter*, vol. LXXVI, 1958, pp. 73–120.

22 Małowist, *Studia z dziejów rzemiosta* . . ., p. 90, and elsewhere.

23 Ehrenberg, *op. cit.*, pp. 50–75.

24 *A.P.C.*, vol. III, *1550–52*, p. 489.

25 P.R.O., S.P.Dom. 12/127, No. 5.

26 *Ibid.*, S.P.Dom. 12/126, No. 24.

27 We deliberately refrain from discussing the innumerable disputes and mutual acts of repression in the Anglo-Hanseatic conflicts, as numerous studies already exist, and we desire to deal with only the basic elements in these conflicts.

28 *The Merchant Adventurers of England: their laws and ordinances, with other documents* . . ., ed. W. E. Lingelbach, *Transactions and reprints . . . University of Pennsylvania*, second series, vol. II, 1902.

29 Ehrenberg, *op. cit.*, p. 323.

30 *Danziger Inventar*, No. 7654, p. 603.

31 *Ibid.*, No. 7119, p. 558. As early as 8 October 1576 Elizabeth wrote to Hamburg on the subject.

32 *Cal.S.P.For.*, *1575–79*, No. 29, p. 22; also 133, p. 114. On 30 May 1578 the Danzigers at Lübeck opposed the extension of the lease of the English residence in Hamburg: *Danziger Inventar*, No. 7654, p. 603.

33 *Cal.S.P.For.*, *1578–79*, No. 131, pp. 112–14. Burghley's memorandum was entitled 'What liberties the Queen's merchants ought to have in the Hanse towns'.

34 *Ibid.*, No. 503, p. 382. It is pertinent to mention that the Merchant Adventurers were represented by Hoddesdon, one of the founders of the Eastland Company: *ibid.*, Nos. 145, 217, 230, 231 and 289; also *Danziger Inventar*, p. 647.

35 P.R.O., S.P.Dom. 12/127, No. 5. See also W.A.P.Gd. 300, No. 51 (Hanse minutes for 1579), ff. 3–4, where there is a list of the privileges won by the Hanse in England 'mit gut und blut'.

36 *Cal.S.P.For.*, *1578–79*, No. 664, p. 495. In a Merchant Adventurers' document of 1579 we read: 'So it is evident that the English nation is not onely used worse than strangers, but worse than Jews.'

37 *Ibid., 1577–78*, p. 429. It is of interest to note that in the course of Danzig's quarrel with King Batory the city appealed to Elizabeth for financial help, though its relations with England were not of the best. The Queen refused the request, appealing to her good relations with the King of Poland and the absence of any guarantee that the money would be returned: *Danziger Inventar*, No. 7440, p. 586.

38 K. Lepszy, 'Stefan Batory a Gdańsk ('Stefan Batory and Danzig'), *Rocznik Gdański*, vol. VI, 1932, pp. 82–136. The basic documents have been published by A. Pawiński in 'Stefan Batory pod Gdańskiem' ('Stefan Batory at Danzig') in *Źródła dziejowe* (*Historical Sources*), vol. III, Warsaw, 1877.

39 A. Szelągowski, *Pieniądz i przewrót cen w XVI i XVII wieku w Polsce* (*Money and the revolution in prices in sixteenth and seventeenth century Poland*), Lwów, 1902, p. 114.

40 Lepszy, 'Stefan Batory a Gdańsk', p. 116; also C. E. Rhode, *Der Elbinger Kreis in topographischer, historischer und statistischer Hinsicht*, Danzig, 1869, p. 263.

41 I. Behring, *Beiträge zur Geschichte der Stadt Elbing*, vol. I, *Zur Geschichte des Danziger Anlaufs*, Elbing, 1900. See also M. Biskup, 'Elbląg w czasach Rzeczpospolitej: z problematyki historiograficznej miasta' ('Elbing in the time of the Commonwealth: on the historiographical problems of the city'), *Przegląd Zachodni* (*Western Survey*), vol. VIII, 1952, Nos. 5–6, p. 193.

42 See E. Keyser, 'Die Tiefe in der Frischen Nehrung', *Elbinger Jahrbuch*, vol. XV, 1938, pp. 9*ff*. The natural difficulties of the port of Elbing were such that English vessels were repeatedly forced to unload and load goods in the roadstead and even 'von Braunsberg und Köningsbergsch Tieffe': W.A.P.Gd., Lib. Port. Elbing, 1599, ff. 12–19, and elsewhere.

43 B.M. MSS 6882, f. 42 (a contemporary English opinion on the importance of English trade to Elbing's development).

44 Rhode, *op. cit.*, p. 65

45 *Kölner Inventar*, pp. 148, 154.

46 Letter from Danzig to the emissaries sent to Warsaw, dated 9 February 1578: *Danziger Inventar*, No. 7556, p. 595.

47 See L. Ennen, 'Der hansische Syndikus Heinrich Sudermann aus Köln', *Hansische Geschichtsblätter*, vol. VI, 1877, pp. 3*ff*.

48 See P. Simson, 'Der Londoner Kontorsekretär Georg Liseman aus Danzig', *ibid.*, vol. XVI, 1910.

49 Elbing letter to the congress of Prussian Hansards, 9 August 1578, and the Prussian Hansards' letter to Elbing, 12 August 1578: *Danziger Inventar*, Nos. 7729 and 7732, p. 608.

50 Minutes of the congress of Prussian Hansards in Danzig, 12–19 August 1578: *Danziger Inventar*, Anh. 38, pp. 904–6.

51 Liseman's letter to the Steelyard, October 1578: *ibid.*, No. 7784, p. 612.

52 Steelyard letter to Danzig: 31 January 1579: *ibid.*, No. 7830, p. 615.

53 Lepszy, 'Stefan Batory a Gdańsk', p. 118

54 Batory's letter to Elizabeth, 7 March 1579: *Danziger Inventar*, No. 7840, p. 616. In this letter the king protested against the activities of the English monopolists, which were detrimental to his subjects and to the Hanse.

55 On 9 April, 1578. Batory had issued a mandate in which he defended English merchants against the chicanery they met with in the Commonwealth: P.R.O., S.P. 88/1, No. 1.

56 *Danziger Inventar*, Anh. 39, p. 906; also Anh. 42, p. 909. How closely Danzig watched the events connected with the English residence in Elbing is revealed by the minutes of the Danzig city council from 1580. W.A.P.Gd. 300, 10, No. 8, ff. 16, 18, 25, 27, 29, etc.

57 Zimmermann to Liseman, 6 June 1579: *Kölner Inventar*, No. 1517, p. 168.

58 Zimmermann to Liseman, 31 October 1579: *ibid.*, No. 1660, p. 185.

59 *Tabeller over skibsfart . . .*, vol. 1, pp. 82–3.

60 Zimmermann to H. Sudermann, 13 December 1579: *Kölner Inventar*, No. 1696, p. 189.

61 Letter from Elbing city council to the Eastland Company, 24 November 1579: *ibid.*, Anh. 127, p. 617.

62 Letter from Danzig city council to its envoys at the Polish court, 14 December 1579, *ibid.*, Nos. 8043, 8044, 8073, pp. 632, 634.

63 W. Kirchner, 'England and Denmark, 1558–88', *Journal of Modern History*, vol. XVII, 1945, pp. 1–15.

64 See letter of the Venctian ambassador, Paulo Tiepolo, to the Doge and Senate, 30 April 1559: *Cal.S.P. Venice, 1558–80*, No. 66, p. 76. See also the same ambassador's letters dated 5 August and 15 December 1559: *ibid.*, Nos. 91 and 119, pp. 117 and 139.

65 Elizabeth's letter to Frederick II, 10 October 1559: *Cal.S.P.For., 1559–60*, No. 60, p. 30.

66 Privy Council letter to Elizabeth: *ibid.*, No. 483, p. 222.

67 Reports from the Venetian ambassador in France, M. Surian, to the Doge and Senate, 31 March and 18 April 1561: *Cal.S.P. Venice*, vol. VII, Nos. 249 and 253, pp. 306 and 309. See Kirchner, 'England and Denmark', pp. 2*f*, where the issue is discussed more fully.

68 Frederick II's letters to Elizabeth, 12 April 1560 and 16 January 1561: *Cal.S.P.For., 1560–61*, Nos. 183 and 884, pp. 114 and 498*f*. C. E. Hill has attempted to present the problem of Danish policy in *Danish Sound dues and the command of the Baltic*, Durham (U.S.A.), 1926, but the work is rather feeble.

69 Hill, *op. cit.*, p. 61.

70 T. Randolph's letter to Burghley, 22 May 1564, and the Danish ambassador's memorial, 6 January 1565: *Cal.S.P.For., 1564–65*, Nos. 412 and 912, pp. 137*f*. and 279.

71 England negotiated with Denmark through Dr John Rogers, who later played an important part in the Eastland Company's attempts to persuade Batory to confirm the English residence in Elbing.

72 B.M., Cotton MSS, Nero B V, ff. 48–55. The document is entitled 'A declaration of the grievances of the Companie of Eastland Merchaunts sustained in the Sounde of Denmarke, and their requests for redresse thereofe.'
73 *Ibid.*, f. 49.
74 *Ibid.*, f. 51
75 *Ibid.*, f. 52.
76 *Ibid.*, f. 54. The Company ended the memorial with the request that 'at least both now and hereafter wee may bee equall with all other nations'.
77 For instance, in 1577 the Netherlands States General complained to Elizabeth about English pirates who were attacking Ostend merchants' vessels carrying cargoes of timber and grain from Königsberg: *Cal.S.P. For., 1577–78*, No. 196, pp. 141*ff.* In 1577 English pirates attacked the ship *Jonas* three miles off Portsmouth; it was carrying a cargo belonging to Edward Osborne, one of the leading members of the Eastland Company: P.R.O., S.P.Dom. 12/106, No. 57.
78 *Cal.S.P.For., 1564–65*, p. 542; also *A.P.C.*, vol. IX, pp. 29–30. See also *Cal.S.P.For., 1577–78*, No. 196, pp. 141*f.*
79 *A.P.C.*, vol. IX, pp. 29*f*; also *Cal.S.P.For., 1579–80*, No. 10, p. 14.
80 *A.P.C.*, vol. X, p. 57.
81 *Cal.S.P.For., 1577–78*, p. 275.
82 *A.P.C.*, vol. X, pp. 83, 193.
83 *Ibid.*, p. 83; see also Deardorff, 'English trade in the Baltic during the reign of Elizabeth' in *Studies in the history of English commerce in the Tudor period*, New York, 1912, p. 249. The author manifestly overestimates the importance of this dispute, attaching to it decisive significance in the genesis of the Eastland Company.
84 *A.P.C.*, vol. X, p. 193.
85 P.R.O., S.P.Dom. 12/127, No. 73.
86 *A.P.C.*, vol. X, p. 275.
87 *Ibid.*, p. 280.
88 *Ibid.*, p. 266.
89 *Ibid.*, p. 277.
90 Letter to Frederick II, in *Forty-fifth annual report of the Deputy Keeper of the Public Record Office*, London, 1885, appendix II, p. 24.
91 *A.P.C.*, vol. XI, p. 205.
92 P.R.O., S.P.Dom. 12/126, No. 24; also *A.P.C.*, vol. XI, pp. 428*f*, vol. XII, pp. 110*f*, 146*ff.*
93 P.R.O., Patent Rolls, 21 Elizabeth, c.66/1185, f. 24.
94 W.A.P.Gd., Archiwum m. Elbląga, III, 255–4, p. 34.
95 The names are taken from the Elbing council letter: P.R.O., S.P. 88/1, No. 4.
96 *Ibid.*; also *Kölner Inventar*, Anh. 127, p. 617.
97 W.A.P.Gd., Archiwum m. Elbląga, minutes of the Elbing council, 1544–1636, No. 1, p. 14. Under the date 23 December 1580 is the entry:

'Englische gleich den Bürgern das Marckt Recht im Einkauff . . . werden erhalten.'

98 *A.P.C.*, vol. XI, p. 378.

99 *Kölner Inventar*, No. 1726, p. 195.

100 Letter dated 30 January 1580: *ibid.*, No. 1724, p. 195.

101 Letter dated 30 January 1580: *ibid.*, No. 1725, p. 195.

102 Letter dated 30 January 1580: *ibid.*, No. 1727, p. 195.

103 Instruction to Dr Rogers, 30 January 1580: *Danziger Inventar*, No. 8081, p. 635. A further instruction was issued to Rogers in August 1580 'to deale with the Towne of Elvinge': B.M., Sloane MSS 2442, ff. 41–43.

104 Letter dated 15 January 1580: *Danziger Inventar*, No. 8072, p. 634.

105 See A. Szelągowski and N. S. B. Gras, 'The Eastland Company in Prussia', *T.R.H.S.*, third series, vol. VI, 1912, p. 171; also Lepszy, 'Stefan Batory a Gdańsk', p. 118.

106 Letter from G. Liseman to J. Neodicus, 1 June 1580: *Danziger Inventar*, No. 8235, p. 648. Also Elbing letter to Danzig, 25 May 1580: *ibid.*, No. 8229, pp. 647*f.*

107 Boratyński, *op. cit.*, p. 191.

108 M. Moller's letter to Danzig council, 17 May 1580: *Danziger Inventar*, No. 8219, p. 646. This Danzig emissary explained the failure of his mission as due, *inter alia*, to the effective steps taken by the English, who tried to avoid trouble in navigating the Sound by giving costly presents to the chancellor and other Danish functionaries.

109 Danzig council instruction to M. Moller, 5 April 1580: *ibid.*, No. 8150, p. 641.

110 Danzig council instruction to K. Lembke and J. Thorbeke, 21 October 1580: *ibid.*, Anh 46, pp. 915*f.*

111 Batory's letter to Elbing, 8 May 1580: *ibid.*, No. 8200, p. 645; also G. Lengnich, *Geschichte der preussischen Lande Königlich Polnischen Antheils*, vol. III, Danzig, 1724, p. 368.

112 See Lepszy, 'Stefan Batory a Gdańsk', pp. 120*ff.*

113 B.M., Nero MSS B II, f. 155–86. Even earlier, immediately after the foundation of the Eastland Company, Elbing had granted England various favourable privileges, concerning which an unsigned and undated document of the Eastland Company says they were more advantageous to English merchants than would have been possible in any other place. This document, dating probably from 1579 or 1580, adds that the English warehouse in Elbing will be able to develop only when it has achieved exclusive right to all England's Baltic trade. 'Iff all Strangers (as well as your Suppliants) might be bound to shipp from hens to Elbing onely and from thens hether there all marchannts and others of these parts would resort to Elbing with theire cuntry commodities, as well to buy our commodities as to sell and vent theirs to the great encrease of traffique and perfect establishment of your supplants residence at Elbing.' —P.R.O., S.P.Dom. 12/146, No. 53.

114 *Danziger Inventar*, Anh. 55.
115 *Ibid.*, No. 8813.
116 On 16 July 1583 Walsingham gave John Herbert an instruction to carry on negotiations with the Elbing council and the Polish court. See: Walsingham's letter to Herbert, 6 July 1583: P.R.O., S.P. 88/1, f. 26, printed in *Elementa ad fontium editiones*, vol. IV, No. 27, pp. 49*f.*
117 *Kölner Inventar*, Anh. 176; also Lengnich, *op. cit.*, vol. III, document No. 72.
118 Simson, 'Die Handelsniederlassung der englischen Kaufleute in Elbing', *Hansische Geschichtsblätter*, vol. XXII, 1916, p. 105.
119 Lepszy, 'Stefan Batory a Gdańsk', p. 123.
120 *Danziger Inventar*, Anh. 64.
121 W.A.P.Gd., Archiwum m. Elbląga, III, 255/252: 'In diesem Jahre [1583—*H.Z.*] verlegten die Engländer ihre Handlung, Societät, und Niederlagen von Danzig gäntzlich nach Elbing zum grössten Nutzen und Emporkommen der Stadt.'
122 *Danziger Inventar*, No. 8814 (note); also Simson, 'Die Handelsniederlassung . . .', p. 124.
123 M. G. Fuchs, *Beschreibung der Stadt Elbing und ihres Gebietes in topographischer, geschichtlicher und statistischer Hinsicht*; vol. II, Elbing, 1852, p. 185.
124 Rhode, *op. cit.*, p. 65: 'Eine Menge Engländer mit bedeutenden Capitalien liessen sich in der Stadt nieder . . .'
125 Chroniclers and historians of Elbing all agree in emphasizing the great importance of the English trade in the growth of the city. See W.A.P.Gd., Archiwum m. Elbląga, III, 255/4, p.43.
126 *Ibid.*, III, 255/186, pp. 1–49. The Brotherhood of St George was of quite an exclusive nature; only the wealthiest merchants could belong to it. See Carstenn, *op. cit.*, p. 303.
127 W.A.P.Gd., Archiwum m. Elbląga, II, 255/186, p. 1.
128 *Ibid.*, p. 11.
129 *Ibid.*, p. 5.
130 *Ibid.*, p. 15.
131 *Ibid.*, p. 33.
132 *Ibid.*, p. 35.
133 *Ibid.*, p. 37.

four *Social factors in the genesis of the Eastland Company*

The formation of so many English trading companies in the second half of the sixteenth century (the Muscovy Company in 1555, the Spanish Company in 1577, the Eastland in 1579, the Levant in 1581, etc) was an expression of the social transformations occurring in the English bourgeoisie during the primitive stage of capital accumulation. Because of the far-reaching importance of this problem it is necessary to preface an analysis of the social composition of the Eastland Company with a brief discussion of those basic social trends which assured the mercantile oligarchy such a considerable predominance in England's foreign trade in the Elizabethan era.

The emergence of organized mercantile interests in the towns of the late Middle Ages usually occurred along two parallel lines of development. To begin with, a specialized mercantile stratum came into being as a separate element, in England recruited frequently from among the most affluent of the craftsmen. This element broke away from production and created exclusively trading organizations, which in turn began to monopolize one or another branch of wholesale trade. These new trading organizations swiftly came to dominate the town authorities, and exploited their political importance in order to extend their privileges and subordinate the craftsmen to themselves. The eminent expert on the history of the English crafts, G. Unwin, long ago emphasized[1] that from the fourteenth century onwards there was a tendency for the English gild organizations to be dominated by their wealthiest members, while on the other hand a process was observable of the poor master craftsmen being rendered dependent on the richer ones, and the weaker gilds on the stronger ones—especially when they were functioning in the same branch of production. In such cases the stronger element took over trading functions, often abandoning workshop activity altogether; in other cases the purchaser–investor, as the supplier of raw materials and the seller of the finished products, became the dominant factor in production. The English gilds, which at first were energetically opposed by the merchants in charge of urban local government, proved incapable of united common action, and as a result of their struggles with the patriciate fell into dependence on the local civic authorities.

The process whereby the wealthy merchant patriciate acquired economic and political privileges in the fourteenth century took various forms.[2] In certain cases the merchant gilds, to which originally the majority of citizens, including craftsmen, could belong, were transformed into increasingly exclusive and closed organizations, with the object of depriving craftsmen of the privilege of carrying on wholesale trade.[3] This happened, for instance, in Newcastle, where the gild excluded from membership all handicraftsmen and street hucksters; also in Shrewsbury, where handworkers were also excluded from wholesale trade. Late echoes of these restrictions are found even in the Eastland Company's privilege, which did not permit craftsmen and retailers to become members.[4] Coventry provides an interesting example: in that town the merchants' gild, after excluding craftsmen, swiftly came to dominate the local government. The ruling group in fifteenth-century Coventry consisted of mercers and drapers; exploiting their authority, they brought the craftsmen occupied in finishing cloth, the clothworkers, into subjection to themselves. But in the fifteenth century this was quite a common procedure; thus the members of the once powerful weavers' gild suffered pauperization, and fell into growing dependence on the cloth merchants.[5] The weavers and other clothworkers grew steadily weaker as a group, especially during the years when the English merchant class was swiftly increasing in importance by virtue of the development of foreign trade; and this phenomenon played a significant part in shaping the social structure of the English citizenry and its organizations.

Though remote in time, these problems of the transformations which occurred both in English crafts and in English trade in the fourteenth and fifteenth centuries are vital to the elucidation of the Eastland Company's social structure. But without going into them in greater detail, we need to point out that even in the fourteenth century English town organizations had developed which brought the generality of the merchants into association, and also brought about the formation of more specialized merchants' associations. The first of the famous livery companies was granted the privilege of incorporation in fourteenth-century London, in the reign of Edward III. These livery companies were the domain of the influential and wealthy London merchant class, after the latter had achieved the subordination of the craftsmen to themselves. Here we may again cite Unwin, who wrote that the strict subordination of crafts to merchants emerged in this form in each of the twelve London livery companies, which had grown out of craft organizations or had craftsmen in their membership.[6] The urban oligarchy which came to dominate the livery companies, and which consisted primarily of that section of the merchant class which had obtained the monopoly of wholesale trade, exerted a growing influence not only on England's trade but also on political authority in England's cities, by occupying all their most important positions and functions.

Colby's investigations have revealed[7] that even at the very beginning of the fourteenth century the functions of the general meetings of town citizens had been taken over by a body of an elite and aristocratic nature, and that by the end of that century the mass of citizens had been completely deprived of the right to vote in town elections. Already at the end of the thirteenth century the citizens of Gloucester and Oxford were complaining that the government of these cities had been arrogated to themselves by 'divites et potentes'; in the fourteenth century the inhabitants of Winchester laid a complaint 'concerning the oppression imposed by twenty-four leading citizens of the town' who had usurped to themselves the right of electing the town officials.[8] The poorer citizens of Newcastle complained of the violence of the merchants' gilds; the inhabitants of York complained that the town government was dominated by the gild of mercer merchants, etc.[9] In London the city aldermen could be recruited only from men 'eminent and prudent', and possessing an estate valued at the large sum of £1,000 sterling. After a time they were appointed for life by the Lord Mayor, who was himself elected by the retiring Lord Mayor and aldermen from among other aldermen designated in agreement with the city council and—of especial importance from the point of view of our study—with the authorities of the more important livery companies. Thus in the towns, but especially in London, a concentration of political authority in the hands of the merchant oligarchy was achieved. In any case, the majority of the aldermen and sheriffs, as well as the mayors without exception, were members of one of the twelve livery companies, which had a permanent monopoly of the government of England's capital city.[10] So that by the fifteenth century, but especially by its turn, the merchant oligarchy organized in twelve gilds had gained the political and economic dominance, going on in the second half of the sixteenth century to exert an equally decisive influence on the trading companies. These it organized with the aim of securing a monopoly of English trade with various parts of the world, with Russia, the Baltic, Spain, the Levant, Africa, etc; not to mention the Merchant Adventurers and their trading operations in the North Sea area.

This 'merchant aristocracy' was not a closed circle; in the fifteenth and sixteenth centuries it was enlarged by any enterprising and wealthy individuals who had enough money to buy their way into it. In those centuries it was a regular thing for new members from among the wealthier master craftsmen to enter the ranks of the merchant oligarchy, in order to abandon crafts for trade and to get rich more quickly. For people of this type the advance to the higher grades took one of two paths: either they purchased membership in one of the twelve livery companies and gave up their former profession, or they began a struggle to achieve the status of a merchants' organization for their own craft gild. The first method was frequently practised in the London gilds, to which, in general, richer and more important citizens were admitted on payment of a decidedly increased enrolment fee. An example of the second method was the coming together of the fullers and shearers in 1528 to form a trade company (the Clothworkers) concerned with cloth finishing, but more especially with trading in finished cloth.[11]

There was a close connection between the trading interests of the London oligarchy organized in the twelve livery companies and the social circumstances attending the genesis of the Eastland Company. The great majority of the founders of the Company, as well as of its various members recorded in the London port books, consisted of wholesalers who belonged to these London gilds. They also dominated the Eastland Company administration and held the decisive power in it.[12] The less affluent merchants, especially those of the northern ports, protested against this domination. For all these reasons it is necessary to give a short account of the various livery companies, so as to form an idea of their status and activities.[13]

A list has survived from 1516 of the twelve London gilds, arranged in order of precedence.[14] It should be explained that in the course of time the medieval nomenclature of these companies came to have little in common with the branch of trading activity actually carried on by their merchant members.[15] As members of the Eastland Company the leather sellers or skinners were just as much occupied with the export of cloth to the Baltic countries or the import of timber, pitch or rye as were the clothworkers or mercers.[16] We even find fishmongers or ironmongers among cloth exporters to the Baltic, and this indicates the purely historical and formal connection between the gild's name and the actual trading activities of its members in the sixteenth century. This observation applies to all the twelve London livery companies, each of which we must now briefly characterize.

1. The *Mercers* were at first engaged in trading in costly woven goods, but as they also handled other kinds of trade, especially in the provinces, they had for long been identified with the conception of merchants generally. This was not so in London, however, where the name did relate mainly to trade in costly woven goods.[17] From Stow's 1598 *Survey of London* it appears that the mercers had their shops chiefly on old London Bridge,[18] and therefore in a spot which was especially convenient for trading with new arrivals in the capital. They were one of the most influential of London's livery companies; they initiated the organization of the Merchant Adventurers,[19] and played the most important role in that company. The data we have obtained concerning 134 London members of the Eastland Company mentioned in the London port books at the end of the sixteenth century reveal that fifteen were mercers, which puts them in third place after skinners (twenty-seven members) and drapers (eighteen members). In the list of founders of the Eastland Company mentioned in Elizabeth's 1579 charter the mercers were numerically second to the skinners. The mercers also played the most important part in the Muscovy Company, in the second half of the sixteenth century.[20]

2. The *Grocers* (spice merchants), who occupy the second place in the 1516 list, came into being as a gild by the fusion of the gilds of merchants engaged in the pepper and spices trade.[21] Later on they greatly extended the range of their trading operations, taking in many other commodities, from wool and cloth to various foodstuffs and other articles.[22] The Grocers did not play any large part in the early years of the Eastland Company; the London port books note only nine names of such merchants in the Elizabethan era. But they held numerically third place in the list of creators of the Muscovy Company.

3. The *Drapers* separated from the Mercers as greater specialization developed in the cloth trade.[23] They played a considerable part in the early history of the Eastland Company. In the London port books there are eighteen names of drapers engaged in the Baltic trade—second in number after the Skinners. They also held second place numerically among the creators of the Muscovy Company.

4. The *Fishmongers* do not appear in the 1579 privilege at all, and only two fishmongers' names are mentioned in the London port books. There is just as little to be said about them in connection with

the early history of the Muscovy Company. In the fourteenth century they were still quite a powerful organization, but they declined considerably from the end of the century and lost their former privileges in the realm of trade in fish and other victuals.[24]

5. The *Goldsmiths*[25] also had very few members of the Eastland or Muscovy Companies in the Elizabethan era. Among the London members of the Eastland Company we have managed to trace only one goldsmith, John Watson, who in 1588 was trading with Elbing,[26] importing wax from that city.

6 The *Skinners*[27] played the most important part in the early period of the Eastland Company's existence. As many as twenty-seven of their number carried on trade with the Baltic from London in the Elizabethan era. We find six skinners also among the first members of the Muscovy Company. The merchants gained a decided predominance in the Skinners, as in other livery companies, ousting the skinner craftsmen from all influence. Even in Elizabeth's time the craftsmen were petitioning for a separate charter, justifying their request on the ground that they had no representation whatever in the government and administration of the Company.[28] Skinners were among the wealthiest and most influential members of the Eastland Company connected with the Baltic trade, e.g. Thomas Allen, William and Thomas Cockayne, Robert Mayott, Francis and Nicholas Pearson, and others.

7. The *Merchant Taylors*[29] existed as a brotherhood of tailors as early as the thirteenth century; in 1326 they organized themselves into a gild and in 1502 received the name of Merchant Tailors, since they traded 'in all parts of the world and the kingdom', selling and buying 'various goods and products, especially woollen cloth', as Henry VII's 1502 privilege says.[30] They had five representatives in the Eastland Company's 1579 charter, and eight merchant tailors are mentioned in connection with the Baltic trade in the London port books of the Elizabethan period. There were seven merchant tailors among the first members of the Muscovy Company.

8. The *Haberdashers* were originally a section of the mercers' gild, but at the beginning of the sixteenth century they gradually absorbed many cap and hat merchants, and changed their name to Merchant Haberdashers. Here, too, as in the case of other gild companies which were originally crafts organizations, the merchants gained the dominance and subordinated the craftsmen to themselves.[31] They were merchant entrepreneurs who imported caps and hats into England, but gradually branched out into trade in other goods.[32] We

find four Haberdashers' representatives in the Eastland Company's 1579 charter; the London port books mention fourteen haberdashers among merchants exporting goods to the Baltic and importing every kind of commodity from that area, with the exception of hats and caps.

9. The *Salters* played a minor role among the London gild companies. The Eastland Company privilege names only two; but in the second half of the sixteenth century eight London salters traded with the Baltic. Bridbury has recently shown[33] that in the sixteenth century salters had little connection with the salt trade—even less than the Grocers and Mercers, for instance. They were engaged in the sale of wine, tin and fish, but above all in the export of cloth; and it is as cloth exporters that they are mentioned in the London port books of this period.[34]

10. The *Ironmongers*[35] had only one representative among the known creators of the Eastland Company. Four representatives of this livery company traded with the Baltic in the second half of the century, and there were four ironmongers among the organizers of the Muscovy Company.

11. The *Vintners*[36] do not figure among the creators of the Eastland Company, but four of them are mentioned in the London port books as carrying on trade with the Baltic.

12. The *Clothworkers* were not included in the above-mentioned 1516 list of London livery companies, the last place in the list being occupied by the Shearmen. The Clothworkers' Company was formed in 1528 by the fusion of the shearmen and fullers in one organization.[37] The Eastland Company's charter names five clothworkers, and the London port books mention thirteen as taking part in London's Baltic trade in the Elizabethan era.

We get some indication of the wealth and the relative position of the various London livery companies in the sixteenth century from the level of their contributions towards supplying the capital with grain. Table 4.1 shows that the mercers, grocers and tailors were the wealthiest livery companies, and the vintners, salters and ironmongers were the poorest. In comparing this table with the 1516 list, which we took as the basis of the order we have adopted in discussing the respective livery companies, one is struck by the definite advance of the tailors and drapers, who rose several places during the sixteenth century.

A similar picture is obtained for the beginning of the seventeenth century if we take the size of the loans imposed on the twelve livery companies by the court in 1604 and 1627–28. This shows the further growth in affluence of the Merchant Taylors, since they then occupied first place, while there was some impoverishment of the Mercers. But the last places were still occupied by the vintners, salters, and ironmongers.[38]

As we have already mentioned, it has not been possible to establish the membership of London livery companies of all the merchants mentioned in the Charter of 1579. Other sources, especially the London port books, have enabled us to obtain information for about

Table 4.1 *London livery companies' contributions to the capital's grain supplies (£)*

Livery company	1520	1546	1566	1574
Mercers	80	150	200	500
Grocers	80	150	175	500
Merchant Taylors	80	150	175	431
Drapers	80	150	150	373
Goldsmiths	80	100	150	375
Fishmongers	80	100	150	250
Haberdashers	70	100	125	315
Clothworkers	–	100	150	275
Skinners	60	100	75	200
Ironmongers	40	66	75	$181\frac{1}{2}$
Salters	16	100	75	$181\frac{1}{2}$
Vintners	20	60	33	$181\frac{1}{2}$

Source N. S. B. Gras, *The evolution of the English corn market from the twelfth to the eighteenth centuries*, Harvard, 1926, pp. 421–3

half the Charter members of the Eastland Company. From these sources we get the following figures for thirty-five identified merchants in the charter of 1579: six mercers, six skinners, five clothworkers, five drapers, five merchant taylors, four haberdashers, two salters, one ironmonger and one leather seller.

The London port books for the years 1565, 1567, 1576, 1587, 1588 and 1599[39] yield further data on the share of the various livery companies in the Eastland Company's Baltic trade. These show twenty-seven skinners, eighteen drapers, fifteen mercers, fourteen haberdashers, thirteen clothworkers, nine grocers, eight merchant taylors, seven salters, four ironmongers, four vintners, two fishmongers and one goldsmith. These figures indicate the dominating rôle of the gild companies in the organization and trade of the Eastland Company: of the 134 London merchants registered in the sources as engaged in trade with Baltic countries in the Elizabethan era, as many as 122, or 91 per cent, were members of livery companies while simultaneously responsible for the entire administration of the Eastland Company.

As we have indicated, the numerous trading companies which came into existence in Elizabethan England were primarily the result of the activity of wealthy London merchants. They united with the object of more certainly securing their interests, and first and foremost of gaining a monopoly more easily, and in associations of various kinds increasing—but at this stage mainly only creating—the basis of their large fortunes.[40] In addition the trading companies were the expression of the economic trends of the Tudor monarchy, which in encouraging their development also gained a convenient means of controlling the trading activities of the English merchant class.[41] In all the trading companies of the Elizabethan era the wealthy London oligarchy had the absolute predominance; these great wholesalers maintained widely ramified trading relations with a considerable part of the known world, while engaged in extensive financial operations, owning their own ships, great warehouses and granaries, and readily buying landed property as a means of investing their capital and of speculation.

From the days of Henry VIII onwards the acquisition of land by merchants who were adding to their wealth was a phenomenon more and more to be observed, as Robert Crowley, a sixteenth-century writer and printer, emphasized:

> To purchase land is all their care
> And all the study of their brain.

T. Lever, a puritan cleric, noted in 1550 that the London merchants were not content only with the trade by which they were growing rich, but invested their capital in the countryside, buying up farms 'out of the hands of worshipful gentlemen, honest yeomen, and poor labouring husbandmen'. This activity must have been on a considerable scale, since Thomas Cromwell even contemplated a law 'that merchants shall employ their goods continually in traffic and not in purchasing lands'.[42] The wills of certain members of the Eastland Company reveal that they owned sometimes numerous manors and other landed property, apart from their London houses (see below).

W. G. Hoskins has collected similar data relating to Elizabethan Exeter.[43]

It is worth drawing attention to yet another source of more than one Elizabethan merchant's fortune. This was privateering, which often yielded enormous profits, especially during the years of Anglo-Spanish rivalry towards the end of the century. English, and more especially London, merchants had considerable shares in the financing of English ships in expeditions against Spanish vessels, and in this way they accumulated often quite substantial fortunes.[44]. For instance John Watts, a modest London draper, one of the earliest members of the Spanish Company, in association with other merchants acquired several ships as well as shares in privateers. Having made a large fortune, he became governor of the East India Company, and later Lord Mayor of London.[45]

Members of the Eastland Company were also among the London merchants who treated privateering as one way of making a fortune. In this connection one must mention first and foremost the first governor of the Company, Thomas Pullison, who had many shares in English ships' pillaging expeditions against Spain, as is witnessed by the loss of £10,000 which he suffered.[46] In 1598 Richard Staper, another member of the Eastland Company, had shares in the pillaging expeditions of five English vessels which captured Spanish imports of provisions, especially grain[47] (see below).

Turning to an analysis of the social composition of the Eastland Company, it should be said that, as in the case of other companies, it was organized primarily by wealthy London merchants who were already carrying on an extensive trade with other areas and markets and who belonged to various other trading organizations. Retailers and craftsmen were excluded from membership of the Company. Analysis of the social composition of the original members of the Company reveals clearly that the wealthy London merchant oligarchy, who had long occupied the leading positions in the capital's political and economic life, played the chief part in its organization.[40] The wealthy mercantile oligarchy[48] not only played the decisive role in the formation of the Elizabethan companies, but later exerted a dominant influence on their structure. They monopolized the companies' administration,[49] as Malynes very critically emphasized early in the seventeenth century, when he drew attention to the fact that all the trade of the Merchant Adventurers 'is come to be managed by forty or fifty persons of that company, consisting of three or four thousand'.[50] Girolamo Lando, the Venetian ambassador in England, wrote at the beginning of the seventeenth century that everything in the English trading companies was decided by a few individuals, that the companies represented the interests of a small group, and that they restricted trade 'to a few tyrannical hands'.[51] The universal tendencies towards oligarchy in the trading companies at the close of the sixteenth century were combated by Edwin Sandys, who in a speech in the House of Commons in 1604 declared that 'it is against the natural Right and Liberty of the Subjects of England to restrain it [trade] into the hands of some few, as now it is'.[52]

The 1579 charter names four representatives of London's wealthy oligarchy at the head of the list of founders of the Eastland Company: Edward Osborne, Thomas Pullison, George Barne and George Bond.[53]

Edward Osborne, who heads the list in the charter, began his career as an apprentice to the wealthy London cloth manufacturer William Hewett, who was Lord Mayor of London in 1559.[54] As a clothworker Osborne reached the dignity of Master in his livery company, about 1554, and he greatly increased his capital through his marriage with William Hewett's daughter. He belonged to several trading companies and played an important part in more than one of them. He was Governor of the Levant Company,[55] and grew extremely rich by trade with the Levant and Spain. He also developed trade with the East Indies.[56] Unfortunately the surviving port books do not reveal his operations in the Baltic trade under the aegis of the Eastland Company. He occupied several positions in London's local government; from 1573 he was an alderman, from 1575 a sheriff, and in 1583 Lord Mayor. He was knighted for his services in 1584, and in 1586 he entered the House of Commons.[57] In the year of the Great Armada he lent the government £500 sterling, a considerable sum for those days.[58]

Thomas Pullison, whom Elizabeth appointed the first governor of the Eastland Company in 1579, was a draper and belonged to the more affluent and influential circles of the London oligarchy. His wealth is indicated by the fact that he estimated that he had lost £10,000 sterling in the southern trade in 1585,[59] though strictly speaking the loss was from privateering activities he had financed. A member of the Spanish Company, he had extensive trading interests in the Iberian peninsula[60] and in the Netherlands.[61] It is difficult to assess his share in the Baltic trade, because of the gaps in the London port books. They tell us only that in 1576 he exported 190 pieces of cheap Manchester cottons to Danzig in two vessels,[62] and that in 1588 he imported 32 cwt of flax and 8 cwt of hemp—comparatively small quantities—from Königsberg.[26] Like Osborne, Pullison held the office of alderman, and was sheriff in 1573[63] and Lord Mayor in 1584.[64] In 1585 he was knighted. At a later date Francis Drake, the famous navigator, lived in his London house.[65]

Unlike the two Lord Mayors of London already mentioned, who were more interested in trade with the Netherlands, Spain and the Levant, George Barne (or Barnes) was chiefly occupied in trade with eastern Europe, and primarily with Russia. He belonged to the Haberdashers' Company, and was the son of George Barne, a London alderman and one of the chief advocates of England's trade with Russia and Africa.[66] Barne was the brother-in-law of Walsingham, Elizabeth's Secretary of State,[67] and a kinsman of the Archbishop of York.[68] He was also related to several of the most influential families in the London oligarchy. He was Governor of the Muscovy Company as many as four times,[69] and Master of his livery company in 1586–87.[70] Barne climbed all the rungs of a London municipal career, from alderman (in 1574–93 with breaks),[63] through the office of sheriff (1576) to Lord Mayor in 1587.[64] He was a member of the House of Commons in the difficult years 1588–89, and was knighted.[71] He had widely ramified trading interests, from the Levant, Spain and Portugal to the Baltic and Moscow. In 1587, jointly with his brother-in-law, Walsingham, he imported 41½ lasts of flax, valued at £500 sterling, from Archangel;[72] this constituted a considerable proportion of the Muscovy Company's flax imports at the time. Barne was also interested in the exploitation of ores and minerals, and had shares in the Company of Mineral and Battery Works.[73] His will, which has been preserved, testifies to his wealth;[74] it reveals that, as was the custom of the contemporary merchant patriciate, he had invested capital in land and had several estates in various counties.

The fourth on the list in the 1579 charter is Alderman George Bond (or Bonde); he too belonged to the Haberdashers' Company. Like Osborne and Pullison, he had a considerable share in trade with the Levant[75] and Spain;[76] we meet with his name among the earliest merchants to engage in trade with Narva, in 1564.[77] Bond was also a member of the Company of Mineral and Battery Works.[78] It would appear that he did not have a large share in the Eastland Company's trade; but in any case the surviving port books do not enable us to make any estimate. In 1578 Bond was Sheriff of London,[64] and in 1587–88 Master of his livery company. He was knighted in 1588.[79] Like Osborne, in 1588 he lent the government £500 sterling.[80]

He was among the wealthiest members of the Eastland Company; in his will he left some £10,000 in cash as well as several landed estates.[81]

The 1579 charter mentions two other persons named Bond: Margaret Bond, the sister-in-law of George Bond, and her son William. Margaret was the widow of William, George Bond's brother, who was a London alderman in 1567–76 and a sheriff in 1567. He, too, was a member of the Haberdashers' Company, and a well-known member of the Merchant Adventurers.[82] He exported cloth to Antwerp, imported wine from France, owned his own ship and carried on trade with the Baltic, Russia and Spain. He left Margaret and her son a considerable fortune, including £4,200 in cash.[83] Margaret Bond, the only woman to figure in the first list of the Eastland Company, was the daughter of the London merchant Thomas Gore, who was a member of the Spanish Company and traded with Morocco.[84]

Christopher Hoddesdon, a London haberdasher, also figures in this group of the most important members of the Eastland Company, merchants engaged on a large scale in the trade of various companies. Hoddesdon had at one time been an apprentice to George Barne senior, and he married Barne's granddaughter, which helped him to achieve a fortune and importance in the City rather more quickly. His participation in the Eastland Company was only one—and that by no means the most important—branch of his trading activities. From the very beginning of the Muscovy Company's existence he was one of the pioneers of trade with Moscow. It is possible that he accompanied Chancellor in his 1553 voyage to Russia; later on, as the Muscovy Company's agent, he spent some years in Narva, Novgorod, Yaroslav and other East European towns, handling the Company's many trading interests,[85] with great benefit, as he wrote, to English merchants.[86] After returning to London in 1562 and developing his private interests, he became, in 1566, England's chief commercial agent in Narva, where in the years 1566–67, and again in 1569–70 he made purchases on behalf of the Muscovy Company, not without considerable benefit to himself. The Company even accused him of exploiting the position entrusted to him for his own profit and benefit. In 1570 he was present at a battle between English ships and Polish privateers.[87] In 1577 he was commissioned to sail to Narva with twelve English ships; on the way this flotilla fell in with seven Danzig privateers, which were blockading Narva. The English side succeeded in scattering the privateers and sent eighty-five of their crews to

Moscow, while their commander, Hans Snark, was transported to England.[88] From 1574, as Elizabeth's financial agent, he performed various functions relating to England's trade with Germany and the Netherlands.[89] In the years 1577–80 he represented the Merchant Adventurers in negotiations for the extension of the lease of the Hamburg residence, and later on in conversations directed towards obtaining an entrepot in Emden.[90] Late in the sixteenth century he was made Governor of the Merchant Adventurers, and in 1603 he was knighted. He was another typical representative of the London merchant oligarchy; he had shares in various English companies engaged in foreign trade, and owned properties in several parts of the country.[91]

Thomas Bramley was also a member of several trading companies, and traded not only with the Baltic but also with Spain, Morocco and even Brazil, combining trading with privateering activities.[92] Richard Staper, a London clothworker and an associate of Edward Osborne, had widely ramified trade relations; he was one of the pioneers of England's Levant and East Indies trade—'perhaps the biggest Mediterranean trader in London', as Stone called him.[93] From 1581 Staper was a member and one of the organizers of the Levant Company,[94] and then of the East India Company. He was a member of the Spanish Company and imported southern commodities from Seville and Malaga. He traded with Genoa and Morocco. He had shares in the profits accruing from the privateering activities of five English ships which in 1598 carried off a quantity of Spanish grain, various kinds of provisions, and arms.[95] The scope of Staper's activities must have been enormous, since in the *Survey of London* in 1598 Stow called him the greatest merchant of his times.[96] But we know nothing about his relations with Baltic countries. Nor do the sources yield any information on this point concerning another member of the Eastland Company, Thomas Wylford, who played a very important part in the Spanish Company and was even its Governor.[97] We know just as little about the share of John Foxall, a London mercer, in the Baltic trade. His main activity was confined within the Merchant Adventurers' organization, but he also engaged in voyages to Narva, which aroused the Muscovy Company's protest in 1564.[98] Foxall was also interested in trade with Spain, as we learn from his complaints when the Spaniards detained his ship in Cadiz in 1576.[99] In 1585 he suffered considerable losses 'from the king of Spain' in this trade.[100]

The members of the Eastland Company which we have dealt with so far, as figuring in the 1579 charter—representatives of the wealthy

London oligarchy, officials of various companies and holding high office in London's government—do not appear to have had any large share in the trading activities of the Company whose foundation they had advanced so actively. They invested their capital rather in the Russian, Spanish and Levant trades, not confining themselves to any one area, thus enlarging their turnover and reducing the element of risk. In their operations the Baltic trade was only a part of the expanding world market, in which from the Elizabethan era onwards English merchants played a more and more vital part.

However, the merchants so far mentioned were not the most numerous group among the founders of the Company. The majority would appear to have been wholesalers who concentrated their trading interests in the areas of the North and Baltic seas, though it cannot be excluded that they had some share in the southern trade.

An example of a merchant occupying a middle place between these two groupings of Eastland Company members was William Cockayne, a London leather merchant and member of the Skinners' Company. For some forty years he carried on an active trade with Poland, while engaged in commerce in the North Sea area. He was the father of a famous alderman and Lord Mayor of London who was the author of a plan to export only finished cloth from England—a plan which during the reign of James I caused much confusion and many complications in the Merchant Adventurers' trade.[101] William Cockayne was also a Merchant Adventurer, and traded with France;[102] but the Baltic zone was an especially important field for his commercial activities. His will, which has survived,[103] reveals that he was a very wealthy man, with considerable liquid cash and owning a number of manors. In 1588 he lent the English government £200 sterling.[80] Late in the sixteenth century he was deeply involved in importing grain from the Baltic; in 1596, with Thomas Offley and the Freeman brothers, he was responsible for some 30 per cent of the total rye imports from Poland to England,[104] and in 1597 he and his sons were among the main English importers of Polish rye.[105]

The London port books give some idea of the extent and nature of Cockayne's trade with Poland. In 1567–68 he shipped from Danzig to London 35 lasts of pitch, 20 lasts of tar, 12 lasts of ashes, 38 cwt of feathers, 28 packs of flax, 3 packs of canvas and 237 cwt of ships' tackle—a cargo of considerable value, and fairly typical, so far as the items were concerned, of English merchants' imports from the Baltic.[106] In 1576, jointly with Nicholas Pearson, Cockayne shipped to Danzig 63,560 skins, especially cony skins, 13 casks of currants and 2 cwt and 20 lb of sugar, in six vessels.[62] In 1587–88 he shipped from Elbing 13·5 lasts of ashes, 979 cwt of ships' tackle, 470 bales of 'spruce canvas', 120 rugs, some 500 cwt of flax, etc, in thirteen vessels.[107]

Among the merchants mentioned in the 1579 charter who were engaged primarily in the Baltic trade, first place must be conceded to Thomas Russell, whom Elizabeth named the first Deputy Governor, and who in 1597 became the Governor of the Eastland Company.[108] From 1565 onwards Russell was 'one of the Queen's Majesties Purveyours',[109] an official supplying the court with provisions. This was an exceptionally profitable office, yielding large returns, among other reasons because the prices of victuals purchased by the Queen's supplier were based on the principle that the people's compulsory contributions to the court, the army or the fleet were to be paid for at lower than market prices.[110] In addition, this official had the possibility of selling on his own account and at a good profit any surplus of goods bought for the court at reduced prices. It is not impossible that this official position was the foundation of Russell's wealth. Like William Cockayne, he was one of those Eastland Company members who for many years carried on trade with the Baltic.

The London port books note that in 1565[16] Russell shipped to Danzig some 100 cloths, mainly expensive broadcloth originating from Suffolk and Gloucester, in four ships. In 1567–68[106] he imported from Poland 46 lasts and 10 casks of pitch, 22·5 lasts and two casks of tar, 25 lasts and 12 casks of ashes, 4 tons of iron, 33 packs of flax, 4 packs of hemp, 75 cwt of various kinds of cordage, one hundred of staves, six hundreds of oaken staves, 3 Danzig chests, etc, involving cargoes of twelve ships. At the end of the sixteenth century he imported various goods from Poland, and his name appears on a 1597 list of London importers of Polish rye.[111] During this time he was engaged in negotiations with Danzig on behalf of the Eastland Company.[112] For many years he had factors working for him in the Baltic area; in Danzig, for instance, he had two agents in residence from time to time.[113] His will indicates the great wealth of this Eastland Company governor; he left £2,033 sterling in cash,[114] willing a large part of it to charitable purposes. For instance, he assigned £748 to the poor,[115] £453 for impoverished members of his livery company,[116] and £267 for the development of higher studies.

The London salter Jerome Beale bought Polish products in Danzig and Elbing for more than twenty years. The port books reveal that in 1568[106] he imported from Poland 20 lasts of pitch, 16 lasts of tar, over seven lasts of ashes, Danzig chests, a small quantity of staves, etc. In 1587[72] he imported 23 lasts of ashes, 11 lasts of pitch, a little flax, hemp, etc. A cargo he bought in Elbing and Königsberg in 1588[26] consisted of 68 lasts of ashes, 3 lasts of tar, a small quantity of flax, hemp, staves, and other goods. In 1588 the total quantity of ashes exported from the Baltic in English vessels amounted to 202 lasts.[117]

Two other merchants mentioned in the 1579 charter played an important part in the Baltic trade for many years, as 'King's merchants for Danske' or 'King's merchants in the east parts beyond the seas'. They resided in Danzig and Elbing, making purchases on the spot for the English court, and primarily for the fleet. In the days of Henry VIII, Edward VI and Mary one of these agents was the William Watson we have already mentioned. He was a London cloth merchant, and Henry VIII used his services in purchasing cordage, masts and other goods needed for shipbuilding from the Danzig council.[118] In 1545 Watson sailed to the Baltic 'upon the Kinges Majestes affayres',[119] buying cordage and other goods to the sum of £713 8*s* 4*d*. In 1547–48 the Acts of the Privy Council mention him as travelling to Danzig 'for cables and other maryne stuf'[120] to a value of about £964. In 1551 the Privy Council commanded Watson to purchase 1,000 lasts of rye and about 330 lasts of wheat in Danzig.[121] In 1576 he exported to Danzig, probably on his own account, 10,000 grey cony skins;[62] in 1587–88 he bought about 17 lasts of ashes, over 1,200 cwt of cordage, 20 lasts of spruce flax, tar, hemp, staves and oak staves, feathers, etc, in Elbing and exported all these cargoes to London in ten ships.[72] One should add that Watson was one of the first members of the Muscovy Company and took part in its original administration. He was a ship owner,[122] which indicates that he achieved considerable wealth in the Baltic and Moscow trade.

One of Watson's successors in the office of king's agent was another charter member of the Eastland Company, the London leather merchant Thomas Allen. He was the son of Richard Allen, gentleman, who was married to the daughter of a London sheriff.[123] Elizabeth's 1561 patent granting Allen the position of 'the Queen's merchant in the East parts beyond the seas for the provision of all materials for the apparellinge and furniture of the Queen's navy and ships' included an annual salary of £33 6*s* 8*d*.[124] The terms of the patent we have quoted clearly indicate the kind of Baltic goods England was chiefly interested in. A list of officials of the English navy for the years 1583–88 includes Allen's name as 'Queen's merchant for Danske', with an annual salary of £30.[125] In 1565 he was granted a licence to sell 240,000 skins in the Baltic countries,[126] this quantity being almost half the total export of skins to the Baltic from England.[127] Elizabeth more than once intervened with the King of Denmark to ensure Allen's safe passage through the Sound,[128] and intervened with the King of Poland also on his behalf.[129] It should be added that Allen was also interested in other possibilities of developing England's trade; he was treasurer of the company which financed Frobisher's attempt to discover the North-west Passage.[130] He owned the *Barke Allen*, 90 tons,[131] and several other ships, as we learn as the result of two of his ships *en route* for Narva being detained by Sweden in 1579, exposing him to losses of £1,000.[132] He undertook voyages to Narva also on behalf of the English court; for instance, in July 1581 he exported a quantity of flax and hemp 'for the Queen's Majesty's use' from that port.[133] His many years in the Baltic trade assured him a considerable fortune; in his will be left several landed properties in various counties and in London.[134] He also probably had interests in trade with the Netherlands and Russia, but nothing definite can be said on these points.

The London port books reveal the extent of Allen's trading operations in the Baltic for various years. In 1565 he exported 180 cloths in five ships to Danzig,[16] and brought back 19 lasts of pitch in two ships.[135] In 1567–68 he consigned to London from Danzig a large and valuable cargo of 55 lasts and 12 casks of pitch, 20 lasts of tar, 49 packs of flax, 20 cwt and two packs of hemp, 19 hundreds of staves, a quantity of oars, deal boards, oak staves, iron, etc, in fourteen bottoms.[106] In 1589 he supplied the English fleet with 46 masts bought in Danzig for £679,[136] and in 1590 he supplied masts to a value of £3,000 sterling.

The London merchant Thomas Sexton employed another member of the Eastland Company in 1579, Blase Freman, as his commercial agent in Danzig from 1555 to 1559.[137] Freman was a leather merchant; we devote more space to his activities in chapter ten, dealing with the organization of England's Baltic trade.

John Collett, a merchant taylor, and Richard Gourney, (or Gurney), a cloth worker, carried on trade with the Baltic for over twenty years.[138] In 1565 Gourney and three other merchants who figure in the 1579 charter, Henry Isham and John Langton, mercers, and William Salkins, a merchant tailor, exported a quantity of cloth to Poland.[16] In 1567–68 Gourney shipped forty-three packs of flax, a small quantity of iron, cordage, hemp, etc, from Poland to London in ten ships.[106] In 1587 he was Deputy Governor of the Eastland Company, with his headquarters in Elbing.[139] In 1594 he became an alderman of the City of London.[140] William Salkins was also a Deputy Governor of the Company,[141] and during the campaign at the Polish court to obtain confirmation of privileges in Elbing he played an important part in the negotiations, especially in 1581.[142]

In the year of the great Armada John Bodleigh, a London merchant tailor, and Hugh Offley, a skinner, imported various goods from Elbing and Riga.[143] Offley was an alderman, a very wealthy man, able in 1588 to lend the government £300 sterling,[80] and to leave the enormous sum of £1,500 to charity in his will.[144] Offley also carried on trade on a large scale with France. He had an agent in Poland named Pattelier, who was an ardent opponent of the attempts to transfer the English warehouse from Danzig to Elbing.[145]

During the months of the Armada another London merchant tailor, Peter Collett, also brought a considerable cargo of Polish goods to London. In 1587 he imported 43·5 lasts of ashes, 5 lasts of pitch, 240 cwt of hemp, over four lasts of flax, 6 cwt of wax, 144 cwt of cordage, 16 cwt of gunpowder, 17 tons of iron, a small quantity of staves and boards, and 11 dozen 'playing tables' from Elbing in 14 vessels.[72]

Richard Lewis, or Lewes, a cloth worker, also maintained trading relations with Poland at this time. He was one of the first Assistants in the Eastland Company administration. From the details of a dispute he had with the Company it appears he was one-third owner of a ship, and was at law for seventeen years with other merchants over his shares in it.[146]

Late in the sixteenth century the London merchant tailor Robert Mayott (or Maiott) also had quite active relations with the Baltic area; in 1576 he exported 20,000 cony and fox skins to Poland,[62] and in 1588 he imported from Elbing to London 28 lasts of pitch and tar, 18 cwt of gunpowder, some 22 lasts of flax, etc, in ten ships.[72]

John Burnell, Robert Hilson, John Langton and Roger Fludd were among Eastland Company members who married Danzig women and even lived in Poland for long periods. Burnell, a London cloth worker, married the daughter of a wealthy Danzig merchant, Peter Kamerlinck. Hilson married another of his daughters.[147] Burnell was one of the wealthiest merchants in London; in his will he left almost £5,000 in cash, as well as landed properties and livestock.[148] He carried on trade with Poland for over thirty years, and was also engaged in trade with France.[149] At the time of the Armada he imported over 22 lasts of flax, 134 cwt of hemp, 8·5 lasts of ashes, 8 cwt of wax, 140 rugs, etc, but especially a large quantity of various kinds of cordage weighing close on 700 cwt, from Elbing to London.[150] Late in the century he imported rye from Poland.[151]

Burnell's brother-in-law, the London mercer Robert Hilson, was connected with the Baltic trade at a rather earlier period. The London port books have an entry recording that in 1567–68 he imported 30 lasts of rye, almost fifty lasts of pitch, a little flax, ashes, timber, and 'sope boxis' from Danzig in twelve ships.[106] He owned an estate in Great Stanmore, to which he retired in his old age. He built a chapel in the local church, and left a bequest for the maintenance of a permanent preacher there. In addition he assigned a sum to purchase children's clothing for the local hospital,[152] and in his will left £382 for the poor.

The third of the merchants above mentioned, the London mercer John Langton, spent over thirty-four years in Poland, especially in 'Crown Prussia', and was an expert on problems connected with trade between England and Poland.[153] He was married to a Danzig woman, but we have no detailed information on his trading operations.

The London cloth merchant Roger Fludd also married a Danzig woman, and he lived permanently in Danzig from about 1560 onward. After thirty years he obtained civic rights in the city.[154] In the years 1574–76 he purchased a quantity of saltpetre and gunpowder for the English court.[155] He was an ardent advocate of abolishing the English residence in Elbing and transferring it to Danzig. Having long been settled in Danzig, where he owned land and other real estate, when the English staple was established in Elbing he was reluctant to transfer to that town, though as a member of the Eastland Company he was under obligation to do so. He appealed to Stefan Batory on the issue, pointing out that Danzig provided much better conditions than Elbing for English trade.[156] In a letter to Danzig at the end of 1584 he attacked the Eastland Company for locating its staple in Elbing and not in Danzig, and for compelling its members to transfer to the new centre. As he was not prepared to submit to the instruction, and remained in Danzig, the Company fined him 100 Hungarian florins, and then a further 200 florins, and threatened to expel him from membership.

The information we have given so far concerning approximately half the London merchants who are named in the 1579 charter confirms our statement that the wealthy London merchants, the great wholesalers carrying on trade with various parts of the world and belonging to several trading companies, played a special part in the formation of the Eastland Company. They were all members of the powerful London livery companies. Apart from this group, the main core of the founder members of the Company were also London merchants and members of the livery companies, who had long-established and continuous trade relations with the Baltic countries, especially with Poland.

We have more meagre information concerning the Company's members who came from the north-eastern ports, Hull and Newcastle; and what we have relates to a later period. As we shall show later, these merchants had a large share in England's Baltic trade. In general their trade was modest by comparison with that of the London wholesalers; the port books show that their Baltic exports and imports were on a much smaller scale. There were exceptions—for instance, wholesalers like Alexander Davison of Newcastle, the member of a long line of wealthy skinners and glovers, the owner of numerous estates and houses,[157] who exported cloth and lead to the Baltic. Another member of the Eastland Company, Robert Beswick, was one of the wealthiest wholesalers in Newcastle at the beginning of the seventeenth century. In 1616 he exported goods valued at over £8,000 sterling to the Baltic, mainly cloth to Elbing. But these were rather exceptional and untypical cases. The Hull and Newcastle merchants, not to mention those of Ipswich and Lynn, could not compare with the London wholesalers in respect of their wealth or their transactions in the Baltic trade. For instance, in 1593 one of the most active Newcastle merchants in Elizabeth's time, Thomas Liddle, imported 8 lasts of flax, 16½ lasts of pitch and 4 tons of iron from Elbing in three ships.[158] In 1598 he imported 80 lasts of rye, etc, from Poland.[159] Another Newcastle merchant, Culbert Beswick, imported 16 lasts of flax, 9 lasts of rye and 2 lasts of pitch from Poland in 1593.[158] In 1598 he despatched to Elbing 298 cheap kerseys, and bought there 26 lasts of flax, 15 lasts of pitch and 45 cwt of hemp. In the same year Christopher Mitford, of Newcastle, sent 10 cheap cloths (dozens), 16 kerseys and 800 items of white skins to Elbing, acquiring in exchange 7 lasts of flax, 4 lasts of pitch and tar, 2 lasts of rye and 2·5 tons of iron.[159] In 1598 the same merchant exported 900 sheepskins to Poland, bringing back 6 lasts of flax, 5·5 cwt of hemp, and 3·5 lasts of tar.[159] These years are the oldest records we have for Newcastle; no Hull books for the same period have survived.

Eastland Company members residing in Ipswich had an even more modest turnover in the Baltic trade. They exported almost exclusively cloth (Suffolk shortcloths) and skins. In 1571 nine Ipswich merchants jointly exported 200 cloths and 8,000 skins to Danzig,[160] quantities which were the equivalent of one London merchant's normal export. In 1603–04 twenty-three Ispwich merchants exported chiefly cloth to Poland,[161] the average per merchant being much smaller than in the case of the London wholesalers.

Late in the sixteenth century Lynn merchants exported mainly cony skins, of no great value, to Poland. For instance, in 1598 only three merchants took part in this export,[162] and their aggregate was nine pieces of cloth and 72,000 skins. No data are available for any earlier years.

Comparison of the London merchants' transactions in the Baltic trade with those of Eastland Company members residing in other ports clearly demonstrates the London wholesalers' predominance and ascendancy; these were the merchants who were primarily responsible for the steps which led to the organization of the Eastland Company.

Notes

1 G. Unwin, *Industrial organization in the sixteenth and seventeenth centuries*, London, 1957 (first published 1904), pp. 21*ff*. The problem of the changes that occurred in English crafts in the fourteenth and fifteenth centuries has been extensively discussed by Małowist, *Studia z dziejów rzemiosła* . . ., pp. 209–78.

2 See A. Law, 'English *nouveaux-riches* in the fourteenth century', *T.R.H.S.*, second series, vol. IX, pp. 49*ff*.

3 M. Dobb, *Studies in the development of capitalism*, New York, 1947, chapter III.

4 P.R.O., Patent Rolls, 21 Elizabeth, c. 66/1185, f. 21.

5 The basis and course of this process has been broadly presented by Małowist, *op. cit.*, pp. 260*ff*.

6 Unwin, *Industrial organization* . . ., pp. 41*ff*.

7 C. W. Colby, 'Growth of oligarchy in English towns', *E.H.R.*, vol. V, 1890, pp. 643*ff*.

8 *Ibid.*, pp. 646*f*.

9 *Ibid.*, pp. 644–8.

10 Dobb, *op. cit.*, p. 116.

11 Unwin, *Industrial organization* . . ., pp. 44*ff*.

12 L. Stone, 'State control in sixteenth-century England', *Ec.H.R.*, vol. XVII, 1947, p. 117, considers that in Elizabethan England companies 'were formed to obtain the maximum profits for a minimum number'.

13 See W. Herbert, *The history of the twelve great livery companies of London . . .*, vols. I–II, London, 1837 (includes many documents); also G. Unwin, *The gilds and companies of London*, London, 1908.
14 See Lipson, *The economic history of England*, vol. I, p. 430.
15 S. Thrupp, 'The grocers of London: a study of distributive trade' in *Studies in English trade . . .*, p. 247.
16 P.R.O., E 190/2/1.
17 See Thrupp, *op. cit.*, p. 289. On the Mercers, see J. Watney, *History of the Mercers' Company . . .*, London, 1914.
18 J. Stow, *Survey of London*, vol. I, Oxford, 1908, p. 81.
19 See E. M. Carus-Wilson, 'The origin and early development of the Merchant Adventurers' organization in London as shown in their own medieval records' in her *Mediaeval merchant venturers: collected studies*, London, 1954, pp. 147*ff*. Down to 1526 the Merchant Adventurers shared a common minute book with the London Mercers. See Dobb, *op. cit.*, p. 123.
20 Willan, *The Muscovy Merchants . . .*, p. 17. Our numerical data concerning the share of the various livery companies in the organization of the Muscovy Company are based on this work.
21 Of earlier works, see J. A. Rees, *The Worshipful Company of Grocers . . .*, London, 1923. The best general work is Thrupp, *op. cit.*, pp. 247–92.
22 Thrupp, *op. cit.*, pp. 262–72.
23 The basic work on the history of the Drapers' Company is the extensive study by A. H. Johnson, based on the original sources: *The history of the Worshipful Company of Drapers*, vols. I–V, Oxford, 1914–22. The medieval and Tudor periods are covered in vols. I–II.
24 Lipson, *The economic history of England*, vol. I, pp. 382*f*.
25 See A. Heal, *The London Goldsmiths, 1200–1800*, Cambridge, 1935. The Goldsmiths' Gild was one of the oldest in London; it existed as early as the beginning of the thirteenth century.
26 P.R.O., E 190/8/1.
27 See J. F. Wadmore, *History and antiquities of the Company of Skinners*, London, 1902.
28 Unwin, *Industrial organization . . .*, p. 44.
29 See C. M. Clode, *The early history of the Guild of Merchant Taylors*, vols. I–II, London, 1888.
30 C. M. Clode, *Memorials of the Guild of Merchant Taylors . . .*, London, 1875, pp. 195*f*.
31 Dobb, *op. cit.*, p. 141.
32 Unwin, *Industrial organization . . .*, p. 106. Among many other commodities they imported wool from Spain.
33 A. R. Bridbury, *England and the salt trade in the Middle Ages*, Oxford, 1955, pp. 145*f*.
34 *Ibid.*, p. 146. In a document dating from the end of the fifteenth century one of the London merchants was referred to as 'a salter, otherwise

called draper', which gives a good indication of this company's evolution in trade.

35 T. C. Noble, *A brief history of the . . . Ironmongers, London,* A.D. *1351–1889*, London, 1889.

36 T. Milbourn, *The Vintners' Company*, London, 1888.

37 Lipson, *The economic history of England*, vol. I, p. 430.

38 R. Ashton, *The Crown and the money market, 1603–40*, Oxford, 1960, pp. 116, 136.

39 P.R.O., E 190/2/1; E 190/3/2; E 190/4/2; E 190/6/4 E 190/7/8; E 190/8/1; E 190/10/11.

40 N. S. B. Gras, 'The rise of big business', *Journal of Economic History*, vol. IV, 1932, p. 389.

41 R. Häpke, 'Die Handelspolitik der Tudors', *Hansische Geschichtsblätter*, vol. XX, 1914, p. 401.

42 Lipson cites various texts illustrating this problem: *The economic history of England*, vol. I, p. 148.

43 W. G. Hoskins, 'The Elizabethan merchants of Exeter' in *Elizabethan government and society: essays presented to Sir John Neale*, London, 1961, p. 176.

44 K. R. Andrews has published an extensive study of this subject: *Elizabethan privateering: English privateering during the Spanish war, 1585–1603* Cambridge, 1964, especially pp. 100–23.

45 *Ibid.*, p. 108.

46 *Ibid.*, p. 112.

47 *Ibid.*, pp. 267*f.*

48 Lipson, *The economic history of England*, vol. II, p. lv. In 1557 the Venetian ambassador wrote that among the Merchant Adventurers and members of the Staplers' Company were owners of property to the value of about £50,000, which, translated into present-day terms, would make them millionaires. As we shall see later, certain members of the Eastland Company also owned fortunes exceeding £10,000 in cash, e.g. George Bond.

49 Unwin, *Studies in economic history* . . ., pp. 168*ff*; also p. 183.

50 G. Malynes, *The maintenance of free trade*, London, 1622, pp. 50–1.

51 *Cal.S.P. Venice*, vol. XVII, p. 434.

52 See *Journals of the House of Commons*, vol. I, London, 1803, p. 218.

53 P.R.O., Patent Rolls, 21 Elizabeth, c.66/1185, f. 21.

54 Stow, *op. cit.*, vol. I, p. 223.

55 A. C. Wood, *A history of the Levant Company*, London, 1935, p. 7.

56 Ramsay, *English overseas trade* . . ., p. 110.

57 Welch's article 'Sir Edward Osborne' in the *Dictionary of national biography*, vol. XIV, London, 1909, does not mention his membership of the Eastland Company.

58 B.M., Lansdowne MSS 56, No. 3.

59 K. R. Andrews, *op. cit.*, p. 112.

60 *Cal.S.P.For., 1583, and addenda*, No. 597, p. 564. In November 1580 the Portuguese fell upon Pullison's ship *Falcon*, which was sailing with goods to Spain.
61 *A.P.C.*, vol. x, pp. 97, 107; also *Cal.S.P.Dom., 1547–80*, p. 490.
62 P.R.O., E 190/6/4.
63 Stow, *op. cit.*, vol. II, p. 184.
64 *Ibid.*, vol. II, p. 185.
65 *Ibid.*, vol. I, p. 231.
66 A. B. Beaven, *The aldermen of the City of London*, vol. I, London, 1908, p. 36; also Hakluyt, *op. cit.*, vol. I, pp. 314–20.
67 C. Read, *Mr Secretary Walsingham and the policy of Queen Elizabeth*, vol. I, Oxford, 1925, p. 26.
68 *An analytical index to . . . Remembrancia, preserved among the archives of the City of London*, A.D. *1579–1664*, London, 1878, p. 181.
69 *Cal.S.P.Dom. and addenda, 1580–1625*, p. 6.
70 Beaven, *op. cit.*, vol. II, p. 40.
71 *A.P.C.*, vol. VIII, p. 287, and vol. XII, pp. 144, 183.
72 P.R.O., E 190/7/8.
73 M. B. Donald, *Elizabethan monopolies*, Edinburgh, 1961, pp. 37, 53, 72.
74 Prerogative Court of Canterbury, 1, Neville.
75 *Select charters of trading companies*, A.D. *1530–1707*, ed. C. T. Carr, *Publications of the Selden Society*, vol. XXVIII, London, 1913, p. 30.
76 *Cal.S.P. Spanish, 1580–86*, pp. 152, 179, 184.
77 Willan, *The early history of the Russia Company*, p. 68.
78 M. B. Donald, *Elizabethan monopolies*, pp. 38, 72, 74.
79 Beaven, *op. cit.*, vol. II, p. 40. Bond was an ancestor of the Duke of Marlborough.
80 B.M., Lansdowne MSS 56, No. 3.
81 Prerogative Court of Canterbury, 30, Harrington.
82 *Cal.S.P.Dom., 1547–80*, p. 246.
83 W. R. Jordan, *The charities of London, 1480–1660: the aspirations and the achievements of the urban society*, London, 1960, p. 331.
84 T. S. Willan, *Studies in Elizabethan foreign trade*, Manchester, 1959, pp. 202*f.*
85 A. F. Pollard, 'Sir Christopher Hoddesdon' in the *Dictionary of national biography*, vol. XXII, London, 1909. Willan, in *The early history of the Russia Company*, p. 34, considers that Hoddesdon went to Russia only in 1555.
86 According to his own statement, in two years he sold goods in Moscow for £13,644 sterling which in England had cost only £6,607; see Willan, *The early history of the Russia Company*, p. 35.
87 Pollard, *op. cit.*, p. 853.
88 P.R.O., S.P. 12 82/4, f. 17. The document is entitled 'Collection of matters touching the Hanse from 1557'.
89 *Ibid.*, S.P.Dom. 12/179, No. 38.

90 *Cal.S.P.For.*, vol. XIV, Nos. 145, 217, 230, 231, 289; also *Danziger Inventar*, p. 647.
91 Prerogative Court of Canterbury, 18, Wood.
92 Willan, *Studies in Elizabethan foreign trade*, p. 292. Bramley had shares in the profits from the piratical activities of the *Samaritain* (160 tons), which in 1590 pillaged a quantity of Spanish wine and Portuguese wheat and salt, among other adventures. See K. R. Andrews, *Elizabethan privateering*, p. 248.
93 L. Stone, *An Elizabethan: Sir Horatio Palavicino*, Oxford, 1956, p. 88.
94 T. S. Willan, 'Some aspects of English trade with the Levant in the sixteenth century', *E.H.R.*, vol. LXX, 1955, pp. 399*ff.*
95 K. R. Andrews, *Elizabethan privateering*, pp. 267*f.*
96 Stow, *op. cit.*, vol. I, p. 118. See also G. Fisher, *Barbary legend: war, trade and piracy in north Africa, 1415–1830*, Oxford, 1957, p. 112.
97 *Cal.S.P.Dom., 1547–80*, p. 687.
98 *Ibid.*, p. 246.
99 *Ibid.*, pp. 519, 574.
100 *Cal.S.P.Dom., 1581–90*, p. 251.
101 See A. Friis, *Alderman Cockayne's project and the cloth trade: the commercial policy of England in the main aspects, 1603–25*, Copenhagen–London, 1927. B. E. Supple has also discussed this question in his *Commercial crisis and change in England, 1600–42*, Cambridge, 1959, pp. 33–51.
102 *Select charters of trading companies*, pp. 64, 80.
103 Prerogative Court of Canterbury, 87, Kidd.
104 Stone, 'Elizabethan overseas trade', p. 53.
105 P.R.O., S.P. 12/263, No. 107. In 1596 he shipped from Poland about sixty-seven lasts of rye, as we learn from a letter of the Lord Mayor of London, written to the Lord Treasurer on 5 October 1596 in connection with the detention at Harwich of a ship belonging to Cockayne. See Corporation of London Record Office, Guildhall, Remembrancia, II, No. 166.
106 P.R.O., E 190/4/2.
107 *Ibid.*, E 190/7/8 and E 190/8/1.
108 *The Acts and ordinances of the Eastland Company*, ed. M. Sellers, London, 1906, p. xiii.
109 *A.P.C.*, vol. VII, p. 241.
110 In the sixteenth and seventeenth centuries the manner in which this office functioned aroused much discontent. See A. Woodworth, 'Purveyance for the royal household in the reign of Queen Elizabeth', *Transactions of the American Philosophical Society*, new series, vol. XXXV, part I, Philadelphia, Pa., 1945.
111 P.R.O., S.P. 12/263, No. 107.
112 B.M., Sloane MSS 25, ff. 2–3.
113 J. Rogers, letter to F. Walsingham, 4 April 1581: P.R.O., S.P. 88/1, No. 11.

114 Jordan, *op. cit.*, p. 334.
115 *Ibid.*, p. 102.
116 *Ibid.*, p. 231.
117 *Tabeller over skibsfart . . .*, vol. IIA, p. 129.
118 *L.P. Henry VIII*, vol. XXI, part I, pp. 107, 660.
119 *A.P.C.*, vol. I, p. 312.
120 *Ibid.*, vol. II, pp. 120, 189, 223.
121 *Ibid.*, vol. III, p. 202.
122 *Ibid.*, *1542–47*, pp. 374, 376.
123 *The visitation of London of the year 1568*, ed. R. Cooke and G. J. Armitage, *Publications of the Harleian Society*, vol. I, London, 1869, p. 53.
124 *Calendar of Patent Rolls*, Elizabeth I, vol. II, p. 127.
125 Historical Manuscripts Commission, Fifteenth report, appendix, part V, London, 1897, p. 106.
126 *Calendar of Patent Rolls*, Elizabeth I, vol. III, p. 255.
127 In 1565 total exports of skins from England to the Baltic amounted to 669,000 items: *Tabeller over skibsfart . . .*, vol. IIA, p. 15.
128 Elizabeth's letters to Frederick II on 28 March 1562 and 5 May 1565: *Forty-fifth annual report of the Deputy Keeper of the Public Record Office*, London, 1885, appendix II, p. 23.
129 *Calendar of Clarendon State Papers*, vol. I, No. 165, p. 486.
130 *A.P.C.*, vol. X, p. 415; also *Cal.S.P.Dom.*, *1547–80*, pp. 608, 621.
131 *A.P.C.*, vol. XIII, p. 83.
132 *Cal.S.P.For.*, *1583–84*, No. 350, pp. 292*f.*; also *ibid.*, *1584–85*, p. 13.
133 *Cal.S.P.Dom.*, *1581–90*, p. 24.
134 Prerogative Court of Canterbury, 27, Harrington.
135 P.R.O., E 190/3/2.
136 *Ibid.*, S.P. 12/225, No. 62.
137 See chapter ten.
138 P.R.O., E 190/4/2, E 190/6/4 and E 190/8/1.
139 Corporation of London Record Office, Guildhall, Repertory, 21, f. 293. A document dated 30 April 1587 calls him 'governor of the Danske merchants', which indicates that, despite the transfer of the headquarters to Elbing, Danzig was still a synonym for Baltic trade in English thinking.
140 *Ibid.*, Repertory, 23, f. 257.
141 *The visitation of London in the year 1588*, p. 22.
142 P.R.O., S.P. 88/1, Nos. 11 and 18.
143 *Ibid.*, E 190/7/8; also E 190/8/1.
144 Jordan, *op. cit.*, p. 169.
145 P.R.O., S.P. 88/1, No. 11. Rogers reported to Walsingham on 4 April 1581 that Offley was 'estemed here a verry riche merchant'.
146 B. M. Lansdowne MSS 160, f. 181.
147 P.R.O., S.P. 88/1, No. 11.
148 Prerogative Court of Canterbury, 58, Haynes.

149 *Select charters of trading companies*, pp. 64, 80.
150 P.R.O., E 190/7/8 and E 190/8/1.
151 *Ibid.*, S.P. 12/263, No. 107.
152 Jordan, *op. cit.*, pp. 99, 332.
153 P.R.O., S.P. 88/1, No. 11: Rogers' letter to Walsingham, dated 4 April 1581. In Rogers' opinion Langton was 'the most expert of all our nation'. He considered that Langton should be the Eastland Company's Deputy Governor, with headquarters in Elbing, and not Salkins, who 'at no tyme hathe . . . bene in this Contrie, and is merely ignorant in the same . . .'
154 *Danziger Inventar*, No. 9984, p. 787.
155 *Ibid.*, Nos. 6736, 6773, 6964, pp. 528, 531, 544.
156 *Ibid.*, No. 9009, p. 715.
157 R. Welford, *Men of mark 'twixt Tyne and Tweed*, vol. II, London, 1895, pp. 21–4.
158 P.R.O., E 190/185/6.
159 *Ibid.*, E 315/485.
160 *Ibid.*, E 190/589/6 (this volume is damaged).
161 *Ibid.*, E 190/598/17.
162 *Ibid.*, E 190/432/5.

five *The organization of the Eastland Company in the Elizabethan era*

It is clear[1] from the charter granted by Elizabeth in 1579 and from other documents that the Eastland Company, like the Levant Company (which in its beginnings was a joint stock company), the Africa Company, and above all the Merchant Adventurers' organization, was one of the so-called regulated companies. In the sixteenth century there was also a second type of trading organization, the joint stock company, among these being the Muscovy and the East India Companies.[2] The organizational prototypes of the English trading companies need to be sought in the medieval *societas*, but more especially in the merchants' gilds, with all their tendencies to be exclusive and monopolistic. Among the various types of organization was the gild headed by one or two elders (aldermen), six brothers and twelve members of the administration ('good and discrete men'), and this type provided the model for the institution of a Governor and a court of assistants in the sixteenth-century trading companies. As we have already indicated, towards the end of the fourteenth and the beginning of the fifteenth centuries charters which constituted the first official recognition of the regulated companies were issued in England. These charters, which dealt with England's trade across the North and Baltic seas, gave the Governor the supreme authority in these companies,[3] and also granted the company the right to draw up statutes and ordinances, powers of legal jurisdiction, etc. The charters, especially those issued to the Merchant Adventurers in the sixteenth century, marked a further step in the development of the company's internal structure. Now the Governor was complemented by a court, consisting of twenty-four assistants ('most sadd, discreet and honest persons') similar to that of the Eastland Company.

Without going more deeply into the genesis of the trading companies and their evolution from the medieval gilds,[4] it should be added that an essential feature of both the above-mentioned types of trading organization was their monopoly, which reserved to them the exclusive right to carry on trade in the area covered by the founding charter. However, in organizational respects there were important differences between the regulated and the joint stock companies. The members of the regulated companies were not in any way restricted in carrying on trade, except by the quite general principles contained in the charter and the company's statutes. These principles only provided a framework, specifying the structure and organization of the company, the area of its trade, and at times the nature of the trade. Within the bounds imposed by this somewhat loose structure the members of the regulated companies carried on trade individually, according to their own judgement and at their own risk. The regulated company did not itself engage in trade, but simply watched to ensure that its members observed the general principles we have referred to, and protected them from the competition of the so-called interlopers, i.e. merchants who, not being members of the company, endeavoured to break its monopoly in the trading area reserved to it. The joint-stock companies were organized on different lines; they had the structure of a centralized company and carried on trade directly through their agents with the prescribed area. The members of this type of company were shareholders who participated in the profits.[5] Of these two types of organization the regulated company was the older. They developed trade between England and the countries nearer at hand, where economic conditions were more stabilized and normal. On the other hand the joint-stock companies, generally speaking, were concerned with trade to more remote countries, where the trading risk was greater and navigation more dangerous.

Elizabeth's charter of 1579 primarily determined the Eastland Company's sphere of activity in some detail—the area reserved to it exclusively, where only English subjects who were its members could carry on trade. The domain of the Eastland Company was Eastland,[6] i.e. the lands lying beyond the Sound, the Baltic countries; the charter specifies them in detail, drawing attention especially to the precise demarcation of the frontier between the Eastland Company's zone and that of the Merchant Adventurers. In accordance with the suggestion, made the previous year, that the Sound and the river Oder should form the western frontier of the Eastland Company's sphere of activity,[7] the 1579 charter recognized its monopoly of trade with Norway, Sweden and Poland, together with their possessions in Livonia, Pomerania and Prussia to the east of the Oder. Among the Baltic ports reserved exclusively to the Company the privilege names (reading from the east) Riga, Reval, Königsberg (Krolewiec),

Braunsberg (Branievo), Elbing (Elbląg), Danzig (Gdańsk), Copenhagen and Elsinore. The Baltic port of Narva was excluded, since it was reserved to the Muscovy Company.[8] Finally, the charter names the Baltic islands (Bornholm, Gotland and others) as also falling within the company's trading area.[9] To the west of the boundary formed by the river Oder was to be a zone common to both the Eastland and the Merchant Adventurers' companies. The charter included Denmark in this area (with the exception of Copenhagen and Elsinore, which, as we have seen, were reserved to the Eastland Company), as well as Jutland, Mecklenburg, Silesia and Moravia, the ports of Lübeck, Wismar, Roztok, Stralsund (Strzalow) and Stettin and 'the whole ryver Odera'.[10] The zone recognized as the two companies' joint trading area extended westward to the Elbe, while the duchy of Holstein, and Hamburg were exclusively the domain of the Merchant Adventurers. Across this area the Eastland Company was granted free transit and exemption from any form of payment to the Merchant Adventurers.

The opening section of the 1579 charter also detailed the reasons for founding the Eastland Company, stating that England would thus secure a better organization of trade and greater economic benefits. It expressed the opinion that the regulation of the English Baltic trade achieved by founding a company would also bring benefits to the merchants who already had long experience in trade with the Baltic. We read, further, that the Company would make it possible to exclude from the Baltic trade those English merchants who had not this experience and who, through their unorganized and inefficient activities, had done the country nothing but harm (the so-called interlopers). By possessing a Baltic company English merchants will be able, says the charter, to defend themselves more effectively abroad against the obstruction of foreign rulers, and against unjustified imposts and increased customs duties.[11]

After defining the area of the Company's activity and stating the reasons for its foundation, the charter names all the sixty-five merchants who were its foundation members (see chapter four). Here it is worth considering the total number mentioned. Taking the Muscovy Company as a basis for comparison, it would seem that the original membership was comparatively small, a fact which may possibly be due to the Eastland Company's known tendency to be exclusive.[12] At the start of its existence the Muscovy Company had 201 members,[13] including seven peers, twenty knights and thirteen esquires, many of whom occupied the highest positions at the royal court, in the government and in the State administration. We do not find any such group of high officials in the Eastland Company; similarly, they were absent from the Merchant Adventurers, in which the highest ranking members were mayors and city councillors.[14] There would appear to be a simple explanation of this fact. The Muscovy Company was a joint-stock company; its members did not directly engage in trade, they only contributed capital, drawing considerable profit from the Company's financial and trading operations. The form of organization of the regulated companies, whose members carried on trade individually, restricted their composition, at least at first. And so they had fewer members, although it must not be forgotten that they expanded quite rapidly; this is to be deduced from Elizabeth's charter dated 20 December 1560, in which only seventeen London merchants are mentioned.[15] In this charter these merchants were given permission to transport commodities between England and Danzig, Hamburg, Lübeck, and other Hanseatic towns, in foreign bottoms, for the same payment as for English ships. We may also recall that only fifty-four merchants are mentioned in the Merchant Adventurers' charter of 1564.[16] Shortly after its foundation the Eastland Company already had many more members than in 1579—the exact number is not recorded—but not as many as the Merchant Adventurers,[17] which according to Wheeler[18] had about 3,500 members in 1601, including families and apprentices.

The charter of 1579 devotes much space to the problem of recruiting members into the Company. It lays down precisely what conditions candidates had to observe in order to be accepted, and how this issue was to be tackled in the future. The prime condition was that only English merchants could be members. This stipulation is also found in the charters of other contemporary companies, for instance the Merchant Adventurers, who decided the issue even more rigorously, excluding from membership any merchant who had married a foreign wife or possessed real estate abroad.[19] The condition was intended to preserve the national character of the company, which—especially in the case of the Merchant Adventurers, whose headquarters were on the Continent—was exposed to the danger of ceasing to represent exclusively English interests. Elizabeth's charter permitted the Eastland Company to acquire real estate up to £100 annual value,[20] and did not restrict marriage with foreign women. As we have already observed, it was common for English merchants to contract mixed marriages in Danzig and Elbing.

A further condition of membership of the Eastland Company

was that the candidate must have had at least eleven years' experience in the Baltic trade. Elizabeth's charter of 1579 included the stipulation that only merchants who had carried on trade with the Baltic areas before January 1568 could be members (also their children and apprentices).[21] Widows of merchants who had fulfilled this qualification could also be accepted, as is indicated by the name of Margaret Bond which figures in the 1579 charter. In a later section of the charter the requirement of an eleven-year standing was modified, an exception being made for merchants residing in the south-western ports of England, such as Bristol, Exeter, Plymouth and Dartmouth, which had not in fact carried on any considerable trade with the Baltic countries.[22]

As in the case of e.g. the Merchant Adventurers,[23] craftsmen and retail merchants were excluded from participation in the Company, this being, as we have already remarked, an expression of the social changes occurring in the English corporations and gilds, and a proof of the predominance of the merchant oligarchy. The charter did not provide any definition of the term 'retailer', but from sources deriving from the Merchant Adventurers' Company, which was similarly organized in many respects, it appears[24] that merchants selling quantities smaller than one piece of cloth, 100 lb of pepper, etc, were reckoned in this category. At the beginning of the seventeenth century the acts and ordinances of the Eastland Company did not allow members living outside London—i.e. in places where trade was less well developed—to trade in smaller quantities of goods than, for example, one barrel of pitch or tar, one bale of flax, half a hundred of deals and other kinds of wood (with the exception of masts, etc.)[25] This condition is further confirmation of the opinion expressed above that the Eastland Company was founded mainly by large wholesalers, who also gathered the governing authority into their own hands.

Acceptance into the Eastland Company involved certain payments. In the case of merchants who had been engaged in the Baltic trade from 1568 onward the 'entrance fee' was £6 13*s* 4*d*, but if this condition could not be met the fee was £20. Merchants in the above-mentioned towns of south-west England who began trading with the Baltic countries after 1568 but joined the company within one year of the issue of the charter also paid the lower entrance fee. Otherwise, they, too, had to pay £20.[26] By comparison with the charges of the Merchant Adventurers, whose membership fee at the beginning of the seventeenth century was about £200 for an independent merchant and £50 from an apprentice,[27] the sum required on acceptance into the Eastland Company was not excessive and it could not have acted as a severe restriction on the recruitment of members.

All the merchants who joined the Company obtained, nominally at least, the same rights and privileges irrespective of whether they had become members through many years of activity in the Baltic trade or were in the company by the right of patrimony from fathers who had been members. This was not the case with, for instance, the Merchant Adventurers, who differentiated between members with a long record of activity and the younger ones.[28]

As in the case of the corporations and gilds, membership of the trading companies was conditional upon a certain length of apprenticeship. The Eastland Company's 1579 charter did not actually resolve this question. But it follows from an Act of the company at the beginning of the seventeenth century that a candidate for apprenticeship had to be sixteen years of age, and the period of service was eight years. A merchant member of the Company was restricted to two apprentices during a period of seven years.[29] The Merchant Adventurers resolved this question in a similar manner, except that only one apprentice could be taken on during the first seven years, two at any one time during the next thirteen years, and three after twenty years.[30] The condition that an apprentice could be affranchised only in the English capital reflected the extent to which the company was centralized in London, and the predominance of the metropolis.[31]

On the eve of the issue of the 1579 charter very great interest and considerable controversy were aroused by the question whether members of other trading organizations, particularly the Merchant Adventurers and the Spanish Company, should be allowed to join the Eastland Company. The merchants of medium rank who carried on Baltic trade mainly from the towns of north and east England (from York, Hull, Newcastle, etc), who had long-standing traditions of trading with Eastland and resisted the domination of the great London wholesalers, were against enlarging the membership in this manner. We find an echo of these discussions and disputes in an anonymous pamphlet of October 1578,[32] whose author, a year before the creation of the Company, criticized the proposal then being put forward that only merchants who had been engaged in the Baltic trade from 1568 onward should belong to the Company, which was already then in process of organization. In this unknown author's opinion such a restriction would wrong many merchants who had started trading with Baltic countries after that date.[33] He was of the opinion that all English merchants actively engaged in Baltic trade in the year of the issue of the charter should be accepted as members. He also declared himself in favour of allowing other people who had not previously traded with the Baltic, but who had expressed the wish to join, to become members if within one year from the date of the issue of the charter they paid a fee of £5. In his view the fee for merchants who joined the Company at a later date should be £40. And he proposed that the same sum should be paid by members of other companies.

Documents relating to the Merchant Adventurers' organization, which at the time was passing through a crisis, reveal that at first they were rather antagonistic to the formation of the Eastland Company. When, on the eve of the issue of the Company's charter, the question of restricting membership was raised, the Merchant Adventurers threatened its members with expulsion if they joined the Eastland Company. But the interests of the wealthy English merchant class did not allow the issue to go as far as an open break, and it was settled by way of a compromise. It was laid down that members of the Merchant Adventurers also could join the Eastland Company, after paying an entrance fee of £10[34] and provided they had all the qualifications mentioned above. Fundamentally both companies were dominated by the same merchant element, the companies had originated from the same social milieu, and were distinguished from each other mainly by their respective spheres of activity. Frequently the same merchants are to be found in the administrations of both companies, a circumstance which often came under attack towards the end of the sixteenth century.[35] More than once, too—especially at the beginning of the seventeenth century—the Governor of the Merchant Adventurers was simultaneously Deputy Governor of the Eastland Company, and merchants, especially of the northern English ports, frequently belonged to both companies, had joint officials and held joint meetings.[36]

The 1579 charter decided the question as to whether members of the Eastland Company could simultaneously belong to other trading organizations, in particular to the Spanish Company and the Merchant Adventurers. The manner in which the corresponding passage is phrased clearly indicates the decisive influence exerted by the wealthy London merchants on the company's structure and organization. Merchants of both the last-mentioned trading organizations were allowed to join the Eastland Company[36] provided they fulfilled the same conditions as other members of the Company. Within one year from the issue of the 1579 charter they were required to pay an entrance fee of £10, a figure rather higher than that required from merchants who were not members of other companies. But if members of the Merchant Adventurers and the Spanish Company had not previously engaged in trade with the Baltic they were required to pay an entrance fee of 40 marks, or £26 13*s* 4*d* sterling.[37]

Certain Acts of the Privy Council indicate that even after the issue of the 1579 charter there was a tendency in the Eastland Company not to allow members of the Merchant Adventurers or the Spanish Company to join; but the Privy Council would not agree to their exclusion.[38] At a Council meeting on 9 August 1580 representatives of the Eastland Company attended to defend their original standpoint that only members of the two specified companies who had engaged in the Baltic trade from 1568 onward could join their company.[39] The Privy Council rejected the demand, and stood by the principle that the only special condition to be imposed on members of the Merchant Adventurers and the Spanish Company who wished to become members of the Eastland Company was the entrance fee of £10:[40] a decision which may be interpreted as further proof of the predominance of the wealthy wholesalers.[41] In 1580 the Governor of the Merchant Adventurers declared that any member of his company could enter the Eastland Company solely on payment of £10,[42] and after this year there was a considerable increase in the Company's membership.

In discussion of the Eastland Company's organization the main problem is that of its governing body, and especially that body's composition and sphere of competence. According to the charter of 1579 the Company was to be headed by a Governor, his deputy, and a court of assistants, consisting of twenty-four persons.[20] The majority of the English trading companies of this period had a similarly constituted governing body. But the Muscovy Company[43] and the Company of Kathai[44] each had two Governors. The Merchant Adventurers, who provided a kind of model for other companies, had essentially the same type of administrative authority as the Eastland Company.[45] (At the beginning of the sixteenth century it still had two Governors.[46]) But, unlike the Eastland Company, whose Governor resided in London, the Merchant Adventurers' Governor resided on the Continent, while his deputy lived in London.[47]

The original members of the Eastland Company's governing body were appointed by Elizabeth in the charter of 1579.[48] As we have seen, Thomas Pullison was the Governor, and his deputy was Thomas Russell, who in practice managed the Company's affairs—it is his name, not that of Pullison, which figures in the Acts of the Privy Council. The first court of assistants consisted of W. Cockayne, R. Hilson, H. Offley, H. Isham, T. Allen, J. Bodleigh senior, J. Burnett, E. Boldero, R. Willys, W. Salkyns, G. Wilson, J. Foxall, W. Watson, W. Barker, R. Strete, W. Bonde, H. Salkyns, J. Collett, N. Pierson, C. Collett, R. Mayott, R. Lewis, E. Burlace and J. Beale (the names are given according to their order in the charter). Thus many wealthy and influential London merchants whom we have already mentioned were members of the Company's governing body. Their decisive influence on the activity of the Eastland Company derived from the nature of its internal structure, which assured the wealthy wholesalers hegemony in this type of trading organization.[49]

The Governor and deputy who headed the Eastland Company were elected by the court of assistants meeting in London and consisting of London merchants. Oligarchic tendencies, which were even stronger than in the Merchant Adventurers, caused the Eastland Company's Governor to be elected by the twenty-four assistants and not, as in the case of the Merchant Adventurers and the Levant Company, by the general court of members. At the end of the sixteenth and beginning of the seventeenth centuries the London court of assistants also elected the Governor residing at the Company's staple in Elbing, and also gave its consent to the establishment of local courts in provincial towns (York, Hull, Newcastle, etc).

The charter did not deal in detail with the Governor's sphere of authority, or his relations with the court of assistants. The document resorts to the rather broad definition 'the Governor, assistants, and fellowship of the Merchants of Eastland', calling the assistants the Governor's counsellors and assistants,[50] and stipulating that the Governor's decisions must receive the approval of at least a majority of the court.[51] However, the Governor was to call meetings of the court of assistants as he deemed necessary, and he acted as the court's chairman,[52] which indicates his decisive role in the Company's administration. This is further confirmed by many later documents, which reveal that he was elected for a long term of office.

The 1579 charter granted the London court of assistants the right to choose the Governor and his deputy, who was usually the head of the Company's staple abroad, and to elect new assistants from all the Company's members. The court also had the right to dismiss the Governor and assistants if they betrayed the trust reposed in them. The elections were to be held once a year, or more frequently if the need arose.[48] In the event of the death of the Governor or an assistant, additional elections were to be organized. Theoretically the Governor and his deputy were elected for one year, but in practice the oligarchic tendencies already mentioned led to the Governor holding his position for year after year, and in certain instances even for life.[53] But the assistants were elected 'for one year or longer, for as long as they shall discharge their obligations well and enjoy the confidence of the Governor or his deputy and the majority of the court of assistants',[48] which once more witnesses to the Governor's dominant position in the Company.

The Governor, together with the court of assistants, had the right to call general meetings of all the members of the Company in London or in some other place, in England or in Eastland, according to his judgement, 'from time to time'.[54] The charter did not specify what matters were to be considered by this general meeting, nor how far the resolutions it passed were binding on the Governor. It says only that, for a resolution to be valid, at least twenty members of the Company must be present, and of these at least thirteen must be assistants.

Nor did the charter settle more precisely the question of the relationship between the London central body and the Company's local branches established in certain towns in the north and east of England which had long had active trading relations with the Baltic countries, such as York, Hull, Newcastle and Ipswich.[55] Before the Eastland Company was founded, these towns had independently carried on a Baltic trade which in many cases was equal to that of London. The foundation of the Eastland Company involved the administration's domination by the London wholesalers, and the merchants of the provincial towns were excluded from influence in it. York in particular led the northern towns' opposition to London; it still retained a considerable share in the Baltic trade, though during the Elizabethan era it lost its former importance. In 1579 at least sixty-six York merchants sailed through the Sound;[56] York merchants played an essential role in the endeavours to form the Eastland Company, and immediately it was founded they protested strongly against the Company administration's neglect of the north-eastern towns.[57] The merchants of York, Hull and Newcastle were not prepared to agree that the London wholesalers alone should decide all questions,[58] and they frequently laid complaints before the Privy Council,[59] declaring that their trade had declined as a result of the London merchants' monopolistic egotistical policies.[60] An ostensible concession was made to the north-eastern ports when they were granted permission to have their own, local courts. But these had no serious influence or significance within the Company, if only because they had no local assistants, without whose participation no important decisions could be taken.

The 1579 charter deals in very general terms with the question of the organization of the Company's staple. As already mentioned, the court of assistants under the Governor's chairmanship, was granted the right to elect a Deputy Governor 'in the partes beyond the seas',[48] i.e. in the town where the staple was established, for an undefined period. This staple director, who had the title of Deputy Governor, or Overseas Governor, was himself to use his own judgement to choose a court consisting of twelve assistants, recruited from the members of the Eastland Company residing in the city where the staple was established.[48] In principle he was not given legislative authority; none the less, the London central authorities could endow him with extensive plenipotentiary powers.[61] In any case, it is evident that the director of the Baltic staple and the local court of assistants enjoyed considerable authority, and they were much more extensively privileged than, for instance, the Company's provincial branches in the north eastern ports of England. The 1579 charter granted the Company's Overseas Governor full jurisdiction not only over members of the Company but also over all the English merchants in the Eastland area. The considerable authority and independence of the governor of the Elbing staple was due above all to its great distance from London and the frequent necessity to take swift decisions. This was especially the case while the Company was making its protracted endeavours at the Polish court to obtain confirmation of its residence in Elbing,[62] as we have already discussed. That the Elbing court of assistants was very active is indicated by the number of meetings it held: in 1600–01 it met thirty times—more than twice a month.[63]

The first director of the English staple in Elbing was Thomas Russell. He was followed by William Salkins, who figures in the Acts of the Privy Council as 'Deputie for the Companie of the East Marchantes at Elbing'.[64] Salkins had no previous knowledge of Poland, had never been in Prussia, and in the opinion of Dr John Rogers, the English ambassador, who was negotiating at the court of King Stefan Batory to obtain confirmation of the Elbing staple for the Eastland Company, revealed a complete lack of discernment in regard to the questions under discussion. Of all the English merchants in Danzig Rogers most highly esteemed John Langton, who, as we have already observed, lived in the Polish Commonwealth for thirty-four years and was completely at home with local problems.[65]

From the Eastland Company's Acts and ordinances at the beginning of the seventeenth century it would seem that it exercised a quite effective jurisdiction over its members residing in Elbing, and empowered the local Governor to send back to England immediately any merchants' sons, as well as apprentices and servants, who proved refractory and violated the regulations.[66] This applied especially to English merchants' sons, who were sent to Eastland from time to time to study the foreign languages which they would have need of later, and to make practical acquaintance, frequently in the capacity of factors, with the organization of the Baltic trade. Other issues connected with the functioning of the Elbing staple have already been discussed in chapter three, when we were considering the course of the England–Elbing negotiations in the years 1581–85. These negotiations did not in fact result in Elbing accepting the full English proposals; none the less the English merchants were assured of very advantageous conditions for their residence and trade in this port.

The jurisdiction of the London Governor and the Company's court of assistants, which is only generally indicated in the charter of 1579, was broad and varied. Above all, the Queen granted the Company the right to issue 'statutes, laws, constitutions and ordinances', and to resort to by-laws to extend and develop the Company's structure, which had been only broadly defined in the charter.[67] The only restriction on these powers was the 1579 condition that they were not to be in conflict with Parliamentary legislation, and were not to violate England's treaties with foreign countries or her international obligations.[52]

In accordance with the charter the Company's jurisdiction over its members was not subject to appeal, and this was further confirmed by the Privy Council in September 1580.[68] However, in consequence of the opposition of the north-eastern towns, which attacked these original wide powers of the Governor and the London court of assistants, at the beginning of the seventeenth century they were considerably restricted. The oldest surviving Acts of the Company indicate that from 1616 onward not only the Governor, with the court of assistants, but the annual general meeting of the members, together with representatives of the provincial branches, were to decide the Company's statutes and ordinances, and, in addition, they were thenceforth subject to confirmation by the Privy Council.[69] The Acts of the Privy Council also reveal that in 1616 the Council ordained that the meetings of the general court of members were to be held once a year, with the participation of the north-eastern towns, each of which was to send at least one delegate.[70]

Among other powers granted to the Company's central authorities the 1579 charter specifies the right to impose financial contributions and payments on English merchants carrying on trade with the Baltic countries, on their goods, and on the ships transporting them.[52] The money thus obtained was to be used for the needs of the entire Company. The Company was also granted the right to exclude from membership any merchants violating the statutes, the right to impose various punishments, and even that of imprisonment where especially serious offences were concerned. The Company's powers of jurisdiction and discipline were in fact extended to cover all the English merchants engaged in the Baltic trade. In this connection the charter assured the Company the aid of English officials and customs officers of various ranks, giving a long list of these at the beginning of its text.[71] Here it may be worth noting that to ensure that all the members of the Company were reminded of their obligations the charter and the later Acts and ordinances were read out to the London general meeting of members twice a year, and at the staple four times a year.[72]

As has already been said, the charter of 1579 empowered the Eastland Company to take action against any English merchants who, though not members, endeavoured to trade illegally in the area reserved exclusively to the Company. This permission arose from the problem of the so-called 'interlopers', which was a burning issue in contemporary trade.[73]

The rapid development of English trade during the Elizabethan era led to the formation of a number of trading companies, whose members enjoyed, in England, a monopoly of trade with the areas reserved to the various companies. Towards the end of the sixteenth century unorganized English merchants could carry on trade only with France and Italy of the more important economic areas of Europe not covered by the monopoly of one or another company. In these conditions, during the second half of the century the English merchants not organized in companies—the interlopers—developed illegal trade on a large scale. Various companies issued severe regulations against them,[74] for example the Muscovy Company in 1555, the Merchant Adventurers in 1564, the Spanish Company in 1577 and the Eastland Company in 1579; [75] the regulations provided for fines, the confiscation of goods and vessels, and even the arrest of the offenders. Considerable light is thrown on the problem of the interlopers and the difficulties the Eastland Company came up against in the attempt to maintain control over English merchants trading with the Baltic by the petition it presented to Walsingham, probably in 1580. From it we learn that setting up a staple at Elbing had not at first yielded such good results as had been expected,[76] *inter alia* because many English merchants consigned their goods not to Elbing but to other Baltic ports (as we have already mentioned, the English staple was completely transferred from Danzig to Elbing only in 1583). So the Eastland Company asked that special regulations should be issued requiring English goods exported to Poland, Prussia and Kashub to be delivered only to Elbing,[77] and exports from Poland to England also to pass only through Elbing. In 1580 the Privy Council assured the Eastland Company of its aid in the struggle against the interlopers,[68] and gave English officials appropriate instructions. The privilege did in fact grant the Company fairly wide powers to deal with this problem, for its right to sequester, commit and fine could not be challenged in the courts.[78]

The severity of the regulations against interlopers arose out of the decided difficulties of the struggle to suppress them, and on the other hand it drew attention to the danger the interlopers constituted for the trading companies despite the seemingly comparatively small volume of their trade. The Eastland Company certainly had its controlled staple at Elbing, and the vast majority of the English trading operations with the Baltic passed through it, but we know from the register of the Sound tolls that English merchants also sent quite large quantities of commodities through Danzig, Königsberg and Riga, places in which the Eastland Company could exert only a small degree of control. In any case not only interlopers but even members of the Eastland Company themselves readily avoided the compulsion to use the staple at Elbing and to make the appropriate payments to the Company, as is testified by a Company letter of 1625[79] in which it stigmatized its members for carrying on trade through the port of Danzig during an epidemic at Elbing, despite an order to refrain from trade during this period.

Evidently the Eastland Company did not make any great effort to ensure that only its members carried on trade with the Baltic, since the interlopers preferred to engage in the Baltic trade illegally rather than pay the comparatively small sum of £20 and become members. In 1624 they even rejected the House of Commons' compromise proposal that they should pay a reduced entrance fee of only £5.[80] At the turn of the sixteenth and seventeenth centuries Ipswich especially was a mainstay of the interlopers, as its merchants had an important share in the export of cloth.

An interesting light is thrown on the problem of the interlopers and the Eastland Company's policy in regard to them by the case of William Gore, which came up early in the seventeenth century. (Material of this kind is lacking for earlier periods.) From two petitions made by the Eastland Company to the Privy Council in July 1622 we learn[81] that in December 1620 a serious epidemic had raged in Königsberg, where many English merchants purchased hemp; it would appear that the epidemic caused as many as a thousand deaths in one week. Other Prussian towns also suffered considerably from it. In these circumstances, in its fear that the epidemic might reach England, the Eastland Company forbade its members to import hemp purchased during this time, 'for feare of infection'. But William Gore disregarded this instruction and sent his cargo of hemp back to England 'in the greatest heat of the plague', for which he was first fined £460—a very heavy punishment—and then, when he refused to pay, expelled from the company. None the less, we learn from the Eastland Company's petitions that Gore continued, as an interloper, to export various commodities to the Baltic, especially cloth, which he dyed and finished in Hamburg. In its petitions to the Privy Council the Company appealed to the Elizabethan charter of 1579, as well as to proclamations issued by James I, and asked the Privy Council to inflict exemplary punishment on Gore with the object of frightening other interlopers off the Baltic trade. It is characteristic that in appealing to James I in 1624 to confirm the Eastland Company's privileges it gave as its main motive the danger to its trade caused by interlopers.[82] From a Privy Council letter of 1629[83] we learn that interlopers exported English products to the Baltic and brought back goods to England not only directly through the Sound but indirectly through Hamburg and Amsterdam as well, which rendered the Company's struggle to stop them even more difficult. The Privy Council's letter of February 1629 confirmed that it was necessary to forbid English merchants who were not members of the Company to carry on any kind of trade with the Baltic, whether directly or indirectly.[84] The customs officials were not to allow shipments brought from the Baltic countries by interlopers to be unloaded or passed through the English customs houses. On this occasion the Privy Council's letter drew attention to one particular form of excess. It appears that the interlopers quite often passed through the English customs products from Baltic countries which they claimed had originated in Holland or Russia (e.g. 'Holland flax' or 'Muscovia hemp').

The problem of the interlopers reveals the difficulties the Eastland Company met with in enforcing its monopoly. The extensive area covered by its Baltic trade made it difficult for the Company's authorities to exercise effective control, and English merchants who were not its members thus had every encouragement to carry on a trade which brought them considerable profit. They constituted an element eroding the rigid principles contained in the charters of the trading companies, principles which were not always applied in practice. By their flexible and energetic activities they also contributed to England's trade expansion.

Notes

1 Cf H. Zins, 'Przywilej Elżbiety I z 1579 dla angielskiej Kompanii Wschodniej' ('Elizabeth I's charter granted to the English Eastland Company in 1579'), *Rocznik Elbląski* (*Elbing Yearbook*), vol. III, 1966. Few documents relating to the Eastland Company in the Elizabethan era have survived, most of its earlier records having perished in the Great Fire of 1666. Those of its Acts and ordinances which have survived are known only from copies kept by its branch at York, and these begin only in 1616.

2 Among works on the subject of the English trading companies Scott's *The constitution and finance of English, Scottish, and Irish joint stock companies*, vol. I, remains of basic importance.

3 *Foedera . . .*, vol. III, p. 66, and IV, pp. 67, 107, 125.

4 Cf R. de Roover, 'The organization of trade' in the *Cambridge economic history of Europe*, vol. III: *Economic organization and policies in the Middle Ages*, ed. M. M. Postan, E. E. Rich and E. Miller, Cambridge, 1963, pp. 116*ff.*

5 G. N. Clark, *The wealth of England from 1486 to 1760*, London, 1957, pp. 48*ff. Circa* 1572 London merchants' investments in this type of company amounted to about £100,000.

6 The *Oxford English Dictionary*, vol. III, Oxford, 1961, p. 21 E, defines Eastland as 'the lands bordering on the Baltic'.

7 P.R.O., S.P.Dom., 12/126, No. 24: '. . . were yt not amysse yf the marchants of the este parties myght have into ther corporacion all the ports in the Sowande and within the same in the easte seas for the better establyshinge of ther traphyque . . .'.

8 Cf chapter two.

9 P.R.O., Patent Rolls, 21 Elizabeth, c. 66/1185, ff. 21–2.

10 *Ibid.*, f. 25.

11 *Ibid.*, f. 21. Possessing an organized company would facilitate the 'redressinge of suche wrongs and injuryes as heretofore hathe bene and hereafter myghte be layde unto and upon yowe by dyvers and sundrye unlawfull and unreasonable taxes, exaccyons and imposicions and other customes in those partes, contrarye to the entercourse betwene us and our noble progenitors and the princes . . . of the said easte countryes . . .'.

12 The figure indicates that only some of the merchants actually trading with the Baltic joined the Eastland Company in 1579, as can be deduced from a document dated 1578 which indicates that in that year 141 English merchants were engaged in the Baltic trade: P.R.O., S.P.Dom. 12/127, No. 73.

13 Cf Willan, *The Muscovy Merchants* . . ., p. 9.

14 *Calendar of Patent Rolls*, Elizabeth I, vol. III, pp. 178*ff.*

15 *Ibid.*, vol. II, pp. 8*ff.*

16 W. E. Lingelbach, 'The internal organization of the Merchant Adventurers of England', *T.R.H.S.*, second series, vol. XVI, 1902, p. 22.

17 B.M., Sloane MSS, f. 6, where there is the remark that towards the end of the sixteenth century the membership of the Eastland Company approached that of the Merchant Adventurers.

18 J. Wheeler, *A treatise of commerce*, London, 1601, p. 57. [Wheeler's figure did not include families and apprentices; he said there were 3,500 freemen of the company.]

19 Lingelbach, *op. cit.*, p. 42.

20 P.R.O., Patent Rolls, 21 Elizabeth, c. 66/1185, f. 21.

21 *Ibid.*, f. 21. Members of the Eastland Company could be persons 'beinge our subjectes or which hereafter shalbe the subjects of us, our heires and successours and beynge mere marchaunts and noe retaylours or handy crafts men which have had and lawfully did use or nowe have and doe lawfully use the trade of marchaundyze out of and from . . . [here follows the demarcation of the territory granted as a monopoly to the company] before the firste daye of Januarye . . . 1568 . . . and their children and also their apprentyces'.

22 The registers of the Sound tolls indicate that of the towns mentioned only Plymouth, Dartmouth and Bristol had carried on a very small trade with the Baltic before 1579. See *Tabeller over skibsfart* . . ., vol. I, pp. 9, 20, 44, 52, 64, 76, 80, 81, 84.

23 Lingelbach, *op. cit.*, p. 35.

24 *The Merchant Adventurers of England* . . ., pp. 11*ff.*

25 *The Acts and ordinances . . .*, p. 19.
26 P.R.O., Patent Rolls, 21 Elizabeth, c. 66/1185, f. 24.
27 *The Merchant Adventurers of England . . .*, pp. 36*ff*. [The fee of £200 was for redemptioners only, and £50 was for a redemptioner's apprentice.]
28 Cf W. Cunningham, *The growth of English industry and commerce during the early and Middle Ages*, Cambridge, 1896, p. 416.
29 *The Acts and ordinances . . .*, p. xxiv.
30 *The Merchant Adventurers of England . . .*, p. 35.
31 *The Acts and ordinances . . .*, p. xxv.
32 P.R.O., S.P.Dom. 12/126, No. 24. The pamphlet was entitled 'An indyfferent plan for all parties interessed, touching Corporacions for trades in forraine Countryes'.
33 *Ibid.*, 12/127, No. 73. A list drawn up in 1578 gives the names of as many as seventy-six merchants who are not included among the founder members of the Eastland Company.
34 *The York Mercers and Merchant Adventurers, 1356–1917*, ed. M. Sellers, *Publications of the Surtees Society*, vol. 129, Durham–London, 1928, p. lxvii.
35 *Tudor economic documents*, vol. II, pp. 55*ff*.
36 In the seventeenth century the two companies were often identified, especially in the north of England, as 'The Merchant Adventurers of the Eastland Company'. Cf *The Acts and ordinances . . .*, p. xxxiii.
37 P.R.O., Patent Rolls, 21 Elizabeth, c. 66/1185, f. 24. One mark equalled 13*s*. 4*d*.
38 *A.P.C.*, vol. XII, pp. 110*f*, 146–50.
39 B.M., Sloane MSS, 25, f. 6. In 1602 the Eastland Company complained that 'any merchantt for a small some of money may be free with us'.
40 *A.P.C.*, vol. XII, p. 149. In these discussions with the Privy Council the Eastland Company's representatives were Thomas Russell, William Barker, John Burnell, Stephen Collett and Dr John Rogers (the last-named as the English government's ambassador and intermediary at the Polish court and in Elbing in the matter of confirming English residential rights in Elbing).
41 In 1580 the Merchant Adventurers protested against any restriction on membership of the Eastland Company, declaring that 'if the will devyze any newe ordenaunces to cutt us from our lybertyes of Spayne, Eastland, or Russia we will not eny weysse consent or yeald thereto': *The York Mercers . . .*, p. 235.
42 *Ibid.*, p. lxvii.
43 Willan, *The early history of the Russia Company*, p. 9.
44 *The three voyages of Martin Frobisher*, ed. R. Collinson, *Publications of the Hakluyt Society*, vol. XXXVI, London, 1867, p. 111.
45 *Tudor economic documents*, vol. III, p. 285.
46 *Acts of the court of the Mercers' Company, 1453–1527*, ed. L. Lyell and F. D. Watney, Cambridge, 1936, p. xiv.

47 Lingelbach, *op. cit.*, pp. 51–8.
48 P.R.O., Patent Rolls, 21 Elizabeth, c. 66/1185, f. 22.
49 Cf Carus-Wilson, *Medieval merchant venturers*, p. 175.
50 P.R.O., Patent Rolls, 21 Elizabeth, c. 66/1185, f. 22. The assistants were to be 'from tyme to tyme assistaunces and ayders of the said governor ... in all causes and matters concernynge the said fellowshipp'.
51 *Ibid.*, f. 23. The Governor was to function 'with the assente and consente of the assistaunts or the greatest parte of them'.
52 *Ibid.*, f. 23.
53 *The Acts and ordinances* . . ., p. xiii.
54 P.R.O., Patent Rolls, 21 Elizabeth, c. 66/1185, f. 3. The privilege calls these meetings 'courtes and congregations'.
55 This is evident from an analysis of the registers of the Sound tolls. Cf also *Extracts from the records of the Merchant Adventurers of Newcastle-upon-Tyne*, vol. II, ed. F. W. Denty, *Publications of the Surtees Society*, vol. CL, Durham–Edinburgh, 1899, p. xix. The complaint laid by the northern towns against the central authority in London under date 5 May 1619 included the statement that the northern towns' trade with the Baltic countries 'hath ben more anciently used there then in any other parte of the kingdome'.
56 P. H. Tillott, 'The City of York', *V.C.H. Yorkshire*, Oxford, 1961, p. 131.
57 *Ibid.*, p. 168*f.*
58 A. Friis, *Alderman Cockayne's project* . . ., p. 172.
59 *A.P.C.*, *1615–16*, pp. 417, 553.
60 *Ibid.*, *1617–19*, p. 442.
61 P.R.O., Patent Rolls, 21 Elizabeth, c. 66/1185, f. 22, '. . . the governour or governours . . . in the said partes beyonde the seas . . . shall have full power and auctoritie to governe in the said domynyons within such boundes and lymyts as to them by the said governour and assistaunts of the said fellowshipp residente in Englande shalbe prescribed and assigned'.
62 Cf *Elementa ad fontium editiones*, vol. IV, *passim*.
63 B.M., Lansdowne MSS 160, f. 179. These meetings were held in the Company's own house, erected on ground given to it by the city of Elbing. Cf. also B.M., Cotton MSS, Galba D XIII, f. 42.
64 *A.P.C.*, vol. XIII, p. 312.
65 P.R.O., S.P. 88/1, No. 11. In a letter to Walsingham Dr Rogers wrote on 4 April 1581 that Salkins 'at no tyme hathe . . . bene in this Contrie [i.e. Poland] and is merely ignorant in the same'. On the other hand, in his view Langton was 'the most expert man of al our nation'.
66 *The Acts and ordinances* . . ., pp. 38*f.*
67 From the wording of the charter it would appear that the right to issue statutes and ordinances was granted to the Governor himself: '. . . the said governour or his deputye to be one from tyme to tyme . . . may and shall make, ordeyne, and stablishe . . . good statutes, lawes, constitucyons

and ordinaunces.'—P.R.O., Patent Rolls, 21 Elizabeth, c. 66/1185, f. 23. But in practice in such matters the Governor acted jointly with the court of assistants.

68 *A.P.C.*, vol. XII, p. 207.

69 *The Acts and ordinances . . .*, p. 156.

70 *A.P.C.*, *1615–16*, p. 574: '. . . every yeare a certaine day be assigned by the Company in London for a courte to be held, wherof the coast townes are to have notice and to sende up one at the least from every of the said townes . . . At which generall meetinge only (and at no other) whatsoever ordinaunces or bylawes shalbe made, shall binde the whole Company . . . provided that they be not put into execution without the approbacion of the Lord Chancellor, Lord Treasurer, and the two Cheife Justices . . .'.

71 P.R.O., Patent Rolls, 21 Elizabeth, c. 66/1185, ff. 21, 25, 26.

72 *The Acts and ordinances . . .*, p. 34.

73 On the subject of the interlopers, see Willan, *Studies in Elizabethan foreign trade*, pp. 34–64.

74 G. Cawston and A. H. Keane, *The early chartered companies*, A.D. *1296–1858*, London, 1896, pp. 250–77; also V. M. Shillington and A. B. Chapman, *The commercial relations of England and Portugal*, London (n.d.), pp. 313–26.

75 P.R.O., Patent Rolls, 21 Elizabeth, c. 66/1185, ff. 23–4: 'We commaunde and also forbydd and prohibet by thes presentes that noe subjecte of us . . . which is not nor shalbe by force of the presentes made free of the said Fellowshipp shall by any manner of meanes at any tyme, hereafter intermeddle in the trade of marchaundyze or by any meanes by and sell or use any traffyque in the said partes of Eastelande . . . upon payne not onely to incurre our indignacyon but also to paye such paynes, forfaytures . . . and also to suffer ymprisonament and such other paynes due to the transgressours of the said statutes . . . of the said Fellowshipp.'

76 *Ibid.*, S.P.Dom. 12/146, No. 51: '. . . residence and settling at Elbing hath not taken so good effecte as yt was hoped'.

77 *Ibid.*: '. . . that such good order may be taken that all stranngers whatsoever that shall shipp any the commodities of this Realme out of the same for Polland, Prusen or Casshubb shalbe bound to delyver the same at Elbing'.

78 *A.P.C.*, *1591–92*, pp. 132*f.* On 22 September 1580 the Privy Council sent a letter 'to the Lord Chiefe Justice and the rest of the Justices of her Majesties Banche that wheras about one yere past it pleased the Queen Majestie by her Charter under the Greate Seale of Englande to erect a Companye of Merchantse trading into the East Partes, to th' intent that suche disorders as happened heretofore in that trade might be avoyded and prevented, granting upon them libertie for that purpose to make actes and orders for their better government, and authoritie to sequester, commit and fine the transgressours thereof . . .'. In this connection

officials 'when they shalbe advertised from the Governour or Deputie of the said Company, thet they have sequestred . . . any suche person, they would forbeare by writt or otherwise to call the said person or cause before them, or graunt any libertie or releasement to anye such person, but suffer the same to be tried and ordered by the Companie of the said Merchauntes according to their Charter'.

79 P.R.O., S.P. 16/41, No. 91: '. . . And when the Companie in the same tyme of sickness kept their goods at Elvinge rather suffering loss, then presumening to breake order wheras in the same tyme of sickness the brethren of York manie waies did advantage themselves by the companies loss. For first they saved custome which they should have paid at Elvinge. Secondlie they paid noe impositions to the Companie which was due at Elvinge, but is not paid at Danske.'

80 *Journals of the House of Commons*, vol. i, pp. 710, 793.

81 P.R.O., S.P. 14/148, Nos. 16 and 108.

82 *Ibid.*, S.P. 14/158, No. 63.

83 *Ibid.*, S.P. 16/160, No. 67.

84 *Ibid.*, S.P. 16/161, No. 25.

six *English Baltic shipping and the role of foreign middlemen*

In the sixteenth century England's Baltic trade was developed mainly from London, though the north-eastern ports, Hull and Newcastle, also had some share. Ipswich, Lynn and Yarmouth were less important. The great majority of English ships sailed to the Baltic from these ports, with Danzig, Elbing, Königsberg, Narva and Riga as their destination, returning with goods from the Baltic countries.

London had long been the most important centre of England's economic life. It developed even more in the sixteenth century, during the years when great geographical discoveries were being made, when the centre of Europe's economic life was shifting from the south to the north and west, and when there was both political and commercial expansion across the oceans. By the late fifteenth century London was already handling about 70 per cent of the country's wool and 60 per cent of her cloth exports.[1] On the eve of the Elizabethan era London, with its population of 100,000, accounted for close on 90 per cent of the total export of cloth,[2], and this dominance continued until the end of the sixteenth century, by which time the population of the capital had grown to some 200,000.[3] The surest testimony to London's ascendancy over other English ports is obtained from a comparison of the receipts from customs duties, collected at the end of the sixteenth century: London, £115,000; Hull, £2,237; Ipswich, £1,553; Yarmouth, £970; Newcastle, £899; Lynn, £269.[4] In 1604 this overwhelming supremacy came under attack from E. Sandys,[5] who wrote that the monopolistic policy of London's merchants had resulted in the capital gaining £110,000, or 91·1 per cent of the total national receipts from customs, while all the other ports accounted for barely £17,000, or 8·9 per cent. However, when comparing London's recorded trade with that of the north-eastern ports it should not be forgotten that there was a much higher incidence of smuggling and customs evasion in the north than in London, which was right under the nose of the court and government.[6] In a famous economic tract written at the beginning of the seventeenth century John Wheeler observed[7] that English merchants bringing goods into the northern ports had 'more advantage, and meanes to defraude her Maiestie of her duties and rightes, than those which ship at London . . . either by false entryes, colouring of strangers goods, corrupting the customers, and other Officers who, for the most part beeing needie persons in those small, and remote Portes of the Realme, are more readie to take rewards'.[8]

The great geographical discoveries of the age, which fundamentally changed England's situation on the world map, had the effect of turning the interests of the London merchants and privateers primarily to the oceanic routes, to the south and west, where, in bitter rivalry and struggle with Spain, the foundations were laid for England's future hegemony. London became the main centre for the initiative and capital of the country's bourgeois merchants, and they successfully exploited the great opportunity which came to England through the new world alignments of power.[9] London had the largest shipping tonnage in the country: over 30 per cent of ships of over 100 tons belonged to London merchants. The capital was the headquarters of all the trading companies, the administration of which was monopolized, as we have said, by the wealthy London merchants. However, this tremendous political and economic ascendancy by no means applied so decisively to Elizabethan England's Baltic trade as a whole, as we shall be demonstrating extensively in later chapters. In certain branches of that trade the north-eastern ports, especially Hull and Newcastle, proved effective rivals to London.

Kingston-upon-Hull was the most important port in Yorkshire. It had inherited the former glory of the area's chief trading centre, the city of York, which had lost all significance as a port owing to its geographical situation. The direct cause of York's decline was the increase in tonnage of the individual ship; for these larger vessels navigation up the rather shallow river Ouse, which links York with the sea, grew more and more dangerous and in time quite impossible. Goods shipped to York and thence to the Baltic had to be trans-shipped to barges at York and then to ships at Hull.[10] Thus the decline of York went hand-in-hand with the advance of Hull, which successfully exploited its opportunity. The decline of York, at one time a very important port, proceeded so rapidly that in the middle of the sixteenth century the city owned only three vessels of over 50 tons. But it must be added that despite its decline as a port its merchants continued to take an active part in the Baltic trade, chartering vessels at Hull and Newcastle, a system which obviously restricted the initiative as well as the income of England's northern metropolis. That York's Baltic trade was quite valuable in the sixteenth century is indicated by the list of sixty-six merchants of the city who participated in this trade in 1579.[11] York also had a considerable share in the local activities of the Eastland Company's northern branches; but on the whole it gradually declined in importance. It was surpassed by Hull, which was the most important northern centre of the Merchant Adventurers and the Eastland Company,[12] and with Newcastle was the chief northern port for Baltic trade in the second half of the century. There is no doubt that a proportion of the goods shown in the port books as carried in Hull ships belonged to York merchants; but as the Hull port books are missing[13] for the second half of the century it is not possible to establish how many of the ships specified in them could be attributed to York merchants. In any case it can be said that the Elizabethan era was a time of prosperity for the Hull merchants, although they complained of the difficulties that arose from privateering raids, and even more of the rapacity of the London merchants[14] who exerted such a powerful influence on the Eastland Company's administration. These merchants achieved an increasing concentration of trade in the capital at the cost of the smaller centres, which, in the case of Hull also, contributed to the decline in England's northern trade, as we read in Hull's 'complaint' of 1575.[15] In the Baltic trade Hull had a large share in the export of cloth, especially cheap kersey, also lead and skins, as well as in the importation of all the basic Baltic ships' stores.

Newcastle-upon-Tyne, the coal port of northern England, also had an important share in England's Baltic trade.[16] In the middle of the sixteenth century its inhabitants numbered about 10,000, and it was one of the largest provincial towns of the time. In addition to coal, lead, grindstones and millstones, skins, wool and salt the Newcastle merchants exported a large quantity of kerseys to the Baltic. The town's imports from the Baltic consisted mainly of naval stores, in much smaller quantities than those imported by Hull.

The other three ports we have mentioned—Lynn, Yarmouth and Ipswich—had a much smaller share in England's Baltic trade in the Elizabethan era. King's Lynn was an important grain port and had a rich agricultural hinterland. Its imports of foreign corn were generally small;[17] rather, the town shipped grain to other English cities, especially London and Newcastle.[18] Lynn also sent English grain abroad, for instance to Spain and Portugal.[19] Analysis of English shipping movements through the Sound indicates that the town maintained active relations with the Baltic, especially in the period preceding the formation of the Eastland Company. The three Lynn port books which have survived from the Elizabethan era[20] show that in 1597–98 only five vessels set sail for Danzig, while thirteen voyaged in the reverse direction. Lynn's exports to Poland consisted chiefly of skins and cloth, while its imports consisted primarily of pitch, various kinds of timber, and flax.[21]

Great Yarmouth had a relatively small share in England's Baltic trade. Like Lynn, it was an important East Anglian grain port; it exported various kinds of skins to the Baltic, and imported pitch, iron, timber, etc.[22]

The other East Anglian port that had some part in this Baltic trade was Ipswich; the town was an important exporter of cloth to Danzig and Elbing, where its merchants maintained agents,[23] as also to Spain and the Netherlands.[24] From the Baltic Ipswich imported mainly timber, potash, and grain.[25]

The Sound toll registers enable us to get a fairly precise idea of the size of English trade in the Baltic and the share of the various ports. Taking these registers as a basis,[26] table 6.1 gives the number of passages of English shipping through the Sound, in both directions, and indicates the English and Baltic ports that participated in Anglo-Baltic trade.[27] It should be added that owing to the nature of the exchange a large number of English ships sailed to the Baltic only in ballast or with a small quantity of goods, which the shipmasters often attempted to conceal from the Sound toll officials, especially in the case of cloth.[28]

Analysis of table 6.1 brings out above all the overwhelming predominance of London, Hull and Newcastle in English Baltic sailings during the second half of the sixteenth century. It was these ports that played the largest part in the attempts to found the Eastland Company and which had the most extensive traditions of trading with the Baltic countries. It is a characteristic fact that London's predominance, which is so obvious when considering England's total foreign trade in this era, was by no means so obvious in regard to the Baltic trade. But it has to be remembered that the Sound registers do not state how many vessels sailed to the Baltic from each of the various English ports: they only give the home ports of the shipmasters. As London merchants frequently chartered vessels registered at other ports it would be wrong to conclude, solely on the basis of shipping movements through the Sound, that London played a small part.

Table 6.1 also enables us to plot more exactly the destinations of

Table 6.1 *English shipping movements through the Sound, 1562–1600, based on the Sound toll registers*

	Into the Baltic, from the west								*Out of the Baltic, westward*								
Year	*Total*	*From London*	*From Hull*	*From Newcastle*	*From Ipswich*	*From Lynn*	*From Yarmouth*	*From other ports*	*Total*	*From Danzig*	*From Elbing*	*From Königsberg*	*From Narva*	*From Riga*	*From Lübeck*	*From Sweden*	*From other ports*
1562	51	28	11	5	3	3		1	52	43	–	–	–	–	2	5	2
1563	71	6	12	39	1	5	1	7	73	67	–	2	1	–	1	1	1
1564	33	10	7	10	1	1		4	33	22	–	1	6	–	4	–	–
1565	29	7	4	8	1	3	1	5	24	17	–	1	4	–	–	–	2
1566	87	23	19	27	2	3	1	12	77	30	–	1	42	3	–	1	–
1567	51	15	9	20	1	1	2	3	53	30	–	–	16	3	–	1	3
1568	53	15	14	17	1	1	1	4	45	28	–	–	13	1	–	–	3
1569	76	17	23	16	2	4	2	12	72	60	–	2	5	4	–	–	1
1574	72	20	16	13	2	6	8	7	74	51	–	1	13	4	2	–	3
1575	81	16	17	20	2	9	2	15	79	74	–	1	–	4	–	–	–
1576	97	17	23	22	3	7	7	18	102	95	–	–	–	4	–	–	3
1577	83	25	10	16	2	9	5	16	80	6	5	60	–	6	–	–	3
1578	152	39	23	23	8	15	10	34	154	114	–	31	4	1	1	–	3
1579	105	30	26	13	3	11	2	20	103	84	1	14	–	2	1	–	1
1580	56	22	16	8	2	3	–	5	57	10	22	25	–	–	–	–	–
1581	74	31	12	7	7	5	3	9	73	2	60	7	–	1	–	–	3
1582	96	27	17	14	15	8	1	14	93	3	86	3	–	–	–	–	1
1583	83	27	19	13	7	8	1	8	81	2	76	1	–	2	–	–	–
1584	89	33	18	16	5	11	1	5	91	3	81	6	–	–	–	–	1
1585	63	22	12	11	6	4	1	7	66	3	57	4	–	–	–	1	1
1586	197	45	37	31	22	13	5	44	196	63	109	17	–	2	–	2	3
1587	254	65	34	27	21	28	8	71	259	102	96	53	–	2	–	–	6
1588	41	11	13	7	1	5	–	4	41	5	29	4	–	2	–	–	1
1589	78	31	17	16	5	4	–	5	79	9	58	7	1	2	1	–	1
1590	64	25	5	16	8	–	1	9	63	6	47	9	–	–	–	–	1
1591	70	23	18	13	6	3	–	7	72	11	59	2	–	–	–	–	–
1592	63	19	12	15	9	1	–	7	61	4	44	11	–	1	–	–	1
1593	82	27	13	15	10	2	2	13	82	8	64	9	–	1	–	–	–
1594	86	32	17	21	7	1	1	7	91	18	66	5	–	2	–	–	–
1595	124	39	23	25	8	3	2	24	123	32	69	21	–	1	–	–	–
1596	72	20	16	17	8	–	1	10	73	7	51	15	–	–	–	–	–
1597	149	35	34	28	14	3	5	30	150	77	57	13	–	1	1	–	–
1598	111	28	28	15	14	5	3	18	110	31	50[a]	29	–	–	–	–	–
1599	78	24	26	10	10	–	3	5	74	6	55	13	–	–	–	–	–
1600	85	26	30	14	9	1	3	2	77	12	46[b]	16	–	1	–	2	–

Notes

[a] Including one ship from Königsberg.
[b] Including three ships from Königsberg.

Source *Tabeller over skibsfart . . .*, vol. 1, pp. 30*ff*.

English ships entering the Baltic. It appears that down to the foundation of the Eastland Company the great majority of English ships were bound for Danzig, but after its foundation Elbing took over the role. These data clearly demonstrate the overwhelming part Poland played in England's Baltic trade and navigation. The great majority of her Baltic trade was concentrated in Danzig and Elbing, and to some extent Königsberg (especially during the Danzig rising); English ships called at other Baltic ports only to a small extent, apart from the temporary activity of sailings to Narva. In the years 1562–79 71 per cent of all English ships passing out of the Baltic through the Sound were returning from Danzig and Elbing; in the period 1580–1603 the figure rose to 84 per cent. The corresponding figure for Königsberg was just over 10 per cent; for other ports it was minimal. Fundamentally England's Baltic trade was trade with Poland, a point we shall be discussing again in later chapters.[29] As we have said, the Narva traffic was ephemeral,[30] England's trade directly with Livonia was on a small scale, while her trade with Sweden and Norway was conducted without reference to the Sound and so does not come within the scope of our survey.

Comparison of the data supplied by the Sound toll registers and the Elbing customs registers for the end of the sixteenth century leads to the conclusion that the data obtained above should not be overestimated, for English vessels took on and sold cargoes sometimes in several ports, but gave only one town as the port of departure. This applies especially to the ports of the Polish hinterland, Danzig, Elbing and Königsberg, with Danzig and Königsberg complementing Elbing in the trade of Eastland Company merchants, despite the existence of the Elbing staple, because of the navigational difficulties of this port. Comparison of the Elbing customs registers with the Sound registers reveals that the latter record a smaller number of English vessels, and this confirms our foregoing conclusion. Evidently the difference between the two sources was due to ships taking on cargo at Danzig as well as Elbing, and giving Danzig as their last laden point when reporting at the Sound. As table 6.2 shows, the difference between the data given by the two sources was especially large in 1587, when, as a result of poor harvests, England experienced serious food shortages and tried to make up her own deficiencies by large imports of Polish rye.

The further conclusion that follows from an analysis of English Baltic shipping movements in our period (see table 6.1) is the relative slowness of its growth. Before the foundation of the Eastland Company the Sound registers note an average of seventy-four English ships passing through the Sound into the Baltic, but ninety-five after 1579. In fact, however, this was a specious increase, associated with several rather exceptional years in England's Baltic trade. The increase in the passage of English ships into the Baltic in 1578 was obviously connected with the abolition of the English residence at Hamburg; but in 1587–88 and again in 1597 it was the result of economic conditions. In these years England experienced crop failures and was forced to increase her imports of Baltic rye to quite

Table 6.2 *Comparison of the number of English ships returning from Elbing, 1585–1600, based on the Sound toll registers and the Elbing customs registers*

Shipmasters' port of origin	1585	1586	1587	1594	1596	1597	1599	1600
Total:								
Sound toll registers	57	109	96	66	51	57	55	46
Elbing customs registers	60	115	106	67	49	66	58	61
London								
Sound toll registers	20	26	23	27	16	16	18	17
Elbing customs registers	16	24	23	21	12	19	19	22
Hull								
Sound toll registers	12	33	24	18	14	24	24	18
Elbing customs registers	13	35	25	21	15	26	24	21
Newcastle								
Sound toll registers	10	12	10	13	10	5	2	3
Elbing customs registers	13	16	8	16	8	8	4	8

Source *Tabeller over skibsfart . . .*, vol. I, pp. 106*f.*, 110*f.*, 114*f.*, 150*f.*, 166*ff*. Also W.A.P.Gd., Lib. port. Elbing, 1585–1600. See H. Kownatzki, 'Die Bedeutung der Sundzoll-listen nach den Elbinger Pfundzoll-listen', *Historisches Jahrbuch*, vol. LVII, 1937, pp. 360*ff.*

a large extent. The poor harvest of 1586 and a rise in the price of grain by about 40 per cent[31] resulted in large imports of grain from Poland,[32] and, following on this, an abnormally large number of English vessels being sent to the Baltic in 1586 and 1587. A similar situation arose in 1596–97, when England again experienced food difficulties due to poor harvests (in 1596 the price of grain rose by some 80 per cent).[33] If we eliminate these rather exceptional periods we can say that the amount of English shipping sailing to the Baltic in the Elizabethan era remained more or less stable, with a slight tendency to rise resulting primarily from the increasing tonnage of ships, which averaged some 60–80 tons.

The Sound toll registers enable us to get some idea of the proportion of English vessels to total Baltic shipping in the second half of the century. It appears that they provided only a few per cent, from 1·5 per cent in 1565 to 7·9 per cent in 1587 (averaging 3·6 per cent) of all the ships that passed through the Sound in this period. In this respect Dutch shipping was overwhelmingly predominant, over 50 per cent, with Hanseatic vessels second.[34] It may be remarked, incidentally, that in Elizabethan England Baltic navigation was regarded as very dangerous, mainly on account of climatic and navigational difficulties.[35] On 24 April 1582 Thomas North wrote to Walsingham, 'There are more losses on that voyage than on any other I know." [36]

Of essential importance in considering English navigation in the Baltic is the problem of the middleman, the share of foreign vessels and merchants in England's trade with the Baltic countries in the latter half of the sixteenth century. Before proceeding further it should be pointed out that, because of the great gaps in the port books of the time,[37] it is difficult to formulate this problem in terms of numbers; one can only point to certain tendencies which emerge clearly. This problem could be more precisely studied only by a consideration of Dutch trade, and this would go beyond the scope of our study, which is concerned with English merchants' direct trade with the Baltic.

We have already discussed the circumstances surrounding the elimination of the Hanse from England's Baltic trade. So far as the Dutch were concerned, the situation was different; during the fifteenth and sixteenth centuries they succeeded in partially capturing the middleman business in England's Baltic imports, especially of grain, timber, hemp, etc. By comparison with Holland, which was foremost in the realm of industry and trade, England at this period was primarily an agricultural country, exporting mainly raw materials, e.g. wool, and semi-manufactures, e.g. unfinished cloth. By comparison with that of the Dutch, England's trade, navigation, shipbuilding and fisheries were all backward.[38] She had an unfavourable trading balance with Holland and had to compensate for this by the export of precious metals, which caused internal deflation and made it difficult for her to carry on trade with the Baltic countries, among others (see below). This complex of problems marked the beginning of English mercantilism and contributed an important chapter to England's economic history in the seventeenth century.

Considered from the point of view of our study, it is necessary to stress the considerable part played by Dutch middlemen in English imports from the Baltic. This was a key problem, and there was no exaggeration in the words of George Downing, the English ambassador to the Hague at the beginning of the seventeenth century, to the effect that if England were to develop her shipping and assure herself such cheap freightage as Holland could give it would mean the end of Amsterdam's importance.[39] But this was only an English diplomat's pious hope; at the time there was nothing to presage the twilight of the Dutch intermediaries, who on account of their low freight charges had won almost 90 per cent of the total Baltic trade. The Dutch system of warehousing Baltic grain in Amsterdam, to sell later to the English at the moment most advantageous to themselves, renders it impossible to obtain even an approximate idea of the extent of this Dutch intermediary service in England's importation of Baltic goods.[40]

As the result of a report by Cranfield,[41] who made a statistical analysis of the Netherlands' share in London's imports in 1619–20 (unfortunately, we have no comparable source for any earlier years), we can gain some idea of the structure of Dutch middleman activities and grasp the mutual relations of particular groups of commodities which the Dutch exported to London both direct from the Netherlands and from other countries. From these data it would appear that, speaking generally, products of the Netherlands themselves exceeded in value the goods the Dutch shipped from other countries to London. This applied not only to industrial goods but also to foodstuffs. Only in regard to raw materials and semi-manufactures is there clear evidence of the role of Dutch intermediaries (see table 6.3).

These data, which relate to a period of incipient depression in English foreign trade, obviously cannot form a basis for conclusions concerning the Elizabethan era, especially as we have no information as to the Baltic area's share in this compilation. But they do reveal a certain general tendency, and characterize the Dutch intermediaries in English trade.

N. Tench, one of the Eastland Company's Governors in the seventeenth century, expressed the opinion that down to Elizabethan times foreigners had an ascendancy over English merchants in the importation of grain from the Baltic. Only Elizabeth, he wrote, desiring to render herself independent of the foreigners, began to give her support to trade, mainly through the development of trading companies.[42] This observation finds repeated confirmation in the source material. In 1547 Henry VIII negotiated not with English but with

Hanseatic merchants for the supply to the English fleet of such items as Baltic masts, cordage, pitch, flax, etc, 'for the furniture of his navie'.[43] In order to encourage English merchants to sail to the Baltic, in 1559 Parliament passed a statute permitting Englishmen importing masts, pitch and grain from Baltic countries in foreign ships, to pay the same customs duty as that levied on goods imported in English ships.[44] And from the middle of the sixteenth century England took various steps to restrict foreign merchants' privileges.[45]

However, in the struggle against foreign predominance in her overseas trade England was at first concerned not with eliminating foreign vessels but with restricting the influence of foreign merchants. Owing to the weakness of the English merchant fleet, which

Table 6.3 *The structure of Dutch middleman services in London's imports, 1619–20*

Type of goods	*Netherland's own products*		*Foreign products carried by Dutch*	
	£	%	£	%
Manufactures	155,410	81·6	66,073	39
Raw materials and semi-manufactures	8,020	4·2	80,841	47·8
Foodstuffs	25,641	13·4	21,127	12·5
Other	1,278	0·8	1,136	0·7
Total	190,349	100·0	169,177	100·0

Source P.R.O., Sackville (Knowle) MSS 6796.

was not adapted to the transport of heavy and bulky Baltic commodities,[46] the Eastland Company was not at first interested in the policy adopted in the Navigation Acts. James I's proclamation of 1615, which had the nature of such an Act,[47] was not welcomed with enthusiasm by the Eastland merchants, who pointed out that Dutch shipping was better equipped and adapted to Baltic transport, and that their freight charges were much lower. The merchants even complained that James's proclamation might cause the ruin of the English Baltic trade.[48] Not until the trade crisis in the 1620s did the Eastland Company become one of the main advocates of restrictions on Dutch intermediaries, both in the realm of transport and by the proclamation of a navigation Act. The Eastland Company's 1620 petition complained that 'the Netherlanders have eaten out the shipping belonging to the Eastern cities, who have left the trade wholly to the Hollanders for transportation of their native commodities into other countries . . .'[49] It went on to declare that the Dutch engaged in trading brokerage in various parts of the world; they took 'freight from one foreign part to another and carry commodities, the least their own but of other countries, whereby they do not only weaken all other nations in their shipping but so in exceeding manner increase their own, which makes them so strong at the seas'.[49] In the view of the authors of the petition the Dutch intermediaries were an especial danger because they undertook the processing of raw materials and semi-manufactures in their own country, and sold them in England only in a finished state. For instance, in the past flax had been imported in an unfinished state, but now the Dutch cleaned it in Holland first, thus depriving hundreds of English craftsmen of work. In these circumstances the Eastland Company advised the King: 'we are of opinion that His Majesty may . . . by proclamation forbid all strangers whatsoever to bring any gruff goods into these dominions other than in English ships except the native goods of their countries . . .'[49] A commission specially set up to investigate these demands entirely supported the proposals and arguments set forth in the petition. The royal commission's report confirmed[50] that the Dutch had already ruined the trade of the Baltic cities, and were now seriously menacing England's trade and navigation in the Baltic. The commission recognized that the only way out of the situation was the proclamation of a navigation Act.

Violet Barbour's researches[51] have revealed in what respects Dutch transport was superior to English. The Dutch built ships much more cheaply, they purchased timber more cheaply, and their freight charges were lower.[52] Moreover, their vessels were much better adapted to Baltic navigation than English vessels, and they carried smaller crews. All these factors enabled them to put up a competition which the English could not meet. We may add that the Dutch displayed greater elasticity and freedom in their trading operations with the Baltic countries: they could pay cash, whereas the English had difficulties in this respect; the Dutch were granted credits by their government, while the English merchants were left to their own resources; they paid low customs duties on ships' stores imported from the Baltic. In sum, although Holland had high labour costs, these were covered by greater productivity, better organization and mechanization. Consequently Holland could build ships more cheaply than England—by about 30 per cent at the end of the sixteenth century, and by as much as 50 per cent in the seventeenth century.[53] The Dutch flyboat (*fluitschip*) proved an especially useful vessel in the Baltic trade. It was a fast, light boat with a single deck and of considerable length, splendidly adapted to the transport of the bulky, heavy Baltic goods. It was so constructed that it needed a comparatively small crew to handle it.[54] This vessel was introduced into service towards the end of the sixteenth century; and in 1620 John Keymer attributed England's failure to compete with Holland in the Baltic to this very type of ship.[55] It needed only one third of the crew of an English ship of the same tonnage, and this reduced freight charges by about £100 sterling on a single Baltic voyage.

Table 6.4 *Number and tonnage of vessels entering the port of London, October 1601–June 1602*

Vessels' registration	*No. of vessels*	*Aggregate burden (tons)*	*Average burden (tons)*
Netherlands	360	9,328	25·91
England	207	15,601	75·36
France	42	1,732	41·24
Hanse	40	2,656	66·40
Scotland	32	1,074	33·50
Denmark and Norway	8	725	90·62
Others	25	1,934	77·36
Total	714	33,050	46·29

Source L. R. Miller, 'New evidence on the shipping and imports of London, 1601–02', *Quarterly Journal of Economics*, vol. XLI, 1927, p. 743.

Down to the Elizabethan age the English fleet was relatively small; but, worst of all, it included hardly any vessels over 100 tons burden adapted to long voyages. In the first half of the sixteenth century the Sound toll registers noted only two such ships.[56] The proximity of the wealthy Antwerp market left the English under no necessity to display any great enterprise in this direction, and they left the transport of Baltic products generally in foreign hands.[57] A change occurred only in the second half of the century, both for economic reasons (the fall of Antwerp, the opening up of new directions of trade) and for political ones (the beginnings of Atlantic expansion). In the years 1571–76 at least fifty-one ships of over 100 tons burden were built in England; in 1577 the country possessed about 130 such ships, and in 1582 about 177.[58] The majority of these vessels belonged to London owners.[59] Stone[60] regards the development of England's Baltic trade as one of the main factors in increasing the tonnage of English vessels in the Elizabethan era. The surviving London port books reveal that by 1567–76 English ships of over 100 tons had a significant share in the country's Baltic trade. In 1567 it was about 30 per cent;[61] in 1576 about 50 per cent.[62] However tonnage was not the most important factor in this problem; it was, rather, the question of freight costs and the adaptation of ships to Baltic navigation.

Table 6.5 *Respective shares of English and foreign shipping in England's Baltic trade, decennial intervals 1565–1605*

Vessels' port of origin	1565		1575		1585		1595		1605	
	A	*B*	*A*	*B*	*A*	*B*	*A*	*B*	*A*	*B*
England	29	24	81	79	63	66	124	123	70	70
Foreign:	2	29	5	89	8	42	10	147	6	52
Netherlands	1	16	1	43	2	14	5	83	1	23
Eastern Friesland	–	–	1	9	–	–	–	3	–	–
Hamburg	–	9	–	–	–	4	–	5	–	–
Lübeck	–	–	–	3	–	2	–	8	1	2
Stettin	–	2	–	4	–	–	–	–	–	–
Danzig	1	1	1	11	–	3	2	28	1	11
Norway	–	–	–	3	1	–	–	2	–	–
Denmark	–	–	2	12	–	12	3	–	–	6
Others	–	1	–	4	5	7	–	18	3	10
Total	31	53	86	168	71	108	134	270	76	122

Notes Direction of voyage: *A* through the Sound eastward, *B* through the Sound westward.

Source *Tabeller over skibsfart . . .*, vol. 1, pp. 22, 54, 110, 173, 237

Data relating to the beginning of the seventeenth century reveal that the average burden of English and foreign shipping entering the port of London in 1601–02 was much below 100 tons; Holland owned the lightest vessels and Norway, Denmark and England the heaviest (see table 6.4).

Because of the great gaps in the English port books we are able to get a more precise indication of the share of foreign vessels in the Baltic trade of English merchants only by referring to the Sound toll registers, and this for the years 1565, 1575, 1585, 1595 and 1605. The ten-year intervals are due to the fact that the registers give more detailed comparisons only for every decade. The data compiled in table 6.5 clearly show that in the realm of exports to the Baltic England availed herself of foreign intermediaries only to a limited extent, but that the situation was quite different in regard to imports from the Baltic, where foreign vessels continued to take a very large share.

The deductions that follow from table 6.5 are fundamental to our further observations on the subject of English trade with the Baltic countries in the next two chapters. It appears that the use of foreign

Table 6.6 *Respective shares of English and foreign shipping in English merchants' Baltic trade (Danish thalers)*

	1565		1575		1585		1595	
	Thalers	%	*Thalers*	%	*Thalers*	%	*Thalers*	%
Exports:								
English vessels	100,646	98·1	187,911	97·6	407,970	95·7	461,211	97·7
Foreign vessels	1,917	1·9	4,451	2·4	18,229	4·3	10,443	2·3
Total	102,563	100·0	192,362	100·0	426,199	100·0	471,654	100·0
Imports:								
English vessels	48,381	33·3	122,753	53·6	221,468	76·4	235,868	49·0
Foreign vessels	96,927	66·7	106,285	46·4	68,700	23·6	246,166	51·0
Total	145,308	100·0	229,038	100·0	290,168	100·0	482,035	100·0

Note The Danish thaler or rixdollar seems to have been worth about 5*s* sterling (cf R. W. K. Hinton, *The Eastland trade and the Common Weal*, Cambridge, 1959, p. 36).]

Source *Tabeller over skibsfart* . . . , vol. IIA, pp. 15, 18, 25, 47, 50, 58, 59, 101.

ships in exports from England to the Baltic amounted to only a few per cent, the figure being highest in 1585, about 11 per cent, and 7·4 per cent in 1595. It follows that the data obtained from the Sound toll registers provide a much more reliable basis for England's Baltic exports than for her imports. In the latter case, foreign shipping was 54·7 per cent in 1565; 52·9 per cent in 1575; 38·8 per cent in 1585; up to 71 per cent in 1595; and 42·6 per cent in 1605, making an average throughout the period of about 50 per cent. Even as late as 1615 foreign shipping carried a large proportion of England's Baltic imports; from the 1620's English vessels increasingly and rapidly eliminated competition in this sphere, owing to the

Navigation Acts. But in the Elizabethan age foreign brokerage, especially Dutch transport, played a considerable role; in reality it was even greater than table 6.5 indicates. For it must not be forgotten that the Sound toll registers contain information only on direct trade, and they still leave us ignorant of the amount of Baltic goods carried by the Dutch to Amsterdam, to sell to England at a later, favourable conjuncture.

The data quoted relate only to the number of English and foreign vessels employed in England's Baltic trade at the given period; they tell us nothing about their respective shares in England's trade.

Table 6.7 *Foreign merchants' imports into London, 1600 and 1609, according to the origin of the goods (per cent)*

Origin of goods	1600	1609
Netherlands and Germany	86·1	63·2
France	8·7	28·1
Spain and Portugal	3·4	7·5
Italy	1·5	0·5
The Levant	0·1	0·1
Other	0·2	0·6
Total	100·0	100·0

Source Compiled on the basis of material made available to the author by Dr A. M. Millard, from an unpublished work entitled 'The import trade of London, 1600–40', Institute of Historical Research, University of London. Commodity values have been equated on the basis of the 1604 *Book of rates.*

Fortunately, the Sound registers enable us to calculate the value of the goods exchanged by English merchants with Baltic countries in their own and foreign ships. It is interesting that these data more or less confirm the conclusions drawn from our analysis of table 6.5, while somewhat diminishing the extent of foreign intermediation in regard to both exports and imports.

As an addendum to table 6.6 it can be added that in 1605 foreign vessels carried only 0·8 per cent of foreign merchants' exports from the Baltic to England, and 32·2 per cent of their imports; in other words, in both directions there was a decline in foreign brokerage.

To conclude this chapter we may well consider the place the Baltic occupied in the total imports into London by foreign merchants. The earliest available data on this subject derive from the very beginning of the seventeenth century; they show that Baltic trade played a very small part by comparison with foreign imports into London from the Netherlands, Germany, France, Spain, Portugal and Italy (see table 6.7). While emphasizing Holland's great predominance in the field of foreign exports to London at the beginning of the seventeenth century, we must not forget that Baltic products constituted a very large proportion of these exports, since quantities were warehoused in Amsterdam to be transported farther west at a later date. These goods, which cannot be measured statistically, appear in the English port books as imported from Holland, and this obscures the total picture and once more highlights the impossibility of establishing the extent of Dutch participation in England's Baltic trade.

Notes

1 P. Ramsey, 'Overseas trade in the reign of Henry VII: the evidence of customs accounts', *Ec.H.R.* second series, vol. VI, 1953, pp. 179*ff.*

2 Schanz, *op. cit.*, vol. II, pp. 86, 102*f.*

3 See A. L. Rowse, *The England of Elizabeth: the structure of society*, London, 1961, pp. 184*f.*

4 H. Hall, *A history of the customs revenue in England*, vol. II, London, 1885, p. 245. Schanz gives a detailed compilation of the customs revenues for the first half of the sixteenth century: *op. cit.*, vol. II, pp. 37, 40, 41, 49, 51, 52, 55, 56.

5 *Journals of the House of Commons*, vol. I, p. 218.

6 See N. J. Williams, 'Francis Shaxton and the Elizabethan port books', *E.H.R.*, vol. LXVI, 1951, pp. 387–95; also H. Zins, 'Angielskie księgi portowe jako źródło do historii handlu XVI wieku' ('English port books as a source for the history of trade in the sixteenth century'), *R.D.S.G.*, vol. XXIII, 1961, p. 154. The Lynn customs officer, Thomas Shaxton, who also engaged in trading operations on his own account, falsified accounts and seals, and even passed through whole cargoes uncustomed. In one year alone he allowed four out of five vessels carrying grain to pass uncustomed.

7 J. Wheeler, *op. cit.*, pp. 60–1.

8 A report by Dawbeney, dated 1570, based on thecontrol of the various ports, included the statement that the London customs officer William

Bird passed through as many as 27,000 pieces of cloth free of duty and aid the Treasury open to the loss of £7,000 on wine imports. See Zins, 'Angielskie księgi portowe . . .', p. 153.

9 Among recent works on this subject see G. J. Marcus, *A naval history of England*, p. 49.

10 A. G. Dickens, 'Tudor York', *V.C.H. Yorkshire*, Oxford, 1961, p. 128.

11 *Ibid.*, p. 131.

12 Rowse, *op. cit.*, p. 162.

13 Some Hull port books exist, but they do not record cargoes, etc.

14 See 'Hull's complaint', dated *c.* 1575, and entitled: 'Sertaine causes of the decay of the traffique in Kyngston upon Hull' in *Tudor economic documents*, vol. II, pp. 49–50.

15 *Ibid.*, p. 49: '. . . by meanes of the sayd Companies (the Government whereof is rewlled onely in the Citie of London) all the whole trade of merchandize is in a maner brought to the Citie of London; whereby all the welthye chapmen and the best clothyers are drawen to London, and other portes hath in a manner no traffique, but falleth to great decay, the smart whereof we feel in our port of Kingston upon Hull.'

16 On Newcastle's development in Tudor times, see S. M. Middlebrook, *Newcastle-upon-Tyne: its growth and achievement*, Newcastle-upon-Tyne, 1950, pp. 44–76.

17 N.S.B. Gras, *The evolution of the English corn market from the twelfth to the eighteenth century*, *Harvard Economic Studies*, vol. XIII, Cambridge, Mass., 1926, p. 276.

18 *Ibid.*, pp. 290, 305*f.*

19 Willan, *Studies in Elizabethan foreign trade*, p. 72.

20 P.R.O., E 190/426/2, E 190/428/7, E 190/432/5.

21 W.A.P.Gd., Lib. port. Elbing, 1586, 1587 and other years.

22 P.R.O., E 190/483/3.

23 In 1614, in *England's way to win wealth*, 1614, p. 23, Tobias Gentleman wrote, though with considerable exaggeration, that 'the Ipswich men be the chiefest merchant adventurers of all England for all the Eastlands for the Suffolk cloths, and they have their factors all the year long in all those places'.

24 *Tudor economic documents*, vol. III, p. 192. In a 1573 document we read: 'Wheare the county of Suffolke (in the which county the said Towne of Ipswiche doth stand) is a county of moche draping of clothe, yet the great number of all that clothe draped there servith for Danzicke and the east partes, and so for Spayne, Portugall and other partes of the South'.

25 P.R.O., E 190/589/6.

26 *Tabeller over skibsfart . . .*, vol. I, pp. 30–181.

27 In addition to the six ports named above as having the largest share in the Baltic trade, Aldeburgh, Harwich, Dartmouth, Southampton and Dover also contributed small shares.

28 A. E. Christensen, 'Der handelsgeschichtliche Wert der Sundzoll-register: ein Beitrag zu seiner Beurteilung', *Hansische Geschichtsblätter*, vol. LIX, 1934, p. 75.
29 See chapters seven and eight.
30 See chapter two.
31 Y. S. Brenner, 'The inflation of prices in England, 1551–1650', *Ec.H.R.*, second series, vol. XV, 1962, No. 2, p. 282.
32 *Tabeller over skibsfart . . .*, vol. IIA, pp. 119, 123.
33 Brenner, *op. cit.*, p. 282. Brenner's work has been subjected to critical discussion by J. D. Gould, 'Brenner on prices: a comment', *Ec.H.R.*, second series, vol. XVI, 1963, No. 2, pp. 351–60.
34 *Tabeller over skibsfart . . .*, vol. I, pp. 30–166.
35 A privilege granted by Elizabeth on 20 December 1560 says that the climatic conditions had deterred many English masters from undertaking voyages to the Baltic: *Calendar of Patent Rolls, Elizabeth*, vol. II, *1560–63*, p. 9.
36 *Cal.S.P.For., Elizabeth, 1581–82*, p. 651.
37 See Zins, 'Angielskie księgi portowe . . .', pp. 146*ff.*
38 Wilson, *Profit and power.*
39 *Ibid.*, p. 96.
40 It is quite exceptional for the London port books to add the comment 'Danske corn' or 'Danske deals' against a Dutch cargo: P.R.O., E 190/4/2.
41 P.R.O., Sackville (Knowle) MSS 6796 (no page numbers).
42 Tench, *Reasons humbly offered by the Governour, Assistants, and Fellowship . . .*, p. 8.
43 *A.P.C.*, vol. II, 1547–50, p. 61.
44 *The statutes of the realm*, vol. IV, London, 1819, p. 375.
45 Early in the second half of the sixteenth century the Venetian ambassador reported from England that these regulations might lead to the ruin of foreign merchants trading with the island. See *Cal.S.P. Venice, 1556 1557*, No. 1011.
46 Elizabeth's 1560 privilege gives the explanation that English merchants imported goods from the Baltic in foreign vessels because they could not obtain suitable English ships for the transport of Baltic products, which were 'very pestringe and grosse': *Calendar of Patent Rolls, Elizabeth*, vol. II, *1560–63*, p. 8.
47 A. Friis, *Alderman Cockayne's project . . .*, p. 184.
48 *A.P.C., 1615–16*, p. 142; also P.R.O., S.P.Dom. 14/118, No. 114.
49 P.R.O., S.P.Dom. 14/115, No. 109. [The petition is printed in R. W. K. Hinton, *The Eastland Trade and the Common Weal in the seventeenth century*, Cambridge, 1959, pp. 168–70.]
50 *Ibid.*, No. 111; also 14/118, No. 142.
51 V. Barbour, 'Dutch and English merchant shipping in the seventeenth century', *Ec.H.R.*, vol. II, 1930, pp. 261–90.

52 On the subject of the Dutch and Hanseatic fleets in the fifteenth century, see Małowist, *Studia z dziejów rzemiosła . . .*, pp. 379*ff.*

53 Barbour, *op. cit.*, p. 275.

54 B. Hagedorn, *Die Entwicklung der wichtigsten Schiffstypen bis ins 19 Jahrhundert*, Berlin, 1914, pp. 102*ff.*

55 P.R.O., S.P.Dom. 14/118, No. 114.

56 *Tabeller over skibsfart . . .*, vol. 1, pp. 5–16.

57 Stone, 'Elizabethan overseas trade', p. 41.

58 M. Oppenheim, *A history of the administration of the Royal Navy and of merchant shipping in relation to the Navy from 1509 to 1640*, London, 1896, pp. 172–5.

59 In 1577 London owned forty-three vessels of 100 tons and over; Newcastle, thirteen; Hull, ten; Ipswich and Harwich, nine; Yarmouth, four; Lynn, two.—*Cal.S.P. Elizabeth, addenda, 1566–79*, p. 441.

60 Stone, 'Elizabethan overseas trade', p. 52.

61 P.R.O., E 190/4/2.

62 *Ibid.*, E 190/6/4.

seven *England's exports to the Baltic*

1 *Preliminary remarks*

This chapter has been divided into two unequal parts, the first of which, much the more extensive, deals with English cloth exports to the Baltic countries, while the second, more compact, considers the export of a dozen or so other commodities, primarily hides, lead, coal, groceries. etc. This division and the unequal proportions of the two parts are not fortuitous. Cloth played such a dominant part in England's exports to the Baltic, and for that matter to other areas of English foreign trade, that without detailed knowledge of its various kinds, its markets, and other problems associated with its disposal it is not possible to achieve a thorough understanding of the entire mechanism of English foreign trade at this time. Textile manufactures represented over 80 per cent, and in some years over 90 per cent, of the value of English exports to the Baltic in the second half of the sixteenth century; in fact the trade was based solely on cloth, and developed only through the sale of English textiles in the countries of the Baltic zone, primarily Poland.

This chapter and the next, which considers English imports from the Baltic area, are based mainly on the port books of the most important east coast ports—London, Hull, Newcastle, Ipswich, Lynn, etc.—the Elbing customs registers dating from the end of the sixteenth and the beginning of the seventeenth centuries, and the Danish Sound toll registers for the years 1562–1600. As after 1580 the greatest part of England's Baltic trade was concentrated on Elbing, as the Eastland Company's entrepot, the Elbing customs registers enable us to achieve a more thorough understanding of many problems than do the port books of the various English east coast ports, which, like those of Elbing, suffer from very considerable gaps. Unfortunately, the Danzig mooring registers have not been preserved, and the only one still existing from the second half of the sixteenth century, that for 1583,[1] does not contain more detailed information.

A critical discussion of the customs records which provide the basis for this chapter must begin by considering the value of the English port books as sources for the history of the English Baltic trade in the Elizabethan era.[2]

The reliability of all forms of customs records has long been the subject of discussion, and various doubts have been expressed. We know that from the earliest days customs officers committed various frauds, took bribes, and in return passed a certain quantity of goods through the customs without duty.[3] This applied equally to England, and narratives and documents of the Elizabethan era frequently mention smuggling and the frauds of dishonest customs officers. Such practices occurred not only in the ports of northern England, distant from the capital, but even in London itself, right under the nose of the court. Contemporary narratives indicate not only that customs officers passed certain quantities of various commodities without duty, but that entire ships, even, slipped through uncontrolled, either taking on in the open sea goods brought out in boats, or availing themselves of other possibilities provided by the long, irregular English coast line.[4] However, there is no way of determining the extent of this smuggling or of the customs officers' frauds. In any case, despite these various reservations the English port books form an invaluable source material, enabling us to make a more exact analysis of the main trends of English foreign trade, its character, dimensions and directions. For instance, they provide the only basis for forming some idea of the English merchants' share in foreign trade, the extent to which foreign middlemen were involved, etc.

Of late there has been a noticeable tendency to take a more critical and sceptical attitude towards the early stories concerning the extent to which smuggling went on. The outstanding expert on the problems of English trade in cloth and wool, E. M. Carus-Wilson, who, with O. Coleman, has published statistics of the English export trade for the years 1275–1547,[5] considers that opinions depreciating the value of the customs records because smuggling was so prevalent were greatly exaggerated and, if anything, unproven.[6] She considers that while the smuggling of luxury articles, such as spices, small in bulk and very expensive, could have been so extensive as to undermine the value of the official statistics, this did not apply to the export of English cloth. The customs duty on cloth was not particularly high, and consequently it was simply not worth risking having the goods confiscated if the attempt to smuggle them was discovered. It must be remembered, too, that the customs officers were personally interested in detecting smuggling, for they received a reward in the form of a considerable proportion of the confiscated goods. In addition, the detailed system of customs control, which was effected by four customs officers reciprocally checking one another, must also have restricted fraud. Nor must it be forgotten that the Crown derived a very important part of its income from customs duties, and so was directly concerned to see that the customs system functioned efficiently. The governors of the trading companies, who defended their members' interests against the competition of the interlopers, were also interested in seeing that there was strict customs control. For instance, we know that in England the Merchant Adventurers supervised the loading of cloth destined for the Netherlands, while the Eastland Company similarly controlled the formalities associated with the Baltic trade both in England and at Elbing. So altogether it would seem that, although the existence of extensive smuggling is not to be underestimated, contemporary accounts which illustrated, sometimes vividly, the extent of customs officers' fraudulent practices were frequently exaggerated. In many cases they even originated from the trading companies themselves, for it was in the companies' interests deliberately to exaggerate the losses they suffered through smuggling, since it provided them with arguments in their fight to maintain their monopoly.

Earlier research into the English customs system at the turn of the fifteenth century has led to similar conclusions: Ramsey[7] has pointed out that it was in the custom's officers' own interests to exercise strict control and to intercept smuggled goods. He further drew attention to the circumstances that the number of customs officers checking each other must have put difficulties in the way of merchants attempting to employ bribery. And taking the risk did not always pay. Taking all these factors into account, Ramsey came to the conclusion that 'the smuggling trade did not represent more than a minute fraction of England's overseas trade'.

Thus there would seem to be agreement that in the case of England's Baltic trade smuggling was not an important element and that the port books provide a sufficiently reliable and essentially unique source for investigations such as we are making. This deduction follows primarily from an analysis of the structure of the Baltic trade. The great majority of the exports consisted of cloth, which, as we have said, was not worth smuggling because of the relatively low customs duty and the great risk of loss in case of discovery. This also applies to other English goods exported to the Baltic, such as hides, lead or coal, which were even more difficult to smuggle. Frauds could certainly occur in the case of foodstuffs, but these were a comparatively small proportion of England's Baltic trade. It was even more difficult to smuggle imports from the Baltic countries into England, for they were bulky, heavy and cheap, e.g. pitch, tar, masts and other kinds of timber, ships' cables, iron, grain, wax and potash. In the case of grain, which we shall be discussing later, the fraud consisted in representing wheat, which was more expensive, as rye, on which the customs duty was only half as great.

Our main difficulty in making use of the English port books consists not in the impossibility of verifying the extent of the smuggling but in the difficulty of obtaining a progressive view of the problems involved because not all the books have survived. In the circumstances a number of problems can be studied only on the scale of the separate ports for which port books have been preserved, and not for England as a whole, because for certain years the surviving port books do not dovetail with one another, and in addition for our period there is a lack of complete figures for total English exports and imports. For their part, the Elbing customs registers do certainly enable us to cover all aspects of English trade, but only in so far as it affected Elbing, which from 1580 onward was the most important port and entrepot in England's Baltic trade; but the English merchants' trading activities were not confined to this one port. An additional difficulty derives from the fact that various years for which English and Elbing customs registers are available do not coincide, so there is no possibility of comparing their data. In these conditions the Sound toll registers, which provide a long and almost unbroken succession of trading statistics for the entire range of Baltic trade, are of especial importance, particularly in the case of England's Baltic exports, in which, as we have already said, foreign middlemen played a relatively small part. Only with the aid of the Sound registers can we obtain a comparative survey of the problems, and grasp the movement and evolution of trade over a longer period.

For many years there has been extensive discussion of the value and importance of the successive volumes of Sound registers issued by Nina Ellinger Bang from 1906 onward, but there is no point in resuming the arguments here. While emphasizing the enormous importance of this source for research into Baltic trade, many writers have also drawn attention to various difficulties that arise in using these registers, *inter alia* difficulties caused by the manner in which they were edited. After the first enthusiastic appreciations of this source publication, especially by D. Schäfer[8] in 1907, G. W. Kernkamp[9] in 1909, E. Baasch[10] and others, increasingly critical opinions began to find expression, first from E. Arup in 1909, then S. van Brakel in 1915,[11] and formulated with especial severity by Astrid

Friis in 1925. The most extensive and thorough discussion of the value of these registers was contributed by A. E. Christensen in 1934,[12] while in the Polish field L. Koczy recalled echoes of the arguments in 1937.[13]

The charges levelled against the Sound toll registers were, in general, of a twofold nature; they related both to the value of the registers as an historical source and to the manner in which they were edited. So far as the first issue is concerned, since Eric Arup made his contribution it has been more and more emphasized that the registers do not provide a complete picture of commercial movement through the Sound, because there was smuggling, not simply of goods, but of entire ships, which slipped past Kronborg in fog or at night without being observed by the Danish customs officers. In addition, it has been confirmed that *en route* from the Baltic to the west certain vessels avoided the Öresund and used the passage between Seeland and the island of Fyen, passing through the strait known as 'Store Baelt' (the Great Belt). Certainly, it is agreed that this traffic was not considerable, yet it was not without importance to the general trade of the Baltic. The Danish writer Astrid Friis was especially vehement in attacking the value of the registers as source material for the history of the Baltic trade.[14] Comparing the data of the English port books for the first half of the seventeenth century with the Sound registers in so far as the export of cloth was concerned, she found serious discrepancies, to the disadvantage of the Sound registers, which showed smaller quantities of cloth than their English counterparts; it followed that the Danish customs officers must have allowed quantities of goods through uncustomed. While expressing scepticism as to the value of the Sound registers because of the element of smuggling, Astrid Friis also questioned the manner and method of their presentation in printed form.

When drawing up her tables the editor of the registers was in error, *inter alia* in considering that the term *Hjemsted* referred to the nationality of the vessel and not that of the shipmaster. For it is necessary to determine the master's nationality, usually according to his place of residence—a more reliable indication than the nationality of the vessel, which tells us nothing about the merchant's origin.[15] In obstinately insisting, despite the criticisms, on her interpretation of *Hjemsted* as indicating the nationality of the vessel, N. E. Bang introduced considerable confusion into the interpretation of the Sound registers. Here we should explain that these registers, like the majority of customs registers, confined themselves to an indication of the shipmaster's native town. None the less, in the absence of other data it is accepted that in the majority of cases certain deductions can be made from the detail given, i.e. the indication of the master's native town; it would be natural for there to be strong links between the ship's owner and the merchants of the given town, on the one hand, and the local shipmasters, on the other. These local men would have been the best known to the merchants, would have inspired most confidence, and would have been constantly at hand.[16]

Another point to be noted is that the rubric *Afgangshavn*, which gives the name of the vessel's last port of call before arrival in the Sound, does not always signify the port from which the vessel collected all the goods on board. During its voyage it frequently put in at several ports, but the registers do not indicate the fact. This was especially true of English trade with the Baltic area; ships usually collected goods from both Elbing and Danzig (so far as the period after 1580 is concerned), and not infrequently from Königsberg as well. A further serious difficulty in using the Sound registers is the absence of any indication of the vessel's destination. We can only assume that English ships loaded with goods from the Baltic returned to their home ports; so far as other countries were concerned—especially Holland, which engaged in middleman activities on a very large scale—the assumption would have little justification. But, speaking generally, one can accept that in the second half of the sixteenth century the still small English fleet engaged in Baltic trade almost exclusively to serve the needs of its own country. So it would seem that vessels entered as 'England' in the Sound registers did in fact carry goods from England to the Baltic and vice versa. And we may add that English vessels mainly carried the goods of English merchants. It simply did not pay foreign merchants to charter English vessels because the freight charges were so high.[17]

To conclude these general observations, it is desirable also to mention the results of the most thorough study of the Sound toll registers undertaken so far, that of A. E. Christensen, who, drawing on the results of extensive research, attempted to verify the reliability and value of this source.[12] After comparing the registers with those of a number of Baltic towns he produced evidence which went some way towards refuting Friis's harsher criticisms. He did indeed confirm that in the case of Rostok, for example, in the first half of the seventeenth century as many as 25·7 per cent of the vessels arriving at and departing from this port were not noted in the Sound registers;[18] but in the case of Stettin he noted quite extensive agreement between the

Stettin and the Sound registers.[19] This applied also to Stockholm and Lübeck,[20] and above all—a fact which is of especial importance for us—to Danzig.[21] We may add that, as we have already mentioned, the data in regard to ships' movements given by the Sound toll and the Elbing customs registers correlate quite closely. Christensen further pointed out that earlier estimates of the extent of navigation through the Great Belt were decidedly exaggerated. From 1429 onward this route was in practice closed to the ships of England and other western countries, and the ban was observed strictly in the fifteenth and sixteenth centuries.[22] In general only Hanseatic vessels made use of the Belt.

Taking into account the carriage of goods through the Sound, Christensen confirmed the existence of smuggling, but found no striking discrepancy between the customs registers of the Baltic ports and the Sound toll records. But he did discover a rather interesting form of fraud practised by merchants engaged in exporting Polish grain to the west. It transpired that, although the Sound registers and Danzig sources—the so-called *Kolekta hiszpańska*—give much the same figures for Polish exports as a whole, there is a great disparity between the figures for rye and wheat. The customs duty on wheat was twice as high as on rye, so it is evident that on arrival at the Sound the merchants gave false information, considerably understating the quantity of wheat actually carried.[23] As a result, if one wished to verify the Sound registers data concerning grain it would be necessary to increase the figure for wheat by about 50 per cent and reduce the figure for rye correspondingly.

Concluding his assessment of the value of the Sound toll registers, Christensen expressed the opinion that of course they should not be treated as a universal source, capable of solving all manner of problems of the northern trade, as certain earlier historians had done. Their prime importance derives above all from the continuity and the extent of their coverage, both geographical and chronological. In view of the gaps in, and haphazard preservation of, other sources, the registers enable us to supply some of their deficiencies, and they frequently provide a valuable form of control against which other material can be checked. 'But usually they are the only source.'[24]

Christensen's opinion can be applied *in toto* to England's Baltic trade. It is true that we have at our disposal a small number of port books for certain English towns, and several Elbing customs registers for the second half of the sixteenth century; but since these provide only sectional information, relating only to certain ports and certain years, despite the various doubts and reservations which arise in utilizing the Sound registers they remain an incommensurably important source of information, especially for England's Baltic exports.

2 *Cloth*

For centuries wool and cloth were the most important products of English crafts and industry, and for centuries the country's role in foreign trade depended almost exclusively on the export of cloth. The disposition of England's socio-economic relations evolved from the late Middle Ages around the problem of cloth production and distribution, so far as concerned both the well known transformation of the English village[25] and the urban evolution from the sixteenth century onwards. In 1553 William Cholmeley compared the role of cloth in English trade to the importance of silver and gold.[26] He pointed out that England was able to develop her foreign trade and provide herself with all the commodities she needed thanks above all to her cloth exports. He further emphasized that the Hanseatic trade in the Baltic, that of the Italian cities in the east, and that of the Spaniards and Portuguese in Africa, Asia and America, all developed largely on account of the English cloth they exported to these parts of the world.[27] John Wheeler, the author of a well known economic treatise in 1601, declared that cloth was a basic English product and a source of the country's importance.[28] In 1606 the great historian of the Elizabethan era, William Camden, called cloth production one of the pillars of the English economy,[29] and the Venetian ambassador in England wrote to the Doge and senate a few years later that cloth constituted the island's main wealth.[30]

Analysis of England's cloth exports to the Baltic needs to be prefaced by at least a brief summary of the main English centres producing various kinds of cloth, indicating those which were concerned primarily with supplying their products to the Baltic area.

Speaking very generally, one can divide English cloth manufacture in the sixteenth century into two basic kinds: (1) cloth woven from carded wool, and (2) cloth woven from combed wool, called worsted.[31] The most important type in the first category was broadcloth, an expensive, high-quality material; it was the main basis of English textile exports, including those to the Baltic area. Another important role was played by kersey, which was also woven from carded wool but was lighter and much less expensive than broadcloth. Among the cheaper kinds of kersey were dozens, which also were exported to the Baltic countries in quite large quantities by English merchants. Other types of woollen manufactures were frieze, medley cloth, etc.

In the second category, the worsteds, were baize (bays), serge and various other types of cloth, none of which, apart from baize, turned up to any extent in Baltic exports during the period we are concerned with. Worsteds were lighter than woollens; they contained a smaller quantity of wool than, for instance, broadcloths. Consequently the heavy and warm woollens made of carded wool, but of no great variety of design and colour, found their best market in the countries of northern and eastern Europe, whereas there was a greater demand for cloths from combed wool, which were lighter and of richer colours, in the warmer countries of the Mediterranean area, Spain, and Portugal.[32]

English broadcloth retained its dominant position for over a hundred years from the middle of the fifteenth century. In the second half of the sixteenth century production achieved a degree of stability, despite occasional fluctuations, though in the seventeenth a steady decline in exports of broadcloth was to set in. Exactly the opposite situation was to be observed in the development of the manufacture and export of cloth from combed wool. From about the middle of the sixteenth century, but more especially from the beginning of the seventeenth, this kind of cloth was sent overseas in increasing quantities. But so far as exports to the Baltic in the second half of the sixteenth century were concerned, broadcloth and kersey continued to dominate the market, though during this period worsteds also turned up in English vessels arriving at Baltic ports.

The most important centre of broadcloth production in England was the south-west, especially Gloucestershire, Wiltshire and Somerset, and to a lesser extent Oxfordshire and Worcestershire. Cloth from these counties was exported to the Baltic region, where it is mentioned in the Elbing customs registers. The same area also produced lighter cloths, especially kersey, for which Wiltshire was particularly noted.[33] Owing to difficulties in obtaining English wool of sufficiently high quality, this south-western centre, which had been producing woollen cloth, transferred at the beginning of the seventeenth century to the production of so-called 'Spanish cloth' from wool supplied by the Iberian peninsula.

To the south and west of the main centre of broadcloth production lay the western part of Somerset and Devon, Dorset and Cornwall, which produced mainly kersey.[34] Here too a cheap variety of kersey, called dozens, was developed; English merchants exported it in large quantities to the Baltic countries.[35]

Berkshire, Hampshire, Kent and the adjacent counties formed a south-eastern area of cloth manufacture, engaged in producing kersey and broadcloth, both of which also found their way to the Baltic countries. The Elbing customs registers mention Hampshire kerseys, for instance.

The variety of broadcloth most frequently found in English vessels bound for Baltic ports was produced in central eastern England, especially Suffolk. Among cargoes consigned to Danzig or Elbing the London port books note that the great majority consisted of Suffolk shortcloth,[36] which, with Gloucester shortcloth, formed the overwhelming bulk of textile exports to the Baltic. From the fifteenth century onwards Suffolk was the largest centre of woollen cloth production, but at this time it did not play any considerable part in the output of worsted cloth. Besides fine quality broadcloth, Suffolk also produced poorer qualities known as sett clothes, also found in the Baltic trade, as is indicated, for example, in correspondence between the London merchant, Sexton, and his Danzig factors in the middle of the sixteenth century.[37] A considerable quantity of the unfinished Suffolk cloth was bought by London cloth manufacturers, who finished it and sold it to London merchants for export. London and Ipswich formed the two most important English markets for Suffolk cloth, and from these cities it was sent primarily to the Baltic.[38] The importance of Ipswich in this respect is indicated by the fact that the Eastland Company had a branch in the town, its members being chiefly exporters of cloth to the Baltic countries.[39]

The centres situated farther north, the West Riding and the rest of Yorkshire, etc.,[40] were of lesser importance in English cloth manufacture in the sixteenth century, and we need not concern ourselves with them, nor with the somewhat later revolution in English cloth production marked by the introduction of the 'new draperies', brought about mainly through the immigration of Dutch and Walloon weavers.

From 1487 onwards, regulations enjoined that only finished cloth was to be exported. But as English standards of finishing and dyeing were not yet high enough to compete with the Continental product, especially that of Flanders, English merchants continued to export a large quantity of unfinished cloth, especially to the North Sea area, where the Merchant Adventurers' Company operated. Although various statutes, mindful of the interests of the English cloth manufacturers, banned the export of white and unfinished cloth, it accounted for the larger part of English textile exports.[41] Such cloth was much easier to dispose of, especially in the Netherlands, where it was readily bought with a view to completing the finishing process for resale at a profit.[42] In resisting plans for the restriction of exports of unfinished cloth the Merchant Adventurers drew attention to the low standards of the English finishing industry, emphasizing that if these plans were put into operation they might lead to a breakdown in English exports.[43] A letter which English cloth manufacturers sent to the Privy Council in 1541[44] clearly indicates the still poor quality achieved by the finishing industry at that time. From the letter one learns that the Dutch were not willing to buy English finished and dyed cloth, and paid two ducats less per roll for it than for unfinished cloth. The fact that in 1577 the Privy Council granted an advantageous privilege to a certain Portuguese inventor who was carrying out experiments in cloth dyeing also speaks for itself.[45] Again, in 1593 the Governor of the Merchant Adventurers complained that on the Continent a piece of English finished cloth cost about ten shillings less than the unfinished kind.[46]

The great demand in the Netherlands for English unfinished cloth was due chiefly to the profits made by the Dutch cloth manufacturers and merchants associated with its finishing and sale. The English merchants themselves exported finished cloth to France, Spain, Italy, Turkey, the Baltic countries and Russia—in other words, to countries where the standards of finished cloth were not, in general, high. To the Baltic the Eastland Company exported only finished cloth, with the exception of 200 pieces of white (undyed) cloth per annum permitted by Elizabeth's 1579 charter.[47] It is worth mentioning that the Eastland Company protested again and again against this restriction, especially from the beginning of the seventeenth century onward, referring in doing so to the example of the Merchant Adventurers. In 1620 John Keymer,[48] pointing bitterly to England's weakness as compared with Holland in the export of cloth to the Baltic, wrote that all the English companies, with the exception of the Merchant Adventurers, exported only finished and dyed cloth, which exposed England to great losses. It was true that it resulted in a greater income from customs duties, and a larger number of English craftsmen found employment in finishing the cloth, but the consequential losses to England were incommensurably greater. Friis's investigations revealed in detail[49] how the Dutch bought unfinished white cloth produced in Wiltshire or Gloucestershire from the Merchant

Adventurers and undertook its dyeing and finishing at home, in the course of doing so lengthening the roll of cloth by several yards. Such a practice, while assuring the Dutch considerable profit, undermined confidence in English textile manufactures, especially as the Dutch furnished the finished cloth with English marks before selling it to the Baltic countries.

Among many arguments put forward by the Eastland Company in a petition dated about 1600[50] in favour of permitting the company to export unfinished cloth to Poland, is the claim that this would not cause any rivalry between the Company and the Merchant Adventurers because of the strictly determined spheres of their activities. The Polish purchaser would also gain, we read in the petition, because the English cloth would be dyed and finished in Poland to suit local tastes, while the Polish cloth merchants would enjoy greater opportunities of selling the cloth not only within the Commonwealth of Poland but also for export,[51] which in turn would stimulate a growth in demand for English cloth in the Baltic area. But the most weighty argument in favour of the export of unfinished cloth was connected with a reminder of the losses which England suffered as the result of the Dutch and Hansards buying cloth from the Merchant Adventurers and finishing it in the Netherlands workshops, then selling it in Poland and other Baltic countries.[52] The Eastland Company's 1602 petition contains similar arguments.[53] It considers that permitting the Company to engage in the unrestricted export of undressed cloth to the Baltic would be a means of overcoming the crisis in this export trade, which had set in at the very beginning of the seventeenth century, and of countering foreign competition.[54]

Passing from these general observations to an analysis of English cloth exports to Baltic countries, one must at once strongly emphasize the enormous importance of this export to the development of England's entire Baltic trade. It can be said that England's trading expansion in the Baltic during the sixteenth century was only possible from the economic standpoint thanks to the extensive opportunities for selling large quantities of cloth, which found a ready market in this area. We need only point out that in 1565 cloth accounted for 76·9 per cent[55] of total English exports to the Baltic, in 1575 75·2 per cent,[56] in 1585 91·4 per cent[57] and in 1595 as much as 92·1 per cent.[58] This situation was maintained at the beginning of the seventeenth century; in 1605 cloth represented 91·6 per cent,[59] and in 1615 as much as 94·4 per cent,[60] of the value of all English exports to Baltic countries. The crisis in the English cloth industry from the

1620's onward, associated *inter alia* with the Cockayne plan,[61] resulted in considerable temporary difficulties in the English export of cloth but did not affect sales to the Baltic. In 1625 cloth accounted for as much as 95·2 per cent of all England's exports to that area.[62] In the second half of the sixteenth century the importance of the Baltic, and especially the Polish, market as an important customer for English cloth was well understood in England, as the numerous pronouncements on the subject testify. To illustrate we need cite only the words of the English ambassador to Flanders, Dr Valentine Dale,[63] who in 1573, in conversation with Catherine de Medici, the mother of Henri de Valois, who had just been elected king of Poland, declared that England had long drawn enormous wealth from her export of cloth to Danzig.[64] In 1603 the Venetian envoy to England, Giovanni Carlo Scaramelli, expressed a similar opinion in a letter to the Doge and senate of Venice.[65]

It would be possible to get a thorough appreciation of the importance of the Baltic market for English cloth exports if we could establish its position in relation to total English exports. Unfortunately, lack of data makes this impossible to calculate. But we can obtain a partial answer from an extremely interesting document which dates from the very end of the sixteenth century, the period of England's largest cloth exports to the Baltic. This document, which gives the figures for the export of cloth from London in 1597–98 according to trading companies and other exporters, reveals above all the importance of exports to the Netherlands and Germany, the area served by the Merchant Adventurers. The members of this company, together with interlopers and foreign merchants, exported as much as 70·6 per cent of the entire export of cloth from London in the year mentioned (see table 7.1). Second place was occupied by the Eastland Company's Baltic market, with 11·3 per cent; third place by the Levant; and then came France and other areas, with the Russian market last of all. But central, eastern and southern Europe were customers for English cloth to a much greater extent because of the middleman activities of the Dutch, and the overland transport of cloth through Germany. But in any case the deductions that can be made from table 7.1 are all the more to the point if we recall London's role in the total exports of English cloth towards the end of the sixteenth century. We know that over 80 per cent of that total was in the hands of London merchants, and this even further emphasizes the importance of the Baltic market.

The Sound toll registers demonstrate England's primacy in the export of cloth to the Baltic by sea in the second half of the sixteenth century. In 1565 her share amounted to 85 per cent, while at the end of the century it was as much as 92 per cent of total Western European cloth exports to the Baltic countries. Second place was occupied by Dutch exports, which increasingly competed with those of England from the beginning of the seventeenth century.

Table 7.1 *Distribution of cloth exports from London, 1597–98*

Exporter	*Broadcloth*		*Kersey*		*Devonshire dozens*		*Total shortcloth*[*a*]	
	Pieces	*%*	*Pieces*	*%*	*Pieces*	*%*	*Pieces*	*%*
Merchant Adventurers	58,053	69·3	13,305	24·4	1,970	14·3	62,980·4	59·8
Eastland Company	11,601	13·9	873	1·6	126	0·9	11,931·5	11·3
Interlopers exporting to Netherlands and Germany	4,951	5·9	6,895	12·7	4,390	31·9	8,346·8	7·9
Turkey Company and others trading the Levant seas	750	0·9	18,031	32·9	95	0·7	6,784·1	6·5
Exporters to France	1,590	1·9	9,233	16·8	5,604[*b*]	40·8	6,046·2	5·8
Foreign cloth exporters to the Netherlands and Germany	2,552	3·0	451	0·8	1,563	11·4	3,115·6	2·9
Barbary merchants	2,394	2·8	–	–	–	–	2,394	2·2
Foreign exporters overland to Venice	161	0·2	5,663	10·3	–	–	2,048·7	1·9
Muscovy Company	1,769	2·1	280	0·5	–	–	1,862·5	1·7
Total	83,821	100·0	54,731	100·0	13,748	100·0	105,509·8	100·0

Notes

[*a*] See note 36.
[*b*] This figure comprises 5,414 Devonshire dozens and 823 so-called plains.

Source P.R.O., S.P.Dom. 12/268, No. 101.

The course of Anglo-Dutch rivalry in cloth exports to the Baltic at the end of the sixteenth century and during the seventeenth, and Holland's gradual exclusion of England from the Baltic market during those years, are clearly revealed in table 7.2, which illustrates the problem by ten-year periods, beginning with 1580 and running to the end of the seventeenth century. It will be seen that the period of England's greatest supremacy in cloth exports to the Baltic was the last two decades of the sixteenth century, when English merchants had over 90 per cent of the trade. In the 1570s the figure had been a little over 80 per cent. Political events, Holland's devastation during the years of her revolution against Spain, and the general crisis in her economy at that time, had no little influence in this respect. From the beginning of the seventeenth century England gradually began to lose her dominant position in the Baltic cloth trade, and the decline

Table 7.2 *Respective shares of England and the Netherlands in cloth exports to the Baltic, 1580–1700*

Years	*England*		*Netherlands*		*Other countries* (%)
	Pieces	%	*Pieces*	%	
1580–89	178,539	93	7,175	4	3
1590–99	265,272	91	21,690	7	2
1600–09	333,483	82	61,993	15	3
1610–19	312,593	70	129,482	29	1
1620–29	317,785	49	299,854	46	5
1630–39	274,591	43	327,857	52	5
1640–49	216,699	35	354,587	58	7
1650–59	104,733	51	74,885	36	13
1661–70	142,248	40	198,047	55	5
1671–80	163,174	40	227,744	56	4
1681–90	209,192	33	423,855	66	1
1691–1700	180,069	42	243,192	57	1

Source *Tabeller over skibsfart*..., vols. IIA and IIB. Our compilation does not extend to earlier years because there is a gap of several years (1570–73) in the Sound toll registers. Cf S. E. Åström, *From cloth toiro n*, vol. I, Helsingfors, 1963, p. 72.

was especially sharp after the great crisis in English cloth manufacture in the 1620's. Parallel with this decline in English textile exports to the Baltic, Dutch exports increased proportionately. It should be added that table 7.2 does not take into consideration a certain quantity of bales of cloth, owing to difficulties in calculating the quantity; the larger proportion of these fell to Dutch exports, which somewhat reduces the size of Holland's share.

Without going more deeply into the causes of Holland's successful rivalry in exporting cloth to the Baltic—the phenomenon relates to a period outside the scope of our inquiry—we need only draw attention to the superior quality of Dutch finishing, as already mentioned, and especially to the Netherlands' superior organization of the trade itself, their lower freight charges,[66] and the Dutch organizations' greater flexibility and independence.[67]

In addition, English exports to the Baltic were based wholly on cloth and were confined to the entrepot of the Eastland Company. This rendered English trade subject to many fluctuations and difficulties not encountered to the same extent by Dutch exports, since the latter covered a very wide range of commodities and developed on a much broader geographical basis. But these issues relate to a later period, and did not apply to the Elizabethan era, when there was a great increase in English cloth exports to the Baltic. In a sense the turn of the sixteenth and seventeenth centuries marked the end of this era, in which English merchants enjoyed complete supremacy in cloth exports to Baltic countries.

Analysis of English cloth exports to the area in the second half of the sixteenth century reveals first and foremost its steady growth, which was noticeably swifter and more clearly defined after the foundation of the Eastland Company. A second striking phenomenon was the English merchants' virtual elimination of foreign middlemen in this export trade. From 1566 down to the end of the century over 95 per cent of England's cloth exports to Baltic countries by the sea route through the Sound (overland transport was probably quite small and cannot be expressed in figures) was carried in English ships, with the exception of the years 1574 and 1590 (see table 7.3). It is worth pointing out that one cannot assume that only English merchants transported cloth to the Baltic in English ships, although in the overwhelming majority of cases this must have been so. Similarly, foreign transport did exist, and it is not to be assumed that English merchants never availed themselves of it. The London port book for 1565 notes that Hanseatic merchants exported from London in English ships about 32 per cent of the entire exports of cloth from the capital to the Baltic that year. Unfortunately, the London port books do not give detailed data for cloth for other years, and it is difficult to say to what extent foreign merchants made use of English transport in later years. It would seem that the tendency was rather the reverse: English merchants were inclined to entrust their Baltic exports to foreign ships. However, there is no doubt of the great preponderance of English merchants and English vessels in the English cloth export trade of the Elizabethan era.

Table 7.3 *Respective shares of English and foreign vessels in cloth exports from England to the Baltic, 1562–1600*

Year	*Total*			*English ships*				*Foreign ships*		
	Bales	*Pieces*	*Ells*	*Bales*	*Pieces*	*Ells*	%	*Bales*	*Pieces*	%
1562	–	7,685·5	–	–	4,850·5	–	63·2	–	2,835	36·8
1563	111	14,036	–	30	9,832	–	67*	81	4,204	33*
1564	29	10,403	1,220	–	7,822	–	73*	29	2,581	27*
1565	3	6,919·5	298	3	6,919	298	100·0	–	–	–
1566	–	9,923·5	–	–	9,431	–	95·0	–	492·5	5·0
1567	9	4,759	–	9	4,240	–	89*	–	519	11*
1568	1	4,450·5	–	–	4,229	–	94*	1	221	6*
1569	2	11,121	–	1	11,019	–	99·0	1	102	1·0
1574	2	14,442	–	–	11,568	–	80·0	2	2,904	20·0
1575	–	8,558	–	–	8,493	–	99·2	–	65	0·8
1576	–	9,809	–	–	9,457	–	96·4	–	352	3·6
1577	–	3,824	–	–	3,821	–	99·4	–	3	0·6
1578	1	6,661	–	1	6,661	–	100·0	–	–	–
1579	–	9,346	–	–	9,328	–	97·7	–	18	2·3
1580	–	7,329	–	–	7,329	–	100.0	–	–	–
1581	–	8,006	–	–	8,006	–	100.0	–	–	–
1582	–	10,947	–	–	10,912	–	99·6	–	35	0·4
1583	–	12,814	–	–	12,812	–	99·9	–	2	0·1
1584	–	18·828	–	–	18,813	–	99·9	–	15	0·1
1585	–	20,695	–	–	20,167	–	97·4	–	528	2·6
1586	–	35,737	–	–	34,393	–	96·2	–	1,334	3·8
1587	18	35,800·5	–	–	35,777	–	99·5*	18	23	0·5*
1588	2	10,819·5	–	–	10,733	–	99·0	2	86	1·0
1589	–	17,563·5	–	–	17,097	–	97·3	–	466	2·7
1590	–	21,233	–	–	10,036	–	47·2	–	11,197	52·8
1591		24,258·5	–	–	23,136	–	95·3	–	1,122·5	4·7
1592	–	15,520		–	15,298	–	98·5	–	212	1·5
1593	1	15,821	–	1	15,557	–	98·3		259	1·7
1594	–	17,574	–	–	17,206	–	98·0	–	388	2·0
1595	–	20,660	3,000	–	19,483	3,000	95*	–	1,177	5*
1596	–	19,577	–	–	16,848	–	86·0	–	2,729	14
1597	–	36,628	–	–	35,164	–	96·0	–	1,464	4
1598	–	47,230	–	–	47,143	–	99·8	–	87	0·2
1599	–	46,771	–	–	46,744	–	99·9	–	27	0·1
1600	–	40,556	–	–	40,538	–	99·9	–	18	0·1

* Approximate figures.

Source *Tabeller over skibsfart . . .*, vol. IIA, pp. 2–196, and vol. IIB, pp. 18–20 and 199.

Down to the early 1580's, and so down to the time when the Eastland Company developed its entrepot in Elbing, total exports of cloth from England to the Baltic were maintained, with exceptions in individual years, at a level considerably below 10,000 pieces per annum. In the last two decades of the sixteenth century there was a perceptible increase, and the growth passed through several phases. Its culminating point was reached in 1586–87, and again at the close of the century. Later we shall discuss in greater detail the link between England's exports of cloth and her demand for grain. A second element to which attention must be drawn was the relationship between her cloth exports to the Baltic and the demand for English cloth in the areas under Spanish domination. More than once an increase in exports of English cloth to the Baltic went hand-in-hand with a crisis in her exports to the Netherlands and Spain.

The two factors just mentioned fully explain the considerable increase in English cloth exports to the Baltic in 1586–87. At the time England's foreign trade had reached a crisis, owing to the political situation, which rendered it increasingly difficult for her to penetrate the Netherlands and German markets. One need only recall that in 1585, as a consequence of the suppression of the Netherlands' revolt, the main cities of Flanders and Brabant, with Antwerp chief of them, fell into the hands of the Spanish vice-regent, the Duke of Parma, and this fact, in conjunction with the sea blockade, did much to restrict England's trade with the Netherlands.[68] The Merchant Adventurers also came up against serious difficulties in their trade with Germany. Admittedly, after the fall of Antwerp, Emden proved a good substitute for a while, but the steadily mounting pressure of the Hansards and of Spain presaged a speedy end to the Emden staple, which in addition met with the opposition of the Dutch, who resented its competition. And it appears from F. J. Fisher's researches that in the years 1586–88 London's total cloth exports fell by over 6,000 cloths per annum by comparison with previous years,[69] a figure accounted for mainly by the decline in cloth exports to the North Sea area. At the same time, data provided by the Sound toll registers reveal that for two of these years, 1586 and 1587, the increase in English cloth exports to the Baltic amounted to some 15,000 pieces per annum, a rise of close on 100 per cent, a figure which points to the close connection and interaction between the English merchants' political and commercial interests in these two markets, which were among the most important for English cloth.

The year 1598 marked a culminating point in the export of English cloth to the Baltic countries. From then on there was a gradual decline (1598, 47,230 pieces; 1600, 40,556; 1601, 37,205·5; 1602, 30,062·5; 1603, 28,846),[70] while, as we have said, Dutch competition grew steadily, especially after 1607.

A key to the explanation of the movement of English cloth exports to the Baltic is provided by correlating them with England's imports of Baltic grain. Analysis of the statistical material reveals their interdependence. The specific nature of England's Baltic trade, foreign exchange problems and other difficulties meant (see chapter ten) that to all intents and purposes cloth was the sole English exchange for Baltic produce. Hence the value of cloth exports provides some indication of England's requirements for Baltic grain and naval stores.

Food supply difficulties in England in 1562 caused a rise in the price of grain and an increase in imports from the Baltic. In 1562 imports amounted to 736 lasts, but in 1563 they were 1,884 lasts. A similar correspondence between exports of cloth and imports of grain occurred in 1576, but even more markedly in the period of serious English harvest failures, the years 1586–87 and 1596–97 (see chapter eight).

London had long been England's most important cloth centre, but it is not possible to demonstrate this ascendancy in detail for the second half of the sixteenth century, owing to the gaps in the English port books. The data provided by the Enrolled Customs Accounts for the first half of the century (they break off at 1547)[5] enable us to compare London with other English ports engaged in this trade in the time of Henry VIII (see table 7.4). It appears that throughout this period, parallel with an increase in the total of cloth exports from England, there was an increase in London's exports and a decline in the relative importance of other English ports.

Unfortunately, corresponding statistics covering the whole of England do not exist for the second half of the sixteenth century. So far as London's share in cloth exports to the Baltic is concerned, our only source material is the registers of the Sound tolls, which, by giving the shipmaster's place of residence and not the port of origin of the goods, to some extent distort the true state of affairs, especially as London made no small use of vessels from Hull, Newcastle and other English east coast ports, as the English port books and the Elbing customs registers both testify. The Sound toll registers establish the share of London vessels in total English cloth exports to the Baltic as follows. In 1565 it was 37·2 per cent; in 1575, 27·6 per cent;

in 1585, 36 per cent; in 1595, 57·4 per cent; in 1605, 19·8 per cent, and in 1615, 20·9 per cent,[71] taking into account all the varieties of cloth as a whole. From these figures it follows that London's predominance, so pronounced in England's sixteenth century trade, was less marked in respect of cloth exports to the Baltic, and that Hull and Newcastle, exporting principally kersey and other cheap varieties of cloth, competed quite effectively with the capital. And these cheaper cloths had a definite influence on the above calculations, which are not too favourable to London.

Table 7.4 *English cloth exports from London and other ports in the first half of the sixteenth century*

Year	*Total ('000 pieces)*	*London*		*Other ports*	
		'000 pieces	*%*	*'000 pieces*	*%*
1510	76	50	65·7	26	34·3
1515	93	65	69·9	28	30·1
1520	98	67	68·3	31	31·7
1525	96	79	82·2	17	17·8
1530	91	71	78·0	20	22·0
1535	92	78	84·7	14	15·3
1540	116	100	86·0	16	14·0
1545	147	136	92·5	11	7·5

Source Based on statistics in G. Schantz, *Englische Handelspolitik*, vol. II, Leipzig, 1881, pp. 76–105, and L. Stone, 'State control in sixteenth century England', *Ec.H.R.*, vol. XVII, 1947, p. 119.

Only one London port book containing full details of cloth exports for the second half of the century has been preserved. This is the port book for 1565,[72] and it provides the basis for table 7.5. Comparison of the data in the 1565 London port book with the Sound toll registers for the same year reveals an unexpected degree of agreement between the two sources so far as the quantity of cloth exported is concerned. The Sound registers mention 2,580 pieces,[73] while the London book gives 2,558 pieces[72] of cloth exported from London to the Baltic in 1565—a very slight difference, especially bearing in mind the known discrepancies in customs registers. Correlation of the two registers also confirms the view that in the 'Hjemsted' ('Home town') column

Table 7.5 *Cloth exports from London to Poland and Russia 1565, according to the London port book (pieces of cloth)*

Name of vessel	*Tonnage*	*Port of origin*[a]	*Master's name*	*Destination of cargo*	*Cargo and its owners*
Saviour	80	London	William Hawle	Danzig	Eleven English Merchants: 205 Ss, 41 Gs, 19 N, worsted, 3 others One Lübeck merchant: 112 Ss, 32 Gs
Barke Graye	70	London	Robert Graye	Danzig	Ten English merchants: 189 Ss, 30 Gs Two Lübeck merchants: 154 Ss, 44 Gs
Jonas	140	Ipswich	John Peres	Danzig	Two English merchants: 41 Ss, 12 Gs, 4 western
Marye George	90	London	William Banner	Danzig	Seven English merchants: 98 Ss, 12 Gs Two Lübeck merchants: 182 Ss, 52 Gs
Swallow	160	London	Stephen Aborrow	Russia	One Muscovy Company agent: 430 kerseys H, 289 Ss
Harrye	160	London	William Aborrow	Russia	One Muscovy Company agent: 400 kerseys H, 28 Ss
Christ	140	Newcastle	John Taylor	Danzig	Eleven English merchants: 215 Ss, 55 Gs, 80 northern kerseys, 9 kerseys H, 13 longcloth, 5 D dozens, 5 others One Lübeck merchant: 98 Ss, 28 Gs
Peter	60	London	John Saffron	Danzig	Four English merchants: 72 Ss, 21 Gs Two Lübeck merchants: 174 Ss, 54 Gs One Danzig merchant: 70 Ss, 20 Gs
Mary George	60	London	Peter Richards	Danzig	Twelve English merchants: 300 Ss, 64 Gs, 18 Wilts s, 72 northern kerseys, 36 dozens, 1 longcloth Three Lübeck merchants: 284 Ss, 19 Gs Two Danzig merchants: 99 Ss, 47 Gs

Notes The vessels' and masters' names are given according to the version in the port book. *C* Coventry, *D* Devon, *Gs* Gloucester shortcloth, *H* Hampshire, *N* Norwich, *Ss* Suffolk shortcloth, *W* Warwickshire, *Wilts* Wiltshire

[a] 'Port of origin' refers to the vessel, not the master. For instance, under the date 30 April 1565 the book states that the ship *Saviour* came from London but the master from Lee.

Source P.R.O., E 190/2/1.

the Sound registers give the place of residence of the shipmaster,[74] not the port of origin of the goods, as certain researchers still believe.

The London port book for 1565 reveals above all the overriding importance of the expensive broadcloth, especially that originating from Suffolk and Gloucester, in that city's exports to the Baltic. Other qualities, such as the cheap kersey or dozens, did not play any great part. We find further confirmation of this fact in the Elbing customs registers for 1586 and 1594.[75] In 1586 *Luński* cloth* represented 50·3 per cent and kersey 47·9 per cent of total exports of textiles from London to Elbing; but in 1594 the corresponding figures were 75·6 per cent for *Luński* cloth and 13·3 per cent for kersey. Comparison of cloth exports to Elbing from London and other English ports towards the end of the sixteenth century reveals the capital's decided predominance in the export of the expensive *Luński* cloth (i.e. broadcloth, or shortcloth, to adopt the customs terminology), while at the same time it had a smaller share in the export of cheap kersey, which was sent to the Baltic more by the merchants of Hull and other north-eastern ports. Other kinds of cloth played little part in this trade.

Another deduction resulting from an analysis of the London port book for 1565 concerns the average quantity of cloth exported per London merchant engaged in the Baltic trade (see table 7.6). In that year twenty-two London merchants exported 1,556 cloths to Danzig including 1,277 broadcloths (1,059 from Suffolk and 218 from Gloucestershire). Thus on average each London merchant was responsible for some seventy cloths. The largest exporters were Thomas Allen, with 180 cloths, Dunstan Walton, with 155, William Vanghardt, with 149, and the first Deputy Governor of the Eastland Company, Thomas Russell, with 121 cloths.

By comparison with the average of seventy cloths per London exporter in 1565, in the same year the Hansards, chartering English vessels, had a higher average loading of textiles. In that year three merchants from Lübeck purchased 1,051 broadcloths in London, an average of 350 each. C. Skynfeld of Lübeck had an especially large share in this total; he exported 628 cloths from London in five vessels (514 Suffolk shortcloths and 114 Gloucestershire shortcloths). But two Danzig merchants loaded 236 cloths on two English ships—an average of 118 apiece. Maurycy Tymmermann, of Danzig, exported

* For an explanation of these and other foreign terms with no equivalent in English see p. 182.—*Translator.*

182 shortcloths from London (132 Suffolk and 50 Gloucestershire shortcloths), while the Danzig citizen G. Giese had a total of fifty-four cloths.

The Sound toll registers reveal that Hull had an important share

Table 7.6 *London cloth exporters to Danzig, 1565, according to the London port book*

Merchant's name [*a*]	*No. of vessels*[*b*]	*Suffolk shortcloth*	*Gloucester shortcloth*	*Other kinds*
Allen, Thomas	4	147	33	
Beswyck, William	2	44	–	19 N worsted
Best, Ezechias	2	78	–	
Boldero, Edmund	3	46	5	3 other kinds of cloth
Carr, Robert	2	5	–	2 worsted, 1 W longcloth
Codd, Bartholemew	1	–	–	18 Wilts shortcloth
Drapen, Clement	1	8	–	
Folck, Richard	5	120	–	
Foxall, John	1	–	–	5 D dozens, 13 longcloth, 5 others
Franckland, William	2	45	10	
Gourney, Richard	1	3	15	
Isham, Henry	1	–	8	72 northern kerseys
Jeames, William	2	54	30	
Langton, John	3	32	22	4 western shortcloth
Lucas, Henry	1	2	–	80 northern kerseys
Mylner, George	2	8	2	9 D dozens
Perkins, Nicholas	1	21	4	9 H kerseys
Russell, Thomas	4	96	25	9 D kerseys, 1 Kent longcloth
Sockyn, William	3	7[illegible]	6	
Sockson, Lawrence	2	32	–	
Vanghardt, William	4	111	38	
Walton, Dunstan	6	135	20	18 D kerseys, 11 others

Notes

D Devon, *H* Hampshire, *N* Norwich, *W* Warwickshire, *Wilts* Wiltshire

[*a*] The merchants' names are given according to the version in the port book.

[*b*] This column gives the number of vessels in which each merchant sent his cloth to the Baltic in 1565.

Source P.R.O., E 190/2/1.

in the export of cloth from England to the Baltic in the second half of the sixteenth century: in 1565 19 per cent of total English exports to the Baltic; in 1575, 25·6 per cent; in 1585, 39·5 per cent; in 1595 26 per cent.[76] In 1605 the percentage was as high as 60·1. This is aggregating all the various kinds of cloth together, and only on analysis of the Elbing customs registers do we find[75] that in Hull's Baltic exports cheap kersey was predominant, while *Luński* broadcloth comprised only a few per cent. And it has to be borne in mind that some of the cloths entered in the Sound registers to Hull's account belonged to London merchants, who made use of Hull vessels to a not inconsiderable extent in their Baltic trade.

On the basis of the surviving English port books we are unable to determine the extent of Hull's cloth exports to the Baltic during the second half of the sixteenth century. The oldest surviving complete Hull port book dates only from 1609,[77] a year for which we lack both Polish customs registers and the more detailed information of

Table 7.7 *Cloth exports from Hull, 1609, and their regional distribution*

Destination	*Kersey*		*Dozens*		*Shortcloth*		*Longcloth*		*Total*	
	Pieces	%	*Pieces*	%	*Pieces*	%	*Pieces*	%	*Pieces*	%
Elbing	27,703	70·9	711	26·1	583	72·9	34	11·1	29,031	67·5
Netherlands	8,570	21·8	963	35·3	58	7·2	89	29·1	9,680	22·5
France	2,249	5·7	193	7·0	49	6·1	6	1·9	2,497	5·8
Germany	550	1·4	697	25·6	–	–	165	53·9	1,412	3·3
Denmark	11	0·05	65	2·0	82	10·2	4	1·4	162	0·4
Danzig	43	0·1	60	2·0	20	2·5	8	2·6	131	0·3
Norway	16	0·05	64	2·0	8	1·1	–	–	88	0·2
Total	39,142	100·0	2,753	100·0	800	100·0	306	100·0	43,001	100·0

Source P.R.O., E 190/312/6.

the Sound toll registers. Taking this Hull book and an unpublished work by B. Hall[78] as our basis, it appears that Poland was the chief customer for textiles despatched from Hull, and that among these kersey was decisively predominant. The Polish ports provided the chief markets for Hull's cloth, with Holland in second place, followed by France and Germany. In 1609 close on 70 per cent of the textiles exported from Hull went to Elbing (see table 7.7).

Table 7.7 confirms the observation that at the beginning of the seventeenth century Hull's share in English cloth exports to the Baltic showed a considerable increase. Comparing the data in this table with the Sound toll registers,[79] we reach the conclusion that in 1609 Hull's share in England's total export of cloth to the Baltic amounted to 74·6 per cent. But these data relate to a rather later period, a time of incipient crisis in the English textile trade. In the second half of the sixteenth century London's predominance was still indisputable.

The earliest detailed data concerning Newcastle's cloth exports to the Baltic derive from English customs records for the years 1594[80]

Table 7.8 *Exporters of cloth from Newcastle upon Tyne to Elbing, 1594 and 1598 (pieces of cloth)*

Merchant's name[*a*]	*Double dozens*		*Kersey*		*Northern kersey*		*Other kinds*	
	1594	1598	1594	1598	1594	1598	1594	1598
Anderson, Cutbert	42	7	50	81	–	–	–	–
Anderson, Francis	54	–	–	–	–	–	–	–
Beckworth, Robert	15	–	–	–	–	36	–	–
Brentwood, Robert	–	16	–	220	–	–	–	–
Brandling, Robert	38	14	14	–	–	–	–	–
Berwick, Cutbert	20	9	–	298	–	–	–	–
Bowes, Anne	14	16	40	60	–	–		–
Clavering, John	11	6	–	–	–	–	–	8[*b*]
Cock, John	8	–	–	–	–	–	14[*b*]	–
Cherwood, William	–	–	–	–	–	15	–	–
Dawson, Henry	21	–	–	–	–	–	–	–
Elison, Robert	–	–	46	–	–	–	–	–
Fenicke, George	–	39	–	20	–	–	–	–
Greenwell, William	12	–	–	–	–	–	–	–
Hedley, Nicholas	38	–	60	–	–	–	–	–
Lawson, Robert	8	–	20	–	–	–	–	–
Lyendly, Nicholas	–	32	–	160	–	–	–	–
Mitford, Christopher	10	–	16	–	–	–	–	–
Nicholas, Roger	–	8	–	–	–	–	–	–
Morpitch, Anthony	11		–	–	–	–	–	–
Sotherer, Thomas	13	–	–	–	–	–	–	–
Stote, Richard	6	64	30	70	–	60	–	–
Selbie, John	–	4	–	32	–	–	–	–
Selbie, William	–	40	–	–	–	–	–	–

Notes
[*a*] The merchants' names are given according to the version in the port book.
[*b*] Single dozens.

Source P.R.O., E 190/185/6 and E 315/485.

and 1598.[81] In 1594 cloth exports from Newcastle to the Baltic were carried in three vessels belonging to that port and were entirely consigned to Elbing. They consisted of kerseys and dozens, and therefore of cheap cloth; this was also the case in 1598, when three English vessels again carried kerseys and a small quantity of dozens to Elbing. In neither case do we find the expensive *Luński* cloth exported from

Newcastle. The Elbing customs registers which have survived confirm this predominance of kersey in Newcastle's exports. In 1586 it amounted to 54 per cent; in 1594 to 34·4 per cent, and its cheaper variety, dozens, 52·4 per cent.[75] Table 7.8 details the nature and extent of cloth exports from Newcastle to Elbing in 1594 and 1598. It throws light on the predominance of the cheaper kinds of cloth in this trade, and at the same time reveals the relatively very small share the Newcastle merchants had in the cloth trade.

After London, the most important town shipping cloth to the Baltic was Ipswich, which sent the cloth manufactures of Suffolk chiefly to Poland, Spain and Portugal, some to the Netherlands, and a little to France.[82] It is true that Ipswich did not become the 'English Antwerp', as the authors of the document 'Ipswich out of England or Antwerpe in England' suggested in 1573,[83] but its cloth trade was extensive. The Ipswich merchants maintained agents permanently in Danzig and Elbing,[84] and played an important part in the life of the Eastland Company.

The state of the surviving sources unfortunately does not permit any really thorough assessment of the position of Ipswich in the export of English cloth to the Baltic. The Sound toll registers do not mention the Ipswich consignments separately (they do so only in the case of London, Hull and Newcastle), and to make matters worse the only Ipswich port book which has survived for the period in which we are interested, one for the year 1571,[85] is damaged. In these circumstances one can determine the extent and nature of Ipswich's cloth exports to the Baltic only by resort to the Elbing customs registers; but as the great majority of England's exports to the Baltic towards the end of the sixteenth century were directed to Elbing, generalization on this basis would appear to be justified. The Elbing registers indicate the great importance of the expensive kinds of cloth in exports from Ipswich. In 1586, of the total of 3,200 pieces of cloth exported from Ipswich to Elbing, *Luński* cloth accounted for 65·6 per cent, and ordinary kersey for 23·9 per cent. But in 1594, of the 1,422½ pieces of broadcloth exported to Elbing in Ipswich ships, *Luński* cloth accounted for 42·6 per cent, Falendish (a kind of broadcloth) for 15·5 per cent, and the balance was made up of, if anything, even more expensive cloth. In 1605 broadcloth accounted for as much as 66·7 per cent of the exports from Ipswich to Elbing.[86]

The Ipswich port book for 1604 shows that a comparatively large number of merchants of this town took part in the export of cloth to Elbing, and that the average of forty-seven cloths per merchant was fairly high, though it was lower than the London average (about seventy cloths). Similarly, only from the Elbing customs registers can one obtain information as to the share of other English ports in cloth exports to the Baltic during the second half of the sixteenth century. They indicate that Lynn did not play any considerable part in this trade; in 1586, 501 cloths were exported to Elbing in Lynn

Table 7.9 *Exporters of cloth from Ipswich to Elbing, 1604 (pieces of cloth)*

Merchant's name [*a*]	*Shortcloth*	*Other kinds*
Barbor, Jerome	56	
Bronrigge, Mathew	215·5	
Borne, William	82	
Brewster, William	42	
Buck, William	4	
Clench, John	49	
Colborne, Thomas	15	
Cutler, Samuel	41·5	2
Evered, John	49·5	
Eldred, John	21	
Goodier, Michael	46	
Green, William	18	
Grippes, Robert	21	
Hewes, Richard	95·5	20
Humphrey, Roger	23·5	13·5
Ingelthorpe, William	70	
Knapp, Robert	8	
Randes, John	123	
Revett, Edward	14	
Selfry, Robert	1	
Sherwood, Thomas	33	
Sneller, Thomas	1	
Snelling, Robert	117	
Snelling, Walter	19	
Woodgate, Thomas	23·5	

Note
[*a*] The merchants' names are given according to the version in the port book.

Source P.R.O., E 190/599/4.

vessels, 71 per cent being ordinary kersey and 15·3 per cent *Luński* cloth.[87] For Yarmouth also the figures were minimal.[88] The same can be said of Aldeburgh, Dover, Harwich, Dartmouth and Southampton.

The Elbing registers enable us to make a comparison of the share taken by the ships of the most important English east coast ports in the export of particular kinds of English cloth. When studying table 7.10 one should not, of course, assume a complete correspondence between the origin of the shipmasters, as noted in the register,

Table 7.10 *The respective shares of various English ports in exports of the chief kinds of cloth to Elbing, 1586, 1594 and 1605 (pieces of cloth)*

Type of cloth and year	*London*	*Hull*	*Newcastle*	*Ipswich*	*Aldeburgh*	*Lynn*	*Dover*	*Harwich*
Ordinary *Luński*								
1586	3,322	–	277	2,114	170	77	555	–
1594	6,174	428	–	606	–	3	–	99
1605	2,376	688	985	1,462	420	–	–	9
Ordinary kersey								
1586	2,022	8,831	1,373	770	239	358	–	–
1594	539	–	–	–	–	–	–	–
1605	100	36	54	40	–	–	–	–
Northern kersey								
1586	1,144	12	–	–	–	60	525	–
1594	536	4,744	227	–	–	–	–	–
1605	285	13,759	5,408	47	11	–	–	–
Double dozens								
1586	39	738	851	12	52	–	–	–
1594	–	224	346	–	–	–	–	–
1605	–	–	46	–	–	–	–	–

Source W.A.P.Gd., Lib. port. Elbing, 1586, 1594 and 1605.

and the place of origin of the goods, since we know that London merchants often made use of transport from other English ports, while conversely the merchants of Hull or Newcastle freighted London vessels, though this occurred more rarely. But if there is no possibility of checking these data, they do, none the less, allow us to obtain approximate understanding of the question with which we are concerned.

Table 7.10 convincingly confirms London's important position in cloth exports to the Baltic; in reality the capital's share was even larger because the London merchants frequently chartered vessels from Hull and other ports. London's predominance is particularly striking in the case of the expensive *Luński* cloth. Apart from the capital, Ipswich also played an important part in this branch of the trade. But kersey was sent to Poland mainly from Hull and, to some extent, from Newcastle.

In concluding these observations on the share taken by the main English ports in cloth exports to the Baltic, we need to present the question comparatively, for London, Hull and Newcastle, over a somewhat longer period, in order to get an idea of the development of the trade. For this we must base our observations on the Sound toll registers. Table 7.11 gives the aggregate of all kinds of cloth, so it

Table 7.11 *The respective shares of vessels from London, Hull and Newcastle upon Tyne in cloth exports to the Baltic, decennial intervals 1565–1625 (pieces of cloth)*

Year	*London*		*Hull*		*Newcastle*		*Other ports*		*Total (pieces)*
	Pieces	%	*Pieces*	%	*Pieces*	%	*Pieces*	%	
1565	2,580·0	37·2	1,318	19·0	1,746·0	21·3	1,287·5	22·5	6,931·5
1575	2,671·0	27·6	2,470	25·6	707·5	7·3	3,805·5	39·5	9,654·5
1585	7,329·0	36·0	8,057	39·5	1,907·0	9·3	3,076·5	15·2	20,369·5
1595	11,312·0	57·4	5,117	26·0	1,114·0	5·6	2,151·0	11·0	19,694·0
1605	5,617·0	19·8	17,072	60·1	3,809·5	13·4	1,903·5	6·7	28,402·0
1615	6,972·5	20·9	12,307	37·0	11,695·0	35·0	2,367·0	7·1	33,341·5
1625	3,075·5	6·2	28,937	58·5	10,127·0	20·5	7,314·5	14·8	49,451·0

Source *Tabeller over skibsfart . . .*, vol. IIA, pp. 15, 47, 101, 161, 223, 287, 353.

has only a quantitative, not a qualitative significance. However, it supplements our observations on this question with material covering a longer period as well as the total export of cloth to the Baltic in English ships. The three ports of greatest importance in the Baltic trade—London, Hull and Newcastle—together accounted for over two-thirds of the country's cloth exports to that area (in 1565, 77·5 per cent; in 1575, 60·5 per cent; in 1585, 84·8 per cent; in 1595, 89 per cent); at the beginning of the seventeenth century they dominated the market by over 90 per cent. Taking only the quantitative data as a basis for comparison, it further appears that towards the end of the sixteenth century London was still predominant, but at the beginning of the seventeenth this predominance fell to Hull. However, such a mechanical comparison of quantities alone is misleading because of the qualitative differences in the various dearer and cheaper kinds of cloth. As we have already said, the London merchants were predominant in the export of expensive broadcloth, a length of which cost about ten times as much as kersey, for example, which the merchants of Hull and Newcastle exported in large quantities.[89]

The expensive English broadcloth had been known in Poland since the end of the fourteenth century.[90] In Polish terminology it later acquired the name '*Luński* cloth' (the Elbing customs registers call it *Lundisch*[91]), probably as a distortion of the name of England's capital, or from the adjective *holenderskji*, or even from the town of Leyden—which, however, seems unlikely. For that matter, not only the origin of the name but the scope of its application in Poland tended to be rather obscure, because English cloth was to a large extent finished in Holland; so in the sixteenth and seventeenth centuries Poland extended the application of the term *Luński* to cover Dutch cloth as well as English.[92] From the middle of the fifteenth century onward much English broadcloth reached Poland *via* Danzig (it is given a place of honour in the *Book of Theudenkus*).[93] It had a certain importance in Baltic trade in the second half of the fifteenth century[94] (see above). In sixteenth century Poland this cloth was regarded as among the best, and the Polish customs houses, especially that of Poznań, show considerable trade in *Luński* cloth,[95] though it was still disproportionately small by comparison with the quantities arriving at Danzig and Elbing. *Luński* cloth predominated at the royal court and was in great demand among the gentry and affluent burghers. The officials of the *starostwos* (districts) often received their remuneration in this cloth; the Cracow city council bought it for its officials and functionaries as part of their remuneration;[96] we find it mentioned as an item of value in the wills of dignitaries;[97] the uniform of officers of the Polish Commonwealth was made of it; the numerous Tatar emissaries arriving in Poland were given gifts of it, etc.

On the basis of the surviving sources it is difficult to get an idea of the distribution of English cloth in Poland in the second half of the sixteenth century, among other reasons because the term '*Luński* cloth' was also applied to English cloth dyed in the Netherlands or even originating elsewhere. Certain kinds of English cloth were imitated by local cloth manufacturers (for example, towards the end of the sixteenth century kersey was produced in Silesia, so the sources do not always distinguish English from Silesian kersey).[98] In any case, we know that the great market for English cloth was

Poznań, which received it from Danzig and then distributed it to various parts of Poland, while part was forwarded in transit to the East, especially to Vilno (e.g. through Lublin), as a commodity exchangeable for furs.[99] The customs register for Kamenets Podolsk* for 1551–52 mentions various cloths which passed through the local customs in that year, *Luński* cloth forming the largest single item.[100] But it would appear from Rybarski's researches that it is very difficult to establish the distribution of English cloth in sixteenth century Poland on the basis of the surviving registers of the Polish internal customs houses.

In the third quarter of the sixteenth century a new, even more expensive kind of English cloth, known in English sources as 'fyne cloth',[101] began to appear in the Baltic markets; in the customs registers it is called *fein Lacken*,[102] and in Crown Poland† as *falendysz*, from the German *fein Lundisch*.[103] In 1580 a piece of this cloth cost as much as £13 in England,[101] whereas a length of broadcloth at that time cost about £9 sterling.[104] However, the Elbing customs registers reveal only very small quantities of *falendysz* towards the end of the sixteenth century (in 1586 323 pieces,[87] and in 1594 316 pieces[105]).

The second main type of cloth exported by English merchants to the Baltic was kersey; the name derives from the village of Kersey in Suffolk, or from the term 'coarse'.[106] It was essentially a poorer and cheaper quality woollen cloth, and was known in Poland from the end of the Middle Ages onward, but becoming widespread principally from the middle of the sixteenth century. Towards the end of that century the weavers of Silesia began to imitate it.[107] Among the numerous kinds of kersey the customs records mention various types of Devonshire kerseys, the cheapest variety of which was called dozens. In 1580 a coarse northern dozen cost £1 6*s* and Devonshire dozens £1 10*s*, while good northern dozens cost £3.[101] In the seventeenth century kerseys, and even the *Luński* cloth, lost their previous high reputation in Poland, and this, in connection with the increase in demand and passion for luxury led to the situation which Stanisław Słupski described in 1618:[108]

* A town in Padolia, now southern Ukraine; in the sixteenth century within the Polish Commonwealth as a result of the union with the Grand Duchy of Lithuania—*Translator.*

† The area of the kingdom of Poland before the union with Lithuania in 1386—*Translator.*

Dziwna rzecz, że dziś karazyj nie znają,
Snać i na lundysz słudzy się gniewają.
Szukają barwy, coby od bławata,
Choć w tym bławacie znajdziesz i jałata
Nie tylko szlachtę.*

But the phenomenon Słupski observed is not confirmed in the customs registers for the end of the sixteenth century (see table 7.12).

This table reveals the great increase in the exports of English kersey towards the end of the sixteenth century, which contributed so greatly to raising the total of English textiles exported during those years to the Baltic countries, especially to Poland. From correspondence between Cranfield and his Danzig factors at the beginning of the seventeenth century it is clear that kersey continued to enjoy good sales in Poland. If it was not possible to sell it elsewhere, Cranfield instructed his agents to send it on to Danzig.[109] However, exports of narrow and broad dozens were in general limited to a few hundred pieces per annum, and they did not play any great part in England's Baltic trade. The Elbing customs registers also reveal that such kinds of cloth as broad and northern *Luński*, red cloth, red kersey, narrow and broad baize, etc, were of little importance (see table 7.13).

Of course, mechanical comparison of the total of the more important kinds of cloth exported in English vessels to the Baltic does

* It's strange that today kersey isn't known,
And probably people grow tired of Lundish.
They seek colours, preferably of silks,
Though in those silks you'll find the rabble
And not only the gentry.

Notes In order to obtain comparative data, bales of cloth (in any case a very small quantity) have been calculated in lengths at the ratio of one bale to eight pieces of cloth (average). Cf. A. E. Christensen, *Dutch trade to the Baltic about 1600*, Copenhagen–The Hague, 1941, p. 441.

[*a*] The Sound toll registers do not always state whether an item is narrow or double dozens. Wherever there is no indication, narrow dozens have been assumed.

[*b*] Instead of dozens the Sound registers for this year note the export of 292 narrow poldavis—a kind of common canvas.

[*c*] These are double poldavis.

Source *Tabeller over skibsfart*..., vol. IIA, pp. 2–211.

Table 7.12 *Exports of the chief types of cloth to the Baltic in English vessels, 1562–1600*

Year	*Luński cloth (broadcloth)*	*Kersey*	*Dozens[a]*	
			Narrow	*Wide*
1562	3,173	1,536	141·5	–
1563	5,513	3,942	151	–
1564	4,589	2,872	343	–
1565	4,290·5	1,868	113	497
1566	6,593·5	2,075	748·5	–
1567	3,248	981	229	33·5
1568	2,234·5	1,985	384	–
1569	5,606	4,473	668	–
1574	4,744	5,603	462	528
1575	4,771	2,880	337	421
1576	5,105	4,067	330	184
1577	1,928	1,567	345	174
1578	2,515	3,171	702	352
1579	3,580	4,748	357	498
1580	3,837	2,974	234	262
1581	3,204	3,701	348	696
1582	4,520	5,279	424	624
1583	5,529	6,330	334	573
1584	9,336	7,959	249	1,145
1585	7,611	11,415	175	875
1586	9,001	22,556	908	1,775
1587	11,120	21,028	1,199	2,071
1588	3,890	5,897	292[b]	690·5[c]
1589	6,762·5	9,130	243	1,028
1590	5,297	4,022	152	446
1591	6,233·5	15,115	469	1,197
1592	6,009	8,312	110	780
1593	7,207·5	7,282	256	823·5
1594	8,679	7,498	200	644
1595	10,097	8,334	159	729
1596	10,458	5,737	88	512
1597	21,536	12,879	120	437
1598	14,674	30,925	429	920
1599	13,633	31,934	570	469
1600	12,054	27,561	452	319

not enable us to get any real idea of the value of this trade, which was so highly differentiated in regard to quality. This problem can be solved only by resort to the Sound toll registers, which give the value of goods in transit through the Sound in Danish thalers for England and several other countries (but not for Holland) at ten-year intervals, beginning with 1565. Apart from other duties, the English also paid the Sound customs one per cent of the value of the transported goods, calculated on the basis of the shipmaster's own declaration. But as the

Table 7.13 *The chief varieties of English cloth exported to Elbing, 1586, 1594 and 1605 (pieces of cloth)*

Type of cloth	1586	1594	1605
Ordinary *Luński*	6,515	7,312	5,937
Falendysz	323	316	10
Packlaken	–	1,399·5	2,016
Northern cloth	53	735	344
Red cloth	8	–	–
Ordinary kersey	13,835	539	230
Northern kersey	1,741	5,507	19,510
Double kersey	–	54	–
Broad kersey	–	19	–
Red kersey	4	–	–
Narrow dozens	133	2,029	310
Double dozens	1,693·5	570	46
Baize	66	138	28·5
Double baize	2	–	–

Source W.A.P.Gd., Lib. port. Elbing, 1586, 1594, 1605

King of Denmark had the right to purchase goods transported through the Sound, one can assume that the shipmasters in general declared the real value of their cargoes.[110] So the toll registers afford us the possibility of comparing the value of the various kinds of goods, and this over a long period—something that cannot be done on the basis of the very incomplete English and Polish materials, which give only the prices of certain kinds of cloth for certain years.[111] Table 7.14 reveals the overwhelming importance of *Luński* cloth in English textile exports to the Baltic countries. Even at the very end of the

Table 7.14 *Quantity and value of the chief types of cloth exported in English vessels to the Baltic, 1575, 1585 and 1595 (pieces of cloth; value in Danish thalers)*

Type of cloth	1575				1585				1595			
	Pieces	%	*Thalers*	%	*Pieces*	%	*Thalers*	%	*Pieces*	%	*Thalers*	%
Broadcloth	4,771	55·8	106,874	75·5	7,611	37·7	254,509	68·2	10,097	51·8	334,430	78·7
Kersey	2,880	33·7	19,894	14·1	11,415	56·6	94,745	25·4	8,334	42·8	68,043	16·0
Double dozens	421	4·9	10,495	7·4	875	4·3	20,855	5·6	729	3·7	18,255	4·3
Narrow dozens	337	3·9	3,332	2·3	175	0·8	1,676	0·5	159	0·8	1,598	0·4
Other[a]	132	1·7	846	0·7	91	0·6	1,227	0·3	164	0·9	2,456	0·6
Total	8,541	100·0	141,441	100·0	20,167	100·0	373,013	100·0	19,483	100·0	424,782	100·0

Notes A small quantity of ells has been ignored in order to obtain comparative data.
[a] This item consists mainly of baize.

Source *Tabeller over skibsfart* . . . , vol. IIA, pp. 15, 24, 46, 57, 101, 161, 176.

sixteenth century, when kersey decidedly surpassed broadcloth in volume, it took second place in terms of value.

Nothing better explains the reason for the English merchants' persistent efforts to establish an entrepot on the Polish coast than table 7.15, which shows the distribution of English cloth to the more important Baltic ports. This table reveals that in the second half of the sixteenth century 69·1–93 per cent of all English cloth exports in English vessels to the Baltic went to the Polish ports of Danzig and

Table 7.15 *The distribution of cloth exports shipped in English vessels to Baltic ports, decennial intervals 1565–95*

Port	1565		1575		1585		1595	
	Pieces	%	*Pieces*	%	*Pieces*	%	*Pieces*	%
Danzig	4,795[*a*]	69·1	7,782	91·16	70	0·3	568	2·9
Elbing	–	–	–	–	18,702	92·7	17,128	87·9
Königsberg	100	1·4	4	0·04	680	3·3	1,732	8·9
Narva	530	7·6	184	2·1	–	–	–	–
Riga	–	–	105	1·2	–	–	55	0·3
Others	1,506·5[*b*]	21·9	466	5·5	715	3·7	–	–
Total	6,931·5[*c*]	100·0	8,541	100·0	20,167	100·0	19,483[*d*]	100·0

Notes In order to obtain comparative data, bales of cloth are calculated in terms of pieces in the ratio of one bale to eight pieces of cloth.
[*a*] To this should be added 298 ells.
[*b*] Including 1,224 pieces to unidentified ports: *Tabeller over skibsfart* . . . , vol. IIB, p. 227.
[*c*] Including three bales of cloth.
[*d*] To this should be added 3,000 ells.

Source *Tabeller over skibsfart* . . . , vol. IIA, pp. 15, 47, 101, 161; vol. IIB, pp. 199, 215–26.

Elbing. If to these we add Königsberg, through which town also goods destined for the Polish Commonwealth were transhipped, it turns out that Poland received 70·5–99·7 per cent of all the English cloth exported to the Baltic; in other words, she was virtually England's sole trading partner in this area (see below for Russia's role).

Poland's overwhelming importance to English cloth exports to the Baltic is also shown by correlating the Sound registers with the Elbing customs registers for the end of the sixteenth and beginning of the seventeenth centuries (see table 7.16). The Elbing customs register for 1594 gives a figure for English cloth exports to that port which is even larger than England's total exports to the Baltic as given in the Sound registers. This may indicate that the English shipmasters managed to smuggle part of their cargoes through the Sound.

It would seem desirable also to consider the place occupied by the Russian market in English cloth exports, especially from the point of view of its possible competition with English textile exports to the Baltic market. It should be said at once that in the light of the surviving data for the Russian market in the second half of the sixteenth

Table 7.16 *Elbing's share of total English cloth exports to the Baltic, 1586, 1594 and 1605, according to the Sound toll registers and the Elbing customs registers (pieces of cloth)*

Year	*Total from England to Baltic according to Sound registers*	*Total from England to Elbing according to Elbing registers*	%
1586	35,737	24,402·5	68·3
1594	17,574	18,689·0	106·4 (*sic*)
1605	28,453	28,432·5	99·9

Source *Tabeller over skibsfart* . . ., vol. IIA, pp. 118, 150, 231; W.A.P.Gd., Lib. port. Elbing, 1586, 1594, 1605.

century that market did not as yet offer any serious competition to the Polish market. The Sound and the London customs records enable us to make such a comparison only for the year 1565, this being possible because the Muscovy Company's consignments to Russia were despatched almost exclusively from London. On the other hand, however, we cannot say to what extent conclusions drawn from such a comparison for only one year can be generalized, especially as the year in question showed something of a decline in English cloth exports to the Baltic (see table 7.17).

Fragmentary data for later years appear to confirm the view that the Russian market was of minor importance for English cloth exports in the second half of the sixteenth century. In 1568 the Muscovy Company consigned some 400 pieces of cloth to Russia, which amounted to barely 10 per cent of English exports to the Baltic.[112] After the loss of Narva Russia obtained English cloth only *via* Archangel, in quantities of 150–400 cloths annually,[113] and towards the end of the sixteenth century over 1,000 cloths—still only a few per cent of total English exports to the Baltic and Eastern Europe.[114] In 1598 English cloth exports to Archangel amounted to 2,049 cloths (including kersey),[115] but in the same year English exports to the Baltic amounted to 47,230 pieces of various kinds of textiles;[116] in other words, the Russian market could not in any sense compare with the Baltic market at this stage.

One possibility of obtaining a more exact comparison of the Baltic and Russian markets for English cloth is afforded by two London port books—for 1565 and 1606—and the account for

Table 7.17 *English cloth exports to the Baltic and Russia, 1565*

Total from England to both areas		*To Danzig*		*To Moscow via Narva*		*via White Sea*	
Pieces	%	*Pieces*	%	*Pieces*	%	*Pieces*	%
8,066·5	100·0	4,795	59·4	530	6·5	1,147	14·2

Note Figures for kersey and broadcloth are combined.

Source *Tabeller over skibsfart* . . . , vol. IIA, pp. 19, 215, 223; P.R.O., E 190/2/1. [This port book covers Easter to Michaelmas 1565.]

1597–98 preserved in the Public Record Office. The data these provide are of only limited scope, since they relate only to London, but they do enable us to obtain a more precise idea of the demand for various kinds of English cloth in Russia during the second half of the sixteenth and the beginning of the seventeenth centuries. In analysing table 7.18, however, it is necessary to remember that, whereas so far as Russia is concerned, the figures correspond more or less to the total of English exports (as already mentioned, the Muscovy Company despatched goods mainly from London), the same cannot be said of the Baltic exports. of which barely 30 per cent were consigned in London ships.

The greater value of the Baltic as compared to the Russian market for English cloth applied mainly to the expensive kinds, especially

Luński broad cloth. Russia was an important customer for kersey, not yielding place to the Baltic areas so far as exports from London were concerned. Taking into account all the various kinds of cloth, we can say that the Baltic took about two thirds, and Russia one third of the total exports from London to these two areas. At the same time, one is struck by the gradual increase in importance of the Russian market,

Table 7.18 *Cloth exports from London to the Baltic and Russia, 1565, 1597–98 and 1606 (per cent)*

Type of cloth	1565		1597–98		1606	
	Baltic	*Russia*	*Baltic*	*Russia*	*Baltic*	*Russia*
Broadcloth	90·0	10·0	86·7	13·3	72·8	27·2
Kersey	16·2	83·8	75·7	24·3	55·7	44·3
Dozens	100·0	–	100·0	–	74·4	25·6
Other	100·0	–	–	–	45·1	54·9

Note The data for 1597–98 cover the period from 29 September 1597 to 29 September 1598.

Source P.R.O., E 190/2/1 and E 190/13/5; also *ibid.*, S.P.Dom. 12/268, No. 101.

even in respect of *Luński* cloth. In the second half of the seventeenth century a poet acknowledged this in the words:

> To Russia and Muscovy likewise goes
> Good store of broad, and narrow Wollen Clothes
> And all the East lands one such is in the trade
> For Wollen Goods, in England which are made.[117]

Parallel with this growing importance of the Russian market, English cloth exporters were to feel the competition of Holland more and more; it gathered in strength from the beginning of the seventeenth century on.[118]

3 *Other commodities*

Cloth played such an overwhelming part in England's exports to the Baltic that all other commodities pale into insignificance beside it. Their aggregate value in total English Baltic exports amounted to about 20 per cent in the years before the foundation of the Eastland Company, but only a few per cent towards the end of the sixteenth century. They formed only a supplement to the cloth exports, whose value amounted to about 90 per cent of England's total Baltic exports. In this section these other exports to Baltic countries will be briefly summarized.

(a) *Skins and hides.* In England's trade with the Baltic, second place after cloth, in terms of value, was taken by the export of skins—especially cony—and hides.[119] English merchants exported a very considerable quantity of these skins to the Baltic, from some half a million before the foundation of the Eastland Company to about a million per annum towards the end of the century. In the second half of the century English exports of skins to the Baltic countries amounted in general to about 80 per cent of total western European exports of this nature, and in this field the only competitors with the English were the Scots, who exported mainly lambskins to the Baltic.[120] The Dutch had a relatively small share in this trade; on the whole it only very exceptionally exceeded 100,000 items per annum (in 1564, for instance), running in general at the level of 10,000–20,000 items per annum, with frequent interruptions and considerable fluctuations. Hanseatic and French exports of skins to the Baltic were equally small. It was the exception for Spanish vessels to turn up in Baltic ports with a cargo of skins and hides. In 1576, for instance, they delivered 27,500 items, and in 1577 as many as 52,000,[121] but these were sporadic visits, and in practice the English did not meet with any serious competition.

The great majority of the skins exported by English merchants to the Baltic were cony, especially grey cony. They accounted for over 90 per cent of this trade. Lambskins (*lamfele*), fox skins and others were of minor importance. But it should be observed that at the end of the sixteenth century, especially after 1590, there was a quite definite increase in exports of lambskins, and in 1597 it amounted to as much as 21·5 per cent, and in 1600 17 per cent, of total English exports of skins to the Baltic countries. Exports of fox skins averaged several hundred per annum, the highest figures being reached in 1574 (2,562 skins) and in 1598 (2,737 skins); in each year they were only a fraction of one per cent of the total trade.

Hides and skins figured largely in Poland's general trade in the second half of the sixteenth century, and, as Rybarski has observed,[122] the volume of the trade in certain kinds of skins and hides bears comparison even with the contemporary scale of trade. Undoubtedly, a large proportion of the skins exported to Poland by the English and Scots passed in transit through that country,[123] especially *en route* to German lands. For it is difficult to believe that, in view of the considerable local production and the large imports

Table 7.19 *Exports of skins from the West to the Baltic, 1562–1600*

Year	Total (items)	From England		From Scotland		From other countries (%)
		Items	%	Items	%	
1562	869,356	641,685	73·8	227,671	26·2	–
1563	874,952	701,605	80·1	173,347	19·9	–
1564	883,184	510,856	57·8	226,196	25·6	16·6
1565	1,061,363	669,000	63·0	337,423	31·7	5·3
1566	850,724	604,522	71·0	224,202	26·3	2·7
1567	1,069,320	870,360	81·3	118,360	11·0	7·7
1568	1,062,986	692,530	65·1	325,236	30·5	4·4
1569	1,085,868	814,016	74·9	263,822	24·2	0·9
1574	952,375	758,412	79·6	182,513	19·1	1·3
1575	870,848	643,503	73·8	223,345	25·6	0·6
1576	978,072	665,033	67·9	241,099	24·6	7·5
1577	785,203	526,042	66·9	181,061	23·0	10·1
1578	915,459	607,717	66·3	291,742	31·8	1·9
1579	856,937	632,900	73·8	216,037	25·2	1·0
1580	922,367	746,810	80·9	174,257	18·8	0·3
1581	897,002	722,508	80·5	173,004	19·2	0·3
1582	1,027,197	833,380	81·1	193,107	18·7	0·2
1583	827,456	609,632	73·6	217,044	26·2	0·2
1584	1,310,621	1,090,970	83·[illegible]	199,201	15·9	0·9
1585	1,148,082	999,086	87·0	142,800	12·4	0·[illegible]
1586	1,334,756	1,104,023	82·7	194,003	14·5	2·8
1587	1,034,551	823,878	79·6	167,835	16·2	4·2
1588	893,831	722,703	80·8	103,178	11·5	7·7
1589	780,996	656,437	84·0	119,599	15·3	0·7
1590	1,064,298	917,604	86·2	136,754	12·8	1·0
1591	1,142,053	1,021,280	89·4	107,948	9·4	1·2
1592	1,092,072	962,650	88·1	100,167	9·1	2·8
1593	1,321,076	1,178,356	89·1	135,080	10·2	0·7
1594	1,340,415	1,162,750	86·7	163,123	12·1	1·2
1595	1,008,969	856,388	84·8	126,721	12·5	2·7
1596	904,423	769,628	85·1	125,884	13·9	1·0
1597	833,457	668,938	80·2	98,190	11·7	8·1
1598	768,613	616,937	80·2	124,179	16·1	3·7
1599	1,150,535	975,490	84·7	156,023	13·5	1·8
1600	972,200	783,622	80·6	154,891	15·9	3·5

Source *Tabeller over skibsfart . . .*, vol. IIA, pp. 2–196.

from the east, there could have been such a huge demand for English skins in Poland itself.[124] None the less, as the complaints of the Danzig tanners show,[125] the skins and leather products imported by the English and Scottish merchants competed with those of the local producers, and were all the more threatening because, like the Dutch, the English penetrated into the villages and distributed skins and leather goods (belts, gloves, stockings, etc.) on the spot, at the same time buying up raw materials at extremely low prices, thus diminishing the quantities which the gentry and the peasants supplied to the Danzig market.

Apart from skins and hides, English merchants sent white tanned

Table 7.20 *The distribution of skin and hide exports to the Baltic in English vessels at decennial intervals, 1565–95*

Port of destination	1565		1575		1585		1595	
	Items	%	*Items*	%	*Items*	%	*Items*	%
Danzig	621,900	91·5	651,103	100·0	–	–	41,177	5·2
Elbing	–	–	–	–	933,368	95·3	623,836	77·7
Königsberg	3,600	0·5	–	–	44,768	4·5	137,600	17·1
Unidentified ports	53,600	7·8	–	–	1,200	0·2	–	–
Others	600	0·2	–	–	–	–	–	–
Total	679,700	100·0	651,103	100·0	979,336	100·0	802,613	100·0

Note Skins and hides are combined.

Source *Tabeller over skibsfart . . .*, vol. IIA, pp. 15, 47, 101, 161; vol. IIB, pp. 215–28.

leather to the Baltic, and were almost the sole exporters of this type. The Scots also engaged in the trade to a small extent. English white leather exports to the Baltic amounted to 5,000–30,000 pieces per annum; in 1584 it reached the exceptional figure of over 76,000,[126] and in 1587 even 95,925 items.[127] The Sound toll registers thus enable us to show the distribution of skin and hides exports carried in English vessels to the Baltic in the second half of the sixteenth century (table 7.20). Almost all this trade went to the Polish ports of Danzig and Elbing, and to a lesser extent to Königsberg, which became more important in this kind of trade towards the end of the century.

The great majority of the skins and hides exported from England to the Baltic passed through London, which in this field greatly surpassed the northern towns, Hull and Newcastle. In 1595 London's share reached 97·8 per cent.[128]

From the London port book for 1576 it appears that the main exporters of skins to Danzig, to which city all the English capital's

Table 7.21 *London exporters of skins to Danzig, 1575, according to the London port book (number of skins)*

Merchant's name[a]	*Cony skins*	*Sheep skins*	*Morkins*[b]	*Fox skin*	*Polecat skins*	*Lamb skins*	*Other*
Burbedge, Anthony	22,200	3,400	3,200	60	–	–	–
Cartwright, Lawrence and partners	60,000	17,300	4,900	1,520	400	–	1 wolf skin
Cockayne, William; Pearson, Nicholas	57,400	6,160	–	–	–	–	–
Collett, Peter	4,500	–	–	90	–	–	–
Corbett, Thomas	7,360	–	600	1,800	–	–	–
Dickenson, R.	8,000	–	120	–	–	720	–
Finch, Henry	2,000	–	–	–	–	–	–
Fladd, Edward	4,000	–	–	–	–	–	
Friar, Elizabeth	26,000	–	–	–	–	–	–
Fryar, M.	5,000	–	–	180	–	–	–
Gorsuch, Alice	51,000	–	–	120	120	–	–
Grace, Peter	–	1,000	–	–	–	–	–
Halle, William	–	1,000	–	–	400	–	–
Hassell, Percival	16,000	–	–	–	–	–	–
Hayes, John	4,000	–	–	–	–	–	–
Jones, Griffin	7,000	–	–	72	–	–	–
Mayott, Robert	19,360	–	–	280	–	–	–
Pensen, John	2,000	2,400	150	–	–	–	150
Symons, Jarvis	14,000	–	–	–	–	–	–
Watson, William	16,000	–	–	–	–	–	–
Wood, Henry	9,600	–	–	48	168	–	24 cat skins
Total	329,420	31,260	8,970	4,170	1,088	720	175

Notes

[a] The merchants' names are given according to the version in the port book.

[b] The *Shorter Oxford English dictionary*, Oxford, 1959, defines 'morkin' as 'a beast that dies by disease or accident'. [The term seems to be confined to sheep and lambs.]

Source P.R.O., E 190/6/4.

exports of skins to the Baltic were consigned in that year, were well known future members of the Eastland Company—William Cockayne, Nicholas Pearson, and especially Lawrence Cartwright (see table 7.21). The great majority of their exports consisted of cony skins, the rest consisting of small quantities of sheepskins, fox skins, skins of polecats and even of cats, lambskins, etc.

In the second half of the sixteenth century English skin exports showed a tendency towards stabilization, though there was some growth in the years 1584–94. Although skins and hides occupied second place after cloth in English exports to Baltic countries their share in the country's total exports to that area was 11·5 per cent in 1565; 7·4 per cent in 1575; 5·9 per cent in 1585; 4·2 per cent in 1595; and 3·8 per cent in 1605, so it clearly declined in importance.[129]

(b) *Lead and tin*. The Sound toll registers reveal that lead took third place after cloth and skins in exports to the Baltic. Its importance to the county's economy was recognised by the author of some sixteenth-century verses in mentioning the most important raw materials of English industry:

> This realm hath three commodities, wool, tin and lead,
> Which being wrought within the realm each man might get his bread.[130]

From the time of the Romans onwards a plentiful supply of the metal had been mined in England (Pliny mentions it), especially in the northern and western counties: in Cumberland, Yorkshire, Northumberland, Derbyshire and Somerset, and in Wales.[131] For many years too, it was exported from England by her own and foreign merchants, both to the Mediterranean area and to the North Sea and Baltic areas. The Danzig mooring registers mention a small importation of English lead as early as the second half of the fifteenth century.[132] In the sixteenth century most of the lead from England was sent to the Baltic *via* Newcastle, as the Sound toll registers[133] and the Elbing customs registers both show.[134] Hull too played no small part in this trade,[135] and Yarmouth and Ipswich were both involved.

In the second half of the sixteenth century English merchants had an overwhelming supremacy in the export of lead to the Baltic; in the 1570's and 1580's they concentrated almost 100 per cent of the trade in their hands. The Dutch and Scots had only a small share, and were in no sense rivals to England (see table 7.22). The Sound toll registers show that England's lead exports to the Baltic reached their highest level in the years 1584–91. From then on there was a steady decline, though the trade did not come to a complete halt until the beginning of the seventeenth century.

In the second half of the sixteenth century the English also enjoyed supremacy in exports of tin to the Baltic, but it played a much more modest part in her total exports. As is well known, tin mining

Table 7.22 *Exports of lead and tin from the West to the Baltic, 1562–1600*

Year	*Lead*					*Tin*				
	Total (Ship-pounds)	*England*		*Other countries*		*Total (Ship-pounds)*	*England*		*Other countries*	
		Ship-pounds	%	*Ship-pounds*	%		*Ship-pounds*	%	*Ship-pounds*	%
1562	159	126	79·2	33	20·8	–	–	–	–	–
1563	923·5	919·5	99·5	4	0·5	–	–	–	–	–
1564	593·5	593·5	100·0	–	–	–	–	–	–	–
1565	656	541	82·4	115	17·6	6	6·0	100·0	–	–
1566	737	705	95·6	32	4·4	9	9·0	100·0	–	–
1567	205	135	65·8	70	34·2	1·5	1·5	100·0	–	–
1568	500·5	423	84·5	77·5	15·5	24·5	0·3	1·2	24·2	98·8
1569	582	561	96·4	21	3·6	3·1	3·1	100·0	–	–
1574	423	423	100·0	–	–	6·6	6·6	100·0	–	–
1575	583	579	99·3	4	0·7	8·4	8·4	100·0	–	–
1576	591	591	100·0	–	–	7	7·0	100·0	–	–
1577	468	468	100·0	–	–	–	–	–	–	–
1578	489	489	100·0	–	–	–	–	–	–	–
1579	333	333	100·0	–	–	5·6	5·6	100·0	–	–
1580	600	600	100·0	–	–	6·2	6·2	100·0	–	–
1581	535	528	98·6	7	1·4	4·6	4·6	100·0	–	–
1582	516	516	100·0	–	–	–	–	–	–	–
1583	471	459	97·4	12	2·6	2·8	2·8	100·0	–	–
1584	1,479	1,476	99·8	3	0·2	–	–	–	–	–
1585	778·5	778·5	100·0	–	–	–	–	–	–	–
1586	531	531	100·0	–	–	22·9	22·9	100·0	–	–
1587	1,529	1,527	99·8	2	0·2	32·3	32·3	100·0	–	–
1588	702	702	100·0	–	–	11·5	11·5	100·0	–	–
1589	1,707	1,695	99·3	12	0·7	19·2	19·2	100·0	–	–
1590	1,563	1,452	92·9	111	7·1	33·5	32·0	95·5	1·5	4·5
1591	1,758	1,713	97·4	45	2·6	85·8	67·3	78·4	18·5	21·6
1592	993	960	96·6	33	3·4	91·3	88·3	96·7	3	3·3
1593	734	732	99·7	2	0·3	36·5	36·5	100·0	–	–
1594	384	381	99·2	3	0·8	28·5	28·5	100·0	–	–
1595	321	302·5	94·5	18·5	5·5	17·5	17·5	100·0	–	
1596	30	30	100·0	–	–	45·5	45·5	100·0	–	–
1597	389	294	75·5	95	24·5	77·5	77·5	100·0	–	–
1598	153	150	98·0	3	2	28	6·0	21·4	22·0	78·6
1599	24	24	100·0	–	–	40	12·0	30·0	28·0	70·0
1600	52	32	61·5	18	38·5	68·5	60·0	87·6	8·5	12·4

Notes
Shippound 'A unit of weight used in the Baltic trade, ranging from 300 to 400 lbs, = 20 lispounds.'
Lispound (Livonia pound) 'A unit of weight (12–30 lbs) used in the Baltic trade and in Orkney and Shetland.'
Shorter Oxford English dictionary, third edition, 1959.—*Translator.*

Source *Tabeller over skibsfart . . .*, vol. IIA, pp. 2–197.

is one of the oldest of England's extractive industries, and its beginnings reach back into the dusk of prehistory, to the expeditions of the Phoenicians and other merchants from the south. In the Middle Ages England had a monopoly of European tin production. From Fowey, Falmouth, Plymouth and Dartmouth cargoes were despatched to Flanders and France, and thence *via* La Rochelle and

Table 7.23 *The distribution of lead and tin exports from England to the Baltic, decennial intervals 1565–95*

Destination	1565		1575		1585		1595	
	Ship-pounds	%	*Ship-pounds*	%	*Ship-pounds*	%	*Ship-pounds*	%
Lead								
Danzig	342·0	63·2	300·0	51·8	–	–	–	–
Elbing	–	–	–	–	777·0	99·8	264·0	87·2
Königsberg	60·0	11·0	–	–	–	–	6·0	2·1
Denmark	–	–	276·0	47·6	–	–	–	–
Narva	10·0	2·0	–	–	–	–	–	–
Other[a]	129·9	23·8	3·0	0·6	1·5	0·2	32·5	10·7
Total	541·0	100·0	579·0	100·0	778·5	100·0	302·5	100·0
Tin								
Danzig	6·0	100·0	–	–	–	–	–	–
Elbing	–	–	–	–	–	–	–	–
Königsberg	–	–	–	–	–	–	–	–
Riga	–	–	8·4	100·0	–	–	13·0	74·2
Other	–	–	–	–	–	–	4·5	25·8
Total	6·0	100·0	8·4	100·0	–	–	17·5	100·0

Note
[*a*] This item consists largely of ports not identified by the editors of the Sound toll registers.

Source *Tabeller over skibsfart . . .*, vol. IIA, pp. 19, 51, 105, 167; vol. IIB, pp. 217*ff*.

Bordeaux to Marseilles and the towns of the Mediterranean. For a long time Calais was the main entrepot for English tin on the Continent. English and Hanseatic sources both refer to the export of English tin to the Baltic.[136] In the sixteenth century, despite the growing production of tin in Germany and Bohemia, England was still the largest exporter. The country's richest deposits of the mineral were found in Cornwall and, to a lesser extent, in Devon.[137]

Tin mining, like all the English mining and smelting industries of the Elizabethan era, displayed definite capitalistic tendencies; the trade was monopolized by a small group of wealthy London wholesalers, who bought the metal from the Cornish miners and sold it at 100 per cent profit.[138]

The main customers for lead and tin exports to the Baltic area were the Polish ports, and then Denmark, in respect of lead, and Riga in the case of tin (see table 7.23). Elbing's greater share in the importation of English lead, but especially of tin, is indicated by the Elbing customs registers. Comparing them with the Sound toll registers, it appears that Elbing took about a quarter of the lead and about half the tin exported to the Baltic in the late sixteenth and early seventeenth centuries.[139] Lead reached Elbing in vessels mainly from Hull and Newcastle; tin came from London, Aldeburgh, Dover, Ipswich and Dartmouth (see table 7.24).

From fragmentary data it appears that Russia also was an important customer for English lead ; despite protests from Poland, the Empire and the Hansards, England supplied Russia with lead, iron, gunpowder, saltpetre and other military materials.[140] Scattered references indicate that England's lead exports to Russia were considerable, in certain years exceeding those to Poland. In 1564 England sent Russia 312 shippounds [52 fothers] of lead,[141] which was not much less than England's exports to Danzig for the same year (342 shippounds). In 1576 the Muscovy Company sent 90 shippounds of lead to Moscow, and 591 shippounds were sent to the Baltic, the Russian proportion of the joint exports to the Baltic and Russia being 13·2 per cent. In 1599 the picture was different. In that year England sent 355·5 shippounds of lead to Archangel, and only 24 to the Baltic.[142]

When we turn to a consideration of tin exports, from the few data which have survived it would seem that Russia played a much greater part in this trade than Poland. In 1562 England exported about thirty shippounds of tin to Russia, and in 1565 only six to the Baltic; in 1599 about sixty-four shippounds went to Russia, and twelve to the Baltic.[143] However, all these data are very fragmentary, and it is difficult to draw any general conclusions from them as to the rivalry between the Baltic and Russian markets for England's lead and tin.

(c) *Military materials.* As we noted in chapter two, England also exported weapons and other military materials to the Baltic and to Russia. English merchants sold ammunition to both Russia and Sweden, but no details of the transactions are known. In 1591 there

Table 7.24 *The respective shares of various English ports in exports of lead and tin to Elbing, 1586, 1587 and 1594*

Port of origin	1586				1587				1594			
	Lead		*Tin*		*Lead*		*Tin*		*Lead*		*Tin*	
	Centners	%	*Centners*	%	*Centners*	%	*Centners*	%	*Centners*	%	*Centners*	%
Hull	119	35·8	–	–	849	79·6	–	–	–	–	–	–
Newcastle	213	64·2	–	–	207	19·4	–	–	228	100·0	–	–
London	–	–	45	100·0	10	1	–	–	–	–	5	100·0
Aldeburgh	–	–	–	–	–	–	40	44·4	–	–	–	–
Dover	–	–	–	–	–	–	30	33·4	–	–	–	–
Ipswich	–	–	–	–	–	–	10	11·1	–	–	–	–
Dartmouth	–	–	–	–	–	–	10	11·1	–	–	–	–
Total	332	100·0	45	100·0	1,066	100·0	90	100·0	228	100·0	5	100·0

Note The centner seems to have been roughly equivalent to the English hundredweight.

Source W.A.P.Gd., Lib. port. Elbing, 1586, 1587, 1594.

is a reference to attempts by the Duke of Pomerania to obtain 100 guns in exchange for the export of saltpetre to England.[144] It seems that the traffic in weapons and war materials to the Baltic was rather sporadic; in general—as we shall be discussing later—it was the English who imported goods necessary for the manufacture of armaments (gunpowder, saltpetre, etc) from the Baltic countries.

(d) *Alum.* English merchants also played an important part in the export of certain minerals to the Baltic, especially alum and red lead. In 1575 English exports of red lead formed the whole of the export to the Baltic (300 lb).[145] Data in the Sound registers testify to the considerable extent of English middleman activities in exporting alum to the Baltic countries. In 1565 England took second place after Holland in this trade (Holland 30 lasts, England, about seven, France about three).[146] In 1585 four lasts of alum sent from England represented 100 per cent of the entire export to the Baltic.[147] A considerable share of England's exports of alum consigned to the Baltic in 1565 went to Narva (40 per cent)[148] and to Danzig (20 per cent).[149] In 1585 all the English alum exports to the Baltic went to Elbing.[150] The 1587 Elbing customs register records that two shipmasters from Ipswich brought 53 centners of alum to the port in that year.[151] Converse instances also occurred. For instance, in 1594 the London vessel *Maria Rosa* took on board 72 centners of alum at Elbing consigned to London.[152] Documents of the Muscovy Company refer to larger shipments of alum from England to Russia in 1591 but do not state the quantity.[153]

Alum was an important element in the process of dyeing cloth, as a mordant,[154] and so the demand for this mineral grew everywhere commensurately with the increase in cloth production. It appeared rather meagrely in the Baltic countries, but from Rybarski's work it seems that in the second half of the sixteenth century there was not a great quantity of it in Poland either.[155] In the fifteenth century the largest alum mines were in Asia Minor, and were controlled by Genoese merchants. The Turkish occupation of the mines in 1455 practically cut off the European market from its largest source of supply, and necessitated a search for new reserves of this valuable material. It was found in Italy, Spain, Germany and other countries, but the deposits in central Italy, outside Tolfa, not far from Civita Vecchia, within the territory of the Papal State, were of the greatest importance; because of them the Papacy became for a time a monopolist of this mineral, leasing its production to various wealthy trading groups, including the Medicis.[156] In the middle of the sixteenth century an association of Italian merchants operating in Antwerp (including Agostino Sauli, Niccolò Palavicino and Battista Spinola) played an important part in the distribution of alum. In 1566 the Pope leased the Tolfa mines for twelve years to the Genoese merchant Tobias Palavicino, who extended his trade in alum to England, where a representative of the Palavicino family was already operating.[157] Horatio Palavicino estimated English imports of Italian alum in 1578 at about 10,000 quintals yearly, which amounted

Table 7.25 *The volume and distribution of coal exports from Newcastle upon Tyne, 1608–09*

Destination	*Coal*		*No. of vessels*	*Average chaldrons per vessel*
	Chaldrons	*%*		
Netherlands	7,875	50·7	176	46
France	3,646	23·7	106	34
Denmark	1,512	9·7	30	50
Germany	1,483	9·5	35	42
Poland	586	3·7	12	49
Norway	300	1·9	11	27
Sweden	107	0·8	2	54
Total	15,509	100·0	372	43

Source B. Hall, 'The trade of Newcastle upon Tyne and the north-east coast', MS, Institute of Historical Research, London, p. 112.

to about 30 per cent of total European demand at that time. Part of these imports was re-exported by the English to the Baltic, an area in which English merchants acted as middlemen. At the start of the seventeenth century England opened up her own works for alum production, especially in Yorkshire.[158]

(e) *Coal.* Coal is also found among the commodities exported to the Baltic by English merchants. It had long been an item in the trade of northern England, and from the fourteenth century on we come across quite numerous references to the subject.[159] English coal was particularly in demand in the Netherlands; France also was an important customer for English coal from the beginning of the fourteenth century. There is even a saying, dating from the middle of the sixteenth century, that France could no more live without coals from Newcastle than could a fish without water.[160] Almost all exports of English coal to the Baltic were consigned from Newcastle.

Data from the beginning of the seventeenth century show that the Baltic market did not occupy the main place in England's coal exports. In this respect Holland, France, Denmark and Germany were of greater importance. Poland occupied fifth place, above Norway and Sweden (see table 7.25). In the Elizabethan era Hull was of minor importance as an export port for coal. In 1609 a total of 360 chaldrons of coal was despatched from this port, 41 per cent of it to

Table 7.26 *Exports of coal from England to Elbing, 1586, 1587, 1594 and 1605*

Port of origin	1586		1587		1594		1605	
	Barrels	%	*Barrels*	%	*Barrels*	%	*Barrels*	%
Newcastle	138	71·8	147	82·3	214·5	100·0	30	100·0
London	–	–	31·5	17·7	–	–	–	–
Yarmouth	30	15·6	–	–	–	–	–	–
Aldeburgh	24	12·6	–	–	–	–	–	–
Total	192	100·0	178·5	100·0	214·5	100·0	30	100·0

Note For purposes of comparison, lasts have been converted into barrels in the ratio of one last to three barrels: cf C. Biernat, *Statystyka obrotu towarowego Gdańska w latach 1651–1815* (*Danzig trade statistics for 1651–1815*), Warsaw, 1962, p. 70; also W. H. Prior, *Notes on weights and measures in medieval England*, Paris, 1924.

Source W.A.P.Gd., Lib. port. Elbing, 1586, 1587, 1594, 1605.

Holland and 31·6 per cent to Elbing.[161] Newcastle's predominance in English coal exports to Poland is best shown by resort to the Elbing customs registers for the end of the sixteenth and beginning of the seventeenth centuries (see table 7.26).

(f) *Grindstones and millstones.* These were also exported to the Baltic from Newcastle. The Elbing customs registers give the following quantities: in 1586, 5 lasts and 108 items; in 1594 24·5 lasts; in 1605, 5 lasts. In 1586 English vessels also brought 6 lasts of grindstones from Aldeburgh.[134]

(g) *Groceries.* In certain years during the second half of the sixteenth century English merchants, almost exclusively of London, played quite a large part as middlemen in the export of groceries to the Baltic countries, above all to Poland. Together with the Dutch, the French and the Portuguese they despatched sugar, currants, pepper, figs, ginger, indigo, cloves, dates, saffron, etc, to the Baltic, mainly to Danzig and Elbing. Some of these goods travelled on in transit through Poland to the south, to Silesia, Bohemia, and the south German lands. Narva and Riga, and Moscow also, received a certain quantity of these goods consigned in English ships, but the data available for these places are only fragmentary.

Table 7.27 *The chief groceries exported in English vessels to the Baltic, decennial intervals 1565–1615 (Danish thalers)*

	1565	1575	1585	1595	1605	1615
Sugar and sugar cane	762	4,893	678·5	3,242	1,026	–
Currants	86	3,551	80	450	1,200	478
Pepper	888	47	–	1,500	–	1,561
Figs	151	1,747	462·5	–	–	77
Ginger	–	70	–	1,161	–	346·5
Rice	38	204	–	–	462	–
Dyes	–	12	–	440	100	–
Indigo	–	–	–	–	650	–
Cloves	–	–	–	360	–	–
Dates	234	–	–	–	–	–
Saffron	30	24·5	–	–	–	–
Nutmegs	50	–	–	–	–	–

Source *Tabeller over skibsfart* . . . , vol. IIA, pp. 24, 57, 113*f*, 177, 241, 304.

England's chief source of grocery supplies was Antwerp, where English merchants bought sugar and other southern products to sell at a profit to the Baltic countries. After the fall of Antwerp in 1585, and the development of English trade with the Levant and Morocco, the English merchants obtained their grocery supplies from the Mediterranean area. Late in the sixteenth century they also sailed to South America for them, especially for sugar.[162] England obtained enormous quantities of groceries through the activities of her privateers on the seas and oceans. We need only mention that in the years 1589–91 alone the value of the sugar the privateers captured was at least some £100,000, which would be equivalent to a quantity of about 30,000 cwt[163] and so more or less the same quantity as England's total annual sugar imports from Morocco. Towards the end of the sixteenth century a large quantity of groceries, originating mainly in America, reached London in this manner. The Elbing customs registers show that sugar, and then almonds, ginger and currants, were the most important grocery items exported to Poland in the late sixteenth century.[164]

(h) *Salt*. England exported hardly any salt to the Baltic. The Sound toll registers show only a few dozen lasts of salt annually from England before 1566, and several hundred lasts in the following years. At the end of the century her salt exports to the Baltic again fell to a few dozen lasts annually, and by comparison with the thousands of lasts of salt which the Dutch transported to the Baltic every year this amount was extremely modest.[165]

(i) *Herrings*. The English merchants' share in the export of herrings to the Baltic was very slight. For many years herrings had been one of the principal items of northern trade; control resting first in the hands of the Hansards, and later with the Dutch, who dominated this branch of Baltic trade in the period under consideration.

(j) *Other goods*. The English port books also contain sparse references to the export of several other kinds of goods to the Baltic, though none was of great importance. Among the items mentioned are gloves (e.g. in 1599, 200 pairs of 'Muscovie gloves' were despatched from London to Archangel[166]) and stockings (in 1599, 180 pairs of stockings, among other items, were sent from London to Elbing,[166] and, in 1604, 40 dozen 'kersey stockings', also to Elbing[167]). Sources mention the export of felt hats to Poland, but there is no telling whether these were of English manufacture or were re-exported from Spain. At this time England was importing quite large quantities of hats from Spain and Portugal, as is evidenced by the privileges granted in 1561 and 1562 to Portuguese merchants to import during these two years 30,000 dozen felt hats from the Iberian peninsula.[168] Scattered references also mention beer being exported to Poland. In 1599 the Governor of the Eastland Company, Thomas Russell, consigned ten barrels of beer from London to Elbing, and in the same year John Collett despatched the same quantity.[166] We find casual mention in the English port books of the export of alabaster slabs to Poland,[169] as well as buffalo horns (2,000 items in 1576), copper,

Table 7.28 *The structure of English exports shipped in English vessels to the Baltic countries, decennial intervals 1565–1605*

	1565		1575		1585		1595		1605	
	Thalers	%	*Thalers*	%	*Thalers*	%	*Thalers*	%	*Thalers*	%
Cloth	78,422	77·9	141,441	75·3	373,013	91·4	424,842	92·1	528,128	91·6
Skins and hides	11,592	11·5	13,944	7·4	24,262	5·9	19,438	4·2	22,085	3·8
Lead	4,182	4·1	4,362	2·3	5,818	1·4	2,739	0·6	–	–
Groceries	2,648	2·6	11,109	5·9	1,441	0·4	7,272	1·6	3,608	0·6
Minerals	1,583	1·6	14	–	810	0·2	–	–	–	–
White leather	885	0·9	1,044	0·5	1,850	0·5	558	0·1	3,325	0·6
Salt	810	0·8	7,768	4·1	320	0·1	726	0·2	1,974	0·3
Tin	300	0·3	552	0·3	–	–	480	0·1	559	0·1
Paper	155	0·2	15	–	–	–	–	–	–	–
Other	69	0·1	7,662	4·2	456	0·1	5,165	1·1	16,775[a]	3·0
Total	100,646	100·0	187,911	100·0	407,970	100·0	461,220	100·0	576,454	100·0

Note
[a] Includes herrings valued at 2,320 thalers.

Source *Tabeller over skibsfart . . .*, vol. IIA, pp. 15, 24, 25, 47, 57, 58, 100, 113, 114, 162, 176, 177, 225, 241, 242

wine and spirits (aqua vitae)[166] and also paper, which England sent mainly to Russia (180 reams in 1564;[141] 626 reams in 1576;[69] 1,335 reams and 80 pounds in 1599.[166] This last item included 280 reams of Spanish paper). The Elbing customs registers also mention the export from England of vinegar, honey[170] and even Venetian sword blades (in 1605, 47 dozen from London).[171]

4 *The structure of English exports to the Baltic countries*

The Sound toll registers enable us to construct a table presenting the fluctuations and structure of all the English exports to the Baltic area in the second half of the sixteenth century and the beginning of the seventeenth (table 7.28). It is possible to present this complete picture of the export trade in tabular form for such a long period because the Sound registers note the prices of English commodities passing through the Sound by means of the duty already mentioned of one per cent *ad valorem* (see above, p. 186) imposed by the King of Denmark. Analysis of the fluctuations in English exports to the Baltic in the second half of the sixteenth century reveals above all that, as we have already pointed out, there was a very definite and rapid rise in these exports from 1565 to 1585. During these twenty years English exports increased fourfold, doubling each decade. The growth in exports was much slower at the end of the century and the beginning of the seventeenth, i.e. during the period of crisis which was developing in all England's foreign trade.

Analysis of the structure of England's exports to the Baltic underlines the tremendous predominance of cloth, exports of which increased throughout the second half of the century, comprising over 90 per cent of the country's exports to the Baltic. Parallel with this phenomenon there was a fall in the importance of other commodities, with skins, lead and groceries at their head. This type of structure, with its enormous predominance of cloth, was not confined to England's Baltic trade, but was present in all her foreign trade. In exports from London in 1565 (the only year with general data that are usable) textiles formed 90·1 per cent, lead and tin 4·7 per cent.[172] Only as the result of her cloth exports was England able to develop her foreign trade to all parts of the contemporary world.

Notes

1 W.A.P.Gd., 300, 19, mooring register for 1583.
2 Cf Zins, 'Angielskie księgi portowe ...' This article discusses the question more broadly and cites the most important literature. [See also N. Williams, 'The London port books', *Trans. London and Middlesex Archaeological Society*, vol. XVIII, 1956; W. B. Stephens, 'The Exchequer port books as a source for the history of the English cloth trade', *Textile History*, vol. I, 1969, pp. 206–13; D. M. Woodward, 'Short guide to records: port books', *History*, vol. 55, 1970, pp. 207–10.] An extensive study of the value of the Sound toll registers for research into the history of trade in the sixteenth, seventeenth and eighteenth centuries has been made by P. Jeannin, 'Les Comptes du Sund comme source pour le construction d'indices généraux de l'activité économique en Europe, XVIe–XVIIIe siècles', *Revue Historique*, vol. CCXXXI, 1964, pp. 55*ff*.
3 N. J. Williams, *Contraband cargoes: seven centuries of smuggling*, London, 1959.
4 For broader discussion of this subject, see Zins, 'Angielski księgi portowe ...', pp. 152*ff*.
5 *England's export trade.*
6 *Ibid.*, pp. 18–33.
7 Ramsey, 'Overseas trade in the reign of Henry VII ...', pp. 176*ff*.
8 D. Schäfer, 'Die Sundzollrechnungen als internationale Geschichtsquelle', *Internationale Wochenschrift für Wissenschaft Kunst und Technik*, vol. I, 1907, pp. 365–74, 401–10.
9 G. W. Kernkamp, 'De Nederlanders op de Ostzee', *Vragen des Tijds*, vol. XXXV, 1909, pp. 65–96.
10 E. Baasch, *Holländische Wirtschaftsgeschichte*, 1927, Jena.
11 S. van Brakel, 'Schiffsheimat und Schifferheimat in den Sundzoll-registern', *Hansische Geschichtsblätter*, vol. XXI, 1915, pp. 211–28.
12 Christensen, 'Der handelsgeschichtliche Wert ...', pp. 28–142.
13 L. Koczy, 'Nowe źródła do dziejów handlu Polski na Morzu Bałtyckim' ('New sources for the history of Polish trade in the Baltic Sea'), *R.D.S.G.*, vol. VI, 1937, pp. 179–213.
14 A. Friis, 'Bemaerkninger till vurdering af Öresundstoldregnskaberne og principerne for deres udgivelse', *Historisk Tidskrift*, R. 9, vol. IV, 1925, pp. 109–82.
15 Christensen, *Dutch trade in the Baltic ...*, pp. 60*f*.
16 M. Bogucka, 'Udział szyprów gdańskich w handlu bałtyckim pierwszej połowy XVII w.' ('Danzig shipmasters' share in Baltic trade in the first half of the seventeenth century'), *Zapiski Historyczne*, vol. XXIX, 1964, No. 4, pp. 16*f*.
17 Cf R. W. K. Hinton, 'The mercantile system in the time of Thomas Mun', *Ec.H.R.*, second series, vol. VII, 1955, No. 3, p. 279.

18 Christensen, 'Der handelsgeschichtliche Wert . . .', p. 37.
19 *Ibid.*, p. 42.
20 *Ibid.*, p. 46.
21 *Ibid.*, p. 52.
22 *Ibid.*, p. 61.
23 *Ibid.*, pp. 90–2.
24 *Ibid.*, p. 138.
25 Cf Małowist, *Studia z dziejów rzemiosła . . .*, pp. 209*ff.*
26 *Tudor economic documents*, vol. III, pp. 134–5. Cholmeley wrote that 'for all marchauntis of this part of the worlde doe and must of necessitie seke our cloth as the chepe marchaundice that marchaundizeth in all quarters of the worlde as well as golde and sylver do'.
27 *Ibid.*, p. 139.
28 Wheeler, *op. cit.*, p. 55. This writer spoke of cloth as the 'principallest commodity of the realme' and the 'credite and creame of the land'.
29 W. Camden, *Britannia; sive florentissimorum regnorum Angliae, Scotiae, Hiberniae chorographica descriptio*, London, 1606, p. 247.
30 *Cal.S.P. Venice, 1610–13*, p. 3.
31 Of recent works, see P. J. Bowden, *The wool trade in Tudor and Stuart England*, London, 1962. Also E. Lipson, *The history of the English woollen and worsted industries*, London, 1921. The problem was discussed extensively with special reference to the northern English cloth centres by H. Heaton, *Yorkshire woollen and worsted industries*, Oxford, 1920.
32 P. J. Bowden, 'Wool supply and the woollen industry', *Ec.H.R.*, second series, vol. IX, 1956, p. 53.
33 G. D. Ramsay, *The Wiltshire woollen industry in the sixteenth and seventeenth centuries*, Oxford, 1943.
34 On the question of Cornish trade see J. C. A. Whetter, 'Cornish trade in the seventeenth century: an analysis of the port books', *Journal of the Royal Institute of Cornwall*, new series, vol. IV, 1964, pp. 388–413.
35 Cf Bowden, *The wool trade . . .*, p. 50.
36 'Shortcloth' was the term for a measure of cloth 24 yards long which was used by customs officers in calculating various kinds of cloth for fiscal purposes; cf B. E. Supple, *Commercial crisis and change . . .*, p. 257. A book of rates dated 1558 fixed the relationships between various kinds of cloth as follows: 1 shortcloth = 1 northern double dozen = 2 Devonshire double dozens = 3 kerseys of any kind = 4 Devonshire single dozens, etc. Cf *A Tudor book of rates*, ed. T. S. Willan, Manchester, 1962, pp. 73*f.*
37 P.R.O., S.P. Supplementary 46/9, f. 20. In 1557 a sett cloth was noted in Danzig at 10–14 florins, whereas a broadcloth cost 24–30 florins.
38 G. Unwin, 'Industries of Suffolk', in *V.C.H. Suffolk*, vol. II, London, 1907, p. 259.
39 *Ibid.*, p. 265.
40 Cf Heaton, *op. cit.*, *passim.*

41 Schanz, *op. cit.*, vol. II, p. 17, and Friis, *Alderman Cockayne's project . . .*, p. 60.
42 Lipson, *The economic history of England*, vol. I, p. 485.
43 *Cal.S.P.Dom., 1598–1601*, p. 208.
44 *L.P. Henry VIII*, vol. XVI, p. 410.
45 *A.P.C., 1575–77*, p. 381.
46 *Cal.S.P.Dom., 1591–94*, p. 321.
47 P.R.O. Patent Rolls, 21 Elizabeth, c. 66/1185, f. 24.
48 P.R.O., S.P.Dom. 14/118, No. 114.
49 Friis, *Alderman Cockaynes' project . . .*, p. 230.
50 *Calendar of the Manuscripts of Major-General Lord Sackville*, pp. 35–8.
51 *Ibid.*, p. 36: '. . . the workmen of Poland having white cloths practise to dye and dress other colours to please the countries far beyond them . . .'
52 *Ibid.*, p. 37.
53 B.M., Sloane MSS 25, ff. 5–6. The Eastland Company's 1602 petition has the title 'The answere of the Companie of Eastland merchaunts with their reasons why rough undrest clothes should be transported to the place where they be resident . . .'
54 The petition mentions the decline in exports of English cloth to the Baltic as about 6,000 pieces per annum.
55 *Tabeller over skibsfart . . .*, vol. IIA, pp. 15, 24.
56 *Ibid.*, pp. 47, 57.
57 *Ibid.*, pp. 101, 113.
58 *Ibid.*, pp. 162, 176.
59 *Ibid.*, pp. 225, 241.
60 *Ibid.*, pp. 289, 304.
61 On the subject of the Cockayne plan see Friis, *Alderman Cockayne's project . . .*, *passim*.
62 *Tabeller over skibsfart . . .*, vol. IIA, pp. 355, 372.
63 Cf the *Dictionary of national biography*, vol. XIII, p. 387.
64 *Cal.S.P.For., 1572–74*, p. 393. In this conversation Elizabeth's ambassador said 'how ancient the amity had been between the Queen's progenitors and the subjects of Poland and . . . what riches did come of the staple that was at Dantzig for cloth'.
65 *Cal.S.P. Venice, 1592–1603*, p. 556.
66 V. Barbour, *op. cit.*, *passim*.
67 J. E. Riemenska, 'Government influence on company organization in Holland and England, 1550–1650', *Journal of Economic History*, supplement X, 1950, pp. 31–9.
68 J. D. Gould, 'The crisis in the export trade, 1586–87', *E.H.R.*, vol. LXXI, 1956, No. 279, p. 212; also Baasch, *op. cit.*, p. 259.
69 F. J. Fisher, 'Commercial trends and policy in sixteenth-century England', p. 153.
70 *Tabeller over skibsfart . . .*, vol. IIA, pp. 200–8.
71 *Ibid.*, pp. 15, 47, 101, 161, 223, 287, 353.

72 P.R.O., E 190/2/1. [This port book covers the period from Easter to Michaelmas 1565, and not the whole year.]
73 *Tabeller over skibsfart* . . ., vol. IIA, p. 15.
74 Cf Brakel, *op. cit.*, pp. 211–28, and Christensen, *Dutch trade to the Baltic* . . ., pp. 55–64.
75 W.A.P.Gd., Lib. port. Elbing, 1586 and 1594.
76 *Tabeller over skibsfart* . . ., vol. IIA, pp. 15, 47, 101, 161, 223.
77 P.R.O., E 190/312/6.
78 B. Hall, 'The trade of Newcastle-upon-Tyne and the north-east coast, 1600–40', typescript in the Institute of Historical Research, London. I must express my gratitude to the director of the Institute for making this doctoral thesis available to me.
79 *Tabeller over skibsfart* . . ., vol. IIA, p. 256.
80 P.R.O., E 190/185/6.
81 *Ibid.*, E 315/485.
82 In a document dating from 1573 and putting forward a plan for establishing a staple at Ipswich and for granting the merchants of that city special trading privileges is the remark: 'Wheare the county of Suffolke (in which county the said Towne of Ipswiche doth stand) is a country of moche draping of clothe, yet the great nomber of all that clothe draped there servith for Dansicke and the east partes, and so for Spayne, Portugall and other partes of the South'—*Tudor economic documents*, vol. III, p. 192.
83 *Ibid.*, pp. 173*ff*.
84 In 1614 Tobias Gentleman wrote in *England's way to win wealth*, 1614, p. 23, that 'the Ipswich men be the chiefest merchant adventurers of all England for all the Eastlands for the Suffolk cloths, and they have their factors all the year round in all those places'.
85 P.R.O., E 190/589/6.
86 W.A.P.Gd., Lib. port. Elbing, 1594 and 1605.
87 *Ibid.*, 1586.
88 *Ibid.*; also P.R.O., E 190/426/2 and E 190/428/7.
89 A document dating from *circa* 1580 entitled 'A speciall direction for divers trades' gives the following prices: for fine cloth [falendisch] £13, the piece, but for Devon kersey only £1 10*s*—*Tudor economic documents*, vol. III, p. 209. At that time a piece of ordinary *Luński* cloth cost £9. Cf J. E. T. Rogers, *A history of agriculture and prices in England*, vol. IV, Oxford, 1882, pp. 587*f*.
90 A. Mączak, 'Rola kontaktów z zagranicą w dziejach sukiennictwa polskiego XVI i pierwszej połowy XVII wieku' ('The part played by contacts abroad in the history of the Polish cloth industry during the sixteenth and early seventeenth centuries'), *P.H.*, vol. XLIII, 1952, No. 2, p. 247.
91 W.A.P.Gd., Lib. port. Elbing, 1586, 1587, 1594, 1599. The Elbing customs registers differentiate *gemein Lundisch*, ('common *Luński*')

breite Lacken ('broadcloth'), *fein Lundisch* (*falendisch*), etc. English sources have no equivalent for the term *Luński.*

92 Cf R. Rybarski, *Handel i polityka handlowa Polski w XVI stuleciu* (*Poland's trade and trading policy in the sixteenth century*), vol. I, Warsaw, 1958, pp. 163*f*. Also Mączak, *Sukiennictwo wielkopolskie* . . ., p. 230.

93 Cf *Księga Theudenkusa* (*Book of Theudenkus*), ed. L. Koczy, Toruń, 1937, pp. 8, 10, 16, 17, etc.

94 Cf Lauffer, *op. cit.*, p. 22.

95 Rybarski, *op. cit.*, vol. I, p. 165; also L. Koczy, *Handel Poznania do połowy wieku XVI* (*Poznanian trade to the middle of the sixteenth century*), Poznań, 1930, pp. 286*ff*.

96 J. Pelc, *Ceny w Krakowie w latach 1369–1600* (*Prices in Cracow, 1369–1600*), Lwów, 1935, p. 69 (introduction).

97 For example, the Bishop of Warmia, Ferber, in his will dated 1537, left two pieces of red *Luński* cloth to his steward. Cf H. Zins, 'Nieznany testament biskupa warmińskiego Maurycego Ferbera' ('A previously unknown will of the Bishop of Warmia, Maurice Ferber'), *Rocznik Olsztynski* (*Olsztyn Yearbook*), vol. I, 1958, p. 232.

98 Cf Mączak, *Sukiennictwo wielkopolskie* . . ., p. 232.

99 Rybarski, *op. cit.*, vol. I, p. 170. But it follows from investigations made by A. Wawrzyńczykowa, in *Studia z dziejów handlu Polski z Wielkim Ksiestwem Litewskim i Rosją w XVI w.* (*Studies in the history of Poland's trade with the Grand Duchy of Lithuania and Russia in the sixteenth century*), Warsaw, 1956, p. 59, that a comparatively small quantity of English cloth appeared on the Lublin market in the second half of the sixteenth century, and that it was exported thence to Lithuania in small quantities.

100 Rybarski, *op. cit.*, vol. I, p. 171.

101 'A speciall direction for divers trades' in *Tudor economic documents*, vol. III, p. 209.

102 W.A.P.Gd., Lib. port. Elbing, 1586, 1587, 1594, etc.

103 Mączak, *Sukiennictwo wielkopolskie* . . ., p. 231.

104 Rogers, *op. cit.*, vol. IV, pp. 587*f*.

105 W.A.P.Gd., Lib. port. Elbing, 1594.

106 W. Beck, *The draper's dictionary: a manual of textile fabrics*, London (n.d.), pp. 179–80.

107 Mączak, *Sukiennictwo wielkopolskie* . . ., p. 232. English kersey was some 20–25 per cent dearer than Silesian.

108 S. Słupski, *Zabawy orackie* (*Orak amusements*), Cracow, 1891, p. 24.

109 R. H. Tawney, 'Lionel Cranfield as merchant and Minister' in *Business and politics under James I*, Cambridge, 1958, p. 55.

110 Cf Hinton, *The Eastland trade* . . ., p. 33.

111 Rogers, *op. cit.*, compares the prices of two kinds of cloth, but only with large gaps. For Poland, see J. Pelc, *Ceny w Gdańsku w XVI i XVII wieku* (*Prices in Danzig in the sixteenth and seventeenth centuries*), Lwów,

1937; also his *Ceny w Krakowie w latach 1369–1600* (*Prices in Cracow, 1369–1600*), Lwów, 1935; S. Hoszowski, *Ceny w Lwowie w XVI i XVII wieku* (*Prices in Lwów in the sixteenth and seventeenth centuries*), Lwów, 1928; W. Adamczyk, *Ceny w Lublinie od XVI do konca XVIII wieku* (*Prices in Lublin from the sixteenth to the end of the eighteenth centuries*), Lwów, 1835, and other volumes in the same series.

112 *Tabeller over skibsfart . . .*, vol. IIA, p. 34; also Willan, *The early history of the Russia Company*, p. 82.

113 Willan, *op cit.*, pp. 175, 180.

114 *Ibid.*, p. 186.

115 *Ibid.*, p. 252.

116 *Tabeller over skibsfart . . .*, vol. IIA, p. 188.

117 J. Trevers, *An essay to the restoring of our decayed trade, etc.*, London, 1675, p. 58.

118 Attman, *op. cit.*, pp. 407*ff.*

119 On the subject of leather production in England at the end of the sixteenth and the beginning of the seventeenth centuries, see L. A. Clarkson, 'The organization of the English leather industry in the late sixteenth and seventeenth centuries', *Ec.H.R.*, second series, vol. XIII, 1960, No. 2, pp. 245–56.

120 *Tabeller over skibsfart . . .*, vol. IIA, pp. 24, 57.

121 *Ibid.*, pp. 51, 61, 65.

122 Rybarski, *op. cit.*, vol. I, p. 87.

123 Cf H. Obuchowska-Pysiowa, *Handel wiślany w pierwszej połowie XVII wieku* (*Vistula trade in the first half of the seventeenth century*), Wrocław, 1964, p. 116.

124 M. Bogucka, *Gdańsk jako ośrodek produkcyjny w XIV–XVII w.* (*Danzig as a production centre in the fourteenth to seventeenth centuries*), Warsaw, 1962, pp. 184*f.*

125 *Ibid.*, p. 89.

126 *Tabeller over skibsfart . . .*, vol. IIA, p. 93.

127 *Ibid.*, p. 123.

128 *Ibid.*, p. 161.

129 *Tabeller over skibsfart . . .*, vol. IIA.

130 Clark, *The wealth of England . . .*, p. 49.

131 *An historical geography of England before 1800*, ed. H. C. Darby, Cambridge, 1951, pp. 256*f.*

132 H. Samsonowicz, *Handel zagraniczny Gdańska . . .*, p. 303.

133 *Tabeller over skibsfart . . .*, vol. IIA, pp. 15, 47, 101, 162.

134 W.A.P.Gd., Lib. port. Elbing, 1586, 1594, 1605.

135 In 1575 the anonymous author of the pamphlet *Sertaine causes of the decay of the traffique in Kyngston-upon-Hull* emphasized that the decline in lead exports through Hull was due, among other things, to the growth in activities of the London merchants, who dominated the trading companies.—*Tudor economic documents*, vol. II, p. 49.

136 *Studies in English trade . . .*, pp. 402–6.
137 *An historical geography of England*, p. 259. In the fourteenth century Cornwall produced over ten times as much tin as Devon.
138 Cf Rowse, *op. cit.*, p. 129. Cf also G. R. Lewis, *The Stanneries: a study of the English tin mines*, Harvard, 1908.
139 *Tabeller over skibsfart . . .*, vol. IIA, pp. 119, 123, 151, 231; also W.A.P.Gd., Lib. port. Elbing, 1586, 1594, 1605.
140 *Cal.S.P.For., 1561–62*, Nos. 112, 156, 217, pp. 59, 90, 126*f*.
141 Willan, *The early history of the Russia Company*, p. 53. [Professor Zins converts fothers into shippounds at the rate of 1 fother = 6 shippounds.]
142 P.R.O., E 190/10/11, and *Tabeller over skibsfart . . .*, vol. IIA, p. 193.
143 *Tabeller over skibsfart . . .*, vol. IIA, p. 105. Also Willan, *The early history of the Russia Company*, p. 253.
144 J. Gerds, a servant of the Duke of Pomerania, to Lord Burghley, 23 December 1591: Historical Manuscripts Commission, *Calendar of the manuscripts . . . Hatfield House*, vol. IV, London, 1892, p. 165.
145 *Tabeller over skibsfart . . .*, vol. IIA, p. 57.
146 *Ibid.*, p. 24.
147 *Ibid.*, p. 113.
148 *Tabeller over skibsfart . . .*, vol. IIB, p. 223.
149 *Ibid.*, p. 215.
150 *Ibid.*, p. 219.
151 W.A.P.Gd., Lib. port. Elbing, 1586, ff. 21, 33.
152 *Ibid.*, f. 31.
153 Willan, *The early history of the Russia Company*, p. 249.
154 Cf L. F. Salzman, *English industries of the Middle Ages*, Oxford, 1923, p. 208; also M. Bogucka, *Gdańskie rzemiosło tekstylne od XVI do połowy XVII wieku* (*Danzig textile crafts from the sixteenth to the mid-seventeenth century*), Wrocław, 1956, p. 129. On the subject of English trade in alum, see R. Jenkins, 'The alum trade in the fifteenth and sixteenth centuries and the beginning of the alum industry in England', *Collected papers*, Cambridge, 1936. Cf. also R. B. Turton, *The alum farm*, Whitby, 1938.
155 Rybarski, *op. cit.*, vol. I, p. 145.
156 Stone, *An Elizabethan . . .*, pp. 41*ff*.
157 *Ibid.*, p. 47.
158 Cf J. U. Nef, 'War and economic progress, 1540–1640', *Ec.H.R.*, vol. XII, 1942, p. 23.
159 J. U. Nef has written a fundamental work on this subject: *The rise of the British coal industry*, vol. I, London, 1932. The organization of English coal mining in the Elizabethan era was discussed by L. Stone, 'An Elizabethan coalmine', *Ec.H.R.*, second series, vol. III, 1950, No. 1, pp. 97–106.
160 Lipson, *The economic history of England . . .*, vol. II, p. 116.
161 B. Hall, *op. cit.*, p. 283.

162 Willan, *Studies in Elizabethan foreign trade*, chapter 5, 'Sugar and Elizabethans', pp. 313*ff*.
163 K. R. Andrews, 'The economic aspects of Elizabethan privateering', *Bulletin of the Institute of Historical Research*, vol. xxv, p. 86; also his: *Elizabethan privateering*, p. 207. Both works discuss in detail the economic aspect of English privateering at the end of the sixteenth century.
164 W.A.P.Gd., Lib. port. Elbing, 1586, ff. 13, 18, 24, 25, 28, 29, 33, 35, 44, 61.
165 Cf Bridbury, *op. cit.*
166 P.R.O., E 190/10/11.
167 *Ibid.*, E 190/599/4.
168 *Calendar of Patent Rolls, Elizabeth I*, vol. II, pp. 185*f*, pp. 313*f*.
169 P.R.O., E 190/6/4.
170 W.A.P.Gd., Lib. port. Elbing, 1586, 1594.
171 *Ibid.*, 1605, f. 29.
172 Stone, 'Elizabethan overseas trade', p. 37.

eight *England's imports from the Baltic*

1 *Preliminary remarks*

In previous chapters we have demonstrated the importance to England of the Baltic area, especially Poland, as a considerable market for the disposal of cloth. Since cloth was by far the biggest item in England's total exports, one could determine fairly precisely the Baltic area's position in England's export trade. It appeared that in this respect the Baltic came second to the North Sea area, taking 11 per cent of London's exports at the end of the sixteenth century.

It is more difficult to establish the importance of the Baltic area in regard to England's imports. Data enabling us to draw a picture of this problem as a whole are lacking; however, the incomplete sources available for London indicate that imports from the Baltic played a small part in the capital's total imports. It would appear from the London port books for 1587–88 that at that time the most important contributions to English imports came from the North Sea area, accounting for 63 per cent, followed by the Mediterranean, Africa and the Levant, which jointly contributed 27 per cent. The Baltic contributed only 5 per cent, and the same figure applied to imports from Russia. If we consider the trade of foreign merchants, the Baltic's share of direct exports to London was apparently even smaller. Taking as our basis the value of goods shipped into London by foreign merchants, the data available for 1599–1600 show that the North Sea area's share was 94 per cent, of which the Netherlands accounted for 59 per cent, Germany 27 per cent and France 8 per cent. The Iberian peninsula supplied 3·5 per cent, Italy 1 per cent, Scotland 0·4 per cent, and the Baltic only 0·2 per cent.[1] If we accept these figures it would seem that the Baltic area contributed only a small proportion of England's imports, whether these were shipped by English or by foreign merchants. But it is easy enough to demonstrate that such a conclusion would be quite erroneous, for two reasons.

First, we must draw attention to the circumstance that these figures relate only to London trade, and do not take the north-eastern ports into account, though, as we have shown, their share in the Baltic trade was considerable. Moreover—and this has to be strongly emphasized—the importance of England's imports from the Baltic cannot be measured and evaluated exclusively in monetary terms. The Baltic's small contribution to the value of English imports was due primarily to the cheapness of its commodities. These were mainly raw materials and semi-manufactures, which obviously could not compete in price terms with the expensive industrial products, groceries and luxury goods of western and southern Europe. The Baltic area's importance to England's imports consisted not in the monetary value of the goods suppled but in their indispensability. While the various costly cloths, wine, spices, etc, of the west and south satisfied the luxury demands of an increasingly affluent society, the Baltic market was an important source of products which were indispensable to England's development and security, products which made it possible for her to develop her fleet, and, in times of poor harvest and food shortage, to feed her people.

We must, further, draw attention to certain serious difficulties one encounters in analysing England's imports from the Baltic. As we have already said, there are serious gaps in the English port books, and, like the Elbing customs registers, they yield only a very partial picture of imports. The Sound toll registers, on the other hand, do not state the destination of the goods. While these registers provide a reasonably safe basis for a discussion of England's exports to the Baltic, which in the Elizabethan age were carried mainly in English ships, they yield fewer data for England's imports from Baltic countries. This fact can be explained easily enough by reference to the widespread use of foreign transport, as we have indicated in chapter six, especially Dutch transport; also by the role of Amsterdam, which constituted a great entrepot for Baltic commodities. The Sound toll registers provide no clue to the extent of Dutch intermediary services, nor do they state the destination of Dutch or any other vessels passing out of the Sound with Baltic goods. In these circumstances, in this chapter we shall be dealing mainly with English merchants' imports from the Baltic (and not England's total imports), transported mainly in English vessels. Wherever the English port books render it possible we attempt to deal with the subject more broadly. The restrictions on our analysis of imports from the Baltic imposed by the deficiencies of the surviving sources suggests that, in all probability, only about half England's imports from the Baltic are covered. While we stress this difficulty, we must none the less point out that in this chapter we are concerned primarily with establishing the nature of the trade and the tendencies it reveals, and not with statistical, quantitative analysis, which for the period we are covering would probably be impossible in any sphere whatever of foreign trade.

First place among England's imports from the Baltic was occupied by naval commodities, which in the aggregate constituted two thirds of the value of English merchants' total imports from this area, Poland being the chief supplier. Within the range of these commodities, and also in England's total imports, flax occupied a particularly important position. A second group of goods consisted of foodstuffs, especially rye. In accordance with this division of imports the present chapter divides naturally into three sections, the first dealing with England's imports of naval commodities, the second with foodstuffs, and the third with all other goods—wax, tallow and potash being prominent in this last group. Such a division departs from the traditional classification according to the primary origin of the goods, whether forestry, animal products, etc.; but it would appear to give a much better idea of the nature of England's imports from Baltic countries.

2 *Naval commodities*

During the second half of the sixteenth century the most important item in England's imports consisted of goods used in building and fitting out ships, including flax, hemp, canvas and cordage, timber, iron, pitch, tar, etc. All these had been imported for very many years. Taking them in the aggregate, and calculated in value terms, their proportion of total English imports from Baltic countries was 74·4 per cent in 1565, 54·7 per cent in 1575, 77·5 per cent in 1585, 56·8 per cent in 1595 and 74·1 per cent in 1605. Thus they accounted for well over half of total imports (see the end of chapter nine).

(a) *Flax and hemp.* In the sixteenth century England's need for flax and hemp, in connection with her developing shipbuilding industry, was increasing. They provided the raw materials for two branches of production strictly connected with this industry, rope-making and sail-making; they were needed for ships' rigging and sails, and they were used for caulking decks, etc.

In the Middle Ages, England cultivated flax and hemp for use in her canvas production, which was quite well developed. However, in the sixteenth century home production proved insufficient to meet the country's needs, and so Henry VIII, and later Elizabeth, imposed an obligation on all owners of more than sixty acres of land to cultivate these two crops.[2] Henry's statute on the question clearly revealed the growing needs of the English navy, as well as those of the fishing fleets, and it provided for the heavy fine of £5 on any landowner who did not comply with its terms.[3] The development of livestock breeding and the increasing cost of land had the effect of depriving flax and hemp cultivation of all profitability. There is a characteristic document dating from 1575 which sets out the benefits accruing to Norwich through foreigners settling in the locality and devoting a large part of their land to flax cultivation, while its manufacture into canvas gave employment to the local population.[4] In March 1576 both houses of Parliament discussed the question of developing flax and hemp cultivation.[5] It would appear from the Acts of the Privy Council that, despite various measures and pressures, the cultivation of these two crops developed very slowly.[6]

The need to save the country the enormous importation of flax in the second half of the century led to further steps being taken at the beginning of the seventeenth century to increase home production. But in general all these efforts failed to achieve any significant results.

It would certainly be an exaggeration to say that flax played a role in England's imports from the Baltic similar to that of cloth in her exports; none the less, the Sound toll registers show that its proportionate value in English merchants' total imports from that area was almost 50 per cent. It was 47 per cent in 1565, 30·8 per cent in 1575, 55·3 per cent in 1585 and 52·9 per cent in 1605.[7] Moreover, the London port books reveal that towards the end of the sixteenth and at the beginning of the seventeenth centuries Poland supplied at least half of London's requirements in flax.[8] In the middle of the seventeenth century the figure rose to 90 per cent.

From 1576 to the end of the century England was the largest importer of Baltic flax (taking only English shipping into account); in this item she outstripped even Holland. Unfortunately, the English port books do not enable us to establish England's imports of flax and hemp from the Baltic over periods of years. Port books have survived only for certain years, and this makes it difficult to estimate the extent and growth of the trade. The Elbing customs registers provide valuable complementary data to those of the English books, though of course their information relates only to this one port—which, however, was the most important in England's Baltic trade at the end of the century. On the other hand, the Sound

Table 8.1 *London's imports of flax and hemp from the Baltic 1568 and 1588, based on the London port books*

	1568							1588							
	Total (lasts)	*Danzig*		*Narva*		*Other*		*Total (lasts)*	*Danzig*		*Elbing*		*Riga*		*Other (%)*
		Lasts	%	*Lasts*	%	*Lasts*	%		*Lasts*	%	*Lasts*	%	*Lasts*	%	
Flax	206	158	76·7	38	18·5	10	4·8	278·6	22·7	8·1	211·8	76·0	32·6	11·5	4·4
Hemp	12	12	100·0	–	–	–	–	134·2	12·0	8·9	75·9	56·5	41·6	31·0	3·6

Source P.R.O., E 190/4/2 and E 190/8/1.

toll registers give only a partial picture, since they record only shipments conveyed in English vessels and ignore the considerable contribution of foreign intermediaries. So they enable us only to form some idea of the share of English vessels in her imports from the Baltic.

The London port books for 1568 and 1588, which in fact are the only complete London books for the second half of the sixteenth century, reveal quite a large increase in imports of flax and hemp from Baltic countries during this period (see table 8.1). The Sound tolls do not distinguish London's share for these two years so it is not possible to make any comparison with the figures obtained from the London port books. In 1568 vessels commanded by English masters

Table 8.2 *Imports of flax and hemp from the Baltic to London, 1568 and 1588, by English and foreign merchants (per cent)*

	1568		1588	
	English	*Foreign*	*English*	*Foreign*
Flax	73·8	26·2	95·7	4·3
Hemp	54·1	45·9	95·0	5·0

Source P.R.O., E 190/4/2 and E 190/8/1.

carried 782·5 lasts of flax westward through the Sound, and this is almost four times as much as London imported from the Baltic, according to the London port book. In regard to hemp imports the two sources reveal that in 1568 London received half the total cargoes. But these deductions have only a limited significance, since London made considerable use of foreign shipping.

Further light is thrown on the nature of England's imports of flax and hemp by examining the question from the point of view of the nationality of the merchants who participated in this trade, dividing them into 'English' and 'foreign', the latter being mainly Hansards. Such a comparison (see table 8.2) reveals that in general the English merchants predominated, though in 1568 the foreign merchants' share amounted to 45·9 per cent of imports of hemp. Comparison of the data for 1568 and 1588 would seem to confirm a process of elimination of foreign merchants by English ones. But it must be pointed out that we are considering only direct imports from the Baltic to England. And we do not know how much flax and hemp of Baltic origin came from the Dutch warehouses in Amsterdam.

The extent to which foreign merchants participated in England's imports of flax and hemp can be fairly closely established for the beginning of the seventeenth century. Comparison of the Sound toll registers with the London port books not only reveals that the Dutch, Hansards and French had a very small share in the trade but also clearly demonstrates the Baltic market's importance as the main

Table 8.3 *England's imports of flax and hemp, 1600, 1609, 1615 and 1622, according to country of origin (lasts)*

Origin	*Flax*				*Hemp*			
	1600	1609	1615	1622	1600	1609	1615	1622
From Baltic to England in English ships	1,697·0	1,307·0	520·0	501·0	463·0	310·5	372	715·5
Foreign merchants to London from								
Netherlands	9·0	6·8	85·4	117·3	143·0	10·0	32	34·4
Baltic area	1·3	2·1	4·4	–	–	13·3	13	5·8
Germany	2·5	0·2	–	0·3	0·5	–	–	5·4
France	–	3·0	0·5	–	–	0·3	–	–
Norway	–	–	–	8·9	–	–	–	–

Source P.R.O., 190/11/3, E 190/14/5, E 190/18/6, E 190/26/2; also *Tabeller over skibsfart . . .*, vol. IIA, pp. 198, 258, 291, 334.

source of England's supply of these important commodities, so vital to the production of cordage and sails. In table 8.3 imports of Baltic flax and hemp as shown in the Sound toll registers are compared with the London port books' data on foreign merchants' imports from the Netherlands, the Baltic, Germany, France and Norway. This delimitation is dictated by the scope of the surviving sources. However, as foreign merchants shipped their goods almost exclusively to London (there is no mention of them in the Newcastle and Ipswich port books) table 8.3 does in practice resolve the question of the Baltic market's share in England's imports of flax and hemp, and, further, reveals the small part played by foreign merchants in this import trade.

Having indicated the Baltic market's great importance to England's imports of flax and hemp, it would be desirable to specify the various ports and regions from which they originated. Analysis of the Sound toll registers shows that almost 90 per cent of the Baltic flax and hemp was transported in English ships from Polish ports, originally from Danzig, but after 1580 from Elbing, when the Eastland Company's staple was established in that city. During the Danzig revolt of 1577 and at the end of the century a considerable quantity of flax and hemp was shipped to England from Königsberg also. Of the other ports, Narva made some contribution,[9] but only in the years 1563–74, while at the end of the century Riga also sent a quantity. There was a definite increase in England's flax imports from the Baltic after the founding of the Eastland Company and again at the turn of the sixteenth century, when there was a general quickening of England's foreign trade and an increased expansion of her shipping. In addition to flax, England imported small quantities of flax seed (linseed) from Poland. The Elbing customs registers for 1594 mention an export of eight barrels, or about half a last.[10] (Table 8.4.)

England occupied second place after the Dutch in the Baltic trade in imports of hemp, which was needed for the manufacture of cordage and sails. In the second half of the century the ports of origin of this item, which in terms of volume was much below the flax exports, corresponded with those given for flax. With regard to hemp also Poland was of basic importance to England, for almost all her imports came from Polish Commonwealth territory. Hemp was originally exported from Danzig, but after 1580 from Elbing and Königsberg, Königsberg's importance in this trade increased particularly at the close of the century.[11] Down to the year the Eastland Company was founded, English vessels carried several dozen lasts of Baltic hemp annually, but from about 1578 the figure was approximately 100 lasts. The highest figure was noted in the last years of the sixteenth century, when it exceeded 300 lasts; in 1600 it amounted to 463.

The bulk of the Baltic flax and hemp was consigned to England in vessels registered at Hull, London and Newcastle. The surviving port books indicate that in 1568 London received 26·5 per cent of England's imports of Baltic flax.[12] Newcastle's oldest complete port book, dated 1594, shows that in that year the port's share was 12·1 per cent of England's total imports of Baltic flax.[13] The sources indicate that flax was of great importance in Newcastle's trade with Poland. It was the most important item in the town's imports, and Newcastle

Table 8.4 *Flax imports from the Baltic in English ships, 1562–1600, according to port of origin*

Year	Total (lasts)	From Danzig		From Elbing		From Königsberg		From Riga		From Narva		Other (%)
		Lasts	%	Lasts	%	Lasts	%	Lasts	%	Lasts	%	
1562	324	315	97·2	–	–	–	–	–	–	–	–	2·8
1563	392	376	95·9	–	–	9	2·3	–	–	2·5	0·6	1·2
1564	503	300	59·6	–	–	18	3·5	–	–	99	19·6	17·3
1565	418	295	70·6	–	–	15	3·6	–	–	84	20·1	5·7
1566	1,117	405	36·2	–	–	15	1·3	35	3·1	619	55·4	4·0
1567	812	382	47·0	–	–	–	–	14	1·7	414	51·0	0·3
1568	782·5	435	55·6	–	–	–	–	–	–	333·5	42·6	1·8
1569	1,007	853	84·7	–	–	10	1·0	3	0·3	140	13·9	0·1
1574	698	475	68·0	–	–	3	0·4	2	0·2	196	28·0	3·4
1575	528	515	97·5	–	–	4	0·7	5	0·9	–	–	0·9
1576	599	584	97·5	–	–	–	–	–	–	–	–	2·5
1577	457	13	2·8	3	0·6	387	84·7	13	2·8	–	–	9·1
1578	695	504	72·5	–	–	128	18·4	2	0·2	42·5	6·1	2·8
1579	909	722	79·4	4	0·4	133	14·6	–	–	35·5	3·9	1·7
[illegible]	[illegible]	[illegible]	[illegible]	[illegible]	[illegible]	[illegible]	[illegible]	[illegible]	[illegible]	[illegible]	[illegible]	[illegible]

1583	1,667	–	–	1,654	99·2	10	0·6	3	0·1	–	–	0·1
1584	1,500	–	–	1,458	97·2	41	2·7	–	–	–	–	0·1
1585	1,252	–	–	1,162	92·8	90	7·2	–	–	–	–	–
1586	1,526	14	0·9	1,341	87·8	169	11·0	–	–	–	–	0·3
1587	1,292	25	1·9	1,022	79·1	185	14·3	9	0·7	–	–	4·0
1588	692·5	32	4·6	538	84·9	25	3·6	12	1·7	–	–	5·2
1589	1,543·5	22	1·4	1,330	89·1	94	6·0	21·5	1·4	10	0·6	1·5
1590	933	11	1·1	835	89·5	72	7·7	–	–	–	–	1·7
1591	1,374	42	3·0	1,289	93·8	15	1·1	–	–	–	–	2·1
1592	1,067	–	–	945	88·0	119	11·0	12·5	1·0	–	–	–
1593	1,393	4	0·2	1,222	87·7	151	10·8	14·5	1·0	–	–	0·3
1594	1,522·5	60	3·9	1,325	87·0	115	7·5	22·5	1·4	–	–	0·2
1595	1,209·5	9	0·7	1,143	94·5	52	4·3	5	0·4	–	–	0·1
1596	1,010	–	–	828	82·0	182	18·0	–	–	–	–	–
1597	997·5	53·5	5·3	851	85·3	89	8·9	3	0·3	–	–	0·2
1598	2,221	31	1·4	1,570	70·7	618	27·8	–	–	–	–	0·1
1599	2,405	–	–	2,181	90·7	224	9·3	–	–	–	–	–
1600	1,697	2	0·1	1,449	85·4	239	14·1	7	0·4	–	–	–

Note Shippounds have been converted into lasts at the rate of six shippounds to one last. Very small quantities of packs have been ignored.
Source *Tabeller over skibsfart* . . . , vol. IIA, pp. 4*ff*, and vol. IIB, pp. 239*ff*.

merchants' import trade with the Baltic dealt almost exclusively with flax, grain playing only a small part. The Elbing customs registers for the end of the century reveal that the great bulk of the flax and hemp was consigned from Elbing to London and Hull, and other ports received only a small share in the trade (see table 8.5).

The London port books enable us to get an idea of the size of the average cargo of flax per London importer. In 1587 it was 4·3 lasts, and in 1588 8·4 lasts, the quantity per individual importer varying widely, from 0·2 to 26·5 lasts. The biggest London importer of flax was William Cockayne, whom we have already mentioned more than once. In the case of Newcastle, in 1594 average imports were 5·4 lasts, and in 1598 5 lasts, the variation per importer ranging from

Table 8.5 *Exports of flax from Elbing to England, 1594 and 1599, based on the vessels' port of destination*

	Flax						*Hemp*					
		London		*Hull*				*London*		*Hull*		
Year	*Total (lasts)*	*Lasts*	*%*	*Lasts*	*%*	*Other (%)*	*Total (lasts)*	*Lasts*	*%*	*Lasts*	*%*	*Other (%)*
1594	969·9	631·4	65·0	307·5	31·7	3·3	22·0	18·0	80·0	1·0	4·5	15·5
1599	1,469·6	563·4	38·3	804·8	54·7	7·0	98·5	90·5	91·9	8·0	8·1	–

Source W.A.P.Gd., Lib. port. Elbing, 1594, 1599.

0·7 to 26 lasts.[14] Table 8.6, which lists the most important London importers of Baltic flax, also reveals England's great dependence on foreign shipping in imports from Baltic countries. At the end of the sixteenth century Russia's exports of flax to England were relatively small, and in this respect the Russian market was no rival to the Baltic one. Only in the years 1566–68 did England obtain approximately the same quantity of flax from Narva as from Polish ports. When sailings to and from Narva ceased, the Muscovy Company imported flax from Russia *via* the northern route, the quantities amounting to 12·8 per cent in 1587 and 9·5 per cent in 1588 of all England's imports from the Baltic and Russia aggregated. In quantitative terms the figures were 188·6 lasts in 1587[15] and 72·4 lasts in 1588.[8] But the Russian market's share was probably larger, for in the foregoing calculations the Sound toll register's figures for all

Table 8.6 *The leading London flax importers, Michaelmas 1587–Michaelmas 1588*

Merchant's name	*Quantity (lasts)*	*Origin of flax*	*No. of vessels*	
			English	*Foreign*
Ashbey, John	3·0	Elbing	1	–
Austin, John	1·5	Elbing	1	–
Barker, Robert	4·5	Elbing	1	1
Beale, Jerome	6·5	Elbing	3	1
Bodleigh, John	1·2	Elbing	1	–
Bond, Nicholas	24·0	Riga		1
Burnell, John	28·7	Elbing	7	2
Carlill, Lawrence	7·5	Elbing, Königsberg	–	2
Clarcke, Roger	6·0	Elbing	3	1
Cockayne, Thomas	11·5	Elbing	2	1
Cockayne, William	36·5	Elbing, Königsberg	4	2
Collett, Peter	9·5	Elbing	2	1
Darell, Thomas	5·7	Elbing	2	–
Delavall, Peter	6·0	Elbing	1	–
Duncken, Jeromy	12·0	Elbing	3	1
Gardener, Thomas	1·0	Elbing	1	–
Grenewell, William	6·0	Elbing	3	–
Golde, Hugh	9·0	Elbing	3	–
Manley, Ralph	24·5	Elbing	4	1
Mayott, Robert	30·7	Elbing, Könisgberg	6	3
More, Hugh	20·7	Elbing	4	2
Prestwood, Thomas	7·0	Elbing	2	–
Pullison, Thomas	1·5	Königsberg	–	1
Silvester, Nathanel	3·5	Elbing	2	–
Stepney, Thomas	2·0	Elbing, Danzig	1	–
Symond, Jarvice	4·5	Elbing	2	–
Waldo, Robert	14·5	Elbing	2	1
Watson, William	24·0	Elbing	2	3

Source P.R.O., E 190/7/8 and E 190/8/1. [These two port books together cover the period from Michaelmas 1587 to Michaelmas 1588.]

England's imports have been compared with information drawn from the London port books covering the proportion of Russian flax. It is true the Muscovy Company shipped its Russian products almost exclusively to London; but—as is shown by the London port book, which gives much lower figures for Narva than those of the Sound registers—a certain amount of the Company's imports evidently went to other English ports,[16] and there is no way of assessing this amount. In any case, in the second half of the sixteenth century the Russian market was still not a serious rival to the Baltic in exports of flax and hemp to England.[17]

(b) *Canvas.* Canvas was quite an important item in England's imports from the Baltic at the end of the sixteenth and the beginning of the seventeenth centuries. In 1595 it amounted to 4·6 per cent and in 1605 to 5·2 per cent of the total value of her Baltic imports. The great bulk of the canvas was despatched from Danzig and Elbing, where, to meet shipbuilding requirements, a canvas making industry had developed, producing ships' sails, among other items. The oldest surviving lists of Danzig canvas makers, dating from the beginning of the sixteenth century, are quite imposing, and allow of the presumption that, including journeymen and apprentices, some 200 people were engaged in the craft at that time.[18] At the end of the century there was a considerable increase in the city's production, partly because Dutch specialists settled in the city. So it is not surprising that Danzig canvas was much sought after by England, especially coarse ticking, which was excellent for sailmaking. Special weavers manufactured it from exceptionally strong and durable yarn.[19]

In addition to importing canvas from Danzig, English merchants obtained it from Cracow, and especially from Silesia and other districts specified in the Elbing customs registers as *hinderland*, i.e. the Polish hinterland.[20] Only in the seventeenth century did England develop her own canvas production on any large scale;[21] until then the imports of Dutch, German, French and Polish canvas were of great importance to her.

London was the chief customer for Polish canvas. In 1568 Thomas Allen imported into London 112 bales and three packs of canvas from Danzig.[22] In 1588 Elbing consigned 782 bales, 279 pieces and 1,800 ells to London. Königsberg consigned 210 bales, Danzig only 2,800 ells.[8] The Elbing customs registers show a considerable increase in consignments to London at the end of the century. In 1594 English ships carried 1,270 bales from Elbing to London, including 400 from Cracow, 460 from Silesia, and 40 from Prussia. In addition they carried 59 cases and packs, and 18,630 pieces of canvas.[23] In 1599 Elbing's exports to London amounted to 1,469 bales, including 1,137 bales of Elbing and 280 of Cracow canvas, plus 89 packs and cases, including a small quantity of canvas from Silesia,[24] as well as 20,433 pieces.

Other English ports imported only very small quantities of canvas from Poland. The Ipswich port book for 1604[25] reports only 2,320 ells of Polish (*hinderland*) canvas and 40 pieces of Silesian canvas. Hull, Newcastle and Yarmouth imported only minimum quantities from the Baltic.

England imported very little canvas from Russia; only four cases in 1566,[26] and almost none in other years.

It is exceptional to find mention in the port books of the import of sails. But in 1594 two sails (*asarulen Seylen*) were consigned from Elbing to London.[27]

(c) *Ships' cordage and yarn.* Cordage and yarn from the Baltic were particularly sought after by England in the sixteenth century. In 1575 imports of these goods amounted to 10·6 per cent, and in 1585 to 8·1 per cent, of the total value of England's imports from Baltic countries. The finest qualities were obtained in Danzig,[28] and it was mainly from this city that Henry VIII[29] and other Tudor monarchs imported cordage. In 1554 the London draper Richard Cragge obtained a privilege to export 300 pieces of cloth to Danzig on condition that in exchange he imported cordage, oars and other ships' commodities into England.[30] In 1555 the Privy Council instructed William Watson to purchase all the available reserves of hemp in Danzig and pass it over to Danzig rope-makers to manufacture into cordage.[31] The commercial correspondence between the London merchant Sexton and his Danzig agents clearly reveals the great importance of cordage in England's imports from the Baltic (see chapter ten). On one occasion the agents gave an order to Danzig rope-makers to turn the entire local reserves of hemp into ship's cordage, paying partly in cash in advance for the work.[32]

Data in the Sound toll registers reveal that in the second half of the sixteenth century England was one of the biggest purchasers of Baltic cordage, and yarn for cordage; in the years 1575 and 1585 she was definitely the largest customer for these goods (see table 8.7). England's predominance in the importation of these goods must have been even greater than is revealed in the above table, since the registers do not enable us to gauge the extent of imports by foreign ships. And it is important to add that the ships' cordage which England imported from Holland was manufactured almost entirely from Polish hemp.[33]

The Sound toll registers make it possible to indicate the regional origin of England's cordage and yarn imports. In 1565 English ships collected 70 per cent from Königsberg and 30 per cent from Danzig;[34] in 1575 the figures were 87·2 per cent from Danzig and 12·8 per cent

Table 8.7 *Exports of cordage, and yarn for cordage, from the Baltic to the West, 1565, 1575 and 1585, according to ships' place of origin*

Ships' origin	1565		1575		1585	
	Shippounds	%	*Shippounds*	%	*Shippounds*	%
England	39	10·5	1,243	58·7	1,551	72·9
Netherlands	187	50·5	43	2·0	87	4·0
France	56	15·2	116	5·4	127	5·9
Scotland	–	–	59	2·7	256	12·0
Danzig	–	–	240	11·2	–	–
Eastern Friesland	–	–	170	7·9	–	–
Hamburg	88	23·8	–	–	24	1·2
Other	–	–	262	12·1	83	4·0
Total	370	100·0	2,133	100·0	2,128	100·0

Note The Sound toll registers for 1595 record five different units of measurement for cordage and yarn, which makes comparison difficult.

Source *Tabeller over skibsfart* . . . , vol. IIA, pp. 17, 49, 103.

from Riga;[35] in 1585 they were 89·7 per cent from Elbing and 10·3 per cent from Königsberg.[36] Thus the Polish Commonwealth supplied the great bulk of England's requirements of cordage and yarn. A similar conclusion is reached from analysis of the London port book for 1567–68. It reveals Danzig's decisive predominance as supplier, and also mentions the most important London importers of Baltic cordage (see table 8.8). On this list we find the names of several well known future members of the Eastland Company, including William Cockayne and Thomas Russell.

Towards the end of the sixteenth century there was a marked decline in the Baltic market's contribution to England's imports of ships' cordage. The Sound toll registers reveal that in 1595 and 1605 a very small quantity of this commodity passed through from Danzig and Elbing. This decline can be explained as due to the growing competition of the Russian market. As early as 1557 English rope-makers had been sent to Moscow to supervise the local manufacture of hemp into cordage, and its tarring before despatch to England.[37] At that time the Muscovy Company expressed the hope that the abundance and cheapness of Russian hemp would make it possible to import cordage, 'as good stuffe from thence, and better cheape then out of Danske . . .'[38] The cordage exported to England from Russia

Table 8.8 *London importers of Baltic cordage, October 1567–October 1568*

Merchant's name	*Quantity (cwt)*	*Origin of goods*	*No. of vessels*	
			English	*Foreign*
Barker, Robert	26	Danzig	–	1
Cockayne, William	185	Danzig	2	1
Collett, Robert	21	Danzig	1	–
Gourney, Richard	70	Danzig	–	1
Hilson, Robert	36	Danzig	1	–
James, William	79	Danzig	2	–
Milner, George	138	Danzig	1	1
Russell, Thomas	175	Danzig	1	1
Vaugham, William	83	Königsberg	–	1
Walton, Dunstan	148	Danzig	2	2

Source P.R.O., E 190/4/2.

was made of flax at first but when it was proved that the result did not last and quickly rotted in damp conditions it was soon replaced by hemp. It was cheaper than Danzig cordage by 2*s* 6*d* per cwt,[39] a point of especial importance to English merchants choosing their supply market. In 1568 England imported 359 shippounds of ships' cordage from Russia; 234 shippounds *via* the northern route, and 125 ship-pounds through Narva. This amounted to rather more than she imported from both Danzig and Königsberg in the same year; the total from these sources was 303 shippounds, made up of 274·4 from Danzig and 25·9 from Königsberg.[22] The partial data of the London port book for 1587, covering only the last quarter of the year, entered 1,509 shippounds of cordage against the Muscovy Company, and only 331 shippounds against the Eastland Company (Elbing 325, Riga 6).[15] From other data we learn that apparently the Muscovy Company obtained 2,847 shippounds of cordage in 1587,[40] this being almost twice as much as the total imports from the Baltic.[41] From the London port book for 1588, which is complete, it would appear, however, that the Baltic continued to compete effectively with Russia in the export of cordage to England. In 1588 merchant members of the Eastland Conpany shipped 1,384 shippounds of cordage from Baltic ports, principally Elbing, while the total Muscovy Company cordage imports in the same year amounted to 1,079 shippounds.[8] But from the end of the sixteenth century onwards the Russian market had the better of this competition, and the data for 1595 reveal a decline in Baltic exports to England, down to 687 shippounds,[42] with a simultaneous considerable increase in exports from Russia, up to 3,000 shippounds.[43] Unpublished research carried out by Dr Millard indicates that in 1630 Russia supplied 90 per cent, and in 1633 97 per cent, of London's requirements in ships' cordage. Earlier data relating to Ipswich give imports of 533·8 shippounds of Moscow cordage and 46·5 shippounds of yarn for cordage in 1603, while there were no imports whatever from the Baltic.[44]

(d) *Iron and other metals.* England found the Baltic area an important source of supply of iron, and together with flax this metal held the leading position in imports of ships' commodities. Taking into account the value of England's total imports from the Baltic, in 1565 iron accounted for 15·8 per cent, in 1575 3·4 per cent, in 1585 6·5 per cent, in 1595 5·7 per cent and in 1605 9·2 per cent.[45] It should be added that England was the biggest Western European customer for Baltic iron shipped through the Sound. Various metals, especially iron—cast iron, forged iron, and steel—were needed in the manufacture of anchors, various kinds of nails, grapnels and hooks, hasps and reinforcements for different parts of a ship, for screws, staples and hinges, and for the production of various kinds of mechanical equipment, such as pumps. Other metals were also used for certain of the above-mentioned items, though to a much lesser extent, e.g. copper, brass, tin, lead, etc.[46]

In the sixteenth century England found it necessary to import iron because of the limitations on home production, which was hampered by a growing shortage of the wood needed for the smelting process. At the time this became such an urgent problem that on the eve of Elizabeth's reign there were some who advised the elimination of iron foundries altogether from England, because they consumed enormous areas of forest. In 1559 it was forbidden to use certain oak, beech and ash timber for iron smelting, and various other regulations were issued with the object of conserving the swiftly diminishing acreage of forest.

For many centuries Sweden was the most important iron producer in northern Europe;[47] she accounted for some 80 per cent of the iron imported into England at the end of the seventeenth and the beginning of the eighteenth centuries.[48] The Sound toll registers do not show any exports of Swedish iron to England in the second half of the sixteenth century, partly because it was consigned to England from ports situated outside the Sound, especially Göteborg, but also because England did not import iron directly from Sweden on any large scale, but bought it from Hanseatic towns, chiefly Danzig.

Iron ore was extracted from many mines in central and western Sweden, and smelted by primitive methods into small balls, called *osemundar*. Thus this kind of iron came to be known as osemund (in Polish, *osmund*). In general these balls were not forged on the spot; Swedish merchants bought them at an absurdly low price and transported them to Stockholm, where they were purchased by Hanseatic merchants, especially from Lübeck and Danzig.[49]

Stockholm trade statistics reveal Danzig's dominant position in the importation of Swedish osemund in the second half of the sixteenth century. In the years 1572–1620 Danzig imported approximately 500–1,000 lasts of osemund annually from Sweden, and this accounted for about 50–70 per cent of all Sweden's exports. During the second half of the century Swedish bar iron also went mainly to Danzig and Lübeck; but from the middle of the seventeenth century it went to Holland and England.[50] Year after year the Danzig merchants imported large quantities of osemund,[51] which they forged into bar iron, selling the product partly to local craftsmen and partly exporting it either up the Vistula to central Poland or by sea to the West, primarily to England. The importance to England of this Danzig trade is indicated by the fact that as late as the eighteenth century the term 'danzic iron' was in use to denote Swedish iron.[52]

From the end of the fifteenth century England ceased to confine herself to Hanseatic middlemen for the importation of Baltic iron, and her merchants took on board a little osemund on the return voyage from Danzig.[53] Data collected by Lauffer relating to the end of the fifteenth century[54] show that at that time exports of osemund from Danzig to England were considerable.

Analysis of data yielded by the Sound toll registers leads to the conclusion that in the years 1562–1600 England almost constantly occupied first place in iron imports from the Baltic, surpassing both Scotland and Holland. After the founding of the Eastland Company there was a definite increase in the country's iron imports from the Baltic, which essentially were from Poland (see table 8.9). At first all

Table 8.9 *Exports of bar iron from the Baltic to the West, 1564–1600, according to shipmasters' country of origin*

Year	*Total (ship-pounds)*	*England*		*Scotland*		*Netherlands*		*Others*	
		Ship-pounds	%	*Ship-pounds*	%	*Ship-pounds*	%	*Ship-pounds*	%
1564	1,387	1,101	79·3	102	7·3	137	9·8	47	3·6
1565	3,113	1,285	41·2	109	3·5	474	15·2	1,245	40·1
1566	1,422	866	60·9	284	19·9	146	10·2	126	9·0
1567	2,164·5	972	44·9	306·5	14·1	214	9·9	672	31·1
1568	730	423	57·9	230	31·5	33	4·5	44	6·1
1569	2,163	1,565	72·3	196	9·0	10	0·4	392	18·3
1574	1,535	573	37·3	381	24·8	191	12·4	390	25·5
1575	1,779	670	37·6	712	40·0	27	1·5	370	20·9
1576	2,297	819	35·6	996	43·3	69	3·0	413	18·1
1577	253	10	3·9	170	67·2	12	4·7	61	24·2
1578	942	308	32·7	429	45·5	31	3·3	174	18·5
1579	2,537	352	13·8	331	13·0	1,408	55·4	446	17·8
1580	2,457	668	27·1	401	16·3	481	19·5	907	37·1
1581	1,481	647	43·6	319	21·5	218	14·7	297	20·2
1582	1,728	794	45·9	370	21·4	137	7·9	427	24·8
1583	3,420·5	2,055	60·0	535·5	15·6	126	3·6	704	20·8
1584	4,116	2,495·5	60·6	735	17·8	183	4·4	702·5	17·2
1585	4,320·5	2,394·5	55·4	457	10·5	330	7·6	1,139	26·5
1586	4,213	2,399	56·9	268	6·3	412	9·7	1,134	27·1
1587	4,853	1,970	40·6	752·5	15·5	444	9·1	1,686·5	34·8
1588	5,450	3,036	60·1	451	8·2	361	6·6	1,602	25·1
1589	7,348·5	4,317·5	58·7	577	7·8	490	6·6	1,964	26·9
1590	6,439·5	2,606	40·4	947·5	14·7	1,130	17·5	1,756	27·4
1591	5,420	2,997	55·3	647	11·9	332	6·1	1,444	26·7
1592	6,494·5	3,467	53·3	606	9·3	445	6·8	1,976·5	30·6
1593	4,641·5	2,080	44·8	478	10·2	333	7·1	1,750·5	37·9
1594	6,669	3,350	50·2	656	9·8	364	5·4	2,299	34·6
1595	4,622·5	2,235	48·3	274	5·9	550	11·9	1,563·5	33·9
1596	5,269	1,870	35·5	476	9·0	1,064·5	20·2	1,858·5	35·3
1597	6,337·5	2,613	41·2	455	7·1	430·5	6·8	2,839	44·9
1598	16,925	5,735	33·8	2,321	13·7	1,572	9·2	7,297	43·3
1599	12,381·5	3,238	26·1	2,782	22·4	3,120	25·2	3,241·5	26·3
1600	8,222·5	4,133	50·2	865·5	10·5	823	10·0	2,401	29·3

Source *Tabeller over skibsfart . . .*, vol. IIB, pp. 13–199.

England's imports of Baltic iron came from Danzig, but after 1579 they came mainly from Elbing. although despite the Eastland Company's regulations English merchants still obtained iron at Danzig and, to a much lesser extent, from Königsberg. But they hardly ever sailed *via* the Baltic to Sweden, though the Dutch, Scots and French, for instance, obtained iron from that country also. Only in the years 1562, 1563, 1586 and 1600 did English vessels take on board a small quantity of iron from Sweden.[55]

The bulk of the Baltic bar iron imported into England was carried in English vessels to London and Hull. Table 8.10 shows the increasing importance of Hull in this respect, but it should be added that vessels from this port were also to a large extent chartered by London merchants for voyages to the Baltic.

Table 8.10 *The respective shares of London, Hull and Newcastle shipping in imports of bar iron from the Baltic, decennial intervals 1565–95*

	1565		1575		1585		1595	
	Ship-pounds	%	*Ship-pounds*	%	*Ship-pounds*	%	*Ship-pounds*	%
London	480	37·3	314	46·8	388·5	16·2	530	23·7
Hull	194	15·0	276	41·2	1,276	53·2	1,227	54·9
Newcastle	202	15·7	–	–	404	16·8	112	5·0
Other ports	409	32·0	80	12·0	326	13·8	366	16·4
Total	1,285	100·0	670	100·0	2,394·5	100·0	2,235	100·0

Source *Tabeller over skibsfart . . .*, vol. IIA, pp. 18, 50, 104, 165.

London's 1588 port book reveals that English merchants and vessels figured most prominently in the capital's imports of Baltic iron. In that year English merchants and shipping were responsible for 79·1 per cent of such imports, while foreign (Danzig) merchants accounted for 20·9 per cent. English vessels carried 70·4 per cent and foreign vessels 29·6 per cent of the iron obtained from Elbing and Danzig.[8] The two surviving Newcastle port books for the close of the sixteenth century show that this town's share in the Baltic iron trade was small, being expressed in the following figures: 1594, 84 shippounds;[13] 1599, 72 shippounds.[56] No Hull port books have survived from the second half of the sixteenth century, and only after an analysis of the Elbing customs registers is the disparity between the data of the Sound toll registers and those of the port books for London and Newcastle explicable. It then appears that the great bulk of Baltic iron was carried to England in Hull vessels (see table 8.11).

It is worth stressing the considerable measure of agreement between the data obtained from the Sound toll registers and those of the Elbing customs registers in the case of England's iron imports, which at the end of the sixteenth century came mainly from Elbing. The 1594 Sound registers give 3,022 shippounds from Elbing, while the Elbing customs register gives 2,844. In 1599 the Sound register gives 3,238 shippounds, and the Elbing customs register 3,328; in each case the difference is comparatively small.

In the second half of the sixteenth century imports of Baltic osemund were of much less importance to England than those of

Table 8.11 *The respective shares of Hull, London and Newcastle shipping in England's imports of iron from Elbing, 1594 and 1599, based on the Elbing customs registers*

Year	*Total (shippounds)*	*Hull*		*London*		*Newcastle*	
		Shippounds	%	*Shippounds*	%	*Shippounds*	%
1594	2,844	1,990	70	724	25·1	130	4·9
1599	3,328	3,062	92	251	7·5	15	0·5

Source W.A.P.Gd., Lib. port. Elbing, 1599.

bar iron. Apart from 1562, when English ships carried 99 lasts of osemund through the Sound (72 lasts from Danzig, 14 from Sweden),[57] English imports of osemund were very small. So far as the general Baltic exports through the Sound are concerned, it is worth noting that Scotland was the main customer for osemund; Holland and the Hanseatic cities took much less.

Late in the century English merchants also imported small quantities of steel from Poland; this seems to refute Rybarski's opinion that at this time Poland imported only steel.[58] The Elbing customs registers give the figure for steel exports from Elbing to London in 1594 as 8 centners,[59] and in 1599 as 53 centners.[60]

England also imported relatively small quantities of copper from the Baltic; it came mainly from Hungary, and passed *en route* through Poland to Danzig and Elbing.

The Elbing customs registers indicate that all the copper exported from Poland went to London: 36·5 shippounds in 1594[61] and 167 shippounds in 1599.[62]

The port books also mention small English imports of lead, although England herself was, as we have shown, a very important exporter of lead to the Baltic. In 1594 English merchants consigned 76 shippounds of lead from the Baltic;[63] in 1598, 193·6 shippounds.[64] In this latter instance England's imports of lead from the Baltic countries exceeded her exports of lead to them. The Baltic lead carried by English ships came mainly from Olkusz, being known as *olkusch bley*.[27]

(c) *War materials.* English merchants also obtained from Poland various iron and steel manufactures needed mainly for equipping the navy and army. The largest imports of such materials occurred mainly at the height of the country's struggle with Spain towards the end of the century. Although not all the items mentioned below were of service for equipping the fleet, it is convenient to group them together in this section.

In the second half of the sixteenth century, down to the 1590's, England was one of the chief importers of Baltic gunpowder. Taking as our basis only English vessels—which connotes a considerably reduced figure—it appears that in the 1570's England took 100 per cent of Baltic exports of this item, and in the 1580's took 50 per cent of all Baltic gunpowder exports to the west. Table 8.12 shows the amounts of gunpowder exported from the Baltic to England in English ships, and their connection with the country's political situation. It is hardly fortuitous that the biggest increase coincided with the year of the Armada and the years when the English fleet was most active. The Sound toll registers for 1588 show 227·5 centners of gunpowder shipped from Poland to England;[65] this was the largest quantity of Baltic gunpowder imported in any one year. At this time, as in other years during the Elizabethan age, gunpowder from Poland accounted for almost the whole of Baltic consignments to England.

Apart from England, the Netherlands and Scotland, the Hanseatic towns—especially Hamburg and Lübeck—and France and Denmark were the chief importers of Baltic gunpowder. It can be added—although the Sound registers do not reveal the fact—that towards the end of the sixteenth century Ireland also obtained supplies of gunpowder from Danzig; she was unable to produce it herself owing to the lack of sulphur in Ulster.[66]

The port books also make occasional mention of English imports of Polish saltpetre. Evidently England's own saltpetre production was very small, since only in 1561 was a privilege issued granting two London entrepreneurs the exclusive right to produce it.[67] We know that in the same year Thomas Gresham shipped saltpetre from the Baltic to England.[68] Letters from Elizabeth to Danzig in 1574 and 1576 indicate that among the importers of Polish saltpetre was Roger Fludd.[69] The 1588 London port book names the London

Table 8.12 *Exports of gunpowder from the Baltic to the West, 1574–96, according to shipmasters' country of origin*

Year	*Total (centners)*	*England*		*Netherlands*		*Scotland*		*Other countries*	
		Centners	%	*Centners*	%	*Centners*	%	*Centners*	%
1574	17	17	100·0	–	–	–	–	–	–
1584	285	148·5	52·1	21·5	7·5	4	1·4	111	39·0
1585	121	56	46·3	–	–	6	4·9	59	48·8
1586	51·5	27	52·4	–	–	9	17·4	15·5	30·2
1588	402·5	227·5	56·5	16	3·9	16	3·9	143	35·7
1589	325·5	209	64·2	–	–	37	11·3	79·5	24·5
1590	175	34	19·4	30	17·1	21	12·0	90	51·5
1591	198·5	41	20·6	13	6·5	6·5	3·2	138	69·7
1592	413	81·5	19·7	170	41·1	22	5·3	139·5	33·9
1594	198	19	10·0	7	3·7	13	6·8	159	79·5
1596[a]	104·5	15	14·3	39	37·3	10	9·5	40·5	38·9

Notes Only those years in which English vessels participated in the trade are given.
[a] Including saltpetre.

Source *Tabeller over skibsfart . . .*, vol. IIA, pp. 45, 95, 104, 121, 129, 133, 137, 141, 145, 153, 183.

merchant Hugh Golde, who on 3 September 1588 shipped 3,100 lb of saltpetre from Elbing to London.[8] The Duke of Pomerania supplied England with a quantity of saltpetre in 1591, and sought to obtain 100 cannon in exchange,[70] which suggests that the amount involved was considerable. But Poland was not England's main supplier of this commodity; a tract written by John Wheeler and dated 1601 indicates that her chief source was Germany.[71]

Apart from gunpowder and saltpetre, England imported various kinds of armaments from Poland. The Elbing customs register, under the date 2 September 1587 shows that the London shipmaster, John Beverly exported 120 pieces of armour (*Harnisch Rüstung*) from Elbing to London.[72] In the year of the Armada the London merchant Richard Gourney, a member of the Eastland Company, shipped ninety coats of mail from Elbing to London.[8] The 1594 Elbing register notes the exports to London of 2,340 sabre blades (*Schabbel klingen*),[27] 2,000 pike hooks (*Spisschacken*) and 50 ship-pounds of iron balls (*eyserne keulen*).[27]

(f) *Timber*. This was another commodity urgently sought after by England in the second half of the sixteenth century. It was needed mainly for the construction of ships' hulls and for masts. Olechnowitz's detailed research has established that for the construction of the average sized naval vessel 4,000 healthy, well grown oak trees were needed—a clear indication of the extent of the demand for timber in an age of rapid increase in ocean navigation.[73]

England was importing Polish timber as early as the fourteenth century.[74] In the fourteenth and fifteenth centuries Hanseatic vessels shipped pine and oak, oak and other staves, and masts to England from Prussia and Norway.[75] In the thirteenth and fourteenth centuries Norway was England's main source of supply, but from the beginning of the fifteenth century this role passed to Prussia.[76] In the sixteenth century Norway again played an important part as an exporter of timber, particularly of masts, to England. However, owing to the gaps in the English port books and the fact of Dutch intermediaries one is faced with great difficulties in attempting a more exact estimate of the size of England's timber imports. Moreover, the Sound toll registers obviously do not contain any data for Norway. It is worth noting that in the sixteenth century Norwegian timber exports were so large that the kings of Denmark took alarm at the rapid thinning of the Norwegian forests, and endeavoured in the interests of their own fleet to restrict the felling of Norwegian oaks and pines.

England's most important source of timber supplies in the Baltic area was Poland. It is a well known fact that at this time the Commonwealth forest reserves afforded great possibilities for the exploitation of raw timber materials.[77] Timber, mainly from Mazovia and Podlasie, Pomerania and the Dobrzyń district, and even from the sub-mountainous dictricts of southern Poland, was floated in large quantities down the Vistula to Danzig.[78] The great extent of Poland's forests made it possible from the earliest times to float lumber rafts down to Danzig on a mass scale, and, together with the export of grain this trade became a source of the Polish and Prussian nobility's affluence.[79] The chief customer for Polish timber was Holland, whose ships carried half, and in certain years even two-thirds, of total Baltic timber exports. The great bulk of the timber passed through Danzig and Königsberg, and to these cities the bountiful forest wealth of the Commonwealth was sent to be exported to the west.

In the sixteenth century various kinds of timber were used for shipbuilding, oak, elm, larch, pine and beech being most in demand. The Polish timber exported to England and other countries was mainly in the form of semi-manufactures, and so in the customs books it is classified in accordance with the nature of the processing and the ultimate purpose of the export. Generally speaking, timber processed for the needs of shipbuilding consisted of staves, which were used for ship hulls, oaken staves, which were the best kind,[80] masts, and various kinds of baulks, deals, planks, etc.

The Sound toll registers reveal that English vessels shipped mainly staves and oak staves, and a few masts, from the Polish ports. Their share in the total Baltic export trade was comparatively small, and in the case of both kinds of staves it amounted to only a few hundreds per annum, with the exception of the years 1593–94 and 1598, when the total exceeded 20 hundreds, and in 1578, when it even reached 45 hundreds of oak staves. English ships loaded the great majority of the staves at Danzig, and later at Elbing and Königsberg. It is an interesting fact that although the English warehouse was transferred to Elbing, Danzig remained England's most important port for shipping Baltic timber. This is easily explained by reference to the organization of Vistula lumber rafts down to its mouth at Danzig, and the natural difficulties of Elbing as a port. (Table 8.13.)

Compared with that of Holland and the Hanseatic towns, English ships' share of Baltic timber exports represented only a small percentage. Even in 1578, when imports of oak staves in English vessels were higher than in any other year in the second half of the century, the figure was only 2·9 per cent of total Baltic exports, whereas Dutch vessels accounted for 39 per cent of the oak staves passing through the Sound, and Danzig vessels 22·9 per cent.

So far as Baltic timber exports are concerned, the Sound toll registers cannot provide any basis for an analysis of England's imports, because foreign intermediaries were especially active in this field (see chapter six as regards England's difficulties in Baltic navigation). The few English port books that have been preserved point not only to the predominance of foreign vessels but also the relatively large participation of foreign merchants in the importation of Baltic

Table 8.13 *Exports of staves and oak staves from the Baltic in English vessels, 1562–1600, according to port of origin (hundreds)*

Year	*Oak staves*				*Staves*			
	Total	*Danzig*	*Elbing*	*Königsberg*	*Total*	*Danzig*	*Elbing*	*Königsberg*
1562	3·0	3·0	–	–	3·7	3·7	–	–
1563	0·5	0·5	–	–	1·0	1·0	–	–
1564	–	–	–	–	12·2	12·2	–	–
1565	–	–	–	–	5·5	5·5	–	–
1566	1·5	1·5	–	–	4·2	4·2	–	–
1567	4·5	4·5	–	–	1·0	1·0	–	–
1568	1·0	1·0	–	–	0·7	0·5	–	–
1569	2·5	2·5	–	–	4·2	3·0	–	–
1574	3·5	3·5	–	–	7·0	5·0	–	–
1575	3·5	3·5	–	–	3·2	3·0	–	0·2
1576	11·5	11·5	–	–	4·2	4·2	–	–
1577	5·0	5·0	–	–	3·0	–	–	3·0
1578	45·0	36·0	–	2·0	14·5	11·5	–	2·7
1579	4·0	4·0	–	–	2·5	2·5	–	–
1580	3·0	3·0	–	–	3·7	3·7	–	–
1581	–	–	–	–	3·9	–	3·7	–
1582	7·0	–	7·0	–	2·7	–	2·7	–
1583	–	–	–	–	1·7	–	1·2	–
1584	3·0	–	3·0	–	2·5	1·0	1·2	0·2
1585	–	–	–	–	0·5	–	0·5	–
1586	2·0	1·0	1·0	–	0·5	0·5	–	–
1587	11·0	6·0	2·0	3·0	4·2	1·7	0·5	2·0
1588	–	–	–	–	0·2	–	0·2	–
1589	2·0	2·0	–	–	2·5	1·7	0·7	–
1590	9·0	–	–	9·0	2·5	–	0·2	2·3
1591	–	–	–	–	1·3	–	1·0	–
1592	4·0	–	–	4·0	2·2	0·5	–	1·7
1593	16·0	9·0	7·0	–	9·5	6·3	3·2	–
1594	23·7	21·5	2·2	–	14·7	10·0	4·7	–
1595	6·5	2·0	2·0	2·5	5·7	3·2	1·0	1·5
1596	0·7	0·2	0·5	–	3·2	1·7	0·5	1·0
1597	10·0	7·7	0·7	1·5	10·5	7·7	0·5	2·3
1598	23·7	19·2	0·5	4·0	7·7	3·2	1·2	2·8
1599	1·5	1·0	0·5	–	3·0	1·5	0·7	0·5
1600	0·5	0·5	–	–	2·8	0·2	0·7	0·5

Source *Tabeller over skibsfart . . .*, vol. IIA, pp. 4–198, and vol. IIB, pp. 98–108, 122–4, 129–34, 239–40, 245, 246–7.

timber.[81] The 1568 London port book reveals that in that year the city received all its imports of Baltic oak staves exclusively from Danzig, to a total of 82·5 hundreds; English merchants were responsible for 62·4 per cent, and foreign merchants 37·6 per cent, of this total. The imports of plain Baltic staves amounted to 64·5 hundreds, the English merchants' share being 64·3 per cent, and foreign merchants' 35·7 per cent. In both cases almost the whole of the trade was carried in foreign vessels, which is why the Sound registers yield such a small figure for English consignments. The dominance of foreign merchants and transport was even clearer in 1588, when foreign merchants had a 98·4 per cent share of the imports of oak staves and 52·3 per cent of imports of plain staves (see table 8.14).

The London port books enable us to determine the ports of origin of the Baltic timber, and they confirm the view that Danzig was the chief source of supply for English merchants (see table 8.15).

Our only opportunity to compare the size of England's timber imports from the Baltic countries and from Norway is provided by the port books of Newcastle, Ipswich, London and Lynn. Their meagre data do indicate a certain equilibrium between these two most important sources of timber supply. (We discuss imports of masts later.) In 1593–94 the Newcastle port book[13] shows imports from Norway of 78 hundred boards, and from Danzig of 13 hundred staves and 5 hundred oak staves. But in 1598 the merchants imported 52·5 hundreds of boards from Norway and 54 hundreds from Danzig, while from Elbing came 8 hundred staves and 1·5 hundred oak staves.[56] Data for Lynn also show that England imported both kinds of staves from Polish ports, and boards from Norway. In 1598 Lynn received 44·5 hundred boards from Norway, but 40 hundred staves and 1·5 hundred oak staves from Elbing, and 15 hundred staves and 0·5 hundred oak staves from Königsberg.[82] The only Ipswich port book dating from the period under consideration and containing data on timber imports shows that in 1572 this port imported only 1·5 hundred Norwegian boards.[83] The 1588 London port book shows an importation of 33 hundred Norwegian boards, this being twice as many as from Danzig.[8]

Norway had a clear predominance in the export of ships' masts. But Poland also supplied England with this product in the second half of the sixteenth century. A letter from the Danzig merchant Henryk Melman to Thomas Cromwell under the date 17 August 1539 reveals that about that time 20 large masts were sent from

Table 8.14 *The respective shares of English and foreign merchants in London's imports of Baltic timber, 1568 and 1588, according to the London port books*

Type of goods	1568					1588				
	Total (hundreds)	*English*		*Foreign*		*Total (hundreds)*	*English*		*Foreign*	
		Hundreds	%	*Hundreds*	%		*Hundreds*	%	*Hundreds*	%
Staves	64·5	41·5	64·3	23	35·7	111	53	47·7	58·0	52·3
Oak staves	82·5	51·5	62·4	31	37·6	18	0·3	1·6	17·7	98·4
Boards	5·5	5·2	94·5	0·3	5·5	–	–	–	–	–
Oars	6·5	6·5	100·0	–	–	1	–	–	1·0	100·0

Note In 1568 the chief importers of Danzig staves were Thomas Allen (18 hundreds), R. Hilson (13·5 hundreds) and W. James (6·5 hundreds), and among foreign merchants A. Bartr[illegible]ck (18 hundreds). In 1568 a shipmaster from Königsberg, T. Bode, imported 21 hundred oak staves from that city. In 1588 the Danzig merchant Kaspar Manheim imported 32 hundreds of ordinary and 11 hundred oak staves from Danzig to London, and the Danzig merchant Maurice Tymmerman 25 hundred ordinary staves and 6·7 hundred oak staves.

Source P.R.O., E 190/4/2 and E 190/8/1.

Danzig to London.[84] In 1540 Henry VIII received 26 masts, valued at £547 sterling, from Danzig, 'with which he was content'.[85]

The Sound toll registers yield no figures concerning the share of English vessels in the transport of Baltic masts, for the simple reason that they were carried entirely in Dutch vessels. Only the English port books yield certain meagre information on the import of masts from Norway and the Baltic. In 1565 London received a hundred large masts from Norway,[86] but not one mast is mentioned as part of any cargo imported at the time from Polish ports.

Only in the years 1587–88 was there a rise in the imports of both Norwegian and Baltic masts,[87] a circumstance which can be attributed to the development of the English fleet during the war with Spain. In 1587–88 English merchants imported 29 large and 197 small masts from Norway to London, and a further 108 hundred spars. The data for Newcastle in 1593 mention the importation of 14 hundred spars from Norway,[13] and a further 80 small masts and 13 hundred spars in 1598.[56] But in that same year Danzig supplied only 5 hundred spars. The oldest surviving port book for Ipswich mentions 20 small Norwegian masts imported in 1571–72.[83]

England also imported oars from the Baltic countries. In 1567–68 two London Merchants, Thomas Allen and William James, shipped 6·5 hundred oars from Danzig to London;[22] in 1575 English vessels carried 2·5 hundred oars from the Baltic,[88] and a further 19 hundred in 1595.[89] In 1588 the Danzig merchant Maurice Tymmermann sold a hundred oars in London.[8] In 1587 London received 0·5 hundred Norwegian oars.[15] Data for Newcastle give the importation of 30·5 hundred oars in 1598, 24 hundred coming from Norway, 4·5 hundred from Elbing, and 2 hundred from Danzig.[56]

The oars were bought not only for use in England but also for re-export. In 1575 English merchants purchased 40 hundred oars in Danzig and then sold them in Africa.[90] This fact recalls the role of the English as middlemen between the Baltic area and western Europe and the Mediterranean, a role difficult to define precisely.[91] The fact that the same merchants often belonged not only to the Eastland Company but also to the Spanish Company and the Merchant Adventurers is a clear pointer to this activity, though English middleman activities on any large scale in European trade developed only in the seventeenth century.[92]

While we are dealing with England's imports of ships' commodities from the Baltic, we need to mention that in the sixteenth century she bought not only the raw materials for shipbuilding but complete

Table 8.15 *London's imports of Baltic timber, 1568 and 1588, according to port of origin*

Type of goods	1568							1588				
	Total (hundreds)	Danzig		Elbing		Königsberg		Total (hundreds)	Danzig		Elbing	
		Hundreds	%	Hundreds	%	Hundreds	%		Hundreds	%	Hundreds	%
Staves	64·5	61·5	95·3	–	–	3	4·7	111	64	57·6	47·0	42·4
Oak staves	82·5	51·5	62·4	–	–	31	37·6	18	17·7	98·3	0·3	0·7
Boards	5·5	5·5	100·0	–	–	–	–	–	–	–	–	–
Oars	6·5	6·5	100·0	–	–	–	–	1	1	100·0	–	–

Source P.R.O., E 190/4/2 and E 190/8/1.

ships from Danzig. For instance, in 1544 and 1545 Henry VIII bought two caravels, each of 400 tons capacity.[93] And in 1588 Francis Drake purchased a vessel of 300 tons capacity for 4,600 ducats.[94]

(g) *Pitch and tar*. England, the Dutch and the Hanseatic cities were the most important importers of Baltic pitch and tar. The pitch was needed for caulking seams in shipbuilding,[95] also for tarring cordage. Pitch and tar were exported from Danzig to England as early as the fifteenth century, as we learn from the researches of Lauffer,[54] Fiedler[96] and Samsonowicz.[97] As English pitch production was very little developed, the country was greatly dependent on imports,[98]

Table 8.16 *Imports of pitch and tar from the Baltic to London, 1568 and 1588, according to port of origin, based on the London port books*

	1568					1588								
	Total (lasts)	*Danzig*		*Königsberg*		*Total (lasts)*	*Danzig*		*Elbing*		*Köngisberg*		*Riga*	
		Lasts	%	*Lasts*	%		*Lasts*	%	*Lasts*	%	*Lasts*	%	*Lasts*	%
Pitch	401·7	315·2	78·4	86·5	21·6	29	7	24·1	12	41·3	10	34·6	–	–
Tar	118·7	97·7	82·3	21·0	17·7	121	68	56·2	15	12·3	3	2·4	35	29·1

Source P.R.O., E 190/4/2 and E 190/8/1.

especially from Norway and Poland. In 1588 Baltic countries met 41 per cent of London's requirements in pitch and tar.

The two surviving complete London port books, for 1568 and 1588, show that almost the whole of England's imports of Baltic pitch and tar came from Danzig and Elbing, and only a small amount from Königsberg and Riga (table 8.16).

Taking the two surviving Newcastle port books, dating from the end of the sixteenth century, as guide, it appears that all that city's imports of Baltic pitch and tar came from Elbing, and were imported exclusively by English merchants. Taking the two items together, in 1594 the import amounted to 93·1 lasts and in 1598 to 52·2 lasts.[99] London accounted for the largest imports of these two Baltic goods; the capital took about half the country's total imports (see table 8.17).

Taking the English port books as basis, and comparing the respective shares of the London and Newcastle merchants in imports of pitch and tar from the Baltic, we see that in London the trade was concentrated in the hands of relatively few merchants, who, with more capital at their disposal, brought in larger quantities. In the case of Newcastle the situation was reversed: a large number of merchants imported small quantities. In 1568 the average quantity of pitch per London importer was 24·3 lasts, and that of tar 13·5 lasts. But in 1594 the average per Newcastle merchant was 4·6 lasts of pitch and tar jointly.

The 1568 London port book shows that in that year the city received 401·7 lasts of pitch, of which English merchants brought in

Table 8.17 *The respective shares of various English ports in imports of pitch and tar from Elbing, 1594 and 1599*

	Total (lasts)	London		Hull		Newcastle		Lynn		Ipswich		Others (%)
		Lasts	%	*Lasts*	%	*Lasts*	%	*Lasts*	%	*Lasts*	%	
Pitch												
1594	479·5	365	76·1	35	7·3	15·5	3·2	64	13·4	–	–	–
1599	152	66	43·4	64	42·1	–	–	–	–	10	6·5	8
Tar												
1594	195	132·5	67·9	12	6·1	30·5	15·8	20	10·2	–	–	–
1599	69·5	32	46	10	14·4	–	–	–	–	10	14·4	25·2

Source W.A.P.Gd., Lib. port. Elbing, 1594, 1599.

78·9 per cent, and foreign merchants—mainly Danzigers—21·1 per cent. The majority of these cargoes were carried in foreign ships, and so the Sound registers for 1568 report only 95 lasts as England's total imports of Baltic pitch. The same London port book shows that in that year foreign vessels delivered as much as 93·1 per cent of the total London imports of Baltic pitch, from Danzig and Königsberg. Danzig vessels carried 42·7 per cent, Königsberg vessels 21·5 per cent, and Dutch vessels 17 per cent. 75·9 per cent of the tar shipped from Danzig and Königsberg in 1568 was consigned by foreign merchants, and only 24·1 per cent by English merchants. Foreign vessels carried a full 100 per cent of these imports. The 1588 data also reveal the dominance of foreign transport in the import of tar, accounting for 90 per cent.

This large part played by foreign merchants and foreign ships in

England's imports of Baltic pitch and tar renders it impossible to draw any conclusions from an analysis of the Sound toll registers. Like timber, pitch was a commodity which required appropriately large ships for its transport. If we consider English pitch imports in English ships, we can point to an increase from 1578 to 1585, i.e. in

Table 8.18 *London importers of pitch and tar from the Baltic, 1568*

Merchant's name	*Pitch*		*Tar*	
	Lasts	*Origin*	*Lasts*	*Origin*
English merchants				
Allen, Thomas	40	Danzig	10	Danzig
Beale, Jerome	20	Danzig	16	Danzig
Boldero, Edmund	15	Danzig	–	
Cockayne, William	20	Danzig	20	Danzig
Collett, Robert	2·5	Danzig	–	
Hilson, Robert	39·2	Danzig	–	
James, William	30	Danzig	–	
More, John	20	Danzig	18	Danzig
Mylner, George	5	Danzig	7	Danzig
Russell, Thomas	45·5	Danzig	32·2	Danzig
Simon, Jarvis	30	Danzig	–	
Vaugham, William	17	Königsberg	1	Königsberg
Walton, Dunstan	33	Danzig	–	
Foreign merchants				
Barfranke, A.	–		13	Danzig
Bode, Thomas	1	Königsberg	3·5	Königsberg
Bred, Joachim	2	Königsberg	2	Königsberg
Dorne, Ludor	66·5	Königsberg	14·5	Königsberg
Rosenberg, M.	15	Danzig	–	

Source P.R.O., E 190/4/2.

the early years of the Eastland Company. Again, towards the end of the century English ships participated to a greater extent in transporting pitch.

3 *Foodstuffs*

(a) *Grain.* Naudé's[100] and Gras's[101] detailed research has demonstrated convincingly that in the Middle Ages and the Tudor period

England was basically self-sufficient in grain supplies, which were transported to her towns from the country's rich agricultural hinterland. The lack of a developed market meant that regulations did not allow of the transport of grain from one county to another without special permission, whether by sea or land, and the few licences issued for such transport testified to the country's slowly increasing integration towards the creation of a general grain market.

Only in times of poor harvests and crop failures was grain imported from abroad. At such times England had long imported grain, mainly from Holland and Germany—during the epidemic of 1258, for instance[102]—or from France, Spain and even Sicily, as happened in 1315.[103] In the fifteenth century Poland also supplied quite large quantities of grain at such times, through the Knights of the Cross and the Hanse.[104] During the Hundred Years' War England kept her garrisons in France supplied to quite a large extent with grain from the Baltic area.[105]

It must be emphasized strongly that England imported rye and wheat in quantity only when there had been a decline in her own production, in years of crop failure, wars, etc. The increase in population also influenced the issue.[106] At such times Danzig played an important part in the supply of grain to England even in the fifteenth century.[107] Some interesting information on the subject is to be found in the writings of the seventeenth century historian Thomas Fuller. He noted that 'one of the first merchants, who, in want of corn, shewed the Londoners the way to the barn-door—I mean, into Spruceland' was Stephen Browne, Lord Mayor of London.[108] Through imports from Danzig he helped to bring about a fall in the price of wheat during the famine prevalent in 1439.[109] Another big importer of Baltic wheat in the fifteenth century was William Canyngs, a Bristol merchant who had his own commercial agents in Danzig.[110]

Besides the Hanseatic ports, especially Danzig, France also played an important part in England's grain imports, as also did Holland in increasing measure.[111] According to the calculations of Unger and Posthumus for Amsterdam, in the sixteenth century 80 per cent of Holland's imports of grain came from Danzig.[112] Only from the 1630's did Russian grain enter into competition with Baltic grain in England's imports (see below).

Despite increasing imports of foreign grain—especially to London—in the sixteenth century, England was self-sufficient in rye and wheat, apart from years of harvest failure. In his description of

England in 1577 William Harrison wrote: 'The bread throughout our land is made of such grain as the soil yieldeth, nevertheless the gentility commonly provide themselves sufficiently of wheat for their own tables, whilst their household and poor neighbours in some shires are forced to content themselves with rye or barley. . . .'[113] The traveller Fynes Moryson, who in the latter half of the sixteenth century visited most of the countries of Europe, including Poland, reported that in his day various kinds of grain were cultivated in all parts of England. 'The English husbandmen eat barley and rye brown bread, and prefer it to white bread as abiding longer in the stomach, and not so soon digested with their labour; but citizens and gentlemen eat most pure white bread, England yielding all kinds of corn in plenty.'[114]

At the beginning of the seventeenth century Francis Bacon observed that whereas England had formerly been 'fed by other countries', in his lifetime, at the end of the Elizabethan and the beginning of the Stuart eras, 'she fed other countries'.[115] Undoubtedly there was some exaggeration in this statement; none the less it can be said that at the end of the sixteenth and the beginning of the seventeenth centuries England had as yet no serious food problems. Fen drainage, adopted on a large scale in the sixteenth and seventeenth centuries,[116] and then the cultivation of waste lands, effectively compensated—at least for the time being—for the various problems which might arise as a result of the enclosures and the rapid development of stock-raising. Even London, with its considerable concentration of population, was supplied with grain mainly from the neighbouring counties, especially Kent, Sussex, Essex and Suffolk.[117] Certainly, about 1564 William Cecil was concerned that 'contrary to former tymes, the realme is dryven to be furnished with forrayn corne, especially the Citee of London',[118] but the remark was made at a time of crop failure. Fisher's investigations have shown that in the Elizabethan era London was to a large extent independent of imports of foreign grain.[119] The capital obtained its food from the neighbouring counties, especially Kent, which met some 75 per cent of its needs. Apart from times of poor harvest England was not yet importing any large quantities of grain.[120] Its cities had well organized agricultural hinterlands, or imported foodstuffs from the counties which specialized in the various branches of farming.[121] In years of crop failure grain imports from the North Sea and Poland time and again led to the avoidance of high prices and difficulties of food supply.[122]

A connection can be clearly demonstrated between increases in imports of Polish grain and years of poor harvest in England at various times in the second half of the sixteenth century. As early as 1546, when there was a food shortage and it was not possible to purchase the necessary amount of grain in the Netherlands, Hamburg and Lübeck, William Watson was instructed to acquire a large quantity in Danzig.[123] A letter from William Damesell to the Privy Council, dated 20 March 1546, reveals that Watson ordered some 300 lasts of rye and 50 lasts of wheat from two Danzig merchants, Adrian and Michal Koschler.[124] In 1551 the Privy Council instructed William Watson, who was the Crown agent in Danzig, to purchase 1,200 lasts of rye and 333 lasts of corn in Poland.[125] There is a characteristic letter from Thomas Smith to Elizabeth, dated 8 November 1562, in which he expresses the fear that owing to the high price of grain there may be disturbances on the part of the Papists. To avoid this, he advised purchasing a large quantity of rye and wheat in Danzig.[126] In fact the Sound toll registers for 1563 report the largest shipments of Baltic grain in English ships in all the 1560's and 1570's: 1,884 lasts of rye, 94·8 per cent of which originated from Danzig.[127] The Acts of the Privy Council for 1576 reveal that at that time, too, grain imports from Danzig helped to lower the price of wheat.[128]

The greatest imports of Polish grain in the second half of the sixteenth century, in the years 1586–87, when England experienced a very serious crop failure, call for separate consideration. The Acts of the Privy Council reveal that the second half of 1586 and the first half of 1587 especially were times of great difficulty in food supplies. In the Acts we read that in Somerset and Gloucestershire the subjects of her royal majesty were threatened with starvation, and that as a result there had been disturbances in those counties even in 1586.[129] A difficult food situation also occurred in Bristol,[130] while letters from the Lord Mayor of London in the same year speak of 'the hard state of the Citie by reason of the scarcetie and want of corne . . . as well through the staie of their provisions made in foren partes by the stopping of the passages through the great frostes that have fallen out this yeare . . .'[131] In November 1586 George Bond, a London alderman and member of the Eastland Company, was instructed to investigate the possibility of supplying London with wheat from anywhere in the country.[132] In April 1587 there was a meeting between London aldermen and several representatives of the Eastland Company to discuss the possibility of importing grain from Danzig,[133] 'for the necessytye of thys cyttye'.[134] On this occasion it was urged that there was a need to obtain some 2,000 lasts of rye and wheat from Poland.[135] It should be added that Wales also suffered a severe food shortage in 1586–87.[136] The difficulties of the time were aggravated by court policy, which was more concerned with supplying the army with corn.[137] For instance, in 1586 England sent a considerable quantity of grain and other foodstuffs to the Netherlands in order to provision the troops stationed there; also to Ireland, where the English garrisons were suffering from the grain shortage.[138] The surest proof of the difficulties England was experiencing in those years is obtained from the rise in prices: in 1586 wheat cost more than twice as much as in 1584, while rye cost three times as much.[139] In London the rise in grain prices was still greater.

It is worth noting in this summary of the serious food shortages of 1586 and 1587 that the Eastland Company agreed by way of exception to allow its trading monopoly to be relaxed in some degree, permitting Bristol merchants who were not members of the Company to import Baltic grain. In a letter of June 1586 the Eastland Company explained this concession by reference to the food problems of the time, and expressed its agreement to Bristol merchants temporarily trading with the Baltic on condition that the sole article of the imports would be grain, brought in for the purpose of 'bringing relief to the subjects of Her Royal Majesty'.[140]

The position improved greatly during the second half of 1587, largely owing to the imports of Polish grain from Danzig and Elbing. In 1586 English ships transported 4,742 lasts of rye from the Baltic, 91·7 per cent of it coming from Danzig and Elbing. In 1587 imports of Baltic grain reached the highest point in all the half-century, 6,383·5 lasts of rye, almost all of which was shipped from Danzig, Elbing and Königsberg.[141] But the comparable figure for wheat in 1586 was 324 lasts, and in 1587 it was 509 lasts. In fact, in accordance with our previous observation, these figures need to be corrected by about 50 per cent in favour of wheat; but of course this does not alter the fact that total English imports of Polish grain in the two crisis years were a vital contribution to the improvement in the situation. In 1588 English ships carried only 108 lasts of rye from Poland, and the good English harvests of that year caused a fall in the price of wheat to the pre-crisis level of 1586.[142]

Polish grain made up for England's deficiency again in the years 1596 and 1597, when there were poor harvests.[143] In 1596 English vessels took on 798·5 lasts of rye in Baltic ports, the bulk of it being from Elbing, Danzig and Königsberg. In 1597 the figure was 2,874 lasts, and in 1598 1,123 lasts, of rye.[144] These years marked the second largest imports of Polish grain in English ships, after the 1586–87 period, during the whole of the Elizabethan era. For these years detailed data are lacking on the proportions of English and foreign imports of grain into England. One document preserved in the Public Record Office reveals that English merchants were responsible for the great bulk of rye and wheat shipments to London (table 8.19). As most of this grain came from the Baltic, the deductions arising from the data in table 8.19 can be extended to cover England's Baltic imports.

While stressing that England imported large quantities of grain from the Baltic only when she herself experienced a temporary food

Table 8.19 *English and foreign merchants' imports of grain to London, 26 October 1596–26 May 1597*

	Total (lasts)	English merchants		Foreign merchants	
		Lasts	%	*Lasts*	%
Rye	5,248	4,422	84·2	826	15·8
Wheat	3,315	2,278	68·7	1,037	31·3
Oats	536	212	39·5	324	60·5
Malt	368	157	42·6	211	57·4
Barley	99	46	46·4	53	53·6

Source P.R.O., S.P.Dom. 12/263, No. 58.

shortage,[145] it is worth mentioning that this deduction not only follows from analysis of the port books but also has some basis in official documents issued in England late in the sixteenth century. In an Elizabethan statute of 1597–98, promoted with the object of improving the state of agriculture,[146] it is stated that England imported grain from abroad only in times of crop failure. Therefore one cannot agree with the opinion, expressed by Hinton, to the effect that in the sixteenth century Baltic grain constituted the chief equivalent to the English cloth exported to Baltic countries.[147] As we have already said, the true equivalent consisted primarily of ships' commodities. Possibly the phenomenon which Hinton noted occurred at a later date and relates to the seventeenth century. Without doubt the role played by imports from Livonia also came later, as Ahvenainen has pointed out.[148] In any case, with only the Sound toll registers and the

English port books to go on, it is difficult to establish the extent of England's imports of Baltic grain with any great precision, mainly because of the part played by Dutch intermediaries and the role of Amsterdam, which by the middle of the sixteenth century had become a large distributing centre for Baltic grain.[149]

A tract written at the beginning of the seventeenth century, and at one time erroneously attributed to Sir Walter Ralegh, throws much light on the role of the Dutch in the contemporary grain trade. Its author was really one John Keymer, and he had some interesting observations to make on the reasons for Holland's domination of the northern trade, especially from England's point of view.[150] Keymer stressed the Dutch policy of free trade and low customs duties, and devoted much attention to the Dutch practice of warehousing Baltic grain in order to sell it later in the west at the most favourable times—when harvests were poor, grain prices were high, etc.

> . . . by their convenient Privileges . . . by which . . . they draw Multitudes of Merchants to trade with them, and many other Nations to inhabit amongst them, which makes them populous . . . To which Privileges they add smallness of Customs, and Liberty of Trade, which maketh them flourish . . .
>
> [They] make Store-houses of all foreign Commodities, wherewith, upon every Occasion of scarcity and Dearth, they are able to furnish foreign Countries with Plenty of those Commodities, which before in Time of Plenty they engrossed and brought home from the same Places.[151]

He drew attention also to the flexibility of the Dutch merchants' trading operations, in which respect they were far superior to the English. For one thing they had at their disposal ready cash in silver, so that they could buy grain cheaply in Danzig and other Baltic ports. This highly profitable method of operating renders it extremely difficult for us to determine the extent of Dutch middleman activities in the case of England's Baltic trade.

A further reason for the predominance of the Dutch in the northern trade, in Keymer's view, was the size and equipment of their fleet. He confirms what we have observed in chapter six, emphasizing that the Dutch possessed ships much better adapted to transporting the heavy Baltic commodities, though they needed only one third of the crews manning English ships, so that their freight charges were much lower. 'By their fashioned Ships called Boyers, Hoy-barks, Hoys, and others that are made to hold great bulk of Merchandise, and so sail with a few men for Profit.'[151] Discussing the extensive range of the Dutch as middlemen, he wrote:

The Merchandises of France, Portugal, Spain, Italy, Turkey, East and West-Indies, are transported most by Hollanders, and other petty States, into the East and North-East Kingdoms of Pomerland, Spruceland, Poland, Denmark, Sweedland, Leifland, and Germany, and the Merchandises brought from the last-mentioned Kingdoms, being wonderful many, are likewise by the Hollanders and other petty States most transported into the Southern and Western Dominions.[152]

Rightly, he did not name England among the States in whose Baltic trade the Dutch played a large part. But undoubtedly he must have had her in mind when he was writing of imports from the Baltic. He was of the opinion that at the beginning of the seventeenth century some 500 Dutch ships arrived at the English coast, whereas hardly fifty English ships put in at Dutch ports, and he went on to argue that if England had her own fleet it would be

far more easy to serve ourselves, hold up our Merchants, and increase our Ships and Mariners, and strengthen the Kingdom; and not only keep our Money in our own Realm, which other Nations still rob us of, but bring in theirs who carry ours away, and make the Bank of Coin and Store-house to serve other Nations as well, and far better cheap than they.[153]

Taking as example her imports of Baltic grain, Keymer pointed out that the losses England sustained as a result of the middleman activities of the Dutch and the merchants of Hamburg and Emden. 'In Amsterdam, he said, there are always some 60,000 lasts of warehoused grain, not counting the quantities intended for sale. The Abundance of Corn groweth in the East Kingdoms, but the great Store houses for Grain to serve the Christendom, and the heathen Countries in the Time of Dearth [are] in the Law-Countries.'[154] He considered that in consequence a single year of high corn prices in England and other Western countries enriched Holland for seven years. With the food crisis at the end of the sixteenth century and the high prices of that time in mind, Keymer considered that in a single year the merchants of Holland, Hamburg and Emden carried some £400,000 out of England in exchange for the grain they imported, with great detriment to England and to the shame of English merchants.[155]

The English port books for the end of the sixteenth century note hardly any imports of Baltic grain, or note them so fragmentarily that they cannot be used as a basis for assessing the overall volume. For instance, the London port book for 1568 mentions only 30 lasts of rye, brought from Danzig by Robert Hilson in an Amsterdam vessel.[22] The 1588 London port book shows no imports at all of Baltic rye and wheat in English vessels.[8] In that year Norway supplied all London's import requirements in grain. Only for 1597 do the English sources make it possible to extract more detailed data on the imports of Baltic grain to London. A document preserved in the Public Record Office lists the names of English merchants who imported into London 1,617 lasts of rye and 61·5 lasts of wheat from the Baltic during the period from 26 May to 15 June 1597 (see table 8.20). These are, of course, only partial data covering less than one month, but they do make it possible for us to realize how under-stated are the figures for English imports of Baltic grain given in the Sound toll registers. The latter note only 2,874 lasts of rye passing through in English ships in the whole of 1597 to all English ports.

Table 8.20 enables two further deductions to be made. First and foremost it confirms the predominance of the large London wholesalers, among whom William Cockayne alone supplied 20 per cent of the total imports of rye and 16 per cent of the wheat in the period covered. Besides Cockayne, Peter Collett, Roger Clarke and John Highlord also imported large quantities. In less than a month these four members of the Eastland Company jointly imported from the Baltic almost half the total London imports of rye and close on 90 per cent of the wheat. The second deduction that can be drawn from table 8.20 is that rye greatly predominated over wheat in English imports from Baltic countries.

Two Newcastle port books dating from 1594 and 1598[99] enable us to determine the extent and the origin of this town's Baltic imports. Unfortunately, the port books of other eastern English ports have not survived for these two years, so we cannot make any comparisons. In 1594 Newcastle received only 44·5 lasts of Baltic rye, entirely imported from Elbing by eight English merchants. The 1598 book shows a much higher figure. In that year the town obtained 645 lasts of rye from the Baltic, of which 71·6 per cent was imported by English merchants and 28·4 per cent by foreigners. Of this quantity Danzig supplied 508 lasts, or 78·7 per cent, and Elbing 137 lasts, or 21·3 per cent.

The Ipswich port book for 1589 notes only 48 lasts of wheat, obtained from Danzig by four merchants of that city.[156]

In view of the very fragmentary nature of the data obtainable from the English port books we have to turn to an analysis of the Sound toll registers for the information they yield on the transport of Baltic corn in English vessels. But it has to be emphasized that,

Table 8.20 *English importers of grain from the Baltic to London, 26 May–16 June 1597 (lasts)*

Merchant's name	*Rye*	*Wheat*
Cockayne, William	329·0	10
Collett, Peter	166·5	40
Clarke, Roger	101·5	5
Highlord, John	92·5	–
Symond, Thomas	77·5	–
Snelling, Robert	76·0	–
Garill, Margaret	74·0	–
Waldo, Robert	66·5	–
Gossedge, Daniel	45·0	–
Burnell, John	44·0	–
Quarles, Edward	43·5	
Lewes, Richard	42·5	–
Willys, Myles	41·5	–
Freeman, Martin	41·0	–
Golde, Hugh	38·5	–
Carr, Robert	37·5	–
Gourney, William	33·5	–
Fryer, Symon	33·5	–
Clethcroe, Henry	29·5	–
Bambridge, John	26·0	–
Cutler, John	26·0	–
Aldersey, John	21·0	–
Brunskyll, Robert	21·0	–
Harryson, Ralph	21·0	–
Rowland, Odell	21·0	6·5
Jackson, Arthur	16·5	–
Pearson, Nicholas	16·5	–
Russell, Thomas	15·5	–
Beale, William	12·5	–
Vaugham, William	6·5	–
Total	1,617·0	61·5

Source P.R.O., S.P.Dom. 12/263, No. 107.

again because of the great part played by Dutch intermediaries, the picture obtained from this analysis is bound to be very incomplete.

The registers reveal that English ships had a very small share in the total amount of grain that passed from the Baltic to the west. The Dutch completely dominated this trade, carrying some two-thirds of the grain that passed through the Sound. The English share amounted to a little over one per cent; only in years of crop failure did it rise to some 10 per cent, as was the case in 1587, when it accounted for 11 per cent of the rye and 10·8 per cent of the wheat. But that was an exceptional year, and in practice English ships played no important part in the Baltic grain trade (table 8.21).

Table 8.21 confirms the opinion already expressed that Baltic grain was of importance to England only in years of food crisis. The imports show considerable fluctuations, with three steep rises in 1563, 1586–87 and 1595–98, all of them periods when England was having serious grain problems because of poor harvests. Except for these years, rye imports were small, and those of wheat minimal. But it must once more be added that the registers under-state the figures for wheat, and it would seem necessary to increase them by some 50 per cent, reducing the figures for rye correspondingly. However, this does not alter the situation much so far as general conclusions and an estimate of the relationship between wheat and rye in English imports are concerned. Rye was by far the larger import. It should also be said that in years of good harvests England not only imported no Baltic grain (e.g. in 1565, 1568, 1579 and 1580) but even exported some of her own to Scotland and Ireland,[157] to the Netherlands,[158] to Spain,[159] Hamburg[160] and elsewhere.

The Sound registers also reveal the complete predominance of the Polish ports in export of Baltic grain in English ships. Over 95 per cent of England's imports of rye and wheat from the Baltic area came from the lands of the Polish Commonwealth *via* Danzig, Elbing and Königsberg. Riga's share was minimal.[161]

By a fortunate chance we have the Elbing customs registers for the years 1586 and 1587, when England's imports to Baltic grain were the largest in the whole of the second half of the sixteenth century. In the case of rye they give figures approximating to those of the Sound toll registers, though in both years the figure is rather lower than that given by Sound registers, by about 300 lasts in 1586 and about 188 in 1587. The disparity may indicate that after leaving Elbing the English ships took on a further quantity of grain at Königsberg or Danzig. The Elbing customs registers show that in

Table 8.21 *Exports of rye and wheat from the Baltic to the West in English vessels, 1562–1600 (lasts)*

Year	*Total*		*From Danzig*		*From Elbing*		*From Königsberg*		*From other ports*	
	Rye	*Wheat*	*Rye*	*Wheat*	*Rye*	*Wheat*	*Rye*	*Wheat*	*Rye*	*Wheat*
1562	736	33	568	30	–	–	–	–	168	3
1563	1,884	77·5	1,787	77	–	–	50	–	47	0·5
1564	26	10	26	10	–	–	–	–	–	–
1565	–	–	–	–	–	–	–	–	–	–
1566	60	–	60	–	–	–	–	–	–	–
1567	20	–	20	–	–	–	–	–	–	–
1568	–	–	–	–	–	–	–	–	–	–
1569	68	–	67	–	–	–	–	–	1	–
1574	402	112	328	112	–	–	26	–	48	–
1575	957·5	46	932	46	–	–	–	–	25·5	–
1576	758	–	742	–	–	–	–	–	16	–
1577	449	–	60	–	125	–	158	–	106	–
1578	378	12	332	12	–	–	46	–	–	–
1579	–	–	–	–	–	–	–	–	–	–
1580	–	–	–	–	–	–	–	–	–	–
1581	13	–	–	–	13	–	–	–	–	–
1582	36	18	12	–	24	18	–	–	–	–
1583	100	–	–	–	70	–	–	–	30	–
1584	59	–	–	–	59	–	–	–	–	–
1585	71	13	–	–	71	13	–	–	–	–
1586	4,742	324	2,057	256	2,292	67	326	–	67	1
1587	6,383·5	509	2,868	282	1,676	162	1,699	64	140·5	1
1588	108	–	–	–	108	–	–	–	–	–
1589	396·5	6	149	6	235	–	12	–	0·5	–
1590	558	–	108	–	279	–	171	–	–	–
1591	409	–	136	–	273	–	–	–	–	–
1592	25·5	–	–	–	25·5	–		–	–	–
1593	326·5	43	50	–	276	43	–	–	0·5	–
1594	583	135·5	166	–	417	130	–	–	–	5·5
1595	1,783·5	353	772	32	422	261	574	59	15·5	1
1596	798·5	54	138	10	454	26	206	18	0·5	–
1597	2,874	40·5	2,021	23	549	17	229	–	75	0·5
1598	1,123	225	773	149	206	43	144	–	–	33
1599	160	–	160	–	–	–	–	–	–	–
1600	797	–	415	–	159	–	211	–	12	–

Source *Tabeller over skibsfart* . . . , vol. IIA, pp. 3–197, and vol. IIB, pp. 98–107, 122*f*, 128–33, 238, 245–7.

both years Ipswich and Hull were responsible for the largest imports of Polish grain, with London, Lynn and Newcastle accounting for rather less (table 8.22).

Towards the end of the sixteenth century London ships markedly increased their share in the importation of Polish grain. The Elbing customs registers show that in 1594 London's share was 74·5 per cent,[162] while the Sound toll registers show 66·1 per cent for 1585[163] and 24·1 per cent for 1595.[164]

Only for the early years of the seventeenth century is it possible to determine to some extent the Baltic market's importance in England's total grain imports. Table 8.23 gives the Sound toll registers' figures for Polish grain exports to the whole of England in English vessels, compared with information drawn from the London Port books on grain imports made by foreign merchants from Holland, Germany, the Baltic, France, Sweden, Denmark and Norway. As the foreign merchants carried their grain and other goods almost exclusively to London, this table can provide a partial picture of the relations between the two groups, though they cannot be grasped in their entirety because of the gaps in the port books.

Table 8.23 reveals the great importance of the Dutch middlemen in London's grain imports, especially those of wheat, and those of rye also in 1609. However, any deductions that can be drawn from this table must be limited, since the Sound registers make no mention of foreign middlemen, and in any case it is obviously not possible to take data relating to the beginning of the seventeenth century as a basis for conclusions concerning the previous period—if only because of the Navigation Acts, which came into force in the reign of James I, and restricted foreign middlemen's activities.

The few surviving English port books for the second half of the sixteenth century indicate that in the Elizabethan era the issue of the Russian rivalry with the Baltic market for the supply of grain to England had not yet arisen. In 1573 London received only three lasts of rye from Russia, in a single English ship.[165] In 1597, a year of poor harvests, the Muscovy Company obtained the Tsar's permission to export 250 lasts of rye, wheat and barley.[166] By comparison with the nearly 3,000 lasts of rye and wheat imported from the Baltic by English shipmasters in the same year, over 90 per cent of which came from Poland, this was not a large amount. The London port books for 1567–68, 1574–75, 1587 and 1588 show no grain shipments whatever from Russia.[167] This is true also of the Newcastle books for 1594 and 1598,[99] the Ipswich books for 1571–72, 1589–90, 1603 and

Table 8.22 *Exports of rye from Elbing, 1586 and 1587, according to English shipmasters' place of residence*

Year	*Total*	*Ipswich*		*Hull*		*London*		*Newcastle*		*Lynn*		*Others*	
		Lasts	%	*Lasts*	%	*Lasts*	%	*Lasts*	%	*Lasts*	%	*Lasts*	%
1586	1,992·7	593·5	29·8	385·5	19·2	299·0	15	176·5	8·8	161·0	8·0	377·2[*a*]	19·2
1587	1,490·7	221·0	14·8	307·5	20·6	179·7	12	109·0	7·3	172·5	11·6	501·0[*b*]	33·7

Notes

[*a*] Of shipmasters from other ports, those living in Aldeburgh (173·5 lasts), Harwich (94·5 lasts) and Yarmouth (49·7 lasts) had the largest share.

[*b*] Including 205·5 lasts for Aldeburgh shipmasters, 196 lasts for York merchants and others.

Source W.A.P.Gd., Lib. port. Elbing, 1594.

1604,[168] and the Lynn book for 1598.[169] Only from the 1630's onwards are increasing quantities of Russian grain mentioned in the London port books, and only from then on can one speak of the growing competition of the Russian market.[170]

When considering grain exports from Poland to London in the second half of the sixteenth century, one has also to remember the severe conflicts which developed between England and Danzig and other cities belonging to the Hanseatic League, since towards the end of the century they were supplying foodstuffs to Spain. England

Table 8.23 *England's grain imports, 1600, 1615 and 1622, according to country of origin (lasts)*

Origin of goods	*Rye*			*Wheat*		
	1609	1615	1622	1609	1615	1622
From Baltic in English ships	1,078·5	2,419·0	3,466·0	252·0	179·0	376·5
Foreign merchants to London from:						
Holland	1,420·6	46·2	1,854·9	676·9	623·4	167·1
Germany	53·3	6·2	232·0	91·6	127·4	202·1
The Baltic	52·5	–	120·4	55·8	–	27·5
France	5	7·6	5·8	–	–	58·5
Sweden	–	–	–	75·8	–	–
Denmark	–	–	–	48·3	–	–
Norway	–	–	–	31·6	–	–

Source P.R.O., E 190/14/5, E 190/18/6, E 190/26/2; also *Tabeller over skibsfart . . .*, vol. IIA, pp. 257, 290, 333.

attempted to weaken her chief enemy by imposing a blockade in order to stop grain shipments from the Baltic to Spain. In a letter dated 18 May 1589 the Privy Council ordered the admirals Norris and Francis Drake to intercept a flotilla of some sixty vessels *en route* from Danzig, Königsberg, Stralsund, Lübeck and other ports with grain intended for Spain and Portugal.[171] The admirals must have taken prompt action, for by 8 August 1589 the Privy Council was considering complaints from Danzig, Lübeck, and other shipmasters whom the English had detained off the coasts of Portugal and Spain.[172] Conflicts arose again and again over this issue during the time of the Armada, and again in 1595, when the Privy Council ordered Admiral Palmer to effect a grain blockade of Spain and to send the confiscated corn to England, where it was badly needed 'in this tyme of dearth'.[173] In connection with these events the English ambassador to Poland, Christopher Parkins, wrote from that country a very interesting letter to Lord Burghley, explaining why Poland was interested in exporting wheat to Spain. Parkins referred first and foremost to the view of the Polish gentry, who maintained that this trade was dictated by the Commonwealth's own economic interests.[174] The Danzigers also expressed this opinion, emphasizing that the issue was solely one of trade and not of politics. But Parkins was of the opinion that Danzig's appeal to the interests of the entire Polish gentry was not in accordance with the truth, and that it might be a matter only of the interests of that section of the gentry whose farms were situated close to the Vistula. Furthermore, Parkins pointed out, it was a matter of complete indifference to the Polish gentry whether the grain they transported down the Vistula was sold to Spain or anywhere else.[175] And as England was waging a life-and-death struggle with Spain she had the right, in his view, to apply the ancient law *in casu extremae necessitatis omnia sunt communia*, which justified the right to confiscate goods supplied to the enemy from abroad, a right allowed by the security and interest of the nation fighting for freedom. He considered such conduct was justified by 'the law of nations'.

In another letter to Lord Burghley, dated July 1595, Parkins assured him that the King of Poland would do nothing which might lead to a deterioration in Anglo-Polish relations, although on the other hand he must care primarily for the interests of his subjects.[176] For that matter, in Parkins' opinion, Poland had no interest in exporting grain to Spain against the wishes of the Queen of England. But despite the English ambassador's endeavours Polish grain was transported to Spain in Danzig ships. This had little to do with the Commonwealth's policy regarding the Anglo-Spanish conflict, but was bound up with the position of the Hanse, and especially with Danzig's own economic interests. But, as we have already said, at an earlier time the question of exporting Polish grain to England and Spain temporarily became one of the factors influencing Stefan Batory's foreign policy.[177]

(b) *Fish* had long been among the foodstuffs England imported from the Baltic area. In the fifteenth century England obtained chiefly sturgeon and eels from Danzig;[54] and in the sixteenth century sturgeon was an essential item in her imports from the Baltic. The London port books reveal that in 1588 87 per cent of the capital's supply of sturgeon came from the Baltic. Danzig was the main supplier, and London also obtained eels from that city (table 8.24).

Danzig's considerable predominance over Elbing in 1588, as revealed by table 8.24, at a date after the Eastland Company's foundation and the transfer of the English entrepot to Elbing, was due to the fact that the great bulk of London's imports of Baltic sturgeon was in the hands of foreign merchants—particularly Danzigers—who, of course, were not affected by the Company's regulations and restrictions. The Elbing customs registers confirm London's predominance in England's sturgeon imports from the Baltic. In 1594

Table 8.24 *London's imports of Baltic sturgeon, 1568 and 1588, according to port of origin, based on the London port books*

	1568				1588					
Merchants	*Total*		*Danzig*		*Total*		*Danzig*		*Elbing*	
	Barrels	%	*Barrels*	%	*Barrels*	%	*Barrels*	%	*Barrels*	%
English	20	18·4	20	18·4	65·3	13	2·3	0·6	63	100
Foreign	89	81·6	89	81·6	439·7	87	439·7	99·4	–	–
Total	109	100·0	109	100·0	505·0	100	442·0	100·0	63	100

Source P.R.O., E 190/4/2 and E 190/8/1.

London received 100 per cent[178] and in 1599 70·7 per cent[179] of sturgeon imports from Elbing. Apart from sturgeon, England also imported eels and stockfish (cod), but in very small quantities.[86] For these goods, also, Danzig was the main supplier.

In the period we are considering England imported no sturgeon or eels from Russia, but she did import a considerable quantity of codling, salmon and fish oil. For instance, in 1568 the Muscovy Company imported 74 barrels of fish oil from Russia,[22] close on 190 barrels in 1587[15] and 84·5 barrels in 1588.[8] Small quantities of fish oil also arrived in England from Poland. The Elbing customs register notes that an English shipmaster shipped two barrels from that city in 1587.[180]

(c) *Various.* Among the food products English merchants imported from Poland was a quantity of flour. In 1586 the Elbing customs registers note 22 lasts and 7 barrels of flour exported in English ships;[181] in 1587 one last and 21 barrels were exported from that city;[182] in 1594, 10·5 lasts;[183] in 1599, 66 stone.[184] The London port books also mention imports of beer from Danzig and Königsberg,[86] as well as various fruits and vegetables, including plums and cucumbers. For instance, in 1587 three London shipmasters took on board 4 vats, 6 centners and 100 stone of plums at Elbing;[185] at the end of 1587 the London port book mentions the importation of 48 cwt of Polish dried plums.[15] In 1588 a London merchant, Lawrence Cargill, imported 38 cwt of plums from Elbing.[8] The importation of 10 barrels of cucumbers from Elbing to London is certified in the Elbing customs register under the date 26 July 1586.[186] The 1568 London port book notes the arrival of 10 cwt of 'onion seeds'.[22]

4 *Other commodities*

(a) *Wax.* In the second half of the sixteenth century England was one of the biggest importers of Baltic wax, the quantity in certain years amounting to over 10 per cent of the total value of the country's imports from Baltic countries: 12·9 per cent in 1575 and 11·8 per cent in 1585. In the sixteenth century wax was one of the main items of Polish and Russian exports to the west, where it was needed mainly for candle production. Even in the fifteenth century Hansards were bringing wax to England, and they were the chief suppliers at the time, as is evidenced by data for 1446–48 and 1479–82.[187] The Danzig mooring books show a considerable trade in wax from that city to England in the second half of the fifteenth century.[188] In the sixteenth century Lublin was an important Polish market for wax sales; wax brought from the Ruthenian and Lithuanian areas[189] came to Lublin, and travelled thence by various routes to the Baltic coast and the west. The trade was also concentrated to a large extent in Warsaw and Lwów. Most of the Polish and Ruthenian, and some Lithuanian, wax was exported to the west *via* Danzig and Elbing, and to a lesser extent through Riga; large quantities were also transported overland, but it is not possible to calculate the relative proportions of sea and land exports.

In the second half of the sixteenth century England was one of the largest importers of Baltic wax, most of it originating from the area of the Polish Commonwealth. Only for a few years did the Dutch occupy the leading position in this trade—down to 1569, and again towards the close of the century. France and Lübeck also had large shares in the trade. From 1575 to 1590 English vessels carried the largest quantities of wax through the Sound, and as these imports

Table 8.25 *Exports of wax from the Baltic to the West, 1574–1600, according to shipmasters' country of origin*

Year	*Total (ship-pounds)*	*England*		*France*		*Netherlands*		*Lübeck*		*Other*	
		Ship-pounds	%	*Ship-pounds*	%	*Ship-pounds*	%	*Ship-pounds*	%	*Ship-pounds*	%
1574	1,674·0	302·5	18·0	1,153·5	68·9	38·5	2·3	39·5	2·3	140·0	8·5
1575	853·5	335·5	39·3	249·5	29·2	39·0	4·5	30·0	3·5	199·5	23·5
1576	377·0	157·5	41·7	79·5	21·0	13·0	3·4	92·0	24·4	35·0	9·5
1577	256·0	107·5	42·0	63·5	24·8	45·0	17·5	21·5	8·3	18·5	7·4
1578	799·0	170·5	21·3	386·0	48·3	185·0	23·1	23·0	2·8	34·5	4·5
1579	602·5	245·0	40·6	185·0	30·7	141·5	23·4	8·0	1·3	23·0	4·0
1580	846·5	237·0	28·0	147·5	17·4	341·0	40·2	18·0	2·1	103·0	12·3
1581	789·0	254·0	32·2	270·5	34·2	213·0	27·0	4·0	0·5	47·5	6·1
1582	540·5	220·0	40·7	235·5	43·5	60·0	11·1	–	–	25·0	4·7
1583	320·5	232·0	72·4	61·5	19·2	16·5	5·1	–	–	10·5	3·3
1584	763·5	586·5	76·8	141·0	18·4	16·5	2·1	–	–	19·5	2·7
1585	754·0	462·5	61·3	70·5	9·3	117·0	15·5	47·0	6·2	57·0	7·7
1586	1,771·0	1,165·0	65·7	89·0	5·0	105·0	5·9	296·0	16·7	116·0	6·7
1587	1,464·5	685·0	46·7	233·0	15·9	64·0	4·3	346·0	23·6	136·5	9·5
1588	1,757·5	131·5	7·4	69·5	3·9	195·0	11·1	581·0	33·0	780·5	44·6
1589	1,884·5	1,076·5	57·1	16·0	0·8	233·5	12·4	361·0	19·1	197·5	10·6
1590	1,775·0	669·0	37·7	22·5	1·2	274·5	15·4	640·5	36·0	168·5	9·7
1591	903·0	202·0	22·3	–	–	247·0	27·3	345·0	38·2	109·0	12·2
1592	1,062·0	181·5	17·1	34·5	3·2	353·5	33·3	403·0	37·9	89·5	8·5
1593	737·0	173·0	23·4	32·0	4·3	251·0	34·0	186·0	25·2	95·0	13·1
1594	536·5	52·5	9·7	60·0	11·1	306·5	57·1	65·0	12·1	52·5	10·0
1595	481·5	19·0	3·9	72·5	15·0	219·0	45·4	126·0	26·1	45·0	9·6
1596	393·5	7·0	1·7	0·5	0·1	182·0	46·2	144·0	36·6	60·0	15·4
1597	510·5	2·0	0·4	1·0	0·2	344·5	67·5	57·0	11·1	106·0	20·8
1598	1,197·0	85·5	7·1	19·0	1·5	807·0	67·4	16·5	1·3	269·0	22·7
1599	1,261·5	183·5	14·5	58·5	4·6	541·5	42·9	104·5	8·2	373·5	29·8
1600	1,719·5	274·5	15·9	145·5	8·4	841·0	48·9	95·5	5·5	363·0	21·3

Source *Tabeller over skibsfart . . .*, vol. IIA, pp. 45–199.

were transported almost exclusively in English ships (the 1587–88 London port books show this), even at a period in which foreign middlemen played a considerable role in England's Baltic trade, the elimination of the possibility of foreign intervention enables us to consider England the largest importer of Polish wax in the 1570's and 1580's (table 8.25).

Apart from 1586 and 1589, when there was a great increase in Baltic wax imports in English vessels, England imported several hundred shippounds of wax from Poland yearly. In 1594–98 there was a sudden fall, but at the very end of the century imports started returning to their former average level. In the last decade of the century there was a clear increase in the Dutch share of the trade, and in this period Holland took the lead in Baltic wax exports. The abrupt fall in wax imports in English ships in 1588 confirms the view that almost the whole of this trade was handled by English merchants in English ships.

The Sound toll registers clearly show the supremacy of Polish ports in England's Baltic wax imports. Down to 1580 over 90 per cent of the commodity was loaded in Danzig by English ships, with the exception of 1577, when, as a result of the Danzig revolt, almost all Polish exports passed through Königsberg. After 1580 Elbing took over Danzig's role. Narva and Riga had only a minimal share in these exports.[190]

Russia, too, was a large supplier of England's wax requirements. In 1555 the Muscovy Company ordered its agents to purchase in Moscow primarily wax, and then flax, tallow, fish oil and certain kinds of furs.[191] It would seem that at the start of the Muscovy Company's existence wax was perhaps the most important item exported to England from Russia. The Company even instructed its agents in Moscow to intervene with the Tsar to persuade him to forbid 'Poles and Inflantides' (Livonians) to travel to Russia for wax.[192] We do not know exactly how much England imported from Russia, but the fragmentary data indicate that in this respect the Russian market was a serious rival to the Baltic. The London port book for 1568 shows an import of 170 cwt of Russian wax *via* the northern route, and a further 8 cwt from Narva. In the same year Danzig consigned 46·5 cwt of wax to London, and a further cwt went from Königsberg.[22] Thus in 1568 Russia accounted for 79·1 per cent, and Polish ports 20·9 per cent, of the aggregate total from both markets. In 1587 a particularly large cargo of wax was consigned from Russia to London: it amounted to some 1,350 cwt, as compared with the 484·5 cwt imported from Elbing.[15] Aggregating the totals for 1587 and 1588, London received 65·7 per cent of its wax from Russia, 33·2 per cent from Polish ports, and 1·1 per cent from Riga.[8] This, of course, is taking into account only the Baltic area and the Moscow market.

(b) *Tallow.* This was another important item in England's Baltic imports, but even more so in her imports from Russia. In those days it was used for candle-making, soap manufacture, unguents of various kinds, etc. In 1565 England imported 512 shippounds of tallow from the Baltic, and this constituted 8 per cent of her total imports from the area. The corresponding Dutch figure was 56·5 per cent, and that for France 33·7 per cent. The Sound toll registers for 1565 clearly demonstrate the Russian market's predominance over the Baltic in tallow exports to England. As much as 94·4 per cent of the tallow carried by English vessels through the Sound in that year came from Narva,[193] and the remaining 5·6 per cent from other Livonian ports. After the closing of the Narva route there was a gradual decline in Baltic tallow exports to England. In 1575 English shipmasters passed 43 shippounds of tallow through the Sound, 69·7 per cent of this coming from Riga.[194] The London port books for the second half of the century reveal that Russia was almost the sole supplier of London's tallow requirements. In 1568 187 shippounds of Moscow tallow arrived in London;[22] in 1587 (figures for three months only) it was 70·9 shippounds;[15] in 1588 it was 55·8 shippounds.[8] The Ipswich port book for 1604 notes the importation of 319 shippounds of Russian tallow.[44]

(c) *Candle wicks.* With wax and tallow is associated the importation of Baltic candle wicks. The London and Elbing customs records reveal that the chief suppliers were the two Polish ports of Danzig and Elbing. In 1588 London received 5·5 cwt of wicks from Danzig, and 3 cwt from Elbing.[8] The London merchant Peter Collett was the biggest importer of candle wicks at this time; he alone imported 4·5 cwts. The Elbing customs register for 1594 shows that in that year London obtained two packs, one case, one barrel and 6,480 wicks in nine ships.[195]

(d) *Ashes and potash.* In the period under consideration England was an important customer for Baltic ashes and potash, especially from 1569 onwards, when imports exceeded 500 lasts per annum. In 1576 it went up to 1,460 lasts, and from then till the end of the century it remained at a high level. All through this period English ships were second to Dutch in the transport of Baltic ashes and potash, but the Dutch had an overwhelming preponderance in these exports. The main sources of England's supply of the two commodities were the two Polish ports, Danzig down to 1580, and

Elbing thereafter. Königsberg also played a large part in this trade. Exports from Narva were significant only during the time the port was open. Ashes and potash were needed chiefly for the manufacture of cloth, soap and glass. The large income the Polish gentry enjoyed from the export of potash is indicated by Ignacy Krasicki's lines:

Gdyby nie było potażu,
Nie byłoby ekwipażu;
Skarb to nie dosyć wielbiony,
Z popiołow mamy galony.[196]

Table 8.26 shows the considerable increase in Baltic ash and potash exports from 1568 to 1588, while revealing the great domination of Polish ports in this export. It appears from the London port books

Table 8.26 *London's imports of ashes and potash from the Baltic, 1568 and 1588, according to port of origin*

Year	*Total (lasts)*	*Danzig*		*Elbing*		*Königsberg*		*Riga*	
		Lasts	%	*Lasts*	%	*Lasts*	%	*Lasts*	%
1568	155	140·7	90·7	–	–	15·0	9·3	–	–
1588	613	252·0	41·1	286·5	46·7	34·5	5·7	40	6·5

Source P.R.O., E 190/4/2 and E 190/8/1.

that importation was largely in the hands of English merchants (82 per cent in 1568, 92·5 per cent in 1588) so far as direct shipments from Polish ports to London were concerned. We do not know the extent of Dutch participation in the trade. In 1568 English transport also predominated over foreign, the share of English vessels being 70·4 per cent, that of foreign vessels 29·6 per cent. In 1588 English vessels carried only 12·6 per cent of the ashes and potash imported into London from the Baltic. But this was an exceptional year, since the entire English fleet was mobilized in the struggle with the Spanish armada.

(e) *Timber products.* English merchants imported various kinds of timber manufactures in quite large quantities, especially from Danzig. We know from M. Bogucka's researches[197] that the sixteenth century Danzig carpenters and joiners were well known for their excellent products—not only furniture but also cases, various types of chests, canteens, caskets, etc. The port books of the second half of the century contain many references to England's importation of these manufactures. Among the items mentioned were tables, various kinds of chests, gaming tables and boards, canteens, wooden screws, spinning wheels, wooden plates, etc.[198]

In 1568 Robert Collett shipped over 100 tables from Danzig to London, and another merchant imported two small writing desks. In 1588 Peter Collett purchased a small writing desk in Danzig, and Robert Mayott one dozen 'women's desks'.

The London port books register the importation of Danzig gaming tables and boards. For instance, in 1568 the London merchant Jarvis Simons brought six 'playing tables'; in 1587 Ralph Menley imported seventy pairs of gaming boards. In 1588 four London members of the Eastland Company—Roger Clarcke, Peter Collett, James Lewis, and Robert Mayott—acquired twenty-seven dozen gaming tables in Danzig. The Elbing customs register for 1586 mentions the export of forty-one gaming boards to England.[199]

Among the importers of 'Danske chests' in 1586 were Thomas Russell (thirty-one chests), E. Arduner, G. Mylner and W. Watson. Altogether they imported forty-five chests and thirty items of chest fitments. In 1588 the Danzig merchant M. Tymmermann exported ten chests to London. The Elbing customs register for 1586 mentions the export to England of 600 wooden screws;[200] the register for 1599 has details of the shipment of twenty screws to Yarmouth.[201]

In 1574 English merchants imported one spinning wheel, and twelve dozen painted wooden plates, from Danzig; in 1586 there were sixty narrow lime boards; in 1588 threescore of caskets, three bottle caskets, etc.

(f) *Skins and furs.* English ships carried only small quantities of these items from the Baltic area, the skins consisting chiefly of goat, lamb, calf, some elk, etc. These imports came mainly from Narva, and were especially large when this port was open. They were supplemented by imports from Riga. In practice imports from Poland *via* Danzig and Elbing developed only after Narva was closed, but even then they never reached any large quantities. Russia's superiority in this branch of exports was indubitable. Through Narva Russia in 1563–1578 sent England several thousand furs annually; in 1566 it was as many as some 50,000. From 1575 onward England's imports of furs and skins from Polish ports reached several hundred per annum, the highest total coming in 1599—about 3,000—and in 1590, when Danzig and Elbing sent 1,000 and Königsberg 1,400.[202] When Narva was closed, English merchants imported furs and skins from Russia *via* the northern route, but the data on these imports are fragmentary. In 1587 the Muscovy Company imported 2,430 sable furs, 1,020 beaver furs, 896 elk skins, 1,750 kid skins, 3,440 cow hides, etc, by the northern route.[15] The London port book for 1588 gives the following imports of pelts and furs from Archangel: 1,180 elk skins; 240 beaver skins; 11,000 squirrel skins; 5,800 cow hides, etc.[8]

(g) *Wool and textiles.* In certain years during the latter half of the sixteenth century and at the beginning of the seventeenth England was among the biggest importers of Baltic wool, obtained mainly from Poland ('Polonia wool'). Wool exports to the West by sea were comparatively small, and down to 1586 they were mainly in the hands of the Dutch and the Hanse. Only after 1589 did English vessels pass through the Sound with increasingly large cargoes of Polish wool; from that year she led in this Baltic trade. In 1589 English ships carried 75 shippounds of wool from the Baltic,[203] in 1591, 270·5 shippounds, and for several following years imports were maintained at the level of some 200 shippounds of wool per annum.[204] At the very end of the century the Dutch again took the leading place in this trade.

Besides wool, English merchants imported various textile manufactures from Poland, including rugs. In 1587 three London merchants purchased 614 rugs in Poland, exporting them *via* Elbing;[15] in 1588 London received seventy 'Polish ruggs' and 430 Hungarian rugs from Elbing.[8] In 1604, 400 Polish rugs reached London from Elbing.[205] In the records we come across sporadic deliveries of dyed cloth from Elbing to London, e.g. in 1599 two cases and 478 pieces were exported.[206] But above all, one notes the export from the Baltic of cheap woven goods, such as camlet and *muchajer* (mohair).*

Muchajer and camlet were classed among the so-called 'Scottish hucksters'' goods. They were thin, woven materials of combed wool, but their origin has not been completely elucidated. The sources refer to Turkish, Venetian, German, Danzig and other *muchajer*, which in most cases could only signify where they had

*'Mohair', *muchajer* and the variants all derive ultimately from the Arabic *mukhagger*. Cf the Russian *mukhoyer*, 'an old Asiatic (Bokharan) woven material, of cotton with silk or wool' (Dal, *Tolkovii Slovar*)—*Translator.*

come from.[207] Both these materials were worn especially by women, as Jeżowski, writing in the middle of the 17th century, confirmed:[208]

> Good *muchajer*, cheap Turkish, fits better
> Than quality damask, Venetian,
> Good camlet or else crimson garment,
> Not a velvet gown expensively worked.

At the beginning of the seventeenth century camlet began to be produced in England, and in the middle of the century gentlemen's clothes were made of it. In 1664 Pepys wrote that he had put on a new suit of camlet, the best he had ever worn.[209]

In addition to mohair and camlet some grogram was also imported into England from Poland (one even comes across the term 'grogram camlet'). The first grogram to be known in England was imported from Turkey and the Levant, and so the term 'Turkey grograins' became attached to it.[210] Finally, we meet with the importation from Poland of certain quantities of 'mockadoes', an imitation velvet made of wool or cotton.[211]

The woven materials just mentioned were imported into England from Poland only in small quantities. The Elbing customs register for 1594 mentions only one bale of Wrocław mohair.[212] The 1587 London port book also specifies very small quantities of mockadoes imported from the Baltic.[87] In 1587–88 two London merchants, William Shacroft and Lawrence Carlill, imported four pieces of this cloth from Elbing, but at the very end of the century England imported larger quantities of camlet and grogram from Poland. In 1599 English ships took on board 192·5 pieces of camlet[213] and 146 pieces of Turkish grogram at Elbing.[213] Among the main London importers of Turkish grogram was Lawrence Carlill, who purchased two pieces in Elbing in 1587,[15] and in 1588 brought sixty pieces of 'grogram chamlotts' (a cross between grogram and camlet) to London from Elbing.[8]

(h) *Dyes.* In the second half of the sixteenth century England imported dyes, especially red, from the Baltic area, to meet the need for dyeing cloth, among other things. It is difficult to draw any distinction between the various kinds of dyes on the basis of the customs records. The Elbing customs registers indicate a quite large export of red dye from Poland to England. In 1586 vessels from London and Hull took on 256 half-tubs of red dye at Elbing.[214] In 1587 English shipmasters collected 76 half-tubs and 60 stone of red dye from Elbing.[215] English port books mention imports of the bright red dye, madder, from Poland. For instance, in 1567 Thomas Allen imported 23 sacks of this dye from Danzig to London,[22] and in 1588 R. Clarcke purchased 16 cwt and R. Cutler 96 cwt of red dye in Poland.[8]

(i) *Feathers.* English merchants imported feathers from Poland. In 1568 William Cockayne obtained 38 cwt of feathers in Danzig.[22] In 1588 total London imports amounted to 107 cwt,[8] of which J. Lewes imported 89 cwt, Peter Collett 15 cwt, and William Watson 3 cwt. Converted into stones, since the Elbing customs registers specify feather exports in this weight, Poland's export of feathers to England was as follows, as shown in the surviving customs books:

1568: 152 stone	1588: 428 stone
1594: 20 stone[216]	1599: 235 stone[217]

If we compare these figures with those for the trade in feathers in the Poznań customs[218] they are seen to be very large quantities.

(j) *Various.* Of the other goods English merchants imported from the Baltic, glass comes first. Extensive building activities in England in the sixteenth century led to a heightened demand for glass manufactures, especially window glass.

> Though the windows were not yet plate glass but lattice, they occupied a much larger area of the wall space than in former times . . . Plain clear glass was now used in the lattices . . .[219]

In the Elizabethan age England continued to import quite large quantities of glass, though she was attempting to develop home production with the help of foreign entrepreneurs, Dutch, Italian and French.[220]

The surviving port books reveal only small quantities of glass exported from Poland to England. In 1588 the merchant John Knapp imported one barrel of glass from Königsberg,[8] and in 1599 English merchants collected twenty cases of glass from Elbing.[221]

Amber was also imported from Poland. In July 1594 a London ship collected 59 lb of amber from Elbing.[222]

5 *The structure of England's Baltic imports*

The Sound toll registers enable us to prepare a table showing homogeneously, in Danish thalers, the movement and structure of England's imports from Baltic countries in the years 1565, 1575, 1585 and 1595 (table 8.27). Throughout the second half of the sixteenth century and the beginning of the seventeenth, naval commodities decisively

Table 8.27 *The structure of English imports shipped in English vessels from Baltic countries, decennial intervals 1565–95*

	1565		1575		1585		1595	
	Thalers	%	*Thalers*	%	*Thalers*	%	*Thalers*	%
Naval commodities								
Flax	22,720·5	47·0	37,700	30·8	122,505	55·3	83,898	35·6
Cordage, yarn	435	0·9	13,084·5	10·6	17,886	8·1	7,781	3·3
Iron	7,630	15·8	4,218	3·4	14,506	6·6	13,460	5·7
Hemp	196	0·4	3,448	2·8	8,959	4·0	7,231	3·0
Pitch, tar	4,247	8·8	8,052	6·6	4,882·5	2·2	9,425	4·0
Canvas	54	0·01	390	0·3	2,954·5	1·3	10,816	4·6
Staves	42	0·01	168	0·15	20	–	505	0·2
Oak staves	–	–	60	0·04	–	–	305	0·1
Oars	–	–	16	0·01	–	–	582	0·3
Osemund	682	1·4	–	–	22·5	0·01	–	–
Foodstuffs								
Rye	–	–	19,249	15·7	2,082	0·9	63,160	26·8
Wheat	–	–	2,070	1·7	585	0·3	19,651·5	8·4
Fish	716	1·5	286	0·2	1,209	0·6	225	0·1
Flour	351	0·7	588·5	0·5	–	–	313·5	0·1
Barley	–	–	–	–	–	–	338	0·1
Other goods								
Wax	1,627·5	3·4	15,892·5	12·9	26,030	11·8	1,150	0·5
Ashes, potash	264	0·5	12,784·5	10·4	10,828	4·9	6,496	2·7
Tallow	5,087	10·6	857	0·7	–	–	–	–
Copper	835	1·7	263	0·3	3,474	1·6	180	0·1
Furs, skins	3,434	7·1	1,351	1·1	127	0·05	–	–
Wool	–	–	–	–	–	–	6,420	2·7
Saltpetre	–	–	1,260	1·0	576	0·2	–	–
Gunpowder	–	–	–	–	840	0·3	–	–
Others	60	0·1	1,015·5	0·8	3,981·5	1·8	3,931·5	1·7
Total	48,381	100·0	122,753·5	100·0	221,468	100·0	235,868·5	100·0

Source Tabeller over skibsfart . . ., vol. IIA, pp. 25, 58–9, 114–17, 177–9, 242–3.

dominated the structure of England's imports from the Baltic. In 1565 their aggregate value equalled 74·4 per cent of all England's imports in English ships; in 1575 it was 54·7 per cent, in 1585, 77·5 per cent, in 1595, 56·8 per cent and in 1605, 74·1 per cent. In this group of commodities, as also in the total imports from the Baltic, flax was the largest item, and was the main basis of such imports Other essential items of ships' stores were cordage and iron.

The importation of foodstuffs in English ships displayed great fluctuations, especially that of grain, which was imported on a large scale only in years of poor harvests. In the group of 'other goods' only the trade in ashes, potash and wax showed a tendency to remain stable. All the other goods of this group revealed a perceptible decline (e.g. tallow, furs and skins), which can be explained by the growing competition of the Russian market. In sum, it should be emphasized yet again that naval commodities were the main basis of England's imports from the Baltic; among these, flax played a similar role, up to a point, to that of cloth in England's exports to the Baltic. In discussing the structure of England's imports from the Baltic we take into account only the Sound toll registers for goods carried in English vessels, and so the foregoing conclusions are of restricted application. English vessels carried through the Sound about half the total goods imported from the Baltic area; the remainder were carried in foreign ships, and we are unable to calculate this section of the trade in such detail. Despite this proviso, table 8.27 does show the general nature of the structure of England's imports from the Baltic, with the added important reservation that it gives greatly reduced data for grain.

While the structure of England's exports to the Baltic did not depart fundamentally from the structure of her exports as a whole (in both cases cloth accounted for over three-quarters of the total), the same cannot be said of the composition of her imports from that area. The data for 1559–60 and 1565–66 show that in terms of value the leading place in England's total imports was occupied by wine, canvas and other linen cloth, and then dyes, necessary for cloth dyeing, alum and oil. Then came groceries, especially sugar and pepper, iron, costly luxury woven goods, etc. Of the most important import items from the Baltic only flax is found on this list. Grain and timber are missing.[223] But it is difficult to come to any more general conclusions on this last question, for in 1565 England imported no grain from the Baltic, while timber imports were exceptionally small. We must repeat that the measure of the importance of Baltic imports in Elizabethan England's foreign trade is not their monetary value, but the usefulness and necessity of the generally cheap Baltic commodities.

Owing to the great extent of foreign intermediaries, table 8.27 affords no possibility of obtaining some idea of overall trends in England's import trade with the Baltic. Taking into consideration the

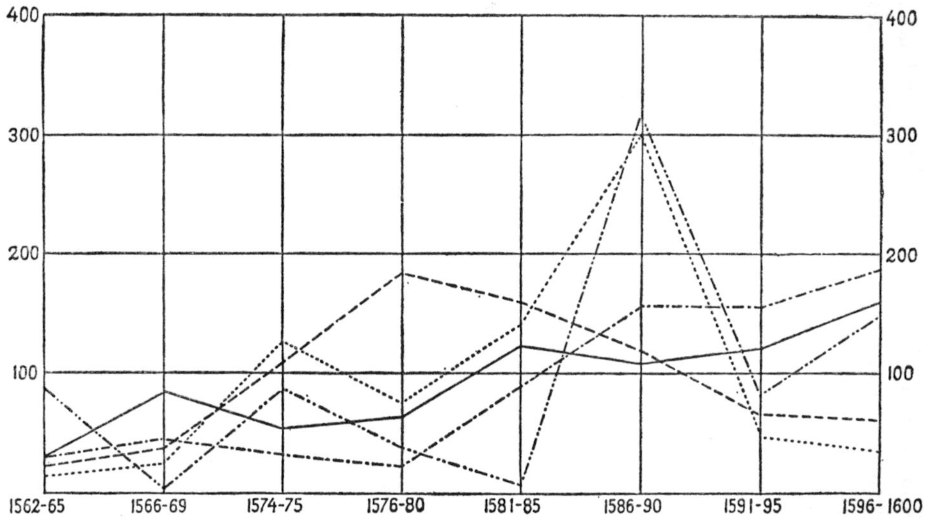

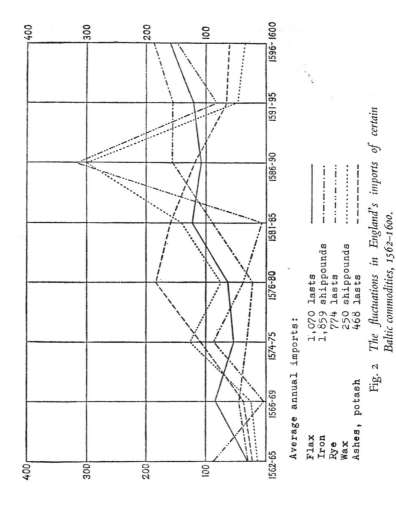

Average annual imports:

Flax	1,070	lasts
Iron	1,859	shippounds
Rye	774	lasts
Wax	250	shippounds
Ashes, potash	468	lasts

Fig. 2 *The fluctuations in England's imports of certain Baltic commodities, 1562–1600.*

data for English merchants' imports of all kinds from Baltic countries, in both English and foreign vessels (table 9.1), we see that in the period 1565–85 England's imports doubled, while in the same period her exports quadrupled. At the end of the century, at a time of increasing conflict with Spain and the development of the English fleet, imports showed a very considerable increase, whereas exports were maintained at the high level of the previous decade.

In conclusion, it is useful to attempt a comparative analysis of the imports in English ships of several of the most important Baltic products, using the five-year indicators of the Sound toll registers as a

Table 8.28 *Average annual imports from the Baltic carried in English vessels, 1562–1600, according to the Sound toll registers' five-yearly indicators*

Years	*Flax* (*lasts*)	*Iron* (*shippounds*)	*Rye* (*lasts*)	*Wax* (*shippounds*)	*Ashes, potash* (*lasts*)
1562–65	409	591	661	50	133
1566–69	930	908	37	72	218
1574–75	613	621	680	319	511
1576–80	701	431	317	184	859
1581–85	1,317	1,675	56	351	753
1586–90	1,181	2,866	2,436	745	563
1591–95	1,313	2,826	626	126	323
1596–1600	1,666	3,522	1,159	111	321
Annual average	1,070	1,859	771	250	468

basis, with the object of grasping the approximate movement of this trade. Although, in view of the part played by foreign intermediaries, we can sketch only a partial picture, it does throw additional light on the question. Table 8.28 reveals that there were fluctuations in the carriage in English ships of the more important Baltic products, together with a definite increase in imports during the last twenty years of the century. However, this remark does not apply to rye imports, which underwent unequal periods of sudden increase and equally sudden decline, nor to ashes and potash (and partly to wax), imports of which were highest in the 1570's and 1580's. While imports of Baltic flax and iron showed a constant upward trend, rye imports fluctuated, according to the English grain harvests. In the case of wax and potash quite serious fluctuations are to be observed. The accompanying graph clearly confirms the foregoing summary of the movement of imports.

If we compare the movement of England's imports from and exports to Baltic countries we clearly see a similar basic trend in both cases. The period 1562–1600 divides neatly into two phases: the first, down to about 1580, reveals a much smaller volume of trade than the second, which covers the last twenty years of the century. The foundation of the Eastland Company and its establishment of an entrepot on the Polish coast marks the clear-cut division between the two phases.

Notes

1 P.R.O. E 190/7/8 and E 190/11/1.
2 Lipson, *The economic history of England*, vol. II, p. 199; also *Tudor economic documents*, vol. II, p. 267.
3 *Tudor economic documents*, vol. II, p. 14.
4 *Ibid.*, vol. I, p. 315.
5 *Cal.S.P.Dom., 1547–80*, p. 519.
6 *A.P.C.*, vol. XIII, pp. 42, 77.
7 *Tabeller over skibsfart* . . ., vol. IIA, pp. 25, 58*f*, 114–17, 242*f*.
8 P.R.O., E 190/8/1.
9 *Cal.S.P., 1581–90*, p. 24.
10 W.A.P.Gd., Lib. port. Elbing, 1594, ff. 58, 59.
11 *Tabeller over skibsfart* . . ., vol. IIA, pp. 4*ff*, and vol. IIB, pp. 98*ff*, 239*ff*.
12 P.R.O., E 190/4/2; also *Tabeller over skibsfart* . . ., vol. IIA, p. 36.
13 P.R.O., E 190/185/6.
14 *Ibid.*, E 190/7/8 and E 190/8/1; also E 190/185/6 and E 315/485.
15 *Ibid.*, E 190/7/8.
16 *Ibid.*, E 190/4/2. The Sound registers for 1568 give the figure of 333·5 lasts for imports of flax from Narva in English ships, whereas the London port book for the same year mentions only 38 lasts.
17 W. Beveridge, *Prices and wages in England*, London, 1939, p. 635, states that only from 1621 onwards did the majority of England's hemp come from Russia.
18 Bogucka, *Gdańskie rzemiosło tekstylne* . . ., p. 33.
19 *Ibid.*, p. 112. See also S. Gierszewski, *Elbląski przemysł okrętowy w latach 1570–1815* (*The Elbing shipbuilding industry in the years 1570–1815*), Danzig, 1961, p. 158.
20 On the subject of the carriage of cloth along the river Vistula, see Obuchowska-Pysiowa, *op. cit.*, p. 108.
21 Lipson, *The economic history of England*, vol. II, pp. 94*ff*.

22 P.R.O., E 190/4/2.
23 W.A.P.Gd., Lib. port. Elbing, 1594. [The 18,630 pieces are based on the assumption that '310 threescores and 30 pieces' means 18,630 pieces.]
24 *Ibid.*, 1599.
25 P.R.O., E 190/599/4.
26 Willan, *The early history of the Russia Company*, p. 73.
27 W.A.P.Gd., Lib. port. Elbing, 1594, f. 36.
28 Writing in the Elizabethan period, the author of the treatise 'A speciell direction for diverse trades' said, '. . . our cables and all our good ropes come from Danska in Pollande'.
29 *L.P. Henry VIII*, vol. VIII, p. 200, and vol. XX, part I, pp. 193*f*.
30 *Calendar of Patent Rolls, Philip and Mary*, vol. I, p. 386, and vol. II, pp. 266*f*.
31 *A.P.C.*, vol. V, p. 236; also *Danziger Inventar*, No. 2947.
32 P.R.O., S.P. Supplementary 46/9, ff. 11, 13 and elsewhere.
33 *Ibid.*, S.P.Dom. 12/283a, No. 88: 'The beste cables are maide at Horne, they work all with Danske hempe . . .'
34 *Tabeller over skibsfart* . . ., vol. IIB, pp. 239, 248.
35 *Ibid.*, pp. 240, 252.
36 *Ibid.*, pp. 245, 248.
37 See Willan, *The early history of the Russia Company*, p. 271.
38 Hakluyt, *op. cit.*, pp. 282*f*.
39 Willan, *The early history of the Russia Company*, pp. 55*f*.
40 *Ibid.*, p. 182.
41 *Tabeller over skibsfart* . . ., vol. IIA, p. 103.
42 *Ibid.*, vol. IIB, pp. 245, 248.
43 Willan, *The early history of the Russia Company*, p. 254.
44 P.R.O., E 190/598/17.
45 *Tabeller over skibsfart* . . ., vol. IIA, pp. 18, 25, 104, 115, 229, 243.
46 See *Rejestr budowy galeony: zabytek z r. 1572* (*Register of galleon construction: a relic from 1572*), ed. A. Kleczkowski, Cracow, 1915, p. 102.
47 See L. F. Salzman, *English trade in the Middle Ages*, London, 1931, chapter XVII.
48 See E. F. Heckscher, *An economic history of Sweden*, Cambridge, Mass., 1954, p. 93; also Aström, *op. cit.*, p. 201.
49 See M. Małowist, *Handel zagraniczny Sztokholmu i polityka zewnętrzna Szwecji w latach 1471–1503* (*Stockholm's foreign trade and Sweden's foreign policy in the years 1471–1503*), Warsaw, 1935, p. 19.
50 Aström, *op. cit.*, pp. 34*f*.
51 M. Bogucka, *Gdańsk jako ośrodek produkcyjny* . . ., pp. 103, 133.
52 B. Zientara, *Dzieje małopolskiego hutnictwa żelaznego XIV–XVII w.* (*History of the Lesser Poland iron foundry industry from the fourteenth to the seventeenth centuries*), Warsaw, 1954, p. 161.
53 Małowist, *Handel zagraniczny Sztokholmu* . . ., p. 41.

54 Lauffer, *op. cit.*, p. 34.
55 *Tabeller over skibsfart* . . ., vol. IIB, pp. 162, 164.
56 P.R.O., E 315/485.
57 *Tabeller over skibsfart* . . ., vol. IIA, p. 5; also vol. IIB, p. 99.
58 Rybarski, *op. cit.*, vol. I, p. 139.
59 W.A.P.Gd., Lib. port. Elbing, 1594, f. 32.
60 *Ibid.*, 1599, ff. 23, 46, 47.
61 *Ibid.*, 1594, ff. 44, 53.
62 *Ibid.*, 1599, ff. 27, 37, 53, 54, 55.
63 *Tabeller over skibsfart* . . ., vol. IIA, p. 153.
64 *Ibid.*, p. 191.
65 *Ibid.*, p. 129.
66 See R. Bagwell, *Ireland under the Tudors*, vol. III, London, 1963, p. 451.
67 *Calendar of Patent Rolls, Elizabeth I*, vol. II, p. 98.
68 *Cal.S.P.For., 1561–62*, pp. 1–2.
69 Elizabeth I to Danzig, 22 April 1574 and 20 February 1576; *Danziger Inventar*, Nos. 6736 and 6964, pp. 528 and 544.
70 J. Gerds, agent of the Duke of Pomerania, to Lord Burghley, 23 December 1591, in Historical Manuscripts Commission, *Calendar of the manuscripts . . . Hatfield House*, vol. IV, London, 1892, p. 165.
71 *Tudor economic documents*, vol. III, p. 283.
72 W.A.P.Gd., Lib. port. Elbing, 1578, f. 42.
73 K. F. Olechnowitz, *Der Schiffbau der hansischen Spätzeit: eine Untersuchung zur Sozial- und Wirtschaftsgeschichte der Hanse*, Weimar, 1960, p. 106.
74 S. Kutrzeba, 'Handel Krakowa w wiekach średnich na tle stosunków handlowych Polski' ('Cracow's trade in the Middle Ages against the background of Poland's trading relations'), *Rozprawy Akademii Umiejętności* (*Transactions of the Academy of Sciences*), Wydział Historyczno-Filozoficzny (Historico-Philosophical Section), second series, vol. XIX, 1903, p. 25.
75 R. G. Albion, *Forests and sea power: the timber problem of the Royal Navy, 1652–1862*, Cambridge, Mass., 1926, p. 153.
76 Postan, '. . . England and the Hanse', p. 140. On the subject of Norwegian timber exports, see E. Bosse, *Norwegens Volkswirtschaft vom Ausgang der Hansaperiode bis zur Gegenwart*, vol. I, Jena, 1916, pp. 34–7. See also A. Soom, 'Der Ostbaltische Holzhandel und Holzindustrie im 17 Jahrhundert', *Hansische Geschichtsblätter*, vol. LXXIX, 1961, pp. 80*ff.*
77 See P. Smolarek, 'Stan i perspektywy badań nad rozwojem szkutnictwa w Polsce (do końca XVII w.)' ('The present state of and future prospects for research into the development of shipbuilding in Poland (to the end of the seventeenth century)', *Kwartalnik Historii Kultury Materialnej* (*Quarterly of the History of Material Culture*), vol. VII, 1959, p. 244, which lists the most important literature.

78 See Z. Binerowski, *Gdański przemysł okrętowy od XVII do początku XIX wieku* (*The Danzig shipping industry from the seventeenth to the beginning of the nineteenth century*, Danzig, 1963, pp. 23–6.

79 See M. Małowist, 'O niektórych cechach rozwoju gospodarczo-społecznego krajów nadbałtyckych w XV–XVII wieku' ('On certain features of the socio-economic development of the Baltic countries in the fifteenth to the seventeenth centuries') in Powszechny Zjazd Historyków Polskich w Krakowie w 1958 (General Congress of Polish Historians at Cracow in 1958), *Referaty i dyskusje* (*Papers and discussions*), vol. II, Warsaw, 1960, p. 92.

80 Rybarski, *op. cit.*, vol. I, p. 49; Binerowski, *op. cit.*, pp. 29, 32. See also *Najstarszy tekst prawa morskiego w Gdańsku* (*The oldest text of marine law in Danzig*), ed. B. Janik, Danzig, 1961, p. 233. On the categories of timber, see J. Broda, 'Staropolskie kategorie drewna w rejonach południowo-zachodniej Małopolski' ('Old Polish categories of timber in the areas of south-west Lesser Poland'), *Kwartalnik Historii Kultury Materialnej*, vol. VIII, 1959, pp. 280*ff*.

81 Material on this subject is to be found in the London port books for 1568 and 1588; P.R.O., E 190/4/2 and E 190/8/1.

82 P.R.O., E 190/432/6.

83 *Ibid.*, E 190/589/6.

84 *L.P. Henry VIII*, vol. XIV, part I, p. 18.

85 *Ibid.*, vol. XV, pp. 126*f*.

86 P.R.O., E 190/3/2.

87 *Ibid.*, E 190/7/8 and E 190/8/1.

88 *Tabeller over skibsfart . . .*, vol. IIA, p. 58.

89 *Ibid.*, p. 178.

90 *Cal.S.P. Simancas*, vol. II, *Elizabeth I, 1568–79*, p. 499. In a letter to Gabriel Zayas dated 18 July 1574 Antonio de Guaras wrote, 'These bad Englishmen, incited thereto by hopes of gain, continue to carry oars to Barbary . . . they have already sold four thousand which I said they had shipped at Dantzig . . .'

91 See Mączak and Samsonowicz, *op. cit.*, p. 213; also M. Małowist, 'Problematyka bałtycka w nowszej historiografii portugalskiej' ('Baltic problems in recent Portuguese historiography'), *P.H.*, vol. LII, 1961, No. 1, p. 19.

92 R. Davis, 'England and the Mediterranean, 1570–1670', in *Essays in the economic and social history of Tudor and Stuart England*, Cambridge, 1961, pp. 129–36.

93 Oppenheim, *op. cit.*, pp. 55*ff*; also K. Lepszy, *Dzieje floty polskiej* (*History of the Polish fleet*), Danzig, 1947, p. 26.

94 *Cal.S.P. Simancas*, vol. IV, *Elizabeth, 1587–1603*, p. 488.

95 Gierszewski, *op. cit.*, p. 67.

96 Fiedler, *op. cit.*, p. 91.

97 Samsonowicz, 'Handel zagraniczny Gdańska . . .', p. 334.

98 D. T. Williams, 'Medieval foreign trade: western ports', in *An historical geography of England . . .*, p. 289.
99 P.R.O., E 190/185/6 and E 315/485.
100 W. Naudé, *Die Getreidehandelspolitik der europäischen Staaten vom 13 bis zum 18 Jahrhundert*, Berlin, 1896, pp. 69*ff.*
101 Gras, *The evolution of the English corn market . . .*
102 D. Macpherson, *Annals of commerce*, vol. I, London, 1806, p. 409.
103 *Ibid.*, p. 482.
104 M. Małowist, 'Polityka gospodarcza Zakonu Kryżackiego' ('The economic policy of the Knights of the Cross'), in *Pamiętnik VII Powszechnego Zjazdu Historyków Polskich* (*Proceedings of the seventh General Congress of Polish Historians*), vol. I, Wrocław, 1948, p. 55.
105 Postan, '. . . England and the Hanse', p. 140.
106 W. Abel, *Agrarkrisen und Agrarkoniunktur in Mitteleuropa vom 13 bis zum 19 Jahrhundert*, Berlin, 1935, pp. 52–7. See also J. C. Russell, *British medieval population*, Albuquerque, 1948, pp. 230–32.
107 Postan, '. . . England and the Hanse', pp. 138–40.
108 Thomas Fuller, *The history of the worthies of England*, vol. II, London, 1840 edition, p. 551.
109 Unwin, *The gilds and companies of London*, p. 338.
110 C. Capper, *The port and trade of London*, London, 1862, p. 45.
111 Naudé, *op. cit.*, p. 81.
112 Małowist, 'The economic and social development of the Baltic countries from the fifteenth to the seventeenth centuries', *Ec.H.R.*, second series, vol. XII, 1959, 2, p. 184.
113 William Harrison, *An historical description of the iland of Britaine*, London, 1577, quoted from Trevelyan, *English social history*, London, 1945, p. 44.
114 Trevelyan, *op. cit.*, pp. 144–5.
115 See Lipson, *The economic history of England*, vol. II, p. 411.
116 See H. C. Darby, *The draining of the Fens*, London, 1940.
117 Gras, *The evolution of the English corn market*, appendix I.
118 *Tudor economic documents*, vol. II, p. 45.
119 F. J. Fisher, 'The development of the London food market, 1540–1640', in *Essays in economic history*, p. 135; also his 'The development of London as a centre of conspicuous consumption in the sixteenth and seventeenth centuries', *T.R.H.S.*, fourth series, vol. XXX, 1948, pp. 37*ff.*
120 This opinion is at variance with another observation by Francis Bacon, who expressed the view that in the days of Elizabeth England was dependent to a dangerous extent on grain imports; see F. J. Fisher, 'Tawney's century', in *Essays in the economic and social history of Tudor and Stuart England*, ed. F. J. Fisher, Cambridge, 1961, pp. 4*f.*
121 See M. M. Postan, 'The trade of medieval Europe: the North', in *The Cambridge economic history of Europe*, vol. II, Cambridge, 1952, p. 196. See also J. Ahvenainen, *Der Getreidehandel Livlands im Mittelalter*, Helsinki, 1963, p. 69.

122 P.R.O., S.P.Dom. 16/203, No. 107: 'Corn did not fall in price until the Eastland Merchants brought in.'
123 *L.P. Henry VIII*, vol. XXI, part I, pp. 98, 201.
124 *Ibid.*, No. 428, p. 201.
125 *A.P.C.*, vol. III, p. 202.
126 *Cal.S.P.For. Elizabeth*, 1562, No. 998, p. 435.
127 *Tabeller over skibsfart* . . ., vol. IIA, p. 8, and vol. IIB, p. 98.
128 *A.P.C.*, vol. XI, p. 287. It appears from the Acts that in 1576 Portsmouth merchants travelled to Danzig for grain, thanks to which 'the price of wheat in all markettes there adjoyninge did presentlie fall and therebie the contrary [*sc.* country] greatly relieved'.
129 *Ibid.*, vol. XIV, pp. 72, 91, 93.
130 *Ibid.*, p. 69. The Acts observe, 'the poorer sortes of people are in danger to famishe.'
131 *Ibid.*, p. 359.
132 B.M., Lansdowne MSS 49, No. 6.
133 Corporation of London Record Office, Guildhall, Repertory, 21, f. 288.
134 *Ibid.*, f. 293.
135 *Ibid.*, f. 363.
136 *A.P.C.*, vol. XV, p. 66.
137 B. Pearce, 'Elizabethan food policy and the armed forces', *Ec.H.R.*, vol. XII, 1942, pp. 39*f*; also Gould, 'The crisis in the export trade . . .', p. 216.
138 Pearce, *op. cit.*, p. 40. The people of Ipswich even started disturbances in protest against the despatch of meat and other food from England to the Netherlands.
139 J. E. T. Rogers, *op. cit.*, vol. V, pp. 269*f.*
140 P.R.O., S.P.Dom. 12/190, No. 60: 'Whereas by reason of the restrayne of trafique into Spain the Merchaunts of Bristoll that used to trade onelye to those parts are nowe destitute of meanes to employe their stocks . . . and for that by reason of the scarcietie of grayne wherby great penurye is fallen amongst the people in those parts and will be moche greater . . . unless some provision be made for them in other countreys . . . We have therefore thought good . . . to lycence the said merchaunts to trade into thease parts [i.e. the Baltic—H.Z.] during the tyme of restraynte onelye with two or three shipps, their retourne being intended to be made onelye with grayne . . .'
141 *Tabeller over skibsfart* . . ., vol. IIA, pp. 119, 123; also vol. IIB, pp. 102, 123, 130–1.
142 The food situation had so greatly improved by this date that gentry of Norfolk applied to the Privy Council for permission to export grain to Holland and Zeeland, and to France: *A.P.C.*, vol. XV, pp. 397, 408.
143 In a letter to the Lord Mayor of London dated 31 October 1596 the Privy Council stated that by that date twenty vessels had arrived in London with Baltic grain. This cargo would be of 'great relief to the inhabitants of the Cytie and Country adjoyning and especially to the

poorest sort'. The Privy Council warned that 'in this tyme of dearth and scarcitie' the grain should not get into the hands of speculators, who, by buying up food and reselling it at high prices, caused 'the oppression of the poor people'.—Corporation of London Record Office, Guildhall, Remembrancia, II, No. 59.

144 *Tabeller over skibsfart* . . ., vol. IIA, pp. 181–9.

145 England brought from Danzig 'greate store of wheat and rye, yf it be scante in England', we read in 'A speciall direction for divers trades', dated about 1575–85 (*Tudor economic documents*, vol. III, p. 201). A cargo of grain brought to London by the Eastland Company was checked for quality by a commission consisting of representatives of the local authorities, gilds and two representatives of the Eastland Company. The commission's task was to investigate whether the corn was in good condition, 'wholesom for the man's body'.—Corporation of London Record Office, Guildhall, Journals, 24, f. 40.

146 *Statutes of the realm*, vol. IV, p. 893.

147 Hinton, *The Eastland trade* . . ., pp. 10, 11, 37.

148 Ahvenainen, *op. cit.*, p. 149.

149 Małowist, 'Z zagadnień popytu . . .', p. 727.

150 Raleigh, *Observations* . . . This tract is also included in Ralegh's *Collected works*, ed. T. Birch, London, 1751, vol. II, pp. 113–36. Our quotations are from this edition (see note 64, chapter one above).

151 *Ibid.*, pp. 113–14.

152 *Ibid.*, p. 171. [Pomerland, Spruceland and Leifland were not kingdoms but principalities.]

153 *Ibid.*, p. 117.

154 *Ibid.*, p. 121.

155 See Naudé, *op. cit.*, p. 337.

156 P.R.O., E 190/593/23.

157 *A.P.C.*, vol. XII, pp. 24, 227; also *Calendar of Patent Rolls, Philip and Mary*, vol. IV, *1557–58*, pp. 74, 76.

158 *A.P.C.*, vol. XII, p. 342.

159 *Calendar of Patent Rolls, Philip and Mary*, vol. IV, *1557–58*, p. 225, and *A.P.C.*, vol. XIII, p. 60.

160 *A.P.C.*, vol. XIII, p. 313.

161 In the seventeenth century also Riga's and Reval's share in the export of Baltic grain was very small. See A. Soom, *Der baltische Getreidehandel im 17 Jahrhundert*, Stockholm, 1961, p. 298. It follows from Soom's calculations that only one per cent of the grain exported from Riga and Reval went to England. This view would appear to refute the opinion expressed by V. Niitemas in *Der Binnenhandel in der Politik der livländischen Städte im Mittelalter*, Helsinki, 1952, p. 137: 'dass der aktive holländisch-englische Handel sich besonders der Kornmärkten der Ostseegebiete zusandte'. This remark should be applied only to Dutch trade.

162 W.A.P.Gd., Lib. port. Elbing, 1594.

163 *Tabeller over skibsfart* . . ., vol. IIA, p. 102.
164 *Ibid.*, p. 162.
165 Willan, *The early history of the Russia Company*, p. 135.
166 *Ibid.*, p. 253.
167 P.R.O., E 190/4/2, E 190/6/3, E 190/7/8, E 190/8/1.
168 *Ibid.*, E 190/589/6, E 190/593/23, E 190/598/17, E 190/599/4.
169 *Ibid.*, E 190/432/5.
170 See the discussion between Bogucka and Hoszowski on the subject of the competition of Russian grain on the Dutch market in *Przegląd Historyczny* (*Historical Survey*), 1962–64; M. Bogucka, 'Zboże rosyjskie na rynku amsterdamskim w pierwszej połowie XVII wieku' ('Russian grain on the Amsterdam market in the first half of the seventeenth century'), *P.H.*, vol. LIII, 1962, No. 4, pp. 611–26; S. Hoszowski, 'W sprawie konkurencji zboża rosyjskiego na rynku holenderskim w pierwszej połowie XVII wieku' ('On the question of the competition of Russian grain on the Dutch market in the first half of the seventeenth century'), *P.H.*, vol. LIV, 1963, No. 4, pp. 688–99; Bogucka, 'Jeszcze o zbożu rosyjskim na rynku amsterdamskim w pierwszej połowie XVII wieku' ('Further observations on Russian grain on the Amsterdam market in the first half of the seventeenth century'), *P.H.*, vol. LV, 1964, No. 1, pp. 118–31.
171 *A.P.C.*, vol. XVII, p. 192.
172 *Ibid.*, vol. XVIII, p. 29.
173 *Ibid.*, vol. XXV, p. 39.
174 P.R.O., S.P.Dom. 46/125, No. 177.
175 *Ibid.* Parkins wrote that grain was accumulated in Poland 'for all forraine Countries as they have neede'.
176 P.R.O., S.P.Dom. 46/125, No. 165.
177 See Nowodworski, *op. cit.*, p. 29.
178 W.A.P.Gd., Lib. port. Elbing, 1594, ff. 11, 12, 17, 31.
179 *Ibid.*, 1599, ff. 19, 20, 23, 34, 55.
180 *Ibid.*, 1587, f. 25.
181 *Ibid.*, 1586, ff. 7, 19, 24, 27, 39, 40, 41, 44, 50, 58.
182 *Ibid.*, 1587, ff. 5, 15, 22, 25.
183 *Ibid.*, 1594, ff. 45, 58, 66, 70.
184 *Ibid.*, 1599, ff. 25, 53.
185 *Ibid.*, 1587, ff. 24, 42, 49.
186 *Ibid.*, 1586, f. 41.
187 Gray, 'English foreign trade . . .', pp. 18, 36.
188 Samsonowicz, 'Handel zagraniczny Gdańska . . ., p. 334. See also Lauffer, *op. cit.*, p. 34.
189 Koczy, *Handel Poznania* . . ., p. 328; also Wawrzyńczykowa, *op. cit.*, p. 44.
190 *Tabeller over skibsfart* . . ., vol. IIA, pp. 45–199; also vol. IIB, pp. 100–108, 122–4, 129–33, 148–50, 156, 241–2, 245, 246, 249, 253*f*, 255.

191 Hakluyt, *op. cit.*, vol. I, pp. 380/91.
192 *Ibid.*, p. 401.
193 *Tabeller over skibsfart* . . ., vol. IIB, p. 254.
194 *Ibid.*, pp. 241, 253.
195 W.A.P.Gd., Lib. port. Elbing, 1594, ff. 45, 47, 51, 54, 57–9, 68.
196

> If it weren't for potash
> There'd be no equipages;
> This treasure is not sufficiently esteemed:
> From ash we get our galloons.

Z. Gloger, *Encyklopedia staropolska illustrowana* (*Illustrated encyclopaedia of old Poland*), vol. IV, Warsaw, 1903, p. 109.
197 M. Bogucka, *Gdańsk jako ośrodek produkcyjny* . . ., pp. 84*ff*.
198 The following remarks on imports of wooden manufactures are based on the London port books: P.R.O., E 190/3/2, E 190/4/2, E 190/7/8 and E 190/8/1.
199 W.A.P.Gd., Lib. port. Elbing, 1586, f. 44.
200 *Ibid.*, f. 16.
201 *Ibid.*, 1599, f. 23.
202 *Tabeller over skibsfart* . . ., vol. IIA, pp. 9–199, and vol. IIB, pp. 98–108, 122–4, 128–33, 148–50, 156, 253–4.
203 *Ibid.*, vol. IIA, p. 133.
204 The Elbing customs registers for 1594 give 170 shippounds and for 1599, 129 shippounds of wool exported from Elbing to England.
205 P.R.O., E 315/467.
206 W.A.P.Gd., Lib. port. Elbing, 1599, ff. 33, 41.
207 Mączak, *Sukiennictwo wielkopolskie* . . ., p. 239
208 W. S. Jeżowski, *Oekonomia albo porządek zabaw ziemiańskich* (*Economy or the order of landowners' amusements*), ed. J. Rostafiński, Cracow, 1891, p. 67.
209 Beck, *op. cit.*, pp. 48–9.
210 *Ibid.*, p. 164.
211 *Ibid.*, p. 225.
212 W.A.P.Gd., Lib. port. Elbing, 1594, f. 5.
213 *Ibid.*, 1599, ff. 8, 19.
214 *Ibid.*, 1586, ff. 19, 21, 23, 25–7, 29, 30, 35–6, 50, 52, 58, 62.
215 *Ibid.*, 1587, ff. 24, 30, 36, 45–6, 60.
216 *Ibid.*, 1594, f. 12.
217 *Ibid.*, 1599, ff. 26, 33, 41, 50–51, 55.
218 Rybarski, *op. cit.*, vol. I, p. 107.
219 Trevelyan, *op. cit.*, p. 157.
220 *Tudor economic documents*, vol. I, pp. 302–04.
221 W.A.P.Gd., Lib. port. Elbing, 1599, f. 23.
222 *Ibid.*, 1594, f. 36.
223 Stone, 'Elizabethan overseas trade', p. 38.

nine *The problem of England's balance of trade with the Baltic*

To be complete, any study of England's trade with the Baltic in the Elizabethan era it must attempt to determine the balance of that trade. If we could solve this problem we might have the surest answer to the question: in the final analysis what effect did the English commercial penetration of the Baltic have from the point of view of the interests of the English merchants?

This is not an easy question to answer, because of the condition and the nature of the surviving sources; moreover, the various sources do not coincide in their dates. Statistics providing a complete picture of England's entire foreign trade in the second half of the sixteenth century are lacking. Another fundamental obstacle to any attempt to estimate the balance of England's Baltic trade is the lack of any comparatively full compilation of prices for the period. The tables compiled by Rogers,[1] Beveridge,[2] and Brenner[3] for England and by Pele for Poland[4] provide data which cover a very insignificant proportion of the goods listed in the English port books.

The only possibility of striking a balance is provided by the Sound toll registers, which give the value in Danish thalers of all the goods carried through the Sound in both directions by English merchants in the years 1565, 1575, 1585 and 1595. As we have already observed, table 9.1 reveals a rapid increase in English exports, which quadrupled over the period 1565–95 and rose especially quickly in the decade following the foundation of the Eastland Company. During the same thirty years imports rose more than threefold, especially towards the end of the century.

If we analyse the figures in table 9·1 closely, we have to conclude that they do not in fact provide a complete picture of England's balance of trade with the Baltic area. As A. Mączak has pointed out (*Zapiski historyczne*, vol. XXXIV, 1969, pp. 117–18), the figures given in the Sound registers deal with wholesale terms at the point of despatch. To attempt to assess the balance of trade on this basis is to ignore two vital factors: the merchant's profit margin, and freight charges. To enable comparative data to be derived with a view to estimating the approximate balance of England's Baltic trade, we need to add a figure for merchants' profits, and in the case of goods carried in foreign ships we need to allow for freight charges. In neither case are exact data available, so we have to resort to estimates.

Table 9.1 *Trial balance of English merchants' Baltic trade, decennial intervals 1565–1625, based on the Sound toll registers (Danish thalers)*

Year	*Exports*	*Imports*	*Balance*
1565	102,563·0	145,308·5	— 42,745·5
1575	192,362·5	229,038·5	— 36,676·0
1585	426,229·0	290,168·0	+136,061·0
1595	471,654·0	482,035·0	— 10,381·0
1605	580,959·0	320,544·0	+260,415·0
1615	561,797·5	337,666·0	+224,131·5
1625	571,515·5	262,935·5	+308,580·0

Source *Tabeller over skibsfart . . .*, vol. IIA, pp. 25, 58, 59, 114, 117, 177, 179, 242, 243, 305, 307, 355, 373.

Studies by M. Bogucka and A Mączak yield average figures for these two factors as follows:

1. Forty per cent profit margin for the difference in prices between Western and Baltic ports for goods carried in English vessels.
2. Twenty-five per cent profit for goods carried in foreign vessels.
3. Fifteen per cent freight charges borne by both categories of vessels.

Adjusting our balance to include these estimated charges, we can arrive at a calculation of the balance of English trade with the Baltic countries over ten-year intervals—the only periods possible—between 1565 and 1615 (see table 9.2).

In the light of the data provided by the Sound toll registers it appears that up to the foundation of the Eastland Company the Baltic trade of English merchants was relatively small in scale, but that after the Company's formation it increased considerably, bringing in over ten times as much profit as in the period before 1579. These deductions, however, are relevant only for direct trade between England and the Baltic carried on by English merchants and shipped in their

Table 9.2 *Estimated balance of English trade with Baltic countries, decennial intervals 1565–1615 ('000 thalers)*

	1565	1575	1585	1595	1605	1615
English exports						
Value of goods shipped to the Baltic in English vessels (prices at the port of despatch)	101	188	408	461	576	555
Value of goods shipped to the Baltic in foreign vessels (prices at the port of despatch)	2	4	18	10	4	7
40% profit to cover the difference in prices at Western and Baltic ports for goods shipped in English vessels	40	75	163	184	230	225
25% to allow for merchant's profit for goods shipped in foreign vessels, less freight charges paid to foreign carriers	0	0	2	1	0	1
Total: net profit on exported goods	143	267	591	656	810	788
English imports						
Value of goods shipped from the Baltic in English vessels (prices at the port of despatch)	48	123	221	236	224	180
Value of goods shipped from the Baltic in foreign vessels (prices at the port of despatch)	97	106	69	246	96	157
Freight charges on goods shipped to England in foreign vessels (15%)	15	16	10	36	15	24
Total: value of imported goods	160	245	300	518	335	361
Difference between exports and imports	−17	+22	+291	+138	+475	+427

Source These calculations are based on *Tabeller over skibsfart . . .*, vol. II, with the adjustments proposed by A. Mączak, 'Angielska Kompania Wschodnia a bilans handlu bałtyckiego w drugiej połowie XVI w.' ('The English Eastland Company and the balance of Baltic trade in the second half of the sixteenth century'), *Zapiski Historyczne*, vol. XXXIV, 1969, p. 119.

own vessels. They do not take into account the role of foreign middlemen, which is difficult to evaluate. It seems necessary also to make a further reservation concerning the decennial intervals. These years cannot be regarded as marking average periods in England's Baltic trade—a proviso which, in view of the considerable fluctuations in the volume of this trade, is of fundamental importance to our general conclusions.[5] It would seem essential to emphasize that there was a strict relationship and a degree of equilibrium between the merchants' Baltic imports and exports. For we have no indication that there was any large transfer of coin or bullion, which is always an adjusting factor in any country's balance of payments.[6] Yet on the other hand the charter Elizabeth I granted to the Eastland Company, in common with other documents, does speak of a serious restriction on exports of coin to the Baltic, and this suggests that a certain number of such transfers were made (see chapter ten).

The question arises, how far can any general conclusions be drawn from the Baltic trade balance of English merchants in the second half of the sixteenth century? This trade was part of a multilateral commerce which England carried on throughout the extensive area of her contemporary world, and only against the background of this multilateral trade could one really estimate the importance of the Baltic trade. But there is no possibility of establishing its value for the sixteenth century, as can be done for later centuries, where the requisite statistics exist. Heckscher, for instance, showed that in the years 1697–1770 England was constantly in deficit in trade with the Baltic; none the less, owing to her favourable balance with Holland, in the eighteenth century England's total foreign trade was in surplus.[7]

The foregoing question links up with the long-discussed theories of the mercantilists, who took the view that not only a country's general balance of foreign trade but also its trading balance with each individual country or area should be favourable. This sort of opinion, that in the sixteenth and seventeenth centuries foreign trade was in essence bilateral, was put forward by Wilson among others.[8] He drew attention to the difficulties inherent in the Baltic trade, a trade which England found necessary because it supplied essential ships' commodities, even though, in his view, it involved an unfavourable balance. England ironed out her deficit in the Baltic trade with the surpluses drawn from other, more profitable directions.

One must, however, make a further point which has not previously been mentioned in this study. It should be added that whilst the imports of bulky, heavy and cheap Baltic products were effected only by sea, within a certain small range the export of cloth or spices could pass overland, and especially *via* Hamburg. It is not possible to express this trade in figures.[9] And it is necessary to recall yet again a second element which cannot be calculated but which involves an increase in the volume of English exports: smuggling, and the activities of the interlopers. It was much easier to smuggle groceries or cloth, valuable yet small in bulk, than barrels of pitch or ships' masts. Despite the consequent adjustments to be made in favour of exports, it is obvious that in the second half of the sixteenth century there were years when England's trade with the Baltic was evidently in deficit, and that the deficits were ironed out by the transfer of coin, etc. A clause in the Eastland Company's 1579 charter permitting English merchants to export only £10 per annum to Baltic countries[10] clearly points to this kind of transaction.[11] A further factor restricting English merchants' profits in the Baltic trade and depriving them of the benefits arising from the cheapness of Baltic products was Dutch competition. Dutch intervention in the trade helped to force down the prices in England of Baltic products.

The absence of data precludes any discussion of England's Baltic trade overall, including that effected through foreign intermediaries. But so far as English merchants' Baltic trade was concerned, we must stress that a serious difficulty in maintaining equilibrium in the trade balance arose out of the nature of England's exports, which in practice consisted of only one product—cloth. Despite the Baltic market's absorptive powers, it was not always easy to dispose of an entire cargo of textiles in Danzig or Elbing in order to find the wherewithal to pay for grain or flax. The correspondence between Thomas Sexton and his Danzig factors, which dates from the beginning of the second half of the sixteenth century and which we shall be examining in the next chapter, clearly reveals England's payments difficulties in Poland and the strict interdependence of exports and imports. Unlike the Dutch, who operated with currency and so had great freedom, flexibility and independence, the English merchants developed their Baltic trade on the rather primitive principle of exchanging exports for imports. Their currency difficulties meant that to a large extent the level of their imports from the Baltic depended largely on the extent of their exports; and this also enforced the maintenance of equilibrium in the trade balance.

English merchants met with a serious difficulty in maintaining this equilibrium in the problem of returns, the commodity equivalent of products sold in the Baltic area. The chief equivalent for cloth was naval commodities especially flax, and then grain and potash. At the beginning of the seventeenth century the Eastland Company was complaining of the shortage of silver in England and the currency debasement in Poland. The Company sought in London to obtain some customs relief for its members, so that in exchange for the cloth sold in Poland they could purchase grain there and transport it to Spain, Portugal and Italy.[12] The Company was granted this form of relief several times in the early years of the century. In 1614 it was permitted to re-export Baltic grain to other countries without paying export duties.[13] In 1621 the difficulties in maintaining equilibrium in the balance of trade with the Baltic were explained as being due, among other things, to the lack of grain imports from Danzig due to the high freight charges and difficulties 'in exchange'.[14] During the trade crisis in the 1620's the Eastland Company complained that at that time flax was the only equivalent for cloth exported to Poland.[15]

The Company's attempts to keep its Baltic trade in surplus are revealed with particular clarity in the case of potash imports. In this instance we also observe English merchants' difficulties in finding a suitable equivalent for cloth exports. The importance of this question in elucidating the workings of the Eastland Company's trade and its attempts to maintain equilibrium obliges us to pay it more than passing attention.

In the early years of the seventeenth century the attempt to apply a new technology to soap production, eliminating the use of ashes and potash, seemed to pose a serious threat to the Eastland Company's Baltic trade. As we have shown, potash was one of the more important commodities English merchants shipped from the Baltic. A letter signed by James I and dated 12 December 1623 speaks of England having paid out large sums in cash for this import.[16] John Bourchier, the author of a plan to restrict imports of potash and ashes and to change to a more economic method of soap production based on home raw materials, even calculated that England paid out annually as much as £30,000 for potash imports.[17] A document in the Public Record Office indicates that at that time two kinds of 'soft soap' were produced in England, selling at 2*d* and 1*d* per lb respectively, and that the Eastland Company imported large quantities of Baltic potash for their production.[18] But there was a far greater demand for the higher-quality 'hard soap' which was imported mainly from Venice and Castile, to be sold on the home market at 6*d*–8*d* per lb. It was also manufactured in England, especially in Devon and Cornwall, but the domestic variety cost 10*d* per lb and was greatly inferior in quality to the imported product. The 1623 plan proposed putting English soap production on a level with that of Venice or Castile, using home-produced raw materials exclusively. A special company, the Society of Soapmakers of Westminster, was organized,[19] but the scheme ended in a scandal, for it transpired that the new soap was much poorer and dearer than that formerly produced. The Soapmakers' Society lost its patent and had to pay compensation. Leaving aside further details as irrelevant here, we need to examine the Eastland Company's arguments against the reorganization of English soap production, hitherto based on Baltic potash, since they provide some interesting sidelights on the subject of attempts to maintain equilibrium in the Baltic trade balance.

During the work of the special commission set up at the demand of the Eastland Company to investigate the question of English soap production,[20] the Company strongly urged that, because of the basic importance of potash as an equivalent for cloth exported to the Baltic, the plan for a new method of soap production without using ashes and potash could have disastrous consequences for English trade. It would reduce cloth exports to the Baltic countries by about 3,000 pieces per annum, since that was the equivalent quantity for imports of potash valued at £30,000, which would come to an end if Bourchier's plan were adopted. The Eastland Company also put forward the argument that stopping imports of potash might lead not only to a disturbance of England's trade balance with the Baltic but also to a drop in income from customs duties and a decline in English navigation in the Baltic.[21] The 1623 letter argues that imports should not exceed exports, in order to 'enlarge our exportation by native commodities . . . and spare our owne treasure, and increase it, by importation of forraine coyne or bullion'. This was a typical mercantilist argument.[21]

The problem of an equivalent for the Eastland Company's exports was raised forcefully in the Company's 1624 petition to the Privy Council. Arising out of the Privy Council's proposal to produce soap from home raw materials, without using foreign potash, we ask, says the petition, 'what compensation might be made unto us for our returnes hereafter, if ashes now about a foreth part of the same were taken away'.[22] Another Company letter in 1624 added that the stoppage of imports of Baltic potash would largely reduce the export of English cloth to the Baltic and cause damage to the country's shipping.[23] In an endeavour to recompense the Company against future losses arising out of the plan for domestic soap production the promise was made that, with a view to ironing out the losses, it would be free to import coin and bullion and to warehouse increased cargoes of Baltic grain in newly built granaries.[24] The Company's reply underlined one of the basic difficulties of the Baltic trade, which was also a source of difficulty in keeping it balanced: the well known contemporary problem of the debasement of the Polish currency, with the complications this gave rise to. A Company letter dated 9 February 1624 states: 'If ashes be taken from us, for want of other commodities we shall be forced, either to carrie out less cloth, or to bring home money, which we may not doe without great loss.' Further on in this extremely interesting letter it is emphasized: 'the common coyne minted in those parts being base, and nowher currant, and dollers and duckets lately risen to more than double their old value'.[23] In the Company's view there would be a loss of potash equivalent to £30,000 sterling; and one could not have a better illustration of the currency difficulties involved in England's Baltic trade.

Once more, in 1634, the Eastland Company petitioned the Privy Council on the matter of maintaining supplies of Baltic potash, arguing that if this import were restricted there would be a breakdown in English cloth exports to the Baltic. The merchants of the Eastland Company, says the petition, both those of London and of Ipswich, export dyed and dressed cloth, completely finished, from which it results that their trade affects not only themselves but many other subjects of His Majesty employed in producing and finishing cloth.[25] Thus emphasizing the national importance of cloth exports to the Baltic, the Company adds that 'money being scarce in the East Countries, the greatest parte mixed and base, and no exchange from thence, their retournes lye wholly in commodities, of which pottashes are the principall parte. When the Companie cannot sell cloth for money nor exchange it for other commodities, they often barter for pottashes, which makes their cloth trade move large and quicke.'[25] The Company closed its letter by emphasizing that it was a peculiar feature of England's Baltic trade that 'in the Eastland trade exportation and importation stand in such relation that the one prospers not without the other. If the importation or use of potashes (a forth parte of the Companie's retournes,) be restrayned, the vent of a fourth parte of the manufactured cloath exported then wil be hindred.'[25] The Polish cloth manufacturers would exploit this opportunity: they had long 'cast an evil eye on English cloth', and if Poland agreed, by way of recompense for the losses arising from restrictions on England's imports of potash, to England importing Baltic coinage to a corresponding value of £30,000 sterling this would not constitute an equivalent. For that coinage would be an equivalent for the restriction of the export of potash, and she would be able to reply to restrict Polish imports of English cloth.[26]

Another difficulty in maintaining an equilibrium between exports and imports in the Baltic trade arose from the fluctuating nature of England's grain imports, which were large only in times of poor harvest, crop failure, sudden famine, wars, etc. 'What shall we do if famine and war come simultaneously?' people asked in seventeenth century England, with the difficulties of the Baltic trade in mind.[27]

These difficulties in keeping the Baltic trade balanced, which the Eastland Company itself stressed so energetically, did not arise so sharply in the second half of the sixteenth century, during the period of England's greatest and most profitable trading expansion in the area. A degree of equilibrium is observable in the Company's exports and imports towards the end of the century, though there were quite wide fluctuations. Taking foreign intermediaries into consideration, it has to be concluded that the balance was favourable to England, and the Baltic trade brought considerable profit to English merchants. Certainly that trade was part of the multilateral commerce which England carried on simultaneously in various markets, and members of the Eastland Company operated in the North and Mediterranean sea areas within the organizations of the Merchant Adventurers, the Spanish Company, etc, thus making up for the losses they suffered in one of their areas of operation. But it must not be forgotten that the nature of the Baltic commodities was such that in general, apart from grain and certain other products, English merchants did not transport Baltic goods farther, since England played the role of intermediary for Baltic products only to a small extent. Thus the importance of the trade to England consisted not in its profitability but in its indispensability to the country's economy and general development. Before England's merchants gathered in the natural resources of the newly discovered expanses of America and the riches of Asia, the Baltic area acted as a great reservoir from which England could draw her necessary raw materials, and as a useful market for the disposal of her cloth. In the Elizabethan era the balance of advantage in the Baltic was still on the side of the English merchants, though not to the same extent as other, newly developing branches of trade.

Notes

1 Rogers, *op. cit., passim.*
2 Beveridge, *op. cit.*, vol. 1, *passim.*

3 Brenner, *op. cit.*, pp. 266–84.
4 Pelc, *op. cit.*, *passim.*
5 See Zins, 'Geneza angielskiej Kompanii Wschodniej (Eastland Company) z 1579 r' ('The genesis of the English Eastland Company'), *Zapiski Historyczne*, vol XXIX, 1964, No. 3, pp. 33*f.*
6 Z. Sadowski, *Pieniądz a początki upadku Rzeczypospolitej w XVII wieku* (*Money and the beginnings of the Commonwealth's decline in the seventeenth century*), Warsaw, 1964, p. 78.
7 E. F. Heckscher, 'Multilateralism, Baltic trade and the mercantilists', *Ec.H.R.*, second series, vol. III, 1950, No. 2, p. 227.
8 C. Wilson, 'Treasure and balance: the mercantilist problem', *Ec.H.R.*, second series, vol. II, 1949, No. 2, pp. 152*ff.*
9 A Merchant Adventurers' petition dated 1578 speaks of English merchants whose goods 'were not vented at Hamburgh but shipped thether to be by the way of Hamburgh transported into the Estseas, which may even as well and as good cheape be transported through the Sound, wherby the navie of this realme shall bee the better maintained': P.R.O., S.P.Dom. 12/127, No. 88. A Privy Council regulation dated 9 March 1636 refers to certain English merchants who, exposing the Eastland Company to great losses, exported cloth and other woven cotton goods indirectly, through Hamburg. The Privy Council ordered them 'to desist from all such indirect and irregular courses for the future': P.R.O., S.P.Dom. 16/315, No. 89.
10 P.R.O. Patent Rolls, 21 Elizabeth, c. 66/1185, f. 26.
11 Attman, *op. cit.*, has drawn attention to this type of practice in the Moscow trade.
12 P.R.O., S.P.Dom. 14/119, No. 139.
13 *Ibid.*, S.P.Dom. 14/178, No. 61.
14 *Ibid.*, S.P.Dom. 14/115, No. 111.
15 *Ibid.*, S.P.Dom. 14/184, No. 65.
16 *Ibid.*, S.P.Dom. 14/155, No. 38.
17 *Ibid.*, No. 41. This document bears the title 'A short note of the benefitt to the King and to the kingdome by the proposition made by Sir John Bourchier touching soap and ashes'.
18 *Ibid.*, No. 42. Some ten London soapmakers had a production of 1,000 barrels per annum.
19 Lipson, *The economic history of England*, vol. III, p. 363.
20 P.R.O., S.P.Dom. 14/164, No. 21. This commission, on which Eastland Company members also sat, was to check and investigate whether the new soap did or did not destroy fabrics, did not do any injury to the laundress's hands, etc. In this connection the London laundresses themselves were to express their opinion.
21 *Ibid.*, S.P.Dom. 14/155, No. 39.
22 *Ibid.*, S.P.Dom. 15/43, No. 61.
23 *Ibid.*, S.P.Dom. 14/158, No. 63.

24 *Ibid.*, S.P.Dom. 14/155, No. 42.
25 *Ibid.*, S.P.Dom. 16/279, No. 70.
26 *Ibid.*, S.P.Dom. 16/279, No. 71.
27 Wilson, 'Treasure and balance . . .', p. 154.

ten *The organization of England's Baltic trade*

In the sixteenth century England's Baltic voyages, like those of the Hansards or the Dutch, were organized to a large extent on the principle of the joint ownership of shipping, the entitlement being either by means of shareholdings or through financial contributions to the vessels' construction.[1] By contributing what, in reality, was not a very large sum to buy a share in a ship, and by the distribution of freight among several vessels, the contemporary merchant lessened the risks arising from loss of the vessel and cargo as a result of storms, pirates or privateers, trading restrictions, etc. As Antonio said in *The Merchant of Venice*,

> My ventures are not in one bottom trusted,
> Nor to one place; nor is my whole estate
> Upon the fortune of this present year.
> Therefore, my merchandise makes me not sad.

As was the universal custom, the merchants of the Eastland Company usually split up goods sent to the Baltic countries, as well as those brought back, into a number of parts, so greatly lessening the risk from loss of the cargo. The correspondence between the London merchant Thomas Sexton and his Danzig factors details this procedure, while the London port books even speak of a cargo sent to the Baltic being distributed into more than a dozen parts and consigned in a dozen or more ships.[2] The various parts of a consignment, usually despatched at one time, were normally of approximately equal value. This was the case, for instance, with goods which Sexton's factors purchased in Danzig in 1556 and 1557.[3]

Merchants carrying on trade with the Baltic were usually either owners of entire ships, such as Thomas Allen[4] or Thomas Pullison,[5] or parts of ships through an association of several merchants. Or, when necessary, they chartered a ship urgently. The principle of shares in ships often led to protracted disputes and litigation, as we learn from the case of Richard Lewis, a member of the Eastland Company who owned one third of a ship and was at law with his associates for seventeen years because of their failure to observe their financial obligations.[6] Pullison,[7] and many other Company members were part owners of ships; their names are frequently mentioned in the Acts of the Privy Council in connection with privateers' attacks and disputes among individual merchants.

Usually merchants sent their goods to the Baltic in various English or foreign ships, chartered sporadically in England's eastern ports, especially London, Hull and Newcastle. They adopted the same procedure in Danzig and other Baltic ports when purchasing local commodities for importation into England. From the correspondence between Thomas Sexton, who did not own his own ship, and his factors it appears that as a rule in such a case several merchants chartered a vessel actually lying in port, on the basis of a charter agreement between the merchants and shipmaster.[8] Then they shared out the freight charges in proportion to their share in the cargo and one of the merchants concluded an agreement with the shipmaster on behalf of them all. For instance, in June 1557 Thomas Sexton entered into such an association with three other London merchants, W. Barker, L. Coxson and W. Burnell, and acted as their representative in an agreement concluded with the shipmaster, John Gosling of Aldeburgh, for the transport of a quantity of iron, flax and other Baltic goods from Danzig to England.[9] The freight charges were usually established jointly between the shipmaster and the merchants, and in general payment was made dependent upon the shipmaster's safe delivery of the entire cargo to its destination. This too led to frequent disputes and litigation, as we learn from Sexton's Danzig agents. For instance, a letter from John Freman to Sexton dated 16 June 1557[10] indicates that Sexton had advised his agents of the despatch to Danzig of a quantity of skins in a ship of which Richard Tomson was master. On the ship's arrival it transpired that there was a shortage of 200 cony skins. As the shipmaster was not prepared to stand the loss and reduce the freight charges appropriately, Sexton's factors refused to pay anything, declaring that the shipmaster would obtain payment from Sexton in London.

Among the various types of association entered into by merchants engaged in the Baltic trade the most common, as appears from the very meagre materials available on the subject, was the so-called *sendeve*, constituting a form of commission.[11] The merchant handed over his goods and a certain sum of money to his collaborator, empowering him to carry on an independent trading transaction in his name in the Baltic ports. Quite often a shipmaster entered into such an agreement. An association of this nature, set up for an immediate trading transaction, had no permanence.[12] Frequently Eastland Company members—especially the less affluent—themselves undertook the sale of their cloth in Danzig or Elbing.[13] As we have already observed, many merchants resided in the Polish ports and arranged transactions to the order of merchants residing in London. (This form of association was called *vera societas.*) The Eastland Company's possession of a permanent entrepot on the Polish coast favoured the development of this kind of association. But the most advantageous organizational form, and the one most widely used in the Baltic trade during the second half of the sixteenth century, was the institution of a travelling, and later of a permanently residing, trading agent, or factor.

The institution of the factor developed in England, as in other countries, in connection with the spread of the 'settled' merchant in foreign trade. It was also due to the vast growth during the Elizabethan era of the scope of operations of the great London wholesalers, who were engaged in trade simultaneously with sometimes distant countries, most frequently with Poland, Holland and Spain, but also with Germany and the Levant, etc. So long as England's commerce was restricted to contact with the nearby Netherlands, English merchants, especially during earlier periods, carried on trade directly, though they had long availed themselves of the mediation of factors and shipmasters, as well as entering into various forms of association, especially of the commission type. We learn from documents of the Merchant Adventurers, who carried on trade with not very remote parts, that the use of factors was widely adopted among them, and their ordinances permited factors to take the place even of English merchants in meetings held at the staple on the Continent.[14] This procedure was also followed by the Merchants of the Staple.[15] As the range of the merchants' trading activities enlarged, the use of factors grew more and more common in the second half of the sixteenth century. This was true not only in the case of joint stock companies, carrying on trade with Russian, the Levant and the Indies almost exclusively through factors, but also of the regulated companies and individual, more affluent merchants in the days preceding the formation of trading companies.

The institution of a permanent agent became indispensable in the Elizabethan era not only because of the wide range of English trade but also because of the actual manner of its organization. As we learn from the correspondence of Sexton's factors, in the middle of the sixteenth century English merchants' trade in Danzig was based to no small extent on credit operations, which called for constant and persistent alertness and close acquaintance with the market and its organization.[16] So not just the rich but also the average prosperous merchant employed factors—sometimes several at once—in the Polish ports; the very wealthy London wholesaler, Thomas Russell, for instance, employed two agents in Danzig for a number of years.[17] And this applied to the moderately well-off London merchant Thomas Sexton, the employer of the Freman brothers, who worked for him in Danzig.

Factoring was often the final phase of a term as a merchant's apprentice; for such a one these *wanderjahre* yielded invaluable experience in the merchant profession. We may take as an example the famous Lionel Cranfield, a merchant member of the Eastland Company and a Minister under James I. At the age of fifteen Cranfield became an apprentice to Richard Sheppard, and six years later, in 1596, he went on Sheppard's behalf as a factor to Stade. There he also watched over the interests of his uncle, William Cranfield. Independently he carried on trading operations in cloth and groceries on his own account.[18] His was not an isolated case, and one frequently comes across examples of factors who, whilst representing their employer's interests, simultaneously traded on their own account. Moreover, such a man might be an associate of a merchant residing in the same city. Lionel Cranfield's father worked in Antwerp in 1551 as Vincent Randall's factor, simultaneously trading in cloth in his own right. In 1559 he was independently engaged in the Dutch trade and employed E. Smith as his Antwerp agent, though Smith was also factor for other English merchants.[19] Thomas Sexton's factors operated in Danzig almost exclusively in their master's interests, although from time to time they executed commission orders for his relatives.[20] The correspondence of Sexton's factors also reveals that one factor sometimes worked for several merchants. In the middle of the century George Lawson worked in Cadiz on behalf of Sexton and another English merchant; in Lisbon John Hilliard was agent for Sexton and several other merchants.[21]

Besides permanent factors, English merchants also employed 'travelling' agents in the Baltic trade, as we learn, once more, from the Sexton correspondence. At times Sexton consigned cloth to the Baltic *via* Hamburg, and he sent his factor, Robert Pope, to take over the cargo in Hamburg and see to its onward despatch to Danzig. Pope was active in Sexton's Danzig trade in May and June 1557; in

September 1558 he was in Portugal and Spain, and again in May 1559.[22] During the same period he attended to several of his employer's interests in England. Thus he acted as a kind of consignor and liaison officer; he complemented and supported the work of Sexton's four main factors, the Freman brothers in Danzig, and Lawson and Hilliard in the Iberian peninsula. Furthermore, in 1559 Sexton sent one of his apprentices to Holland to learn Dutch, with the intention that the youth should become his factor in the Netherlands.

Certainly we still know very little about the methods by which English factors were trained in the Elizabethan era. But one may assume that they acquired their knowledge and experience in practice, serving a certain term and learning their profession from more than one merchant. Towards the end of the century they also had a printed handbook, *The Merchants Avizo*, written in 1589 by John Browne, a Bristol merchant.[23] This work contained many practical suggestions which could be of assistance to the young factor, often a merchant's son, travelling abroad on commercial affairs. It also included a number of model business letters and specimens of receipts, accounts and certificates which the factor had to draw up in the course of his activities. It appears, too, from this handbook that the factor received 2·5 per cent on the transactions he carried through; this brought him a considerable income, and encouraged him to be energetic. In practice a factor's income was even higher, because he also carried on trade on his own account (quite apart from the numerous opportunities of cheating his employers which arose.) Sometimes the latter were hundreds of miles distant, and they had only the factor's correspondence to keep them closely informed of the situation in any given market, the prices ruling in it, the losses actually or ostensibly sustained by the factors, etc.

Examples of correspondence between English merchants and their Baltic factors in the sixteenth century are a rarity, so the series of letters from Thomas Sexton's agents, written in Danzig in 1555–59, are invaluable source material. Fortunately, they have been preserved in the Public Record Office. As they reveal many details of the work of English factors in Danzig and enable us to get a closer look at the organization of England's Baltic trade, they warrant careful consideration.[24]

Thomas Sexton, on whose behalf the factors Blase and John Freman functioned in Danzig for five years, was one of the more affluent London merchants. He came from a family of cloth manufacturers, but he himself was a member of one of the livery companies most deeply engaged in the Baltic trade, the Skinners. He carried on trade with Poland, Spain and Portugal, and had trading interests in the Netherlands.

The earliest of the letters from Blase Freman, the elder of the two brothers and later a member of the Eastland Company, is dated 20 April 1555. He wrote the majority of the letters which have survived. This letter contains a detailed report on the factors' trading operations in Danzig.[25] Sexton's letters to his Danzig agents have not survived, but judging by their replies they carried out his instructions very precisely, and in addition kept him supplied with detailed information on goods, prices, difficulties in buying and selling, etc. In the letter just mentioned Blase Freman reported to Sexton on the purchase in Danzig of the following goods, which had been consigned to London in four vessels: eight bales of flax, twelve cables, forty-two hawsers, twenty-five shippounds of iron, ninety-three single and 214 double ratlines, two chests and two packs of 'playing tabulls'. He also informed his master of the purchase of a further twenty cables and forty hawsers, which he planned to send by the next boat. He had obtained 960 stone of cable yarn, including only 660 stone for cash. He ended the letter, as he did almost all he wrote, with a detailed statement of commodity prices in Danzig. As these supply very full complementary data to those of Danzig sources, we set them out in table 10.1.

Blase Freman's next letter to Sexton, dated 30 August, 1556,[26] clearly shows the work of a commercial factor. He had sent to London five cables and fifteen hawsers, the total weight being close on 36 cwt, also a sack of feathers and one 'peper cask', shipping the goods by the Danzig vessel *Margytt*.[27] About the same time he received 3,800 cony skins from London, but they were of poor quality and condition. As he had only nineteen pieces of *Luński* broadcloth and twenty-two of narrow cloth in Danzig, and temporarily had no purchasers for them, he complained that he did not know how he would manage in this difficult situation, especially as at that time the price of cony skins in Danzig had fallen from 27 to 25 florins per 1,000, and the majority of those he had received recently were 'so ettyn with worms . . . that I cane get no mony for them'.[26] In this letter, as in many others, Freman complained of the quality of and deterioration in the goods London sent him. He advised consigning them *via* Hamburg, and gave his master much advice as to the quality of the kinds of cloth enjoying the greatest demand

Table 10.1 *Prices in Danzig, 1555–*

Date	*English commodities*			*Polish commodities*		
	Cloth		*Cony skins*	*Pitch*	*Tar*	*Ashe*
	Broad	*Narrow*				
	Pieces Florins	*Pieces Florins*	*'000 Florins*	*Lasts Florins*	*Lasts Florins*	*Last. Florir*
1555						
20 April	26–30	15–16	24	15	12–13	–
30 August	–	–	–	17	11·5	20
1556						
10 September	28	–	25·5	17·5	12·5	20
7 October	26–30	–	26	17	13	22
1557						
1 January	27–30	13–14	26	19	13	23
13 April	25–29	12	26	18	13	24
10 May	26–29	–	25–25·5	17	13	22
13–16 June	25–29	–	25·5	18	14–14·5	23–2
28 June	25–27	10–11	25	18	13–15	23–2
3 July	24–27	10	–	18	15	23
14 July	–	–	26	17	13	23
20 July	24–26	–	25·5	17–18	12–13	22–2
15 August	26–29	–	26	17	11	22
24 August	25–29	10	26	17–18	12	22–2
8 September	26–28	–	–	17	12	22–2
14 October	26–29	10	26	15	11	20
1 November	26–29	–	26	15	10	20
20 December	26–29	10	–	14	9	20
1558						
22 January	26–29	9	26	12	9	18
1 October	29–30	–	30	12	9	12
1559						
7 July	–	–	–	12	10	17
23 July	–	–	–	12–14	10	17

Note Sexton's factors noted the prices of many commodities in Danzig
1937, gives only the price of rye, and then only for 1555 and 1556 in the per
Pelc's data and those of the English factors in regard to the price of a last of
quarter of that year, whereas the factors noted 28 florins a last in the th
average prices, whilst Sexton's factors quote the price of the day, so doubt
in those days—though one cannot entirely repress the suspicion that
obtaining greater profit for themselves.

ed on Sexton's factor's correspondence

'heat	*Rye*	*Flax*	*Hemp*	*Yarn*	*Oak staves*	*Staves*
its of measurement and money values						
asts *orins*	*Lasts* *Florins*	*Stones* *Small marks*	*Stones* *Groschen*	*Stones* *Groschen*	*Hundreds* *Florins*	*Hundreds* *Florins*
28	14	124	20	26	–	–
50	28	105–106	34	40	21	22
50	28	106	36	43	22	23
–	30	116	36	44	–	–
–	35	120	43–44	53	22	23
53	38	132	38–40	50	–	–
60	30	132	36	48	–	–
58	43–44	135–136	36–45	48–50	24	29
53	44–47	136	34–36	46–47	–	–
–	–	136	34	46	–	–
50	46–48	133–134	36	46	–	–
53	46–47	130	34	46	–	–
36	26	–	35	44	–	–
40	30	118–120	32	45	–	–
–38	26	118	33	43	20	–
–	–	–	24	34	20	–
–	–	100	24	34	–	–
–	–	96	24	34	–	–
–	–	96	24	33	–	–
–	–	–	–	–	–	–
–	–	110	–	36	–	–
–	18–19	110	–	–	48–50	–

years 1555–59. But J. Pelc, in *Ceny w Gdańsku w XVI i XVII w.*, Lwów, ered by the Freman correspondence. There is a striking disparity between 556. Pelc gives 21 florins in the first quarter and 20 florins in the second rter. (There are no data for any earlier period.) It is true that Pelc quotes disparity can be explained by the great price fluctuations which occurred ors might deliberately have led their master into error with a view to in Danzig. He assured Sexton that despite the temporary difficulties and lack of cash he would endeavour to purchase as much yarn for cordage as possible. He took the opportunity to complain of the high price of hemp in Danzig. This letter also ended with a list of prices for certain Polish commodities of interest to English merchants.

Thus the London merchant would gain a fairly exact picture of the situation on the Danzig market, and would be provided with a guide for directing his future trading operations. We need to point out once more that because of the factors' distance from London and the frequent fluctuations in the Baltic trade they enjoyed considerable independence and freedom to take swift decisions on whether and when to buy or sell. Sexton's factors were engaged not only in acquiring raw materials and semi-manufactures but also—as in the case of hemp—in making arrangements for their conversion into the cordage and lines needed for ships' rigging.[28] For instance, in the autumn of 1556 Freman gave an order to the Danzig rope maker B. Frytte to manufacture yarn into cordage from all the raw materials in his possession, which Frytte was to do in the course of the winter. The quantity totalled 300 stone, and the manufacturing charge was 40 groschen per stone.[29] The factors gave a similar order to the Danzig rope maker Hans Lobkyne for 400 stone of yarn. They could pay for only half this quantity in cash immediately, and the balance was to be paid in the winter. By such means the brothers incurred a debt of 1,000 florins, and in consequence they urged their master to send them a larger quantity of cloth, which they received from London shortly after. Down to the end of August they had received 103 broadcloths, sixteen narrow cloths, and twenty cloths of other kinds.[30] They managed to sell the cloth easily enough, but at only a small profit, as the price in Danzig at that time was not very high: 28 florins a cloth. During the winter of 1556–57 the factors sold, altogether, 152 broadcloths out of a total of 163 received, also all twenty-eight narrow cloths and forty-seven cloths of other kinds. The Freman correspondence indicates that the price of English cloth in their day ranged from 13 to 15 florins for poorer quality red, and from 16 to 24 florins for grey, rising to 30 florins for the best kind of *Luński* broadcloth.

With the money obtained by the sale of cloth Blase Freman purchased various Polish products. In addition to the 700 stone of yarn for cordage already mentioned, he ordered 1,000 stone from one of the Danzig rope makers. He was to take delivery of part at Easter and part at Whitsun, at a price of 1,686 florins, which he had obtained by the sale of his goods at the market on St Dominic's day. For the same price he purchased a further 1,000 stone of yarn from Hans Lobkyne and 600 stone from A. Fulke at a cost of 1,040 florins. He also bought thirteen lasts of hemp and handed it to Danzig rope makers to be converted into ships' cordage. In March 1557 he was able to inform Sexton that he had a cargo of 4,000 stone of yarn for cordage ready for shipment to England.[32]

As the foregoing survey of the activities of Sexton's Danzig factors indicates, essentially cloth was almost the only English export against which ships' commodities and grain could be obtained in Poland. In 1557 the Freman brothers sold in Danzig 152 costly *Luński* cloths, twenty-eight narrow cloths and forty-seven cloths of other kinds. Altogether they obtained 4,280 florins for the cloth sold in Danzig. During this same period they sold about 100,000 cony skins, for 2,550 florins.[33] Thus from the sale of cloth and skins the brothers obtained 6,830 florins, or about £1,308.[34]

We learn from his agents' correspondence that Sexton imported from Poland not only ships' cordage and yarn for ropes, but also flax, hemp, pitch, iron, ashes and a small quantity of grain. He did order 100 lasts of rye, but his factors failed to obtain more than ten lasts, and that at the high price of 38 florins per last.[35] From April to June 1557 relations between England and Danzig were strained, so the English agents' position grew quite difficult, and they came up against various restrictions on trade. In any case, it would seem that Sexton's balance of trade with Poland in 1557 was unfavourable. The goods purchased in Danzig cost him some 9,000 florins, or about £1,800. So his imports exceeded his exports by a sum of about 2,000 florins, or some £400. But 1557 was a particularly difficult year for England's Baltic trade, and besides, we cannot draw any conclusions from the figures cited, as it is not certain whether the surviving Freman letters constitute the whole of their correspondence.

The Freman letters indicate the close and frequent correspondence maintained between the London merchant and his Danzig factors. The need for security forced the factors not only to split up their London shipments into several parts consigned by a number of ships, but also to add to them written reports in several copies. Between 27 June and 4 July 1557 the Freman brothers wrote as many as eighteen letters to their master, sending them by seven ships. These letters were not absolutely identical, but they all contained the same basic information, relating not only to that part of the cargo to which the letter was attached but also to the whole of the agents' trading activities of recent days. They were sent independently of the cargo, by the hand of shipmasters voyaging to London. They took at least two weeks on the voyage; in other words, it was some five weeks before the factors received replies from London. This also implies that they had considerable plenipotentiary powers.

We have already said that in England's sixteenth century Baltic trade the institution of the permanent factor was the more necessary because this trade was to a large extent reminiscent of barter—only after goods imported from England had been sold could the factors obtain the commodities their employer needed, buying in Danzig or Elbing—and the credits they obtained in the Polish ports only partially alleviated the inadequacies of this somewhat primitive form of exchange. So the agents were constantly anxious about the quality of the textiles sent from England.[36] At times when they failed to sell cloth and skins in the Polish ports they had to resort to credits from Danzig merchants and usurers, especially when it was necessary to make a quick purchase because of favourable prices.[37]

The organization of the Danzig market and the seasonal nature of the local markets were another factor compelling the English agents to act swiftly and energetically in their trading operations.[38] In practice, only in the summer, especially at the market held on St Dominic's day, were any large transactions put through in Danzig. At such a time it was difficult for English merchants to compete with the local buyers, who offered a greater variety of goods in exchange, not to mention the fact that English merchants were affected by various restrictions, especially during periods of Anglo-Hanseatic conflict. Moreover, certain goods could be bought only for cash, and so Sexton's factors repeatedly drew their employer's attention to the difficulties they were experiencing in their work.

In the second half of the century English merchants made use of various forms of credit in their Baltic trade. Very few documents dealing with this subject exist, but it seems that the most frequently adopted method was a simple bill of exchange, which consisted in the drawer entering into an obligation to pay a certain sum within a certain time. This form of bill of exchange, presented by the debtor, was a primitive credit instrument applied universally in the feudal world. We also come across bills of exchange with endorsements in the English Baltic trade: a receipt would be given on the back of the bill of exchange associated with the nomination of a plenipotentiary to collect the amount outstanding on the bill.[39] Sexton's Danzig factors also resorted to payment transfers; for instance, in

June 1557 Sexton was presented in Danzig with a bill of exchange drawn by Robert Lewytt for a sum of 19 marks which Lewytt owed Sexton in London.[9] In general it appears that in the total trading operations of English merchants credit exchange did not as yet play any large part (a point we shall be discussing below); but the difficulties the English had in paying with silver meant that to them the exchange of goods was much more important than credit and bill-of-exchange transactions, so that the Dutch had obvious advantages and greater flexibility in trading with the Baltic area. In the Elizabethan period England's Baltic trade was distinguished by a fairly balanced relationship between imports and exports, not involving the necessity for the transfer of large amounts of specie. Only in years when England imported large quantities of Baltic grain, either direct from Poland or *via* the Dutch, was there any big flight of specie from the country. But this occurred mainly in the seventeenth century.

A number of statements by merchants and writers on economics at the beginning of the seventeenth century point very definitely to the bilateral element in England's Baltic trade, in which credit and bills of exchange played as yet no large part. At the beginning of the century English merchants emphasized that their export trade to the Baltic countries 'was entirely covered by products of the Eastern countries'. The question of potash, discussed in the previous chapter as an important equivalent for the Eastland Company's goods in exports to the Baltic, clearly points to the direct and decided predominance of commodity exchange over credits and bills of exchange in that trade. G. Malynes, a contemporary writer on economics, noted in 1601 that at that time England did not as yet trade with Poland on the basis of cash transactions, although English merchants took small quantities of silver to Danzig and Elbing. Even this happened rarely, owing to the great fluctuations in the value of Polish money and the exchange rates, which were unfavourable to England. He wrote that the exchange of exports for imports was the most advantageous.[40] This statement is not in contradiction to our data on the transactions of Sexton's Danzig factors, which in any case relate to a rather earlier period. It is evident that the factors worked to no small extent on a credit basis, but obviously this was only within the scope of the Polish money market. That correspondence reveals that in Danzig English merchants paid cash, partly in florins, for purchases made locally, but that they also partly obtained credits to be paid off later. For instance, in September 1556 the factors incurred a debt of 1,000 florins to Danzig rope makers as a result of the failure of cloth to arrive in time from London.[41] We do not know the conditions on which the Freman brothers borrowed from the Danzigers, but in view of the remark Blase Freman made in this connection—'I pray God I may be able to make mony to pay for ytt'[42] —one could deduce that conditions were not very favourable to the debtors. It has to be added that Sexton's factors attempted to exchange Polish thalers for gold or French crowns in Amsterdam and Antwerp, but met with difficulties.[43] The exchange could have been effected, but only at a loss of 5*d* per £ sterling.

Despite temporary difficulties, such as occurred when Sexton's factors were writing at the beginning of the second half of the sixteenth century, i.e. in years of repressive Hanseatic measures against English merchants in the Baltic area, it must be pointed out that in Elizabethan times there was a quite substantial increase in the stock of specie in England. This came about partly as a result of the development of her foreign trade and the favourable course of the 'revolution in prices', partly through the pillages of English privateers and corsairs, who captured cargoes of Spanish silver.[44] Certainly, even towards the end of the century, there were complaints about the lack of silver currency, and voices were raised in protest against the export of metal currencies abroad. But only at the beginning of the next century did this problem become urgent.[45] From then on English merchants complained more and more frequently of the decline in their Baltic trade because they had nothing with which to pay for goods imported from the area.[46] The difficulties the Eastland Company met with in this period largely explain the sources of England's weakness in the Baltic in her rivalry with Holland. The manufactures of her textile industry were the main commodity offered in exchange for Baltic products, so it was a bilateral trade, as we have already seen. But Holland's Baltic trade was part of a broad international commerce centred on Amsterdam.[47] The Dutch had a tremendous advantage over the English with regard to navigation and the actual organization of trade, which they based to a large extent on credit and bill-of-exchange operations plus cash.[48] Hence they did not suffer from the effects of Baltic inflation to the same extent as the English. In addition, the Dutch applied a system of advances against future deliveries, thanks to which they could react more flexibly to the conditions on the Baltic market than the English, who were heavily dependent on the immediate situation.[49]

The shortage of source materials (as we have said, the Acts and ordinances of the Eastland Company have been preserved only from 1616 onward) unfortunately prevents our entering upon a more detailed discussion of the organization of England's Baltic trade in the second half of the sixteenth century, especially the problems of credit and bill-of-exchange operations, specie transfer and cash transactions. These issues have been the subject of more study in the case of the seventeenth century, but it is not permissible to apply conclusions drawn from a later period to the Elizabethan era because from the time of the crisis in the Baltic trade in the reign of James I a different situation arose.

In conclusion, it is of interest to recall the manner in which the Eastland Company exercised control over the technical aspects of the Baltic trade, especially to ensure merchants' and shipmasters' observance of certain contributions both to the Eastland Company and to the customs authorities in the Sound and at Elbing. To reduce the possibility of shipmasters' indulging in trickery and to avoid any disputes with Denmark over the Sound customs control which might arise in consequence, Elizabeth's 1579 charter reserved to the Company the right to demand that shipmasters sailing to the Baltic should deposit a surety as a guarantee that they would observe all the Company's regulations and pay the customs dues demanded. Before setting out for the Baltic, the master of a ship chartered by Company members went to the Company treasurer, who gave a receipt for the sum of £50 sterling against the payment of customs dues in the Sound, in Poland and under the Duke of Prussia. He also bound himself not to take on board goods belonging to merchants who were not members of the Company, and to carry the cargo entrusted to him direct to Elbing, not to any other Baltic port. Then, after making a declaration to the Company treasurer or other representative that before sailing he would report the exact value of the goods taken on board, the master was given a certificate entitling merchants who were members of the Company to load his ship. With these activities were associated appropriate accounts and receipts, one, for instance, containing an exact list of the goods the master was taking to the Baltic. After being certified by the English customs and sealed, this document was to be presented to the Sound customs and to the governor of the English entrepot in Elbing, who had the right and duty to check on the cargo brought and to extract the appropriate payments from shipmasters and merchants.[50] To avoid these dues, members of the Company repeatedly preferred to unload the goods brought from England at Königsberg or Danzig, as we discover by comparing the London port book with the Elbing customs register for 1587.[51]

The English port books clearly indicate that English ships sailed to the Baltic mainly in convoys, and returned home in the same manner, so as to make defence easier against the attacks of privateers and the other dangers of Baltic navigation. In times of especial danger, particularly towards the end of the sixteenth century and again on the eve of the Thirty Years War, these flotillas were given a kind of naval escort to protect them against attacks. In 1628 the Eastland Company complained to Charles I of the great losses inflicted on it by Spain, and asked at the same time for escorts to accompany its ships sailing to and from the Baltic.[52] The author of one such proposal even suggested that it was necessary to engage ten ships with total crews of 1,000 men for these escorts.[53]

The period for English ships to sail to the Baltic lasted in general from April to September,[54] though one comes across cases of vessels being sent to the Baltic in other months,[55] which applied especially to London merchants' trade. The Elbing customs registers indicate a period from April to November as the main season for English ships sailing to the Baltic, the period being determined by navigational and climatic as well as trading factors.[56]

The fairly loose form of organization adopted by the Eastland Company meant that its members were not hindered by any rigid restrictions and prohibitions. They carried on their trade according to their own judgement and at their own risk, observing only the Company's organizational framework as fairly generally formulated in the charter of 1579, which defined its structure and monopoly without going into the question of the actual organization of the trade.

Notes

1 See Małowist, *Studja z dziejow rzemiosła . . .*, p. 379; C. Brämer, 'Die Entwicklung der Danziger Reederei im Mittelalter', *Z.W.G.*, vol. LXIII, 1922, p. 141; also R. de Roover, 'The organization of trade' in *The Cambridge economic history of Europe*, vol. III, Cambridge, 1963, pp. 105*ff*, 116–18.

2 P.R.O., E 190/6/4 and E 190/7/8. There is a detailed discussion of the problems raised by the English port books in J. R. Jones, *London's import trade with France during the reign of Elizabeth*, Philadelphia, Pa., 1944, pp. 1–14.

3 Letter from J. Freman to Thomas Sexton, 20 December 1557, and from B. Freman to Sexton, 14 August 1558: P.R.O., S.P. Supplementary 46/9, ff. 91, 102.
4 *A.P.C.*, vol. XIII, p. 83.
5 *Cal.S.P.For., Elizabeth I, 1583, and addenda*, No. 597, p. 564.
6 B.M., Lansdowne MSS 160, f. 181.
7 *A.P.C.*, vol. X, p. 124, and vol. XI, p. 29.
8 There is extensive discussion of this kind of association in Christensen, *Dutch trade to the Baltic . . .*, pp. 105–40.
9 P.R.O., S.P. Supplementary 46/9, f. 48.
10 *Ibid.*, f. 36.
11 On the subject of the various types of association and their organization, see N. W. Posthumus, *De oosterse Handel te Amsterdam, 1485–90*, Leiden, 1953; also, G. Mickwitz, *Aus Revaler Handelsbüchern: zur Technik des Ostseehandels in der ersten Hälfte des 16 Jahrhunderts*, Helsinki, 1938. In Polish literature the question has been extensively discussed by H. Samsonowicz, *Badania nad kapitałem mieszczańskim . . .*, pp. 33–42. This also gives the most important writings on the subject. [On the *sendeve* see *Studies in English trade in the fifteenth century*, pp. 147–8.]
12 Christensen, *Dutch trade to the Baltic . . .*, p. 222*f*.
13 *A.P.C.*, vol. V, p. 236.
14 *The Merchant Adventurers of England*, p. 20.
15 *The ordinance book of the Merchants of the Staple*, ed. E. E. Rich, in *Cambridge studies in economic history*, Cambridge, 1937, pp. 106, 188.
16 See M. M. Postan, 'Credit in medieval trade', *Ec.H.R.*, vol. I, 1928, pp. 234–61.
17 J. Rogers, letter to Walsingham, 4 April 1581: P.R.O., S.P. 88/1, No. 11.
18 See Tawney, *op. cit., passim*.
19 Willan, *Studies in Elizabethan foreign trade*, p. 12.
20 P.R.O., S.P. Supplementary 46/9, ff. 12–14, 41, etc.
21 *Ibid.*, ff. 22, 103–04.
22 *Ibid.*, ff. 28, 103, 126.
23 J. Browne, *The merchants avizo*, ed. P. McGrath, Boston, Mass., 1957.
24 The author is planning to deal more extensively with this correspondence in a separate work, and to prepare the complete letters of the Sexton agents for publication.
25 P.R.O., S.P. Supplementary 46/9, f. 2.
26 *Ibid.*, f. 6.
27 Sexton also traded with Spain, and presumably he needed Danzig barrels for spices and fruits.
28 On Danzig's importance as a rope-making centre, see Bogucka, *Gdańsk jako ośrodek produkcyjny . . .*, pp. 57*f*, 62.
29 P.R.O., S.P. Supplementary 46/9, ff. 11, 13: letters from B. Freman to Sexton, dated 7 and 23 October 1556.
30 *Ibid.*, f. 20: Freman's letter dated 1 January 1557.

31 *Ibid.*, f. 98.
32 *Ibid.*, ff. 19, 20, 21, 98.
33 The Fremans' correspondence indicates that the price of one piece of cloth was approximately equal to the price of 1,000 cony skins in Danzig.
34 P.R.O., S.P. 12/106, No. 6, gives the following comparative values of Polish and English currency in 1575: 1 thaler = 4*s* 3*d*; 1 florin = 3*s* 10*d*; 1 large mark = 2*s* 6*d*; 1 small mark = 2*s*; 1 grosch = 1·5*d*.
35 *Ibid.*, S.P. Supplementary 46/9, f. 99.
36 In a letter dated 7 October 1556 Blase Freman wrote: 'I pray you let your clothes you send be most blue and assyers, dark collers and good, or ells I had as lefe have none.' He was especially anxious to receive broadcloth manufactured in Suffolk, for which there was a good demand in Danzig: *ibid.*, f. 11.
37 On the subject of loans and credits granted to foreign merchants in Danzig, see Samsonowicz, *Badania nad kapitałem mieszczanskim* . . ., pp. 74*f*.
38 In July 1557 Blase Freman complained to Sexton, 'I wolld a sentt for a 6,000 marks more [yarn for cordage] than I have yf I colld have wares for longe tyme butt soche wares as you wolld have I cannott gett butt shortt tyme': P.R.O., S.P. Supplementary 46/9, f. 62.
39 A bill of exchange of this nature, presented in 1536 by N. Storye, a factor working for the Ipswich merchant Thomas Lappage, to William Watson, a factor of the London Merchant F. Overton, drawn for a sum of £6, is in P.R.O., High Court of Admiralty 24/5, No. 33. A specimen bill of exchange dated 1617 and presented by two Elbing merchants to a London merchant for a sum of 1,000 zlotys is in *The Acts and ordinances*. . . ., p. 49.
40 G. Malynes, *A treatise of the canker of England's commonweal*, London, 1601, pp. 69–70: 'In Poland, Lithuania, Prussia, etc, other countries adiacent, when they abound with corn, money is very scarce . . . presently great store of ready money cometh from all places thither, which maketh the price of corne rise, the money also being risen to a great value; and yet our English commodities do rather fall with them in price, or remaine unsold, the monies being transported thither onely for the employment of corne. And although we have not an ordinaire exchange with any of these countries, which sometimes is made accordingly to the Florin of thirty grosses, and therefore some ready money (one would thinke) might be brought over in returne of our commodities, yet the same is not done, for that the tolleration of monies to go currant with them farre above their value, hindreth the same; in regard whereof our commodities might be sold accordingly, and then shall we not onely with adventure make needfull and necessary commodities . . . but also in ready money.'
41 P.R.O., S.P. Supplementary 46/9, ff. 11, 13, 20, etc.
42 *Ibid.*, f. 13.

43 *Ibid.*, f. 109.

44 See J. D. Gould, 'The trade depression of the early 1620's', *Ec.H.R.*, second series, vol. VII, 1954, No. 1, p. 86.

45 J. D. Gould, 'The Royal Mint in the early seventeenth century', *ibid.*, vol. V, 1952, pp. 241*f.*

46 P.R.O., S.P.Dom. 14/131, No. 55. The Eastland Company considered that the decline in its Baltic trade was caused by 'the want of meanes of retournes for our merchants . . . because they can neither sell for ready money, nor in barter for vendible commodities'.

47 See Bogucka, 'Z problematyki gospodarczo-społecznej Niderlandów . . .', p. 122.

48 See R. de Roover, *Money, banking and credit in medieval Bruges*, Cambridge, Mass., 1948.

49 See M. Małowist, 'A certain trade technique in the Baltic countries in the fifteenth to the seventeenth centuries', in *Poland at the eleventh International Congress of Historical Sciences in Stockholm*, Warsaw, 1960, p. 114.

50 *The Acts and ordinances* . . ., pp. 55*ff.*

51 P.R.O., E 190/7/8; also W.A.P.Gd., Lib. port. Elbing, 1587.

52 P.R.O., S.P.Dom. 16/105, No. 72.

53 *Ibid.*, S.P.Dom. 16/105, No. 91.

54 *Ibid.*, E 190/2/1, E 190/6/4, E 190/8/1.

55 *Ibid.*, E 190/6/3, E 190/7/8, E 190/10/11. In 1574 London customs officers dealt with vessels arriving from Danzig in December and January. This happened again in 1587–88 and 1589, when many ships arriving from the Baltic in the winter months were subjected to customs controls.

56 W.A.P.Gd., Lib. port, Elbing, 1586, 1587, 1594, 1599, 1602. In 1594 English ships delivered cargoes to Elbing even in December.

Conclusion

The foundation of the Eastland Company in 1579 was the central factor in England's relations with the Baltic area in the sixteenth century. It came at the final and decisive phase of England's struggle with the German Hanse, and was a proof of the victory of the modern Tudor monarchy over the medieval League, which had for long been disintegrating. This struggle, which I have indicated as continuing from the end of the fourteenth to the end of the sixteenth centuries, constituted a kind of axis of England's Baltic policy: England's position in world trade and navigation to a large extent depended on its resolution. I have sought to show the reasons why England was interested in the Baltic area, and to stress her essentially commercial motives. That is why the greatest part of this book has been concerned with the issue of the country's Baltic trade, of which in this respect the Polish market was the main and most important area for English activity in the Elizabethan era.

Analysis of England's Baltic trade in the second half of the sixteenth century has justified the conclusion that the great bulk of that trade was conducted with the Polish Commonwealth, and that other economic areas in the Baltic region, such as Sweden, and Russia, still played but a small part in it, their importance increasing only in the seventeenth century. Trade with Poland was important to England both from the point of view of cloth exports (in this field the Eastland Company was second only to the Merchant Adventurers) and of imports, especially raw materials and semi-manufactures, which England needed in the years of the birth of her might and of her naval expansion. In the sphere of imports of ships' commodities England's dependence on Poland and Norway was considerable, and one can say without exaggeration that her struggle for a position in world trade and navigation reached its earliest decision in the Baltic. To some extent the breakdown of the Hanse monopoly became a prerequisite to her future world expansion.

An attempt has also been made to reveal the social bases of this process, to investigate just what internal factors of English society became the driving force of the country's expansion in the Baltic. Analysis of the Eastland Company's social composition has made it possible to illustrate the role of the wealthy middle class which was one of the pillars of the Elizabethan monarchy, the class of the great wholesalers of London and several other cities who traded with Poland and Russia, the North Sea area and the Mediterranean, the Levant and Africa on such a large scale in the second half of the sixteenth century. These merchants created strong trading organizations and paved the way for England's later naval, commercial and political expansion. Taking the Eastland Company as an example, certain problems of the structure and functioning of this type of organization have been discussed, since England owed her economic and political advance in modern times to such organizations in a degree greater than that of any other country.

Only a small space has been devoted to England's political contacts with the Baltic area, and this deliberately, since in the main they are well known, and in the period under consideration were still somewhat sporadic. Their basis was mainly trade, and they have been illuminated from this angle. On the other hand, various episodic examples of England's transient interest in Polish political events or those of other countries have been left untouched, since they are known through previous studies and do not form an essential link in England's commercial policy in the Baltic. The work has been written from the point of view of the English historical process, and analysis of the source and factual materials has been conducted first and foremost from this aspect.

In conclusion, we may well consider also the importance of England's Baltic trade to the Baltic countries, and the attitude one should take to that trade from this aspect. It needs to be stated that the Baltic trade of England, Holland and other Western European countries reacted on the economic and social conditions of the Central and Eastern European countries in a manner unfavourable to their further development. The Western countries' expansion in the Baltic, which took the form of exploitation of the region's great agricultural and forestry reserves, certainly created a powerful stimulus to the advance of agriculture, forestry, etc. But it also gave a fairly clearly defined direction to that advance, towards a one-sided agricultural development and a feeble growth—even at times a severe retrocession—in industrial production.[1] This was due to the excessive exports of grain, timber and raw materials simultaneously with considerable imports of industrial commodities. In this connection the level of prices for agricultural and industrial products in sixteenth century Poland was much less favourable to industrial production than the corresponding situation in the West; and at the turn of the century Polish industry was beginning to break down. The influx of foreign manufactures, even of those which Poland was not herself producing in sufficient quantities at the time, was bound to react unfavourably on the prices of Polish craft products; on the other hand the mass exportation of Polish foodstuffs and raw materials, in conjunction with other factors, raised the craftsmen's cost of living and the costs of production.[2] In Poland the level of prices of agricultural and craft articles was more unfavourable than in the West, *inter alia* because of the mass exports of grain and various forestry and livestock products. The great crisis and rise in prices that occurred during the second half of the sixteenth century increased the unfavourable situation for Polish crafts still further.

One needs to draw attention to yet another factor when estimating England's Baltic trade from the aspect of the interests and the development of the Baltic countries. While one must confirm that these countries had a favourable foreign trade balance during this period,[3] it needs to be emphasized that the surplus remained chiefly in the hands of the rich merchants of the several port cities, first and foremost those of Danzig.[4] This encouraged the growing economic dependence of the agricultural producers in the hinterland on the wealthy seaboard wholesalers, and the concentration of large properties in the hands of merchants. The gentry also drew considerable profit from this trend. Since in the existing conditions it did not pay to invest the profits from exports in industry, the Baltic area became a kind of economic colony of the West, as Małowist has pertinently said.[5] Only to Sweden did this observation not apply; but Sweden had a different economic structure and a poorly developed agriculture, hardly sufficing for its own needs.

Notes

1 Małowist, 'A certain trade technique . . .', pp. 114*f*.

2 M. Małowist, *Rzemiosło polskie w okresie Odrodzenia* (*Polish craft industry in the time of the Renaissance*), Warsaw, 1954, pp. 53*ff*.

3 Christensen, *Dutch trade to the Baltic* . . ., p. 428, emphasizes the Baltic countries' profitable trade balance with the West at the turn of the sixteenth century, and goes on to say that the West's deficit was ironed out

by resort to specie, as a result of which 'the Sound was one of the roads along which the huge treasures of the large Spanish silver fleets were spread all over Europe'.

4 See S. Hoszowski, 'Rewolucja cen w Polsce w XVI–XVII wieku' ('The revolution in prices in Poland in the sixteenth and seventeenth centuries'), in *VIII Powszechny Zjazd Historyków Polskich*, vol. VI, *Historia gospodarcza* (*The eighth General Congress of Polish Historians*, vol. VI, *Economic history*), Warsaw, 1960, p. 119.

5 Małowist, 'O niektórych cechach . . .', p. 103.

Bibliography

Hitherto England's relations with the Baltic area in the second half of the sixteenth century have not greatly interested historians, a circumstance to which Zakrzewski drew attention as long ago as 1887,[1] while Małowist stressed it again and again, both before the last war[2] and in recent years.[3] This observation applies equally to both English[4] and Polish scholars,[5] and one needs only to study the general surveys covering the second half of the century or sketches of the Baltic problems of the period to realize how little this problem has been subjected to interpretation and analysis so far.

For the sixteenth and seventeenth centuries England's political relations with Poland have been discussed most fully by Jasnowski,[6] in a publication based almost exclusively on the Calendars of State Papers. This work, which was written mainly in order to acquaint the foreign reader with the state of Anglo-Polish relations in Tudor and Stuart times, is of a general nature and barely touches on economic issues. Boratyński went into more detail in regard to certain aspects of England's Baltic policy, but only in connection with the question of Stefan Batory's attitude to the Hanse and the Netherlands, and the work is of limited scope.[7] Borowy was interested for many years in Polish–English relations in the sixteenth century, but apart from a number of minor contributions to the subject, he was unable to publish the larger work which he had in hand.[8] Studies by Kot[9] and Szumska[10] deal with cultural problems. Przezdziecki's remarks on the political relations between Poland and England are of a popular nature.[11]

England's political relations with Denmark in the Elizabethan era have been discussed with concision by Kirchner,[12] who also outlined the problem of the importance to England of the Narva navigation.[13] Szelągowski gave much consideration to this question,[14] while of English historians T. S. Willan's contributions call for special mention. There is quite an extensive literature on England's relations with Russia in the second half of the sixteenth century, both in Russian (it has been surveyed by Lubimenko)[15] and in English (especially Professor Willan's recent studies). But there has been no comprehensive survey of England's trading relations with the Baltic area during the period we are considering, if we ignore two works of a popular nature by Deardorff and Ramsay, which we shall discuss below.

An earlier period of England's relations with the Baltic was covered by the economic historian M. M. Postan in a work which dealt with England–Hanse economic and political relations in the fifteenth century (down to 1475).[16] The ensuing period, to the middle of the sixteenth century, was covered in a monograph by Schanz before the close of the nineteenth century;[17] although in more than one respect out of date today, this thorough-going study, based on primary sources, dealt with English foreign trade down to the middle of the sixteenth century and discussed in some detail England's trading relations with the Baltic area during this early Tudor period. The next phase of England's relations with the Baltic, in the seventeenth century, has received more extensive study. Some years ago R. W. K. Hinton devoted much attention to this period, more especially to the part played by the Eastland Company and Baltic trade in the English economy from 1620 to the end of the seventeenth century.[18] A monograph by the Danish professor Astrid Friis[19] is also of much importance for the first half of the seventeenth century; she was concerned primarily with English cloth exports to the Netherlands, Germany and Poland. A recent publication by the Finnish historian, Åström, covers England's trading relations with the Baltic, and especially with Sweden, in the second half of the seventeenth century.[20]

On the other hand, research into England's relations with the Baltic in the Elizabethan era has been on a much more modest scale. Students have shown more interest in other trends of English foreign trade under the Tudors,[21] for instance the trade with Russia, to which Professor Willan has devoted a number of works in recent years,[22] and before him Page,[23] Wretts-Smith,[24] Yakobson,[25] and others. The history of England's early trade with the Levant and of the Levant Company has aroused considerable interest among English historians, as is instanced by the monographs by Epstein[26] and Wood,[27] not to mention a large number of minor contributions. England's trade with Africa has recently been exhaustively studied by Willan.[28] The Merchant Adventurers' Company and its trading relations with the Netherlands and Germany are of perennial interest to English students, though, if we exclude the works of Carus-

Wilson[29] and Ramsey,[30] relating in any case to earlier years, only Unwin[31] has undertaken a full-length history of this company in Elizabethan times.

The first writer to show an interest in issues connected with the Eastland Company was Sellers, who in 1906 published a volume of its seventeenth century Acts and ordinances, prefacing them with a long introduction.[32] The only material relating to the Elizabethan era in this publication consists of fragments of Elizabeth's 1579 charter issued to the Eastland Company, and these suffer from numerous errors and omissions. Sellers' introduction discusses Eastland Company organization in the seventeenth century, and deals only very generally with its earlier history. Hitherto this publication has been the main source of information concerning the Company, and other writers on English economic history, such as Lipson,[33] have used it as their main basis for observations on the subject. But it does not provide much material relating to the Elizabethan era, and has absolutely nothing on the problem of England's trading relations with Baltic countries in the second half of the sixteenth century.

The only attempts to deal with this problem from the aspect of the entire complex of trading relations have been Deardorff's treatise, published in 1912,[34] and G. D. Ramsay's sketch, which is of a popular nature.[35] Despite the title of her work, Deardorff did not make any detailed analysis of England's trade with the Baltic, and she handled the entire problem very generally and superficially, only in fact discussing references to the subject found in the printed Calendars of State Papers, which meant relying on descriptive sources. She completely ignored both the English customs records and the Sound toll registers, which are fundamental to the problem, not to mention the Elbing customs registers. Her book contains no discussion of the economic background to England's relations with Baltic countries, and moreover it gives a faulty account of the genesis of the Eastland Company. She adduces the problem of piracy, a quite secondary and fortuitous factor, as the decisive element in the creation of the Company, and on the other hand she fails to appreciate fully the social, commercial and political background to the Company's foundation.

Some years ago a popular sketch on the subject of England's economic relations with the Baltic from the fourteenth to the eighteenth century was published by G. D. Ramsay, as already mentioned. This sketch contained no new material but gave an interesting general discussion of this topic. Recently the present writer has dealt with the problem of the birth of the Eastland Company[36] in a work based on English sources. The same author has dealt separately with the complex of issues connected with Elizabeth's 1579 charter to the Company.[37]

The only aspect of the Company's early history which has aroused any considerable interest among historians so far is the question of the English entrepot in Elbing and the company's attempts at Stefan Batory's court to have its residence and privileges in that city confirmed. Arising out of the policy of the city of Danzig, which guarded its privileges jealously, this problem has been the subject of several works by both Polish and German historians, who have presented it mainly in a local context, from the aspect of Hanse interests and Polish policies, without regard for the broader background and in general without acquaintance with English sources. This remark relates above all to the works of the very worthy investigator of Danzig's history, P. Simson, who devoted a special article to the problem of the English residence in Elbing,[38] and also occupied himself more closely with the activities of the main advocate of Hanseatic interests in the conflict with England, G. Liseman.[39] Simson also devoted much space to this question in his history of Danzig;[40] but most of all, as the editor of the Danzig documents on Hanse history in the sixteenth century, he made available the most important of the Danzig materials on the problem in the form of digests.[41] Among earlier German contributions to the subject of the Eastland Company's Elbing residence must be mentioned an article by Neumann, in 1857,[42] but this is of no great value. So far as the problem of the English entrepot in Elbing is concerned, an article by Fiedler[43] is of greater importance, as it also gives an outline especially of Danzig's political relations with England over several centuries.

In Polish historiography the issue of the Eastland Company's residence in Elbing has chiefly interested Szelągowski, whose book on the commercial rivalry of England, Germany, Russia and Poland has already been noted. In this work he gave an erroneous account of the genesis of the Eastland Company, wrongly deciphering the date in Elizabeth's charter and putting the foundation of the Company back by eleven years to 1568.[44] In consequence he interpreted the circumstances of its foundation quite arbitrarily. The article Szelągowski wrote jointly with N. S. B. Gras on the subject of England's efforts to obtain official approval for the entrepot in Elbing is of more importance.[45] It is a paper read to the Royal Historical Society, and presents briefly only the political side of the problem, reporting the English diplomatic endeavours at Batory's courts and Danzig's counter-action. The most extensive discussion in Polish, based on source material, of England's and the Elbing city council's endeavours to have the Eastland Company warehouse transferred to that city is to be found in Lepszy's work on Stefan Batory and Danzig.[46] He surveyed the problem against the broad background of Polish Baltic policy in the times of Batory. Among smaller contributions one may also mention an article by Borowy,[47] which, however, influenced by Szelągowski, repeats that writer's error in dating the beginning of the Company.[48]

The present work is based primarily on English archives in the Public Record Office and the British Museum, the Prerogative Court of Canterbury and the Corporation of London Record Office (Guildhall).

The Public Record Office yielded the largest quantity of source materials, especially the State papers and the port books. The State papers include extensive correspondence between the English Chancellery and various private persons, diplomatic correspondence with foreign countries (in the Foreign section), and correspondence, etc, concerning the country's internal problems (in the Domestic section). This enormous collection yielded information of fundamental importance on the subject of England's relations with the Hanse, Denmark, Poland (the Polish section is classified separately) and other countries at the time of the organization of the Eastland Company and in subsequent years. Letters from Elizabeth, William Cecil, Walsingham and other English statesmen, reports from Elizabeth's emissaries at the Polish court, from Danzig and from Elbing, correspondence with Hanseatic cities, letters from English merchants and petitions from the Eastland Company all throw great light on the English and the general background of England's relations with the Baltic and on the early experiences of the Eastland Company. With the State papers as a basis it was also possible to collect biographical materials concerning the leading London merchants who played the most important part in forming the company, became members of its administration and developed commercial relations with the Baltic and other areas of the known world on a larger scale. Among the private correspondence to be found in this group, letters from two factors of the London merchant Thomas Sexton, written from Danzig in the years 1555–59, proved unusually valuable, since they threw more light on the organization of England's trade with Poland.

A second collection in the Public Record Office is the Exchequer group, which includes the port books for London, Hull, Newcastle, Ipswich, Lynn and other ports on the east coast which played the most important role in England's trade with the Baltic countries. Until now these books have hardly been drawn upon at all for an analysis of England's trade with the Baltic in the Elizabethan era, and as basic source materials they proved unusually valuable in considering England's trade, its nature and extent, the part individual merchants played in it, etc. Unfortunately, a complete series was not available, for many have been lost, or suffered such serious damage in the nineteenth century that the picture obtained from them serves often for exemplification rather than for statistical analysis.[49]

The Manuscript Department of the British Museum enabled us to supplement only to a certain extent the basic source material available mainly in the Public Record Office. The British Museum documents, which in general are badly catalogued, contain many transcriptions of archival materials preserved in the Public Record Office, but at times they do complement those materials.

The resources of the Prerogative Court of Canterbury (in Somerset House), which includes merchants' original wills, provided valuable data on the question of the wealth of the London merchants and their social status.

The City of London archives (the Corporation of London Record Office, Guildhall) contain original documents on the domestic history of the English capital, the economic policy of the City authorities, etc. which were also drawn upon.

Among Polish archives the resources of the Wojewodzkie State archives in Gdansk and the documents of the City of Elbing archives included in them were mainly used. In these collections the materials of greatest relevance to our subject are the Elbing port customs registers (only one of the similar Danzig registers has been preserved), dating from the end of the sixteenth and the beginning of the seventeenth centuries, the city council records, and Elbing manuscripts which throw light on the importance of the English trade to the development of that city.

Among the considerable quantity of printed sources laid under contribution the registers of the Sound tolls were of particular importance to our studies, since they provide the only possibility of obtaining a complete picture by resort to comparative methods of many problems arising out of the Baltic trade, and that over a long period.[50] (A critical discussion of the value of the Sound registers will be found in the introduction to chapter seven.) Only by collating an analysis of the English data and the Polish customs books plus the Sound toll registers did it become possible to present and analyse English merchants' Baltic exports and imports during the second half of the sixteenth century.

Among the printed English sources drawn upon one must put in the forefront the great series of Calendars of State Papers, which include sections relating to England's internal policies (Domestic) and her foreign policy (Foreign), and in addition separate series based on Spanish, Venetian, Roman, etc, materials. These abstracts are of varying value; the later parts are more trustworthy than the series deriving from the end of the nineteenth century. Those of the Foreign section are very extensive, and constitute a contemporary, very precise paraphrase of the originals, and not an abstract in the strict sense of the word; but those of the Domestic section are briefer. As a rule the indexes to the older volumes are badly compiled and have many omissions, and so one is not freed from the disagreeable task of going through whole volumes, most of them decidedly large. All the series of Calendars of State Papers are lacking in any kind of critical apparatus, and have been published 'in the raw'. Recently Talbot has drawn upon the resources of the Polish section in the Public Record Office (State Papers, Poland, 88) to publish in a similar manner, but *in extenso*, sources concerning relations between England and Poland in the time of Elizabeth.[51] In this work the many volumes of the series of documents of Henry VIII's time, published in the form of abstracts under the title *Letters and papers, foreign and domestic, of the reign of Henry VIII*, have also been laid under contribution.

Various English royal privileges, to be found in the form of extensive abstracts in the many volumes of the Calendars of the Patent Rolls, have also been taken into account. The details of the charter granted to English merchants trading with the Baltic at the turn of the fourteenth century have been taken from Rymer's *Foedera* . . .[52]

The Acts of the Privy Council of England, the many-volumed series of protocols of the Privy Council, proved to be an immeasurably important source, for they revealed very precisely England's attitude to various problems of internal and foreign policy in the Elizabethan era.

Among the various publications of source material concerning the English trading companies one must mention first and foremost the *Acts and ordinances of the Eastland Company* issued by M. Sellers in

1906. Besides printing extracts from Elizabeth's 1579 charter to the Eastland Company this volume contains later material dating from 1616, since the Company's earlier documents, like those of many other similar organizations, perished in the great fire of London in 1666. For comparative purposes, in discussing the organization of the Eastland Company the printed documents of the Merchant Adventurers have also been used.[53]

Among Hanseatic sources we have made use chiefly of the Hanse sixteenth century documents: those relating to Danzig edited by P. Simson[41] and those of Cologne edited by Höhlbaum.[54] These contain abstracts and often entire documents relating to the Hanse history of this period. In our discussion of England's relations with the Baltic in the fourteenth and fifteenth centuries use was made of both the basic publications of Hanseatic documents: *Hanserecesse*[55] and *Hansisches Urkundenbuch*,[56] but only to a limited extent because of the introductory nature of our first chapter. (The innumerable data contained in both these sources, each consisting of many volumes, concerning England's everyday disputes with Hanse would have disproportionately enlarged and obscured the presentation of the basic tendencies in earlier Anglo-Hanse relations).

Among Polish printed sources use has been made of the documents in the Zamoyski archives[57] and in Heidenstein's[58] and Bielski's chronicles,[59] the collection of political writings from the time of the first interregnum[60] and others.

Notes

1 W. Zakrzewski, *Stefan Batory, Przegląd historyi jego panowania i program dalszych nad nią badań* (*Stefan Batory: survey of the history of his reign and a programme for further research into it*), Craców, 1887, p. 101.

2 M. Małowist, 'Baltic affairs in the sixteenth and seventeenth centuries in the light of historical literature', *Baltic and Scandinavian Countries*, vol. III, 1937, No. 3, p. 427.

3 M. Małowist, 'Z zagadnień popytu na produkty krajów baltyckich w Europie zachodniej w XVI wieku', *P.H.*, vol. L, 1959, p. 741.

4 See, for example, the basic general histories of England in the Tudor era: J. A. Williamson, *The Tudor Age*, in *A history of England*, ed. C. Oman, vol. v, London, 1953; G. R. Elton, *England under the Tudors*, in *ibid.*, vol. IV, London, 1955; J. B. Black, *The reign of Elizabeth, 1558–1603*, in the *Oxford history of England*, vol. VIII, Oxford, 1959; A. L. Rowse, *The England of Elizabeth: the structure of society*, London, 1951, and his *The expansion of Elizabethan England*, London, 1955.

5 See, for example, W. Konopczyński, *Kwestia bałtycka do XX w.* (*The Baltic question down to the twentieth century*), Gdańsk, 1947; W. Sobieski, *Der Kampf um die Ostsee*, Leipzig, 1933; H. Bagiński, *Polska a Bałtyk* (*Poland and the Baltic*), London, 1942, and other works of the same type.

6 J. Jasnowski, *England and Poland in the sixteenth and seventeenth centuries*, Oxford, 1948.

7 L. Boratyński, 'Stefan Batory, Hanza i powstanie Niderlandów' ('Stefan Batory, the Hanse and the Netherlands uprising'), *P.H.*, vol. VI, 1908. H. Jablonowski completely ignored Polish–English relations in the time of Batory in his 'Die Aussenpolitik Stephan Bathorys', *Jahrbücher für Geschichte Osteuropas*, vol. II, 1937, pp. 11–80, though he did discuss Batory's relations with Moscow, Turkey, the Habsburgs, the Scandinavian countries, etc, at some length.

8 W. Borowy, 'Anglo–polonica. Wiadomość o nieukończonej pracy i zniszczonych materiałach' ('Information on an unfinished work and destroyed materials'), *Sprawozdania Towarzystwa Naukowego Warszawskiego* (*Reports of the Warsaw Scientific Society*), section II, 1946, pp. 1–9.

9 S. Kot, *Anglo–polonica: Angielskie źródła rękopiśmienne do dziejów stosunków kulturalnych Polski i Anglii* (*English manuscript sources for the history of cultural relations between Poland and England*), Warsaw, 1935, and other works by this author.

10 U. Szumska, *Anglia a Polska w epoce humanizmu i reformacji* (*England and Poland in the age of humanism and the Reformation*), Lwów, 1938.

11 R. Przezdziecki, *Diplomatic Venturers and adventurers: some experiences of British envoys at the Court of Poland.* London, 1953.

12 W. Kirchner, 'England and Denmark, 1558–88', *Journal of Modern History*, vol. XVII, 1945, pp. 1–15. The period after 1588 has been handled by E. P. Cheyney, 'England and Denmark in the later days of Queen Elizabeth', *ibid.*, vol. I, 1929, pp. 9–39.

13 W. Kirchner, *The rise of the Baltic question*, Delaware, 1954; also his 'Die Bedeutung Narvas im 16 Jahrhundert', *Historische Zeitschrift*, vol. 172, 1951.

14 A. Szelągowski, *Z dziejów współzawodnictwa Anglii i Niemiec, Rosji i Polski* (*From the history of the rivalry between England and Germany, Russia and Poland*), Lwów, 1910.

15 I. Lubimenko, 'Anglia a Rosja w XVII w.' ('England and Russia in the seventeenth century'), in *Angielska rewolucja burżuazyjna XVII wieku* (*The English seventeenth century bourgeois revolution*), vol. II, Warsaw, 1957, pp. 376*ff.*

16 M. M. Postan, 'The economic and political relations of England and the Hanse, 1400–75', in *Studies in English trade in the fifteenth century*, ed. E. Power and M. M. Postan, London, 1951, pp. 91–153.

17 G. Schanz, *Englische Handelspolitik gegen Ende des Mittelalters mit be-*

sonderer Berücksichtigung des Zeitalters der beiden ersten Tudors Heinrich VII und Heinrich VIII, vols. I–II, Leipzig, 1881.

18 R. W. K. Hinton, *The Eastland trade and the Common Weal in the seventeenth century*, Cambridge, 1959.

19 A. Friis, *Alderman Cockayne's project and the cloth trade: the commercial policy of England in the main aspects, 1603–25*, Copenhagen–London, 1927.

20 S. E. Åström, *From cloth to iron: the Anglo-Baltic trade in the late seventeenth century*, vol. I, Helsinki, 1963.

21 H. Zins, 'Angielska historiografia elżbietańska', *Odrodzenie i Reformacja w Polsce*, vol. VIII, 1963, pp. 182*ff*.

22 T. S. Willan, *The early history of the Russia Company, 1553–1603*, Manchester, 1956; *The Muscovy Merchants of 1555*, Manchester, 1953; 'The Russia Company and Narva, 1558–81', *Slavonic Review*, vol. XXXI, 1953; 'Trade between England and Russia in the second half of the sixteenth century', *E.H.R.*, vol. LXIII, 1948.

23 W. Page, *The Russia Company from 1553 to 1660*, London, 1913.

24 M. Wretts-Smith, 'The English in Russia during the second half of the sixteenth century', *T.R.H.S.* fourth series, vol. III, 1920, pp. 72–102.

25 S. Yakobson, 'Early Anglo-Russian relations, 1553–1613', *Slavonic Review*, vol. XIII, 1935, pp. 598–610.

26 M. Epstein, *The early history of the Levant Company*, London, 1908.

27 A. C. Wood, *A history of the Levant Company*, London, 1935.

28 T. S. Willan, *Studies in Elizabethan foreign trade*, Manchester, 1959, pp. 92–312.

29 Cf E. M. Carus-Wilson, 'The origin and early development of the Merchant Adventurers' organization in London', *Ec.H.R.*, vol. IV, 1933, No. 2.

30 P. H. Ramsey, 'The Merchant Adventurers in the first half of the sixteenth century, 1496–1550', unpublished Ph.D. thesis, University of Oxford.

31 G. Unwin, 'The Merchant Adventurers' Company in the reign of Elizabeth', in *Studies in economic history: the collected papers of George Unwin*, ed. R. H. Tawney, London, 1958.

32 *The Acts and ordinances of the Eastland Company*, ed. M. Sellers, London, 1906.

33 E. Lipson, *The economic history of England*, vol. II, London, 1961, pp. 315*ff*.

34 N. R. Deardorff, 'English trade in the Baltic during the reign of Elizabeth', in *Studies in the history of English commerce in the Tudor period*, New York, 1912.

35 G. D. Ramsay, *English overseas trade during the centuries of emergence: studies in some modern origins of the English-speaking world*, London, 1957.

36 H. Zins, 'Geneza angielskiej Kompanii Wschodniej (Eastland Company) z r. 1579', *Zapiski Historyczne*, vol. XXIX, 1964, No. 3, pp. 7–42.

37 H. Zins, 'Przywilej Elżbiety I z 1579 r. dla angielskiej Kompanii Wschodniej', *Rocznik Elbląski*, vol. III, 1966.

38 P. Simson, 'Die Handelsniederlassung der englischen Kaufleute in Elbing', *Hansische Geschichtsblätter*, vol. XXII, 1916, pp. 87–143.
39 P. Simson, 'Der Londoner Kontorsekretär Georg Liseman aus Danzig', *ibid.*, vol. XVI, 1910.
40 P. Simson, *Geschichte der Stadt Danzig*, vol. II, 1918.
41 P. Simson (ed.), '*Danziger Inventar*, 1531–1591', in *Inventare hansischer Archive des 16 Jahrhunderts*, vol. III, Munich–Leipzig, 1913.
42 T. Neumann, 'Die englische Handels-Sozietät', *Neue Preussische Provinzial-Blätter*, vol. XII, 1857, pp. 141–8.
43 H. Fiedler, 'Danzig und England. Die Handelsbestrebungen der Engländer vom Ende des 14 bis zum Ausgang des 17 Jahrhunderts', *Z.W.G.*, vol. LXVIII, 1928.
44 Szelagowski discovered his error after the book had been printed, and he corrected it in a final note, on pp. 304–5, but was unable to alter the text at that stage. The error was repeated by certain other Polish historians, including S. Kutrzeba, 'Handel i przemysł Gdańska' ('Danzig's trade and industry'), in *Gdańsk. Przeszłość i teraźniejszość* (*Danzig, its past and present*), ed. S. Kutrzeba, Lwów, 1928, p. 134, and elsewhere. Cf also R. Przezdziecki, *op. cit.*, p. 27.
45 A. Szelągowski and N. S. B. Gras, 'The Eastland Company in Prussia, 1579–85', *T.R.H.S.*, third series, vol. XI, 1912, pp. 163–84.
46 K. Lepszy, 'Stefan Batory a Gdańsk', in *Rocznik Gdański* (*Danzig Yearbook*), vol. VI, 1932, pp. 82–136.
47 W. Borowy, ' "Kompania Wschodnia" i kampania wschodnia, Karta z historii stosunków polsko-angielskich', *Wiedza i Życie*, Nos. 6–7, 1936, pp. 402–08.
48 *Ibid.*, p. 404.
49 Cf H. Zins, 'Angielskie księgi portowe jako źródło do historii handlu XVI wieku ('English port books as a source for the history of trade in the sixteenth century'), *R.D.S.G.*, vol. XXIII, 1961, pp. 145–6. See also J. H. Andrews, 'Two problems in the interpretation of the port books', *Ec.H.R.*, second series, vol. IX, 1956, pp. 119–22.
50 *Tabeller over skibsfart og varetransport gennem Öresund, 1497–1660*, ed. N. E. Bang and K. Korst, vols. I and II, A and B, Copenhagen–Leipzig, 1906–33.
51 'Res Polonicae Elisabetha I Angliae regnante conscriptae', ed. C. Talbot, in *Elementa ad fontium editiones*, vol. IV, Rome, 1961. See a review of this publication by H. Zins in *Zapiski Historyczne* (*Historical Notes*), vol. XXVIII, 1963, pp. 833–5.
52 *Foedera, conventiones, litterae et cuiuscunque generis acta publica inter reges Angliae et alios quosvis imperatores, reges, pontifices*, etc., ed. T. Rymer, vols. III–IV, The Hague, 1740.
53 For example, *The Merchant Adventurers of England, their laws and ordinances with other documents . . .*, ed. W. E. Lingelbach, *Transactions and reprints . . . University of Pennsylvania*, second series, vol. II, 1902.

54 K. Höhlbaum (ed.), '*Kölner Inventar*', in *Inventare hansischer Archive des 16 Jahrhunderts*, vol. II, Leipzig, 1903.
55 *Hanserecesse*, Abt. 1, ed. K. Koppmann, vols. I–VIII, Leipzig, 1870–97; Abt. 2, ed. G. Ropp, vols. I–VII, Leipzig, 1876–92.
56 *Hansisches Urkundenbuch*, ed. K. Höhlbaum, K. Kuntze and W. Stein, vols. I–VIII, Halle–Leipzig, 1876–1907.
57 *Archiwum Jana Zamoyskiego*, ed. W. Sobieski, J. Siemieński and K. Lepszy, vols. I–IV, Warsaw–Cracow, 1904–48.
58 R. Heidenstein, *Dzieje Polski od śmierci Zygmunta Augusta do roku 1594*, vols. I–II, St Petersburg, 1857.
59 M. Bielski, *Kronika*, vol. III, Sanok, 1856.
60 *Pisma polityczne z czasów pierwszego bezkrólewia*, ed. J. Czubek, Cracow, 1906.

Index